DATE DUE

OC 12 '01			
NO 2 01			
DE 1 9 08			

THE
STATE
OF
ASIAN
AMERICA

The State of Asian America

Activism and

Resistance in

the 1990s

Edited by
Karin Aguilar-San Juan

Foreword by David Henry Hwang

Afterword by M. Annette Jaimes

SOUTH END PRESS
BOSTON, MA

Cover design by Wen-ti Tsen
Cover photo by Donna Binder, Impact Visuals. Protest at opening
night of "Miss Saigon."
Text design and production by the South End Press Collective
Printed in the U.S.A.
First edition, first printing

Library of Congress Cataloging-in-Publication Data
The State of Asian America: activism and resistance in the 1990s/
edited by Karin Aguilar-San Juan.
p. cm. -- (Race and resistance series)
Includes index.
ISBN 0-89608-477-9: $40.00.-- ISBN 0-89608-476-0 (pbk.): $16.00
1. Asian Americans--Politics and government. 2. Asian Americans-
-Ethnic identity.   I. Aguilar-San Juan, Karin, 1962- II. Series.
E184.06S71993
305.8'95--dc20

93-8510
CIP

South End Press, 116 Saint Botolph St., Boston, MA 02115
00 99 98 97 96 95 94   2 3 4 5 6 7

CONTENTS

Acknowledgements

Over 20 writers contribute to this book; thanks goes first to them. Some of them are close friends, others I recognize only by the sound of their voices over the telephone, but all have demonstrated through their work an interest in community building and activism that I admire and respect.

It's a privilege and a pleasure to thank the South End Press Collective, of which I was a part from 1989 to 1993. Cynthia Peters was not satisfied until each writer tackled the toughest political questions, displaying her own awesome political courage; Sonia Shah without fanfare took over my business tasks and then generously produced two pieces for this book. Dionne Brooks, Steve Chase, Loie Hayes, and Carlos Suarez-Boulangger were friendly comrades even as I became more consumed in the book and less attentive to the details of our collective work life. As interns, Lynn Lu, Homay King, and Antonia Kao did valuable research and interviews that helped shape the book's contents.

My parents, who laid my political foundations, have waited patiently 30 years for this moment. Though my father, Sonny San Juan, worries that the fact of his inclusion in this book might be seen as an act of nepotism, he and my mother, Delia Aguilar, have encouraged me all along the way, shamelessly promising to put the book on their course syllabi.

Finally, Debbie Karlan has been a friend and partner during the last months of completing this book. Her companionship has sustained me, and for that, I am thankful.

A Note About Terms

In the title of this anthology, the term Asian American is used to include U.S. citizens of Pacific Islander roots. Though convenient, this shorthand makes invisible the unique concerns of Pacific Islander Americans. Consequently, many writers within this book use the longer appellation, "Asian/Pacific Island American." Because our community is still growing and we are in the midst of defining our own experiences, no term is perfect—the fact that one contributor is Asian Canadian makes one wonder how accurate even the longer term can be.

Some writers refer to "Pilipinos"; this is not a mistake. This spelling is a recognition that letter "f" is not used in the native languages and is used to respect the native culture. However, other writers use "Filipinos," perhaps to recognize the anglicization of the language and to validate the experience of Filipino Americans.

At the risk of confusing the reader, I have let each writer's choice of terminology stand.

FACING THE MIRROR

DAVID HENRY HWANG

Glenn (a white supremacist): I'm not going to shoot anyone who's not Chinese! Now—
Pastor (Glenn's follower): But maybe ... I am?
Glenn: No ... race is—based on color—OK, well, maybe that can change, but—genetics! It's firmly rooted in genetics!
Linda (an Asian American woman): Scientifically, that's not true either.
Glenn: Then it's faith! As long as you believe you're white, you'll never turn Chinese!!

With my 1993 play *Face Value,* I sought to question the mythology of race. The plot hinges on two Asian Americans who go in white face to disrupt the opening night of a Broadway musical in which an Anglo actor has been cast as a Chinese. Obviously, this premise recalls the *Miss Saigon* casting controversy of 1990, when the British actor Jonathan Pryce was cast as a "Eurasian." In *Face Value,* matters are further complicated with the arrival of two white supremacists, who believe the lead actor actually *is* Asian, and kidnap him for stealing jobs from white people. The result is a farce of mistaken identity, suggesting that race is a construct that has no inherent meaning other than that which we choose to assign it.

Face Value was thoroughly panned in its Boston tryout, and closed on Broadway in previews. Though I concede the play had artistic flaws (I'm currently rewriting it for a future production), I also felt the material struck a chord that made white Boston critics nervous and defensive.

The struggle to balance art, commerce, and political activism has preoccupied me throughout my career as a playwright and screenwriter. Some Asian Americans find my work progressive and ground-breaking, others accuse me of perpetuating stereotypes and selling out to the white establishment. My intention is to hold my art up as a mirror to my own evolution as an Asian American. "Evolution" is the operative word here. I do not believe that I will ever become a "fully actualized" Asian American, indeed such a state would be death, creatively and politically. The only constant in our lives is change, and as we approach the new challenges of the 1990s, we must reevaluate and question old assumptions to progressively harness such change.

As I consider the state of Asian America in the 1990s, many of the assumptions that had once seemed inviolate to me are open to reconsideration. Primary among these, in my view, is the desirability of nationalism and isolationism. At one point in my life, I wanted only to write about Asian Americans, work only with Asian American artists, and aim exclusively toward Asian American audiences. I don't mean in any way to disparage that period, for it helped to heal many of the wounds Euro-American racism had inflicted on me. Having passed through that period, however, it now seems to me imperative to engage society at large, to grapple with it, challenge it, bully and cajole it toward change.

As a native of Los Angeles, I felt the profound limitations of the isolationist/nationalist model during the 1992 uprising that followed the first Rodney King verdict. In the wake of simmering tensions between African American and Korean American communities in New York as well as Los Angeles, repressed hostilities exploded into outright violence. One cannot help but feel that "multiculturalism," as defined during the late 1970s and 1980s, had not been sufficiently inclusive; it operated under the assumption of a Euro-majority nation. Under such circumstances, to "explain ourselves" seemed a pathetic attempt to win favor from whites, the very people who had taught us self-loathing.

In the 1990s, however, we see the rise of a new demographic reality: a nation with no majority race. Certainly whites continue to control a wildly disproportionate amount of power in the United States; that injustice has not changed. But the fact that people of color will soon numerically dominate this nation means that in "explaining ourselves," we are now building bridges to Latino, African, and Native Americans as well as those of European origin. The need to forge such bonds speaks to the explosion of another belief from an earlier decade: the myth of "Third World" solidarity. White America has traditionally set minorities to war against each other over scraps from its pie. As Anglos react to their shrinking powerbase, such battles will become fiercer and more common-place. Thus, "multiculturalism," it seems to me, must evolve into a sort of "interculturalism" which attempts to outline commonalities as well as differences. For example, the question, "What do Asian American and African American cultures have in common?" has not yet been properly posed. In the past we may have replied, "We're all non-white." Such a reactionary response is of limited value as we approach the new millennium.

In fact, the 1990s seem to me to question the very definition of Asian America itself. With increasing bi- and multiracialism among our children, with the expanding diversity of Asian Americans among us, the boundaries of our community have become blurred. When a Caucasian woman who was adopted and raised by working-class *nisei* parents argues with a college student whose parents are wealthy Japanese diplomats, who is the "real" Asian American? Does it matter? Addressing such questions forces us to confront an issue many of us have sidestepped: class. To say that an upper-class Chinese-American corporate lawyer has more in common with a newly arrived Laotian cabdriver than, say, a wealthy African American Ivy Leaguer is a necessary lie. It is necessary because Asians are perceived monolithically in America and must therefore band together. It is a lie, however, because it ignores the line that class cuts through our community and that many Asian Americans, myself included, have often swept under the carpet.

In *Face Value,* I attempted to deal with some of these ambiguities, the fact that definitions of race are meaningless, except as a reaction to the meaningless racism of society as a whole. I believe this message was particularly uncomfortable for whites. Some of my Anglo friends told me the first act of my play made them feel "guilty." One Caucasian woman leaving a performance was overheard saying, "How could they do a play about race in the 1990s and make it about Asians? Asians don't have any problems!" The notion that racial distinctions may be absurd can be disturbing even to Asian Americans. But, in my experience with *Face Value,* it is far more disturbing to whites. Unsurprising, since power in America has historically been distributed along racial lines, and Anglos now feel their influence diminishing before new demographic and cultural realities.

In fact, what most irks white America in the 1990s is that it is increasingly losing control of the political agenda. In the sixties and seventies, white liberalism could be dispensed from above, the majority magnanimously handing over a larger piece of the pie to powerless minorities. In the nineties, people of color are making our own rules, re-defining a national identity that certainly includes European Americans, but as only one element in a diverse picture. As we move toward empowerment, however, we find ourselves facing an entirely new set of realities and responsibilities. It is this evolution that makes the following essays so vital and necessary. In the 1990s, Asian American activism and resistance looks into the mirror, and discovers something frightening and wonderful: Our faces are changing.

—Los Angeles, California
June 1993

LINKING THE ISSUES

From Identity to Activism

KARIN AGUILAR-SAN JUAN

One hot summer weekend in July 1992, I took the train from Boston to New York City to meet Yuri and Bill Kochiyama, an elder Japanese American couple with a long history of activism on a wide range of issues—including notable personal and political alliances with the African American community. (In 1993, they were presented with the Asian American Studies Association's Outstanding Service Award for their community work.) In the course of researching themes and contributors to this anthology, several friends had advised me to look them up.

For 30 years, the Kochiyamas have lived in Harlem, a stone's throw from the #1 train stop. Inside, an entire wall of their apartment is devoted to fliers announcing rallies and fundraisers, posters, photos, and art work from friends and supporters: "Hands Off Cuba Video Summit/Cultural Exchange," "Remember Vincent Chin—10 Years After," and a letter from the David Wong Support Committee, led by Yuri Kochiyama.[1] In the dining room, above a loving shrine to a daughter who was recently killed in a car accident, hovers a framed photo of Malcolm X. "He was a personal friend," Yuri explains. In the hallway, awards and commemorative plaques cover the wall. Two plaques, one labeled "The Malcolm X

Award, In Honor of Our Shining Prince" and the other signed "Thank You from the Black Liberation Movement" struck me as momentous. After all, it was 1992, the year of the Los Angeles riots, a year we will remember for racial conflict and upheaval, not harmony. The Kochiyamas' association with Harlem's African American community, dates back to the 1960s. It is marked by constructive and passionate dialogue with Black activists and provides an important counterexample to those individuals who would argue that Asian Americans lack common ground with other people of color.

I felt moved by the Kochiyamas' commitment to struggles of liberation for all peoples, a commitment that clearly I am not the first to recognize. In the Asian American media, they have been the subject of interviews and essays too numerous to mention. Moreover, they made me feel at home, though I was a perfect stranger. Over breakfast, I asked the Kochiyamas how they prioritize their work. By community? By region? "By issue," Bill responded, matter of factly. Like other activists and radical scholars whose work we cover in this volume, their analysis of the roots of social and economic injustice drives them to embrace causes that cross racial, cultural, and even national boundaries. My visit with the Kochiyamas was brief, only long enough to give me a glimpse of the significance of their lives and work, of the continuing need for Asian American activism, and of the need to make our stories known among Asians and non-Asians alike.

****

We're approaching the twenty-first century, and sheer growth makes us visible. In the last decade, the Asian American population nearly doubled, making us the nation's fastest-growing "minority." Across the country, we represent just under 3 percent of the total population, compared to 12 percent for African Americans and 9 percent for Latinos. In certain regions, Asian Americans comprise a much larger portion of the population: Honolulu, Hawaii is 60 percent Asian, hardly surprising considering its location in the Pacific. A stunning 10 percent of California's population traces their roots to Asia (or the Pacific). The University of California at Los Angeles projects that it will be an Asian American campus by the year 2000. Even in Boston, Massachusetts, Asian Americans comprise nearly 3 percent of the total population, and politicians now consider us an important "voting bloc." For the first time, candidates in the city's 1993 mayoral race attended a reception held specifically for them on the evening of the Asian American Unity Dinner. Asian American community leaders briefed the candidates on some of their more urgent concerns, including violence in the high schools, bilingual education, and the need for expanded community services for recently arrived refugees.

But as Glenn Omatsu observes in Chapter 1, despite our demographic growth and "the growing numbers of people interested in our communities, there has not been a corresponding growth in consciousness about what it means to be Asian American." Unlike African Americans, most Asian Pacific Americans today have yet to articulate the "particularities" of issues affecting our communities, whether these be the debate over affirmative action, the controversy regarding multiculturalism, or the very definition of priorities in American society. In part, that is due to the fact that a majority of us are immigrants or refugees and, as such, lack access to the political and economic structures that are necessary for full participation in society. Whatever the cause, Omatsu points out there is an ideological vacuum here, and progressives will compete with neo-conservatives, mainstream conservatives, and others to fill it.

In Search of a Proper Image

With *The State of Asian America,* we present contemporary examples of Asian American activism and resistance. We unearth, examine, and celebrate our rich tradition of organizing in the hope that all of us, Asian and non-Asian alike, may better see the meaning of—and the need for—constructive resistance to racist injustice and oppression. To put such examples at everyone's fingertips is no small task: We should not underestimate our invisibility either in U.S. politics in general, or on the left. The mainstream media unabashedly reproduces the myth of Asians as the nation's model minority, suggesting for example that the class privilege, social status, and political perspectives that some Asians bring with them when they arrive on U.S. shores are shared by all Asians in this country. Instead, our experience is far from monolithic. Myths about Asian Americans belittle the damage done by the discrimination we face, obscure the complexity of our experience, and make our contributions to the struggle against racism invisible.

The notion that we are the nation's "model minority" unfortunately pervades even so-called progressive establishments. Frequently white activists tell me they don't know any Asian activists and ask me, perhaps somewhat anxiously, to provide them with names. But leftist Asians and other people of color also reproduce the myth that we shun political work. In the early stages of shaping this book, I described it to a prominent Native American activist intellectual. He responded with surprise that the anthology would focus on activism because, as he put it, "Asian Americans don't usually do that kind of thing." Stereotypes run deep, even among friends.

The lack of visible activist role models prevails within the Asian American community as well. At a forum on Asian American activism at Brown University in March 1992, student organizer Leslie Paik prefaced the discussion by observing that "when we mention the phrase 'Asian American activist,' no image comes readily to mind." Although she might have had a point, the comment is troubling. The past three decades *do* contain many examples of Asian American activists, organizers, scholars, writers, and artists who've spent their lives combatting racism and exploitation, as well as sexism, homophobia, environmental destruction, media stereotypes, domestic violence, hate crimes, police repression, and U.S. imperialism.

The fact that much of the academic work in our community has lost its activist edge is ironic, since the initial creation of Asian American Studies programs depended on the work of community and grassroots activists (see Chapter 18). By articulating an activist agenda, we could give new vigor to Asian American Studies and other university programs, as well as augment the academic literature produced to date; among them, *Strangers from a Different Shore* and *Asian Americans: An Interpretive History*, two comprehensive history books that are now standard classroom texts, accomplish a great feat by providing scholarly renditions of our history.[2] The goals of this book and of those, while clearly different, are not necessarily in contradiction: in the early stages of planning this book, Ron Takaki encouraged me to make this book unique and helped to identify crucial activist themes in our communities.

Other academics also recognize the need to keep the link between theory and practice alive. The theme of the Ninth National Conference of the Asian American Studies Association held in San Jose, California in May 1992 was "Diversity, Representation, and Empowerment." I spoke on a panel on activism along with two radically minded students, an AIDS educator, and a labor activist. Three of us were gay, lesbian, or bisexual. As Filipinos, South Asians, and Asians of blended heritage, we represented ethnic and cultural groups that have low visibility in the Asian American academic community. We were committed Asian American activist intellectuals, immersed to varying degrees in community struggles. (The two individuals who organized the panel did not speak but were also role models: they were gay and lesbian, of Filipino heritage, and deeply aware of the value of community work.)

As activists, what we could share with those steeped in academic life probably appeared pedestrian. We discussed how class, race, gender, and sexuality intersect, both in our lives and in our work. In various ways, we admonished Asian American intellectuals not to bury themselves in their books, not to become satisfied with victories of minute dimensions. Our audience, clearly concerned about the issues we raised, responded in one of two ways. The first response was despair. Several graduate students expressed frustration with their academic work and their inability to infuse it with a political purpose, a feeling our discussion exacerbated. The second response came from a young Filipino undergraduate: "You know who my role model is? Malcolm X! Now that brother was down!" Frankly, I was excited to discover one more college-age Asian American who rejected mainstream expectations, inspired instead by Malcolm X and the revolutionary politics he professed. I was especially proud that a Filipino American made this comment, since as a community, Filipino Americans need desperately to decolonize our minds and face the realities of racism and imperialism in our lives.

But that young man's comment also disappointed me. Unlike the Kochiyamas, whose alliances with the African American community are the result of a sophisticated political consciousness and a long history of activism, his remark seemed naive. For progressive Asian Americans, our models of activism are often built on the African American experience, or on the experience of white people. Our own remarkable acts of resistance—as plantation workers, railroad crews, miners, factory operatives, cannery workers, farmers, garment workers, shopkeepers, "ethnic entrepreneurs," union organizers, student activists, writers and artists, cultural critics, and radical academicians—remain invisible, even to ourselves.

Moving Beyond Black and White

The Asian American community needs desperately to articulate itself within current dialogues on race. Discussions of race in the United States are often cast solely in black and white terms, and often are conducted only by blacks and whites. This book aims to widen the parameters of those discussions by offering a range of Asian American perspectives on race and racism.

In an article titled "An Asian Pacific Perspective on the Los Angeles Rebellion," Scott Kurashige, a graduate student activist at UCLA, writes "The public view of Asian Americans is a lot like that of Casper the Ghost: we're either white or we're invisible."[3] Since white society is constantly erasing us and, worse, we have among us years of internalized racism to overcome, we need to learn about ourselves and our heritage to build our pride. Fighting racism requires a positive reclamation of our Asian roots, and an assertion of our heretofore unacknowledged contributions to U.S. society. In 1969, at the height of the civil rights movement and the protests against the Vietnam War, Amy Uyematsu wrote:

> Asian Americans have assumed white identities ... the values and attitudes of the majority of Americans. Now they are beginning to realize that this nation is a "White democracy" and that yellow people have a mistaken identity....
>
> The "Black is Beautiful" cry among black Americans instilled a new awareness in Asian Americans to be proud of their physical and cultural heritages. Yellow power advocates self-acceptance as the first step toward strengthening personalities of Asian Americans.[4]

The rallying call for "yellow power" put forth an image of unity and strength for Asian Americans at a time when the U.S. government was committing mass genocide in Vietnam, Laos, Cambodia, and other parts of Southeast Asia. Our hopes to create a pan-ethnic Asian American community had everything—and nothing—to do with that war. On the one hand, by asserting our identity as one Asian race, we tried to put aside our differences. These differences—of ethnicity, immigrant status, education, occupation, income, religion, language, gender, sexual orientation, and politics—had in previous decades posed obstacles to unified action. Some activists, moved by dreams of a separatist utopia, might have actually hoped to obliterate those differences by invoking "yellow power."

On the other hand, we were bound together as Asians by the war. U.S. foreign policymakers were pursuing their own visions of a race utopia. By the end of the Vietnam War, two million U.S. troops had marched across the globe, ostensibly to force Southeast Asia once and for all to submit to U.S. domination. They killed over one million Vietnamese people and left the land in ruins.[5] Race clearly played a central role in justifying the war (the fact that the enemy was often defined by race caused special conflicts among Asian American veterans).[6] The history of racist foreign policy has a lot to do with why Asian Americans are here in the first place. By expanding the debate on race to include our experience, we can refine our critique of imperialism and colonialism, and build crucial alliances across race.[7]

Beyond Identity Politics and Cultural Retrieval

In the 1990s, we must take care not to subsume ourselves solely in efforts to build Asian American pride. Reducing race to a matter of identity, rather than expanding our experience of racism into a critique of U.S. society, is detrimental to our movement. In the Asian American community, we often make the dangerous mistake of equating the process of acquainting ourselves with our ethnic, linguistic, religious, or historic roots with activism against racism. If in our desire simply to claim our identity, we overlook, for example, the ways that race is connected to imperialism (not just in Asia but in Latin America and the Middle East), then we hover perilously close to the trap of defining race as a biological rather than a social construct. There is no Asian "essence," no genetic quality that makes us inherently distinct from individuals of other races.

True, we must assume that *something about our Asian heritage* binds us together if we are to identify our community in racial, or ethnic, terms. But we should view our identity as Asian Americans as a product of a particular historical period and a myriad of economic and social events, and not a biological fact. So we are left with the task of both asserting race and *at the same time* challenging its categorization of people by skin color. What we are after is the power to articulate and define our experiences in all their complexity.

Thinking about race and community building in this way is a necessary first step to dismantling institutional racism in the United States. The fact is that in the 1990s, as in the 1960s, race—and more specifically, institutions based on white supremacy—in the United States continue to play a central role in a political and economic order that extends far beyond individual psyches, shaping domestic social policies and justifying military intervention and aggression abroad.

Liberals can, and many do, think about race as a source of difference that U.S. society can acknowledge and accommodate without disturbing the status quo. In contrast, radicals view race as a principle upon which U.S. society is hierarchically organized, and racism as a process by which race is transformed into power—or powerlessness. After all, while by some economic indicators Asian Americans are better off than other people of color, moving up a class is not the end of racism because the social processes that translate race into privilege or poverty are still in place, especially for everyone else.

Unfortunately, conservatives—both non-Asians and Asians—are dominating the current discussions about race today. As a response to the civil rights movement, conservatives have co-opted the meaning of racial equality. They warn against the conservative ideologues who define race as ethnicity—or even, simply, "difference"—and that therefore "optimistically predict the gradual absorption of distinct groups into the mainstream of American political, economic, and cultural life."[8] These assimilationist views prevail in academic literature on the subject of race, and in national forums of debate.[9] The emergence of Asian American neo-conservatives serves as an interesting illustration of how the right wing has co-opted race (see Chapter 1). Neo-conservatism poses a special challenge to progressive Asian Americans because our activist history is so hidden. For instance, even though I have been surrounded by progressive communities since my youth, I heard about the Kochiyamas only in 1992. The new generation of Asian Americans—new immigrants, recent college graduates, and youth—is probably equally unaware of our collective history of resistance. Educated during the Reagan/Bush era, many see themselves as marginal to the Asian American struggle. Some are struggling to assert their Asian heritage, often without a larger context in which they might see connections to other issues, and other communities. In Chapter 11, R. Radhakrishnan touches on the experience of young Indian Americans who have been driven to affiliate as people "of color" or "Third World" people because they have been excluded from the mainstream but not because they have developed a critique of racism—or of the poverty and violence racism often implies. As a result, many of these young people define their political activism solely in terms of asserting their identity, and are driven to accept essentialist notions of race and ethnicity.

This shortsightedness is by no means limited to any particular community. When Filipino students congregated at Mount Holyoke College in November 1992, I saw a similar gap in political consciousness.[10] I wondered how many of them believed they would single-handedly surmount racism and become rich and successful. They discussed the problems Filipinos face in the business world without any critique of capitalism, as if the number of Filipino graduates joining the ranks of this nation's elite eclipsed the number in less glamorous professions, like nurses aides and bellboys. Other than affirming their Filipino heritage, these students voiced no explicit critique of corporate values or U.S. foreign policy. Identity politics—while they have created occasional possibilities for dark-skinned individuals to move up the socioeconomic ladder—unfortunately have seduced many people into putting their identity issues at the center of the debate, while shunning the more substantive issues of racism and class oppression.

Bringing It All Back Home: A Personal Perspective

For Filipino Americans, linking racism to U.S. foreign policy could be a simple matter of reviewing our colonial history. For me, a Filipina born and raised in New England and the daughter of academics, this link could not have been more clear. I was 10 years old in 1972, the year Philippine President Ferdinand Marcos declared martial law, suspended the writ of habeas corpus, and put Congress out of session. It was the same year my aunt Mila Aguilar, a poet and journalist based in Manila, changed her name and disappeared into the underground. She did not resurface for 13 long years, during which my family and I—along with thousands of Filipinos exiled in the United States and abroad—attended countless anti-martial law meetings, demonstrations, readings, and fundraisers in the hope that we might help bring democracy back to the archipelago. Even here, we paid a heavy price for our right to protest: in 1981, assassins thought to be Marcos hit men brutally murdered Silme Domingo and Gene Viernes, labor leaders who were also involved in the anti-martial law movement based in Seattle, Washington.

The downfall of the Marcos regime in 1986 and the election of Corazón Aquino as President signaled the end of an era, not only in the Philippines, but also in the Filipino community in the United States. For the first time in 20 years, my father could return to his land of birth without fear of imprisonment or torture or, upon his return to the United States, surveillance. That year, I traveled throughout the Philippines, investigating the plight of pineapple farmers, fishing communities, sugar workers, and prostitutes. That visit was not my first, but so much had happened since 1972—in the country, in my family, in my own life—that the trip constitutes a major turning point. After only 3 weeks in the archipelago, I realized how the repression and poverty plaguing the nation during the dark years of martial law were tied into a global system that keeps the Third World poor and oppressed.

In this somewhat unusual context, my identity as a Filipina American was fused with a cynicism about U.S. foreign policy. Indeed, I thought of my Filipino nationality as being in direct opposition to the U.S. government's imperialistic machinations in my parents' land of origin. In the 1970s, my teachers and class-mates corroborated my thoughts. Despite whatever affection they might have felt for me, they treated me as a foreigner. I also developed a perspective on economic development that made it difficult for me to embrace capitalism, or the inequities that result from profit-oriented growth. I came to see racism and imperialism as strictly intertwined.

Being a woman, and a lesbian, has allowed me to see the links between other issues, including gender roles and militarism. Imagine my frustration, then, at the 1993 March on Washington for lesbian/gay/bisexual/transgender rights. There, activists put the spotlight on the "ban against gays in the military," as if our status as "first-class" citizens would be established if only we could maim and kill side-by-side with heterosexuals. As the contingents of gay and lesbian veterans paraded by, the crowd around me was roused to a jingoistic fervor I found distasteful and narrowminded, so contrary to the principles I thought were the basis for our gay liberation.

In some queer settings—conferences for writers or for activists, women's music festivals, ACT UP demonstrations, and events organized around AIDS—community leaders are working to address racism and to increase racial diversity, but when it comes to the military ban, this concern vanishes. Political scientist Cynthia Enloe argues that

> It's one thing to acknowledge that many gay men and lesbians have served in the military as very competent people, sometimes fighting in wars or performing peacetime services that are indeed socially valuable, but that is not most of what the U.S. military does. The Panama invasion is not sacrificing for your country.[11]

She points out that homophobia and heterosexism on the part of government policy makers and the media have forced lesbians and gay men to focus on the military ban in this way, shoving aside what are our real concerns: AIDS, housing, same-sex benefits, racism, sexism, and so on. As in the Asian American community, gay community activists need to link individual affirmation with a greater social agenda for equity and justice.

Nevertheless, the ban gives us an opportunity to critique militarism from a number of vantage points. In the Philippines, the U.S. military (now eclipsed slightly by Pepsi in its role of representing the evils of the U.S. empire abroad) has had a visible impact on local society. Once home to the U.S. Navy's Seventh Fleet, Subic Base was a popular "rest and recreation" playground, providing navy men with ample drugs and prostitutes. (An international movement to dismantle this and other U.S. bases in the Philippines ended when Mt. Pinatubo erupted and forced Subic's evacuation.)

The connections between militarism, imperialism, homosexuality, and desire are captured in *Macho Dancer*, a 1988 film directed by the late Lino Brocka, the Philippines' most prominent filmmaker. In it, Pol, a young man from the province, is deserted by Larry, his U.S. soldier lover. Pol finds a job in a gay bar featuring "macho dancers," call boys known for their sinewy, undulating moves. At Mama Charlie's, he meets Noel, and they perform the "shower" number together—in skimpy bikinis, they dance, suds, and rinse each other off for the viewing pleasure of the sophisticated residents of metro Manila—and eventually become friends. While they love each other, life has made them too numb to become lovers.

What is truly agonizing about this film for me as a Filipina and a lesbian is that for all the supposedly steamy sex in the macho dancers' netherworld, there is very little room for sex as an expression of love, or desire, in the sense that we talk about it in the United States. Here, the crux of lesbian and gay organizing is sexual desire, and the freedom to express it as we wish. But how can we even talk about sexual desire in the Philippines, or in any Third World country that, desperate for foreign exchange, lures tourists from developed nations with the promise of beautiful and willing flesh?

By centering the U.S. movement for gay rights around gaining access to the military, activists fail to recognize how militarism destroys for some exactly what we seek for ourselves. Like Enloe, I encourage gay activists to push beyond "end the ban" sloganeering so that we may establish our own inclusive agenda for liberation.

Conclusion

South End Press created this Race and Resistance Series to present useful and contemporary analyses of race in the United States for progressive readers of all races. The first volume, edited by M. Annette Jaimes (see Afterword) analyzed the Native American struggle for sovereignty. This anthology, the second in the series, presents an Asian American perspective on a broad range of issues that are of concern to activists and scholars.

Indeed, publishing a book like this for the Asian American community is not an original idea. In 1988, the Asian American Resource Workshop (AARW), a grassroots organization based in Boston's Chinatown, proposed a reader they hoped would pick up where *Roots: An Asian American Reader* and *Counterpoint—Perspectives on Asian America* left off. Although the AARW lacked the energy and resources to complete the book project, South End Press believed they made a strong case for a new Asian American reader.

Within academia, where this book will have a substantial audience, and in other settings, certain groups within our community have experienced relatively more visibility and power. An important purpose of this book is to challenge some of the traditional hierarchies that shape the Asian American community, not only with regard to race but also with regard to ethnicity, gender, sexuality, and professional status. Although this collection has taken a step in the right direction, as editor, I see many opportunities to improve where I have not succeeded. An essay on AIDS and health issues, more voices from the grassroots, a piece focused on gender and sexuality—these are some ideas for future writers. There are also many issues raised here that need further debate: Should we form pan-Asian coalitions? When and where? What does race mean? What is the role of electoral politics in our movement?

More than ever, we need to speak, write, publish, and organize. Fortunately, this book will not be the last on the topic of activism, and though I have great confidence in the power of the printed word to document and augment our political work for the well-being of our community, I sincerely hope our activism does not end here.

Boston, MA
July 1993

Notes

1. A 29-year-old Chinese national with a poor grasp of English, Wong was incarcerated in 1984 for robbery, and then falsely accused of killing an inmate in 1986.
2. Ronald Takaki, *Strangers from a Different Shore: A History of Asian American* (New York: Little, Brown, 1990) and Sucheng Chan, *Asian Americans: An Interpretive History* (Boston: Twayne, 1991).
3. *Forward Motion,* Vol 11, No. 3, July 1992, special issue on Asian Americans and Pacific Islanders.
4. *Roots: An Asian American Reader* (UCLA, Asian American Studies Center, 1971), 9-10.

5. Howard Zinn, *A People's History of the United States,* (New York: Harper and Row, 1980), 555.
6. "Which Way Home: Asian American Vietnam Veterans," radio documentary produced by Gina Hotta, July 1991. The host, Francisco Garcia, a veteran of African American and Chicano descent, interviews Chinese and Filipino veterans. This tape is available from Crosscurrent Media, 346 Ninth Street, 2nd floor, San Francisco, CA 94103.
7. In a four-part, front-page series (July 14-17, 1991), *Boston Globe* reporter Charles A. Radin interviewed a group of teenage boys about their hopes and aspirations for adult life. The first three episodes portrayed the trials and triumphs of four black and Latino boys, referred to by pseudonym and photographed only in silhouette. The fourth and last part, titled "With help, a dream is realized," hit a home run for the model minority myth. A large, front-page photo spanning nearly three column widths and taken in broad daylight shows Loc Tran, a Vietnamese immigrant boy who graduated as class valedictorian at the same high school the other interviewees attended. Radin doesn't talk about the U.S. war in Vietnam, but he does cite Tran's patriotism, presumably as a lesson for the black and Latino boys. "We students are so lucky to live in America," Tran told his classmates on graduation day. "Our country is the best in many ways."
8. Michael Omi and Howard Winant, *Racial Formations in the United States: From the 1960s to the 1980s,* (New York: Routledge, 1990) 10.
9. The Manhattan Institute, a right-wing thinktank, is an example of such a forum. Associates include prominent people of color: Shelby Steele, African American author of *The Content of Our Character: A New Vision of Race in America* (New York: St. Martins Press, 1990) and Linda Chavez, author of *Out of the Barrio: Toward a New Politics of Hispanic Assimilation* (Basic Books, 1991). In May 1993, the Institute held a conference titled, "The Asian American Prospect: Paragons or Pariahs Pursuing the American Dream." The forum featured neo-conservatives Dinesh D'Souza, author of *Illiberal Education: The Politics of Race and Sex on Campus* (New York: Free Press, 1991) and Arthur Hu, columnist for *Asian Week.*
10. The 1992 Filipino Intercollegiate Networking Dialogue allowed students to focus on a number of topics, including feminism, AIDS, homosexuality, gender roles, and the role of U.S. transnational corporations in the Philippines. Students did express a range of political viewpoints, although no one critiqued the corporate perspective directly as far as I know.
11. "Heterosexist Masculinity in the Military: Soj Talks with Cynthia Enloe," *Sojourner: A Woman's Forum,* June 1993.

I

Riots, Roses, and Racism

Some Burning Issues in the 1990s

1

THE 'FOUR PRISONS' AND THE MOVEMENTS OF LIBERATION

Asian American Activism from the 1960s to the 1990s

GLENN OMATSU

According to Ali Shariati, an Iranian philosopher, each of us exists within four prisons.[1] First is the prison imposed on us by history and geography; from this confinement, we can escape only by gaining a knowledge of science and technology. Second is the prison of history; our freedom comes when we understand how historical forces operate. The third prison is our society's social and class structure; from this prison, only a revolutionary ideology can provide the way to liberation. The final prison is the self. Each of us is composed of good and evil elements, and we must each choose between them.

The analysis of our four prisons provides a way of understanding the movements that swept across America in the 1960s and molded the consciousness of one generation of Asian Americans. The movements were struggles for liberation from many prisons.

They were struggles that confronted the historical forces of racism, poverty, war, and exploitation. They were struggles that generated new ideologies, based mainly on the teachings and actions of Third World leaders. And they were struggles that redefined human values—the values that shape how people live their daily lives and interact with each other. Above all, they were struggles that transformed the lives of "ordinary" people as they confronted the prisons around them.

For Asian Americans, these struggles profoundly changed our communities. They spawned numerous grassroots organizations. They created an extensive network of student organizations and Asian American Studies classes. They recovered buried cultural traditions as well as produced a new generation of writers, poets, and artists. But most importantly, the struggles deeply affected Asian American consciousness. They redefined racial and ethnic identity, promoted new ways of thinking about communities, and challenged prevailing notions of power and authority.

Yet, in the two decades that have followed, scholars have reinterpreted the movements in narrower ways. I learned about this reinterpretation when I attended a class recently in Asian American Studies at UCLA. The professor described the period from the late 1950s to the early 1970s as a single epoch involving the persistent efforts of racial minorities and their white supporters to secure civil rights. Young Asian Americans, the professor stated, were swept into this campaign and by later anti-war protests to assert their own racial identity. The most important influence on Asian Americans during this period was Dr. Martin Luther King, Jr., who inspired them to demand access to policymakers and initiate advocacy programs for their own communities. Meanwhile, students and professors fought to legitimize Asian American Studies in college curricula and for representation of Asians in American society. The lecture was cogent, tightly organized, and well-received by the audience of students—many of them new immigrants or the children of new immigrants. There was only one problem: the reinterpretation was wrong on every aspect.

Those who took part in the mass struggles of the 1960s and early 1970s will know that the birth of the Asian American movement coincided not with the initial campaign for civil rights but with the later demand for black liberation; that the leading influence was not Martin Luther King, Jr., but Malcolm X; that the focus of a generation of Asian American activists was not on asserting racial pride but reclaiming a tradition of militant struggle by earlier generations; that the movement was not centered on the aura of racial identity but embraced fundamental questions of oppression and power; that the movement consisted of not only college students but large numbers of community forces, including the elderly, workers, and high school youth; and that the main thrust was not one of seeking legitimacy and representation within American society but the larger goal of liberation.

It may be difficult for a new generation—raised on the Asian American codewords of the 1980s stressing "advocacy," "access," "legitimacy," "empowerment," and "assertiveness"—to understand the urgency of Malcolm X's demand for freedom "by any means necessary," Mao's challenge to "serve the people," the slogans of "power to the people" and "self-determination," the principles of "mass line" organizing and "united front" work, or the conviction that people—not elites—make history. But these ideas galvanized thousands of Asian Americans and reshaped our communities. And it is these concepts that we must grasp to understand the scope and intensity of our movement and what it created.

But are these concepts relevant to Asian Americans today? In our community—where new immigrants and refugees constitute the majority of Asian Americans—can we find a legacy from the struggles of two decades ago? Are the ideas of the movement alive today, or have they atrophied into relics—the curiosities of a bygone era of youthful and excessive idealism?

By asking these questions, we, as Asian Americans, participate in a larger national debate: the reevaluation of the impact of the 1960s on American society today. This debate is occurring all around us: in sharp exchanges over "family values" and the status of women and gays in American society; in clashes in schools over curricular reform and multiculturalism; in differences among policymakers over the urban crisis and approaches to rebuilding Los Angeles and other inner cities after the 1992 uprisings; and con-

21

tinuing reexaminations of U.S. involvement in Indochina more than two decades ago and the relevance of that war to U.S. military intervention in Iraq, Somalia, and Bosnia.

What happened in the 1960s that made such an impact on America? Why do discussions about that decade provoke so much emotion today? And do the movements of the 1960s serve as the same controversial reference point for Asian Americans?

The United States During the 1960s

In recent years, the movements of the 1960s have come under intense attack. One national bestseller, Allan Bloom's *Closing of the American Mind,* criticizes the movements for undermining the bedrock of Western thought.[2] According to Bloom, nothing positive resulted from the mass upheavals of the 1960s. He singles out black studies and affirmative-action programs and calls for eliminating them from universities.

Activists who have continued political work provide contrasting assessments. Their books include Todd Gitlin's *The Sixties: Years of Hope, Days of Rage;* James Miller's *"Democracy Is in the Streets": From Port Huron to the Siege of Chicago;* Ronald Fraser's *1968: A Student Generation in Revolt;* Tom Hayden's *Reunion: A Memoir;* Tariq Ali's *Street Fighting Years;* George Katsiaficas' *The Imagination of the New Left: A Global Analysis of 1968* and special issues of various journals, including *Witness, Socialist Review,* and *Radical America.*

However, as Winifred Breines states in an interesting review essay titled "Whose New Left?" most of the retrospects have been written by white male activists from elite backgrounds and reproduce their relationship to these movements.[3] Their accounts tend to divide the period into two phases: the "good" phase of the early 1960s, characterized by participatory democracy; followed by the post-1968 phase, when movement politics "degenerated" into violence and sectarianism.

"Almost all books about the New Left note a turning point or an ending in 1968 when the leadership of the movement turned toward militancy and violence and SDS [Students for a Democratic

Society] as an organization was collapsing," Breines observes. The retrospects commonly identify the key weaknesses of the movements as the absence of effective organization, the lack of discipline, and utopian thinking. Breines disagrees with these interpretations:

> The movement was not simply unruly and undisciplined; it was experimenting with antihierarchical organizational forms... There were many centers of action in the movement, many actions, many interpretations, many visions, many experiences. There was no [organizational] unity because each group, region, campus, commune, collective, and demonstration developed differently, but all shared in a spontaneous opposition to racism and inequality, the war in Vietnam, and the repressiveness of American social norms and culture, including centralization and hierarchy.[4]

Breines believes that the most important contributions of activists were their moral urgency, their emphasis on direct action, their focus on community building, and their commitment to mass democracy.

Similarly, Sheila Collins in *The Rainbow Challenge,* a book focusing on the Jesse Jackson presidential campaign of 1984 and the formation of the National Rainbow Coalition, assesses the movements of the sixties very positively.[5] She contends that the Jackson campaign was built on the grassroots organizing experience of activists who emerged from the struggles for civil rights, women's liberation, peace and social justice, and community building during the sixties. Moreover, activists' participation in these movements shaped their vision of America, which, in turn, became the basis for the platform of the Rainbow Coalition 20 years later.

According to Collins, the movements that occurred in the United States in the sixties were also part of a worldwide trend, a trend Latin American theologians call the era of the "eruption of the poor" into history. In America, the revolt of the "politically submerged" and "economically marginalized" posed a major ideological challenge to ruling elites:

The civil rights and black power movement exploded several dominant assumptions about the nature of American society, thus challenging the cultural hegemony of the white ruling elite and causing everyone else in the society to redefine their relationship to centers of power, creating a groundswell of support for radical democratic participation in every aspect of institutional life.[6]

Collins contends that the mass movements created a "crisis of legitimation" for ruling circles. This crisis, she believes, was "far more serious than most historians—even those of the left—have credited it with being."

Ronald Fraser also emphasizes the ideological challenge raised by the movements due to their mass, democratic character and their "disrespect for arbitrary and exploitative authority." In *1968: A Student Generation in Revolt,* Fraser explains how these concepts influenced one generation of activists:

[T]he anti-authoritarianism challenged almost every shibboleth of Western society. Parliamentary democracy, the authority of presidents...and [the policies of] governments to further racism, conduct imperialist wars or oppress sectors of the population at home, the rule of capital and the fiats of factory bosses, the dictates of university administrators, the sacredness of the family, sexuality, bourgeois culture—nothing was in principle sacrosanct...Overall...[there was] a lack of deference towards institutions and values that demean[ed] people and a concomitant awareness of people's rights.[7]

The San Francisco State Strike's Legacy

The retrospects about the 1960s produced so far have ignored Asian Americans. Yet, the books cited above—plus the review essay by Winifred Breines—provide us with some interesting points to compare and contrast. For example, 1968 represented a turning point for Asian Americans and other sectors of American society. But while white male leaders saw the year as marking the decline of the movement, 1968 for Asian Americans was a year of birth. It marked the beginning of the San Francisco State strike and all that followed.

The strike, the longest student strike in U.S. history, was the first campus uprising involving Asian Americans as a collective force.[8] Under the Third World Liberation Front—a coalition of African American, Latino, American Indian, and Asian American campus groups—students "seized the time" to demand ethnic studies, open admissions, and a redefinition of the education system. Although their five-month strike was brutally repressed and resulted in only partial victories, students won the nation's first School of Ethnic Studies.

Yet, we cannot measure the legacy of the strike for Asian Americans only in the tangible items it achieved, such as new classes and new faculty; the strike also critically transformed the consciousness of its participants who, in turn, profoundly altered their communities' political landscape. Through their participation, a generation of Asian American student activists reclaimed a heritage of struggle—linking their lives to the tradition of militancy of earlier generations of Pilipino farmworkers, Chinese immigrant garment and restaurant workers, and Japanese American concentration camp resisters. Moreover, these Asian American students—and their community supporters—liberated themselves from the prisons surrounding their lives and forged a new vision for their communities, creating numerous grassroots projects and empowering previously ignored and disenfranchised sectors of society. The statement of goals and principles of one campus organization, Philippine-American Collegiate Endeavor (PACE), during the strike captures this new vision:

> We seek ... simply to function as human beings, to control our own lives. Initially, following the myth of the American Dream, we worked to attend predominantly white colleges, but we have learned through direct analysis that it is impossible for our people, so-called minor-

ities, to function as human beings, in a racist society in which white always comes first ... So we have decided to fuse ourselves with the masses of Third World people, which are the majority of the world's peoples, to create, through struggle, a new humanity, a new humanism, a New World Consciousness, and within that context collectively control our own destinies.[9]

The San Francisco State strike is important not only as a beginning point for the Asian American movement, but also because it crystallizes several themes that would characterize Asian American struggles in the following decade. First, the strike occurred at a working-class campus and involved a coalition of Third World students linked to their communities. Second, students rooted their strike in the tradition of resistance by past generations of minority peoples in America. Third, strike leaders drew inspiration—as well as new ideology—from international Third World leaders and revolutions occurring in Asia, Africa, Latin America, and the Middle East. Fourth, the strike in its demands for open admissions, community control of education, ethnic studies, and self-determination confronted basic questions of power and oppression in America. Finally, strike participants raised their demands through a strategy of mass mobilizations and militant, direct action.

In the decade following the strike, several themes would reverberate in the struggles in Asian American communities across the nation. These included housing and anti-eviction campaigns, efforts to defend education rights, union organizing drives, campaigns for jobs and social services, and demands for democratic rights, equality, and justice. Mo Nishida, an organizer in Los Angeles, recalls the broad scope of movement activities in his city:

Our movement flowered. At one time, we had active student organizations on every campus around Los Angeles, fought for ethnic studies, equal opportunity programs, high potential programs at UCLA, and for students doing community work in "Serve the People" programs. In the community, we had, besides [Asian

American] Hard Core, four area youth-oriented groups working against drugs (on the Westside, Eastside, Gardena, and the Virgil district). There were also parents' groups, which worked with parents of the youth and more.[10]

In Asian American communities in Los Angeles, San Francisco, Sacramento, Stockton, San Jose, Seattle, New York, and Honolulu, activists created "serve the people" organizations—mass networks built on the principles of "mass line" organizing. Youth initiated many of these organizations—some from college campuses and others from high schools and the streets—but other members of the community, including small-business people, workers, senior citizens, and new immigrants soon joined.

The *mass* character of community struggles is the least appreciated aspect of our movement today. It is commonly believed that the movement involved only college students. In fact, a range of people, including high-school youth, tenants, small-business people, former prison inmates, former addicts, the elderly, and workers embraced the struggles. But exactly who were these people, and what did their participation mean to the movement?

Historian George Lipsitz has studied similar, largely "anonymous" participants in civil rights campaigns in African American communities. He describes one such man, Ivory Perry of St. Louis:

Ivory Perry led no important organizations, delivered no important speeches, and received no significant recognition or reward for his social activism. But for more than 30 years he had passed out leaflets, carried the picket signs, and planned the flamboyant confrontations that made the civil rights movements effective in St. Louis and across the nation. His continuous commitment at the local level had goaded others into action, kept alive hopes of eventual victory in the face of short-term defeats, and provided a relatively powerless community with an effective lever for social change. The anonymity of his activism suggests layers of social protest activity missing from most scholarly accounts, while the persistence of his involvement undermines prevailing academic judgments about mass protests as outbursts of immediate anger and spasmodic manifestations of hysteria.[11]

Those active in Asian American communities during the late 1960s and early 1970s know there were many Ivory Perrys. They were the people who demonstrated at eviction sites, packed City Hall hearing rooms, volunteered to staff health fairs, and helped with day-to-day operations of the first community drop-in centers, legal defense offices, and senior citizen projects. They were the women and men who took the concept of "serve the people" and turned it into a material force, transforming the political face of our communities.

The 'Cultural Revolution' in Asian American Communities

But we would be wrong to describe this transformation of our communities as solely "political"—at least as our society narrowly defines the term today. The transformation also involved a cultural vitality that opened new ways of viewing the world. Unlike today—where Asian American communities categorize "culture" and "politics" into different spheres of professional activity—in the late 1960s they did not divide them so rigidly or hierarchically. Writers, artists, and musicians were "cultural workers," usually closely associated with communities, and saw their work as "serving the people." Like other community activists, cultural workers defined the period as a "decisive moment" for Asian Americans—a time for reclaiming the past and changing the future.

The "decisive moment" was also a time for questioning and transforming moral values. Through their political and cultural work, activists challenged systems of rank and privilege, structures of hierarchy and bureaucracy, forms of exploitation and inequality, and notions of selfishness and individualism. Through their activism in mass organizations, they promoted a new moral vision centered on democratic participation, cooperative work styles, and collective decision-making. Pioneer poet Russell C. Leong describes the affinity between this new generation of cultural workers and their communities, focusing on the work of the Asian American Writers' Workshop, located in the basement of the International Hotel in San Francisco Chinatown/Manilatown:

> We were a post-World War II generation mostly in our twenties and thirties; in or out of local schools and colleges ... [We] gravitated toward cities—San Francisco, Los Angeles, New York—where movements for ethnic studies and inner city blocks of Asian communities coincided ... We read as we wrote—not in isolation—but in the company of our neighbors in Manilatown pool halls, barrio parks, Chinatown basements ... Above all, we poets were a tribe of storytellers ... Storytellers live in communities where they write for family and friends. The relationship between the teller and listener is neighborly, because the teller of stories must also listen.[12]

But as storytellers, cultural workers did more than simply describe events around them. By witnessing and participating in the movement, they helped to shape community consciousness. San Francisco poet Al Robles focuses on this process of vision making:

> While living and working in our little, tiny communities, in the midst of towering highrises, we fought the oppressor, the landlord, the developer, the banks, City Hall. But most of all, we celebrated through our culture; music, dance, song and poetry—not only the best we knew but the best we had. The poets were and always have been an integral part of the community. It was through poetry—through a poetical vision to live out the ritual in dignity as human beings.[13]

The transformation of poets, writers, and artists into cultural workers and vision makers reflected larger changes occurring in every sector of the Asian American community. In education, teachers and students redefined the learning process, discovering new ways of sharing knowledge different from traditional, authoritarian, top-down approaches. In the social-service sector, social workers and other professionals became "community workers" and under the slogan of "serve the people" redefined the traditional counselor/client relationship by stressing interaction, dialogue, and community building. Within community organizations, members experimented with new organizational structures and collective leadership styles, discarding hierarchical and bureaucratic forms where a handful of commanders made all the decisions. Everywhere, activists and ordinary people grappled with change.

Overall, this "cultural revolution" in the Asian American community echoes themes we have encountered earlier: Third World consciousness, participatory democracy, community building, historical rooting, liberation, and transformation. Why were these concepts so important to a generation of activists? What did they mean? And do they still have relevance for Asian American communities today?

Political analyst Raymond Williams and historian Warren Susman have suggested the use of "keywords" to study historical periods, especially times of great social change.[14] Keywords are terms, concepts, and ideas that emerge as themes of a period, reflecting vital concerns and changing values. For Asian Americans in the 1980s and 1990s, the keywords are "advocacy," "access," "legitimacy," "empowerment," and "assertiveness." These keywords tell us much about the shape of our community today, especially the growing role of young professionals and their aspirations in U.S. society. In contrast, the keywords of the late 1960s and early 1970s—"consciousness," "theory," "ideology," "participatory democracy," "community," and "liberation"—point to different concerns and values.

The keywords of two decades ago point to an approach to political work that activists widely shared, especially those working in grassroots struggles in Asian American neighborhoods, such as the Chinatowns, Little Tokyos, Manilatowns, and International Districts around the nation. This political approach focused on the relationship between political consciousness and social change, and can be best summarized in a popular slogan of the period: "Theory becomes a material force when it is grasped by the masses." Asian American activists believed that they could promote political change through direct action and mass education that raised political consciousness in the community, especially among the unorganized—low-income workers, tenants, small-business people, high school youth, etc. Thus, activists saw political consciousness as rising not from study groups, but from involving people in the process of social change—through their confronting the institutions of power around them and creating new visions of community life based on these struggles.

Generally, academics studying the movements of the 1960s—including academics in Asian American Studies—have dismissed the political theory of that time as murky and eclectic, characterized by ultra-leftism, shallow class analysis, and simplistic notions of Marxism and capitalism.[15] To a large extent, the thinking was eclectic; Asian American activists drew from Marx, Lenin, Stalin, and Mao—and also from Frantz Fanon, Malcolm X, Che Guevara, Kim Il-sung, and Amilcar Cabral, as well as Korean revolutionary Kim San, W. E. B. DuBois, Frederick Douglass, Paulo Freire, the Black Panther Party, the Young Lords, the women's liberation movement, and many other resistance struggles. But in their obsessive search for theoretical clarity and consistency, these academics miss the bigger picture. What is significant is not the *content* of ideas activists adopted, but what activists *did* with the ideas. What Asian American activists *did* was to use the ideas drawn from many different movements to redefine the Asian American experience.

Central to this redefinition was a slogan that appeared at nearly every Asian American rally during that period: "The people, and the people alone, are the motive force in the making of world history." Originating in the Chinese revolution, Asian American activists adapted the slogan to the tasks of community building, historical rooting, and creating new values. Thus, the slogan came to capture six new ways of thinking about Asian Americans.

- Asian Americans became active participants in the making of history, reversing standard accounts that had treated Asian Americans as marginal objects.

- Activists saw history as created by large numbers of people acting together, not by elites.

- This view of history provided a new way of looking at our communities. Activists believed that ordinary people could make their own history by learning how historical forces operated and by transforming this knowledge into a material force to change their lives.

- This realization defined a political strategy: Political power came from grassroots organizing, from the bottom up.

- This strategy required activists to develop a broad analysis of the Asian American condition—to uncover the interconnections in seemingly separate events, such as the war in Indochina, corporate redevelopment of Asian American communities, and the exploitation of Asian immigrants in garment shops. In their political analyses, activists linked the day-to-day struggles of Asian Americans to larger events and issues. The anti-eviction campaign of tenants in Chinatown and the International District against powerful corporations became one with the resistance movements of peasants in Vietnam, the Philippines, and Latin America—or, as summarized in a popular slogan of the period, there was "one struggle, [but] many fronts."

- This new understanding challenged activists to build mass, democratic organizations, especially within unorganized sectors of the community. Through these new organizations, Asian Americans expanded democracy for all sectors of the community and gained the power to participate in the broader movement for political change taking place throughout the world.

The redefinition of the Asian American experience stands as the most important legacy from this period. As described above, this legacy represents far more than an ethnic awakening. The redefinition began with an analysis of power and domination in American society. It provided a way for understanding the historical forces surrounding us. And most importantly, it presented a strategy and challenge for changing our future. This challenge, I believe, still confronts us today.

The Late 1970s: Reversing Direction

As we continue to delve into the vitality of the movements of the 1960s, one question becomes more and more persistent: Why did these movements, possessing so much vigor and urgency, seem to disintegrate in the late 1970s and early 1980s? Why did a society in motion toward progressive change seem to suddenly reverse direction?

As in the larger left movement, Asian American activists heatedly debate this question.[16] Some mention the strategy of repression—including assassinations—U.S. ruling circles launched in response to the mass rebellions. Others cite the accompanying programs of co-optation that elites designed to channel mass discontent into traditional political arenas. Some focus on the New Right's rise, culminating in the Reagan presidency. Still others emphasize the sectarianism among political forces within the movement, or target the inability of the movement as a whole to base itself more broadly within communities.

Each of these analyses provides a partial answer. But missing in most analyses by Asian American activists is the most critical factor: the devastating corporate offensive of the mid-1970s. We will remember the 1970s as a time of economic crisis and staggering inflation. Eventually, historians may more accurately describe it as the years of "one-sided class war." Transnational corporations based in the United States launched a broad attack on the American people, especially African American communities. Several books provide an excellent analysis of the corporate offensive. One of the best, most accessible accounts is *What's Wrong with the U.S.*

Economy?, written in 1982 by the Institute for Labor Education and Research.[17] My analysis draws from that.

Corporate executives based their offensive on two conclusions: First, the economic crisis in the early 1970s—marked by declining corporate profits—occurred because American working people were earning too much; and second, the mass struggles of the previous decades had created "too much democracy" in America. The Trilateral Commission—headed by David Rockefeller and composed of corporate executives and politicians from the United States, Europe, and Japan—posed the problem starkly: Either people would have to accept less, or corporations would have to accept less. An article in *Business Week* identified the solution: "Some people will obviously have to do with less ... Yet it will be a hard pill for many Americans to swallow—the idea of doing with less so that big business can have more."

But in order for corporations to "have more," U.S. ruling circles had to deal with the widespread discontent that had erupted throughout America. We sometimes forget today that in the mid-1970s a large number of Americans had grown cynical about U.S. business and political leaders. People routinely called politicians—including President Nixon and Vice President Agnew—crooks, liars, and criminals. Increasingly, they began to blame the largest corporations for their economic problems. One poll showed that half the population believed that "big business is the source of most of what's wrong in this country today." A series of Harris polls found that those expressing "a great deal of confidence" in the heads of corporations had fallen from 55 percent in 1966 to only 15 percent in 1975. By the fall of 1975, public-opinion analysts testifying before a congressional committee reported, according to the *New York Times,* "that public confidence in the government and in the country's economic future is probably lower than it has ever been since they began to measure such things scientifically." These developments stunned many corporate leaders. "How did we let the educational system fail the free-enterprise system?" one executive asked.

U.S. ruling elites realized that restoring faith in free enterprise could only be achieved through an intensive ideological assault on those challenging the system. The ideological campaign was combined with a political offensive, aimed at the broad gains in democratic rights that Americans, especially African Americans, had achieved through the mass struggles of previous decades. According to corporate leaders, there was "too much democracy" in America, which meant too little "governability." In a 1975 Trilateral Commission report, Harvard political scientist Samuel Huntington analyzed the problem caused by "previously passive or unorganized groups in the population [which were] now engaged in concerted efforts to establish their claims to opportunities, positions, rewards, and privileges which they had not considered themselves entitled to before." According to Huntington, this upsurge in "democratic fervor" coincided with "markedly higher levels of self-consciousness on the part of blacks, Indians, Chicanos, white ethnic groups, students and women, all of whom became mobilized and organized in new ways." Huntington saw these developments as creating a crisis for those in power:

> The essence of the democratic surge of the 1960s was a general challenge to existing systems of authority, public and private. In one form or another, the challenge manifested itself in the family, the university, business, public and private associations, politics, the government bureaucracy, and the military service. People no longer felt the same obligation to obey those whom they had previously considered superior to themselves in age, rank, status, expertise, character, or talents.[18]

The mass pressures, Huntington contended, had "produced problems for the governability of democracy in the 1970s." The government, he concluded, must find a way to exercise more control. And that meant curtailing the rights of "major economic groups."

The ensuing corporate campaign was a "one-sided class war": plant closures in U.S. industries and transfer of production overseas, massive layoffs in remaining industries, shifts of capital investment from one region of the country to other regions and other parts of the globe, and demands by corporations for concessions in wages and benefits from workers in nearly every sector of the economy.

The Reagan presidency culminated and institutionalized this offensive. The Reagan platform called for restoring "traditional" American values, especially faith in the system of free enterprise. Reaganomics promoted economic recovery by getting government "off the backs" of businesspeople, reducing taxation of the rich, and cutting social programs for the poor. Meanwhile, racism and exploitation became respectable under the new mantle of patriotism and economic recovery.

The Winter of Civil Rights

The corporate assault ravaged many American neighborhoods, but African American communities absorbed its harshest impact. A study by the Center on Budget and Policy Priorities measures the national impact:

- Between 1970 and 1980, the number of poor African Americans rose by 24 percent from 1.4 million to 1.8 million.

- In the 1980s, the overall African American median incomes was 57 percent that of whites, a decline of nearly four percentage points from the early 1970s.

- In 1986, females headed 42 percent of all African American families, the majority of which lived below the poverty line.

- In 1978, 8.4 percent of African American families had incomes under $5,000 a year. By 1987, that figure had grown to 13.5 percent. In that year, a third of all African Americans were poor.[19]

- By 1990, nearly half of all African American children grew up in poverty.[20]

Manning Marable provides a stark assessment of this devastation in *How Capitalism Underdeveloped Black America:*

What is qualitatively *new* about the current period is that the racist/capitalist state under Reagan has proceeded down a public policy road which could inevitably involve the complete obliteration of the entire Black reserve army of labor and sections of the Black working class. The decision to save capitalism at all costs, to provide adequate capital for restructuring of the private sector, fundamentally conflicts with the survival of millions of people who are now permanently outside the workplace. Reaganomics must, if it intends to succeed, place the onerous burden of unemployment on the shoulders of the poor (Blacks, Latinos and even whites) so securely that middle to upper income Americans will not protest in the vicious suppression of this stratum.[21]

The corporate offensive, combined with widespread government repression, brutally destroyed grassroots groups in the African American community. This war against the poor ripped apart the social fabric of neighborhoods across America, leaving them vulnerable to drugs and gang violence. The inner cities became the home of the "underclass" and a new politics of inner-directed violence and despair.

Historian Vincent Harding, in *The Other American Revolution,* summarizes the 1970s as the "winter" of civil rights, a period in which there was "a dangerous loss of hope among black people, hope in ourselves, hope in the possibility of any real change, hope in any moral, creative force beyond the flatness of our lives."[22]

In summary, the corporate offensive—especially its devastation of the African American community—provides the necessary backdrop for understanding why the mass movements of the 1960s seemed to disintegrate. Liberation movements, especially in the African American community, did not disappear, but a major focus of their activity shifted to issues of day-to-day survival.

The 1980s: An Ambiguous Period for Asian American Empowerment

For African Americans and many other people of color, the period from the mid-1970s through the Reagan and Bush presidencies became a winter of civil rights, a time of corporate assault on their livelihoods and an erosion of hard-won rights. But for Asian Americans, the meaning of this period is much more ambiguous. On the one hand, great suffering marked the period: growing poverty for increasing numbers of Asian Americans—especially refugees from Southeast Asia; a rising trend of racist hate crimes directed toward Asian Americans of all ethnicities and income levels; and sharpening class polarization within our communities—with a widening gap between the very rich and the very poor. But advances also characterized the period. With the reform of U.S. immigration laws in 1965, the Asian American population grew dramatically, creating new enclaves—including suburban settlements—and revitalizing more established communities, such as Chinatowns, around the nation. Some recent immigrant businesspeople, with small capital holdings, found economic opportunities in inner city neighborhoods. Meanwhile, Asian American youth enrolled in record numbers in colleges and universities across the United States. Asian American families moved into suburbs, crashing previously lily-white neighborhoods. And a small but significant group of Asian American politicians, such as Mike Woo and Warren Furutani, scored important electoral victories in the mainstream political arena, taking the concept of political empowerment to a new level of achievement.

During the winter of civil rights, Asian American activists also launched several impressive political campaigns at the grassroots level. Japanese Americans joined together to win redress and reparations. Pilipino Americans rallied in solidarity with the "People's Power" movement in the Philippines to topple the powerful Marcos dictatorship. Chinese Americans created new political alignments and mobilized community support for the pro-democracy struggle in China. Korean Americans responded to the massacre of civilians by the South Korean dictatorship in

Kwangju with massive demonstrations and relief efforts, and established an important network of organizations in America, including Young Koreans United. Samoan Americans rose up against police abuse in Los Angeles; Pacific Islanders demanded removal of nuclear weapons and wastes from their homelands; and Hawaiians fought for the right of self-determination and recovery of their lands. And large numbers of Asian Americans and Pacific Islanders worked actively in the 1984 and 1988 presidential campaigns of Jesse Jackson, helping to build the Rainbow Coalition.

Significantly, these accomplishments occurred in the midst of the Reagan presidency and U.S. politics' turn to the right. How did certain sectors of the Asian American community achieve these gains amidst conservatism?

There is no simple answer. Mainstream analysts and some Asian Americans have stressed the "model minority" concept. According to this analysis, Asian Americans—in contrast to other people of color in America—have survived adversity and advanced because of their emphasis on education and family values, their community cohesion, and other aspects of their cultural heritage. Other scholars have severely criticized this viewpoint, stressing instead structural changes in the global economy and shifts in U.S. government policy since the 1960s. According to their analysis, the reform of U.S. immigration laws and sweeping economic changes in advanced capitalist nations, such as deindustrialization and the development of new technologies, brought an influx of highly educated new Asian immigrants to America. The characteristics of these new immigrants stand in sharp contrast to those of past generations, and provide a broader social and economic base for developing our communities. Still other political thinkers have emphasized the key role played by political expatriates—both right-wing and left-wing—in various communities, but most especially in the Vietnamese, Pilipino, and Korean communities. These expatriates brought political resources from their homelands—e.g., political networks, organizing experience, and, in a few cases, access to large amounts of funds—and have used these resources to change the political landscape of ethnic enclaves. Still other analysts have examined the growing economic and political power

39

of nations of the Asia Pacific and its impact on Asians in America. According to these analysts, we can link the advances of Asian Americans during this period to the rising influence of their former homelands and the dawning of what some call "the Pacific Century." Finally, some academics have focused on the significance of small-business activities of new Asian immigrants, arguing that this sector is most responsible for the changing status of Asian Americans in the 1980s. According to their analysis, Asian immigrant entrepreneurs secured an economic niche in inner city neighborhoods because they had access to start-up capital (through rotating credit associations or from family members) and they filled a vacuum created when white businesses fled.[23]

Thus, we have multitiple interpretations for why some sectors of the Asian American community advanced economically and politically during the winter of civil rights. But two critical factors are missing from the analyses that can help us better understand the peculiar shape of our community in the 1980s and its ambiguous character when compared to other communities of color. First is the legacy of grassroots organizing from the Asian American movement, and second is the dramatic rise of young professionals as a significant force in the community.

A stereotype about the movements of the 1960s is that they produced nothing enduring—they flared brightly for an instant and then quickly died. However, evidence from the Asian American movement contradicts this commonly held belief. Through meticulous organizing campaigns, Asian American activists created an extensive network of grassroots formations. Unlike similar groups in African American communities—which government repression targeted and brutally destroyed—a significant number of Asian American groups survived the 1980s. Thus far, no researcher has analyzed the impact of the corporate offensive and government repression on grassroots organizations in different communities of color during the late 1970s. When this research is done, I think it will show that U.S. ruling elites viewed the movement in the African American community as a major threat due to its power and influence over other communities. In contrast, the movement in the Asian American community received much less attention due to its much smaller size and influence. As a result, Asian American grassroots formations during the 1970s escaped decimation and gained the time and space to survive, grow, and adapt to changing politics.

The survival of grassroots organizations is significant because it helped to cushion the impact of the war against the poor in Asian American communities. More important, the grassroots formations provided the foundation for many of the successful empowerment campaigns occurring in the 1980s. For example, Japanese Americans built their national effort to win reparations for their internment during World War II on the experiences of grassroots neighborhood organizations' housing and anti-eviction struggles of the early 1970s. Movement activists learned from their confrontations with systems of power and applied these lessons to the more difficult political fights of the 1980s. Thus, a direct link exists between the mass struggles of activists in the late 1960s and the "empowerment" approach of Asian Americans in the 1980s and 1990s.

But while similarities exist in political organizing of the late 1960s and the 1980s, there is one crucial difference: Who is being empowered? In the late 1960s and 1970s, activists focused on bringing "power to the people"—the most disenfranchised of the community, such as low-income workers, youth, former prisoners and addicts, senior citizens, tenants, and small-business people. In contrast, the "empowerment" of young professionals in Asian American communities marks the decade of the 1980s. The professionals—children of the civil rights' struggles of the 1950s and 1960s—directly benefited from the campaigns for desegregation, especially in the suburbs; the removal of quotas in colleges and professional schools; and the expansion of job opportunities for middle-class people of color in fields such as law, medicine, and education.

During the 1980s, young professionals altered the political terrain in our communities.[24] They created countless new groups in nearly every profession: law, medicine, social work, psychology, education, journalism, business, and arts and culture. They initiated new political advocacy groups, leadership training projects, and various national coalitions and consortiums. They organized political caucuses in the Democratic and Republican parties. And they joined the governing boards of many community agencies. Thus, young professionals—through their sheer numbers, their penchant for self-organization, and their high level of activity—defined the Asian American community of the 1980s, shaping it in ways very different from other communities of color.

The emergence of young professionals as community leaders also aided mass political mobilizations. By combining with grass-roots forces from the Asian American movement, young professionals advanced struggles against racism and discrimination. In fact, many of the successful Asian American battles of the past decade resulted from this strategic alignment.

The growing power of young professionals has also brought a diversification of political viewpoints to our communities. While many professionals embrace concerns originally raised by movement activists, a surprisingly large number have moved toward neo-conservatism. The emergence of neo-conservatism in our community is a fascinating phenomenon, one we should analyze and appreciate. Perhaps more than any other phenomenon, it helps to explain the political ambiguity of Asian American empowerment in the decade of the 1980s.

Strange and New Political Animals: Asian American Neo-Conservatives

Item: At many universities in recent years, some of the harshest opponents of affirmative action have been Chinese Americans and Korean Americans who define themselves as political conservatives. This, in and of itself, is not new or significant. We have always had Asian American conservatives who have spoken out against affirmative action. But what is new is their affiliation. Many participate actively in Asian American student organizations traditionally associated with campus activism.

Item: In the San Francisco newspaper *Asian Week,* one of the most interesting columnists is Arthur Hu, who writes about anti-

Asian quotas in universities, political empowerment, and other issues relating to our communities. He also regularly chastises those he terms "liberals, progressives, Marxists, and activists." In a recent column, he wrote: "The left today has the nerve to blame AIDS, drugs, the dissolution of the family, welfare dependency, gang violence, and educational failure on Ronald Reagan's conservatism." Hu, in turn, criticizes the left for "tearing down religion, family, structure, and authority; promoting drugs, promiscuity, and abdication of personal responsibility."[25]

Item: During the militant, three-year campaign to win tenure for UCLA Professor Don Nakanishi, one of the key student leaders was a Japanese American Republican, Matthew J. Endo. Aside from joining the campus-community steering committee, he also mobilized support from fraternities, something that progressive activists could not do. Matt prides himself on being a Republican and a life member of the National Rifle Association. He aspires to become a CEO in a corporation but worries about the upsurge in racism against Asian Pacific peoples and the failure of both Republicans and Democrats to address this issue.

The Asian American neo-conservatives are a new and interesting political phenomenon. They are new because they are creatures born from the Reagan-Bush era of supply-side economics, class and racial polarization, and the emphasis on elitism and individual advancement. And they are interesting because they also represent a legacy from the civil rights struggles, especially the Asian American movement. The neo-conservatives embody these seemingly contradictory origins.

- They are proud to be Asian American. But they denounce the Asian American movement of the late 1960s and early 1970s as destructive.

- They speak out against racism against Asian Americans. But they believe that only by ending affirmative-action programs and breaking with prevailing civil rights thinking of the past four decades can we end racism.

- They express concern for Asian American community issues. But they contend that the agenda set by the "liberal Asian American establishment" ignores community needs.

- They vehemently oppose quotas blocking admissions of Asian Americans at colleges and universities. But they link anti-Asian quotas to affirmative-actions programs for "less qualified" African Americans, Latinos, and American Indians.

- They acknowledge the continuing discrimination against African Americans, Latinos, and American Indians in U.S. society. But they believe that the main barrier blocking advancement for other people of color is "cultural"—that unlike Asians, these groups supposedly come from cultures that do not sufficiently emphasize education, family cohesion, and traditional values.

Where did these neo-conservatives come from? What do they represent? And why is it important for progressive peoples to understand their presence?

Progressives cannot dismiss Asian American neo-conservatives as simple-minded Republicans. Although they hold views similar at times to Patrick Buchanan and William Buckley, they are not clones of white conservatives. Nor are they racists, fellow travellers of the Ku Klux Klan, or ideologues attached to Reagan and Bush. Perhaps the group that they most resemble are the African American neo-conservatives: the Shelby Steeles, Clarence Thomases, and Tony Browns of this period. Like these men, they are professionals and feel little kinship for people of lower classes. Like these men, they oppose prevailing civil rights thinking, emphasizing reliance on government intervention and social programs. And like these men, they have gained from affirmative action, but they now believe that America has somehow become a society where other people of color can advance through their own "qualifications."

Neo-conservative people of color have embraced thinkers such as the late Martin Luther King, Jr., but have appropriated his message to fit their own ideology. In his speeches and writings, King dreamed of the day when racism would be eliminated—when African Americans would be recognized in U.S. society for the "content of our character, not the color of our skin." He called upon all in America to wage militant struggle to achieve this dream. Today, neo-conservatives have subverted his message. They believe that racism in U.S. society has declined in significance, and that people of color can now abandon mass militancy and advance individually by cultivating the content of their character through self-help programs and educational attainment, and retrieving traditional family values. They criticize prevailing "civil rights thinking" as over-emphasizing the barriers of racism and relying on "external forces" (i.e., government intervention through social programs) to address the problem.

Asian American neo-conservatives closely resemble their African American counterparts in their criticism of government "entitlement" programs and their defense of traditional culture and family values. But Asian American neo-conservatives are not exactly the same as their African American counterparts. The growth of neo-conservative thinking among Asian Americans during the past 25 years reflects the peculiar conditions in our community, notably the emerging power of young professionals. Thus, to truly understand Asian American neo-conservatives, we need to look at their evolution through the prism of Asian American politics from the late 1960s to the early 1990s.

Twenty-five years ago, Asian American neo-conservatives did not exist. Our community then had only traditional conservatives—those who opposed ethnic studies, the antiwar movement, and other militant grassroots struggles. The traditional conservatives denounced Asian American concerns as "special interest politics" and labeled the assertion of Asian American ethnic identity as "separatist" thinking. For the traditional conservative, a basic contradiction existed in identifying oneself as Asian American and conservative.

Ironically, the liberation struggles of the 1960s—and the accompanying Asian American movement—spawned a new conservative thinker. The movement partially transformed the educational curriculum through ethnic studies, enabling all Asian Americans to assert pride in their ethnic heritage. The movement accelerated the desegregation of suburbs, enabling middle-class Asian Americans to move into all-white neighborhoods. Today, the neo-conservatives are mostly young, middle-class professionals who grew up in white suburbs apart from the poor and people of color. As students, they attended the elite universities. Their only experience with racism is name-calling or "glass ceilings" blocking personal career advancement—and not poverty and violence.

It is due to their professional status and their roots in the Asian American movement that the neo-conservatives exist in uneasy alliance with traditional conservatives in our community. Neo-conservatives are appalled by the violence and rabid anti-communism of reactionary sectors of the Vietnamese community, Chinese from Taiwan tied to the oppressive ruling Kuomintang party, and Korean expatriates attached to the Korean Central Intelligence Agency. They are also uncomfortable with older conservatives, those coming from small-business backgrounds who warily eye the neo-conservatives, considering them as political opportunists.

Neo-conservatives differ from traditional conservatives not only because of their youth and their professional status but most important of all, their political coming of age in the Reagan era. Like their African American counterparts, they are children of the corporate offensive against workers, the massive transfer of resources from the poor to the rich, and the rebirth of so-called "traditional values."

It is their schooling in Reaganomics and their willingness to defend the current structure of power and privilege in America that gives neo-conservative people of color value in today's political landscape. Thus, Manning Marable describes the key role played by African American neo-conservatives:

> The singular service that [they] ... provide is a new and more accurate understanding of what exactly constitutes conservatism within the Black experience ... Black conservatives are traditionally hostile to Black partici-

pation in trade unions, and urge a close cooperation with white business leaders. Hostile to the welfare state, they call for increased "self-help" programs run by Blacks at local and community levels. Conservatives often accept the institutionalized forms of patriarchy, acknowledging a secondary role for Black women within economics, political life and intellectual work. They usually have a pronounced bias towards organizational authoritarianism and theoretical rigidity.[26]

Marable's analysis points to the basic contradiction for African American neo-conservatives. They are unable to address fundamental problems facing their community: racist violence, grinding poverty, and the unwillingness of corporate and government policymakers to deal with these issues.

Asian American neo-conservatives face similar difficulties when confronted by the stark realities of the post-Reagan period:

- The neo-conservatives acknowledge continuing discrimination in U.S. society but deny the existence of institutional racism and structural inequality. For them, racism lies in the realm of attitudes and "culture" and not institutions of power. Thus, they emphasize individual advancement as the way to overcome racism. They believe that people of color can rise through merit, which they contend can be measured objectively through tests, grades, and educational attainment.

- The neo-conservatives ignore questions of wealth and privilege in American society. In their obsession with "merit," "qualifications," and "objective" criteria, they lose sight of power and oppression in America. Their focus is on dismantling affirmative-action programs and "government entitlements" from the civil rights era. But poverty and racism existed long before the civil rights movement. They are embedded in the system of inequality that has long characterized U.S. society.

- The neo-conservatives are essentially elitists who fear expansion of democracy at the grassroots level. They speak a language of individual advancement, not mass empowerment. They propose a strategy of alignment with existing centers of power and not the creation of new power bases among the disenfranchised sectors of society. Their message is directed to professionals, much like themselves. They have nothing to offer to immigrant workers in sweatshops, the homeless, Cambodian youth in street gangs, or community college youth.

- As relative newcomers to Asian American issues, the neo-conservatives lack understanding of history, especially how concerns in the community have developed over time. Although they aggressively speak out about issues, they lack experience in organizing around these issues. The neo-conservatives function best in the realm of ideas; they have difficulty dealing with concrete situations.

However, by stimulating discussion over how Asian Americans define community problems, the neo-conservatives bring a vibrancy to community issues by contributing a different viewpoint. Thus, the debate between Asian American neo-conservatives and progressives is positive because it clarifies issues and enables both groups to reach constituencies that each could not otherwise reach.

Unfortunately, this debate is also occurring in a larger and more dangerous context: the campaign by mainstream conservatives to redefine civil rights in America. As part of their strategy, conservatives in the national political arena have targeted our communities. There are high stakes here, and conservatives regard the Asian American neo-conservatives as small players to be sacrificed.

The high stakes are evident in an article by William McGurn entitled "The Silent Minority" appearing in the conservative digest *National Review*.[27] In his essay, he urges Republicans to actively recruit and incorporate Asian Americans into party activities. According to McGurn, a basic affinity exists between Republican values and Asian American values: Many Asian immigrants own small businesses; they oppose communism; they are fiercely pro-defense; they boast strong families; they value freedom; and in their approach to civil rights, they stress opportunities not government "set-asides." McGurn then chastises fellow Republicans for their "crushing indifference" to Asian American issues. He laments how Republicans have lost opportunities by not speaking out on key issues such as the conflict between Korean immigrant merchants and African Americans, the controversy over anti-Asian quotas in universities, and the upsurge in anti-Asian violence.

McGurn sees Republican intervention on these issues strategically—as a way of redefining the race question in American society and shifting the debate on civil rights away from reliance on "an increasingly narrow band of black and liberal interest groups." According to McGurn:

> Precisely because Asian Americans are making it in their adoptive land, they hold the potential not only to add to Republican rolls but to define a bona-fide American language of civil rights. Today we have only one language of civil rights, and it is inextricably linked to government intervention, from racial quotas to set-aside government contracts. It is also an exclusively black-establishment language, where America's myriad other minorities are relegated to second-class citizenship.[28]

McGurn's article presages a period of intense and unprecedented conservative interest in Asian American issues. We can expect conservative commentaries to intensify black–Asian conflicts in inner cities, the controversy over affirmative action, and the internal community debate over designating Asian Americans as a "model minority."

Thus, in the coming period, Asian American communities are likely to become crowded places. Unlike the late 1960s, issues affecting our communities will no longer be the domain of progressive forces only. Increasingly, we will hear viewpoints from Asian

American neo-conservatives as well as mainstream conservatives. How well will activists meet this new challenge?

Grassroots Organizing in the 1990s: The Challenge of Expanding Democracy

> Time would pass, old empires would fall and new ones take their place, the relations of countries and the relations of classes had to change, before I discovered that it is not quality of goods and utility which matter, but movement; not where you are or what you have, but where you have come from, where you are going and the rate at which you are getting there.[29]
>
> —C.L.R. James

On the eve of the twenty-first century, the Asian American community is vastly different from that of the late 1960s. The community has grown dramatically. In 1970, there were only 1.5 million Asian Americans, almost entirely concentrated in Hawaii and California. By 1980, there were 3.7 million, and in 1990, 7.9 million—with major Asian communities in New York, Minnesota, Pennsylvania, and Texas. According to census projections, the Asian American population should exceed 10 million by the year 2000, and will reach 20 million by the year 2020.[30]

Moreover, in contrast to the late 1960s—when Chinese and Japanese Americans comprised the majority of Asian Americans, today's community is ethnically diverse—consisting of nearly 30 major ethnic groups, each with a distinct culture. Today's community is also economically different from the 1960s. Compared to other sectors of the U.S. population, there are higher proportions of Asian Americans who are very rich and very poor. This gap between wealth and poverty has created a sharp class polarization in our community, a phenomenon yet to be studied.

But the changes for Asian Americans during the past 25 years have not been simply demographic. The political landscape has also changed due to new immigrants and refugees, the polarization between rich and poor, and the emergence of young professionals as a vital new force. Following the approach of C. L. R. James, we have traced the origins of these changes. We now need to analyze where these changes will take us in the decade ahead.

Ideologically and politically, activists confront a new and interesting paradox in the Asian American community of the 1990s. On the one hand, there is a great upsurge of interest in the community and all things Asian American. Almost daily, we hear about new groups forming across the country. In contrast to 25 years ago, when interest in the community was minimal and when only progressive activists joined Asian American organizations, we now find a situation where many different groups—including conservatives and neo-conservatives, bankers and business executives, and young professionals in all fields—have taken up the banner of Asian American identity.

On the other hand, we have not seen a corresponding growth in consciousness—of what it means to be Asian American as we approach the the twenty-first century. Unlike African Americans, most Asian Americans today have yet to articulate the "particularities" of issues affecting our community, whether these be the debate over affirmative action, the controversy regarding multiculturalism, or the very definition of empowerment. We have an ideological vacuum, and activists will compete with neo-conservatives, mainstream conservatives, and others to fill it.

We have a political vacuum as well. In recent years, growing numbers of Asian Americans have become involved in community issues. But almost all have come from middle-class and professional backgrounds. Meanwhile, vast segments of our community are not coming forward. In fact, during the past decade the fundamental weakness for activists has been the lack of grassroots organizing among the disenfranchised sectors of our community: youth outside of colleges and universities, the poor, and new immigrant workers. Twenty-five years ago, the greatest strength of the Asian American movement was the ability of activists to organize the unorganized and to bring new political players into community politics. Activists targeted high-school youth, tenants, small-business people, former prison inmates, gang members, the elderly, and workers. Activists helped them build new grassroots organizations, expanding power and democracy in our communities. Can a new generation of activists do the same?

To respond to this challenge, activists will need both a political strategy and a new ideological vision. Politically, activists must find ways to expand democracy by creating new grassroots formations, activating new political players, and building new coalitions. Ideologically, activists must forge a new moral vision, reclaiming the militancy and moral urgency of past generations and reaffirming the commitment to participatory democracy, community building, and collective styles of leadership.

Where will this political strategy and new consciousness come from? More than 50 years ago, revolutionary leader Mao Zedong asked a similar question:

> Where do correct ideas come from? Do they drop from the skies? No. Are they innate in the mind? No. They come from social practice, and from it alone ... In their social practice, people engage in various kinds of struggle and gain rich experience, both from their successes and their failures.[31]

In the current "social practice" of Asian American activists across the nation, several grassroots organizing projects can serve as the basis for a political strategy and new moral vision for the 1990s. I will focus on three projects that are concentrating on the growing numbers of poor and working poor in our community. Through their grassroots efforts, these three groups are demonstrating how collective power can expand democracy, and how, in the process, activists can forge a new moral vision.

The three groups—the Chinese Progressive Association (CPA) Workers Center in Boston, Asian Immigrant Women Advocates (AIWA) in Oakland, and Korean Immigrant Worker Advocates (KIWA) in Los Angeles—address local needs. Although each organization works with different ethnic groups, their history of organizing has remarkable similarities. Each organization is composed of low-income immigrant workers. Each has taken up more than "labor" issues. And each group has fashioned very effective "united front" campaigns involving other sectors of the community. Thus, although each project is relatively small, collectively their accomplishments illustrate the power of grassroots organizing, the creativity and talents of "ordinary" people in taking up difficult issues, and the ability of grassroots forces to alter the political landscape of their community. Significantly, the focus of each group is working people in the Asian American community—a sector that is numerically large and growing larger. However, despite their numbers, workers in the Asian American community during the past decade have become voiceless and silent. Today, in discussions about community issues, no one places garment workers, nurses' aides, waiters, and secretaries at the forefront of the debate to define priorities. And no one thinks about the working class as the cutting edge of the Asian American experience. Yet, if we begin to list the basic questions now confronting Asian Americans—racism and sexism, economic justice and human rights, coalition building, and community empowerment—we would find that it is the working class, of all sectors in our community, that is making the most interesting breakthroughs on these questions. They are doing this through groups such as KIWA, AIWA, and the CPA Workers Center. Why, then, are the voices of workers submerged in our community? Why has the working class become silent?

Three trends have pushed labor issues in our community into the background during the past two decades: the rising power of young professionals in our community; the influx of new immigrants and refugees, and the fascination of social scientists and policy institutes with the phenomenon of immigrant entrepreneurship; and the lack of grassroots organizing by activists among new immigrant workers.

Thus, although the majority of Asian Americans work for a living, we have relatively little understanding about the central place of work in the lives of Asian Americans, especially in low-income industries such as garment work, restaurant work, clerical and office work, and other service occupations. Moreover, we are ignorant about the role that labor struggles have played in shaping our history.[32] This labor history is part of the legacy that activists must reclaim.

In contrast to the lack of knowledge about Asian American workers, we have a much greater understanding about the role of young professionals, students, and, most of all, small-business people. In fact, immigrant entrepreneurs, especially Korean immigrants, are perhaps the most studied people of our community. However, as sociologist Edna Bonacich notes, the profile of most Asian immigrant entrepreneurs closely resembles that of workers, due to their low earning power, their long work hours, and their lack of job-related benefits. Thus, Bonacich suggests that while the world outlook of Asian immigrant entrepreneurs may be petit bourgeoisie, their life conditions are those of the working class and might better be studied as a "labor" question. Asian immigrant small businesses, she contends, play the role of "cheap labor in American capitalism."[33]

Other researchers have only begun to investigate the extent of poverty among Asian Americans and the meaning of poverty for our community. In California, the rate of poverty for Asian Americans rose from about 10 percent in 1980 to 18 percent in 1990. But more important, researchers found that there are higher numbers of "working poor" (as opposed to "jobless poor") in the Asian American community than for other ethnic groups. Thus, in contrast to other Americans, Asian Americans are poor not because they lack jobs but because the jobs they have pay very low wages. According to researchers Dean Toji and James Johnson, Jr., "Perhaps contrary to common belief, about half of the poor work—including about a quarter of poor adults who work full-time and year-round. Poverty, then, is a labor question."[34]

Activists in groups such as KIWA, AIWA, and the CPA Workers Center are strategically focusing on the "working poor" in the Asian American community. KIWA—which was founded in 1992—is working with low-income Korean immigrants in Los Angeles Koreatown, including garment workers and employees in small businesses. AIWA—founded in 1983—organizes Chinese garment workers, Vietnamese garment and electronics workers, and Korean hotel maids and electronics assemblers. And the CPA

Workers Center—which traces its roots to the landmark struggle of Chinese garment workers in Boston in 1985—is composed primarily of Chinese immigrant women. Although their main focus is on workers, each group has also mobilized students and social service providers to support their campaigns. Through these alliances, each group has carried out successful community organizing strategies.

The focus of the three groups on community-based organizing distinguishes them from traditional unions. Miriam Ching Louie of AIWA explains this distinction:

> AIWA's base is simultaneously worker, female, Asian, and immigrant, and the organization has developed by blending together several different organizing techniques. As compared to the traditional union organizing strategy, AIWA's approach focuses on the needs of its constituency. *Popular literacy/conscientization/transformation* [based on the teachings of Paulo Freire] is a learning and teaching method which taps into people's life experiences as part of a broader reality, source of knowledge, and guide to action. *Community-based organizing* takes a holistic view of racial/ethnic people and organizes for social change, not only so that the people can win immediate improvements in their lives, but so that they can also develop their own power in the course of waging the fight.[35]

AIWA's focus on grassroots organizing is illustrated by its "Garment Workers' Justice Campaign," launched in late 1992 to assist Chinese immigrant women who were denied pay by a garment contractor. AIWA organizers shaped the campaign to respond to the peculiar features of the garment industry. The industry in the San Francisco Bay Area is the nation's third largest—following New York and Los Angeles—and employs some 20,000 seamstresses, 85 percent of them Asian immigrant women. The structure of the industry is a pyramid with retailers and manufacturers at the top, contractors in the middle, and immigrant women working at the bottom. Manufacturers make the main share of profits in the industry; they set the price for contractors. Meanwhile, immigrant women work under sweatshop conditions.

In their campaign, AIWA and the workers initially confronted the contractor for the workers' backpay. When they discovered that the contractor owed a number of creditors, they took the unusual step of holding the garment manufacturer, Jessica McClintock, accountable for the unpaid wages. McClintock operates 10 boutiques and sells dresses through department stores. The dresses—which garment workers are paid $5 to make—retail in stores for $175. AIWA and the workers conducted their campaign through a series of high-profile demonstrations at McClintock boutiques, including picketlines and rallies in 10 cities by supporters. AIWA designed these demonstrations not only to put pressure on McClintock and educate others in the community about inequities in the structure of the garment industry, but also to serve as vehicles for empowerment for the immigrant women participating the campaign. Through this campaign, the women workers learned how to confront institutional power, how to forge alliances with other groups in the community, and how to carry out effective tactics based on their collective power.[36]

Thus, through its activities promoting immigrant women's rights, AIWA is expanding democracy in the community. It is bringing labor issues to the forefront of community dicussions. It is creating new grassroots caucuses among previously unorganized sectors of the community, and forming new political alignments with supporters, such as students, young professionals, labor unions, and social service providers. Finally, AIWA is developing a cadre of politically sophisticated immigrant women and promoting a new leadership style based on popular literacy, community building, and collective power.

Similarly, in Boston, the CPA Workers Center is expanding democracy through its grassroots efforts around worker rights. The Center emerged out of the Chinese immigrant women's campaign to deal with the closing of a large garment factory in Boston in 1985.[37] The shutdown displaced 350 workers and severely impacted the local Chinese community due to the community's high concentration of jobs in the garment industry. However, with the assistance of the Chinese Progressive Alliance, the workers formed a labor-community-student coalition and waged an 18-month campaign to win job retraining and job replacement. Lydia Lowe, director of the CPA Workers Center, describes how the victory of Chinese immigrant women led to creation of the Workers Center, which, in turn, has helped other work place campaigns in the Chinese community:

> This core of women activated through the campaign joined with community supporters from the CPA to found a community-based workers' mutual aid and resource center, based at CPA ... Through the Workers Center, immigrant workers share their experience, collectively sum up lessons learned, find out about their rights, and develop mutual support and organizing strategies. Today, the Workers Center involves immigrant workers from each of its successive organizing efforts, and is a unique place in the community where ordinary workers can walk in and participate as activists and decision-makers.[38]

Moreover, forming the Workers Center reshaped politics in the local Chinese community, turning garment workers and other immigrant laborers into active political players. "Previously the silent majority, immigrant workers are gaining increasing respect as a force to be reckoned with in the local Chinese community," states Lowe.

In Los Angeles, the formation of KIWA in March 1992—only a month before the uprisings—has had a similar impact. Through its programs, KIWA is bringing labor issues to the forefront of the Asian American community, educating labor unions about the needs of Asian American workers, and forming coalitions with other grassroots forces in the city to deal with inter-ethnic tensions. KIWA is uniquely positioned to take up these tasks. Out of the multitude of Asian American organizations in Los Angeles, KIWA distinguishes itself as the only organization governed by a board of directors of mainly workers.

57

KIWA's key role in the labor movement and community politics is evident in the recent controversy involving the Koreana Wilshire Hotel.[39] The controversy began in late 1991 when Koreana Hotel Co. Ltd., a South Korean corporation, bought the Wilshire Hyatt in Los Angeles. The change in ownership meant that 175 unionized members, predominantly Latino immigrants, were out of jobs. Meanwhile, the new hotel management hired a new work force, paying them an average of $1.50 per hour less than the former unionized work force. The former workers, represented by Hotel Employees and Restaurant Employees (HERE) Local 11, called upon labor unions and groups from the Asian American, African American, and Latino communities to protest Koreana's union-busting efforts. Local 11 defined the dispute as not only a labor issue, but a civil rights issue. With the help of groups such as KIWA and the Asian Pacific American Labor Alliance, Local 11 initiated a letter-writing campaign against Koreana, began a community boycott of the hotel, and organized militant actions outside the hotel, including rallies, marches, and a picket line, as well as civil disobedience at the nearby Korean consulate. In each of these actions, Local 11 worked closely with KIWA and members of the Asian American community. Due to the mass pressure, in late 1992 the Koreana management agreed to negotiate with Local 11 to end the controversy and rehire the union members.

Throughout the campaign, KIWA played a pivotal role by assisting Local 11 build alliances with the Asian American community. In addition, KIWA members promoted labor consciousness in the Korean community by urging the community to boycott the hotel. KIWA members also spoke at Local 11 rallies, mobilized for picket lines, and worked with the union in its efforts to put pressure on the South Korean government. By taking these steps, KIWA prevented the controversy from pitting the Korean community against Latinos and further enflaming inter-ethnic tensions in Los Angeles.

Also, through campaigns such as this one, KIWA is educating Asian immigrants about unions; training workers around the tasks of political leadership; and creating new centers of power in the community by combining the resources of workers, young professionals, and social service providers.

Thus, through grassroots organizing, KIWA—like AIWA and the CPA Workers Center—is expanding democracy in the Asian American community. Moreover, the three groups collectively are reshaping community consciousness. They are sharpening debate and dialogue around issues and redefining such important concepts as empowerment. What is their vision of empowerment, and how does it differ from prevailing definitions?

The Twenty-first Century: Building an Asian American Movement

> [A] movement is an idea, a philosophy … Leadership, I feel, is only incidental to the movement. The movement should be the most important thing. The movement must go beyond its leaders. It must be something that is continuous, with goals and ideas that the leadership can then build on.[40]
>
> —Philip Vera Cruz

In the late 1960s, Asian American activists sought to forge a new approach to leadership that would not replicate traditional Eurocentric models—i.e., rigid hierarchies with a single executive at the top, invariably a white male, who commanded an endless chain of assistants. In their search for alternatives, activists experimented with various ideas borrowed from other movements, but most of all, activists benefited from the advice and guidance of "elders" within the Asian American community—women and men with years of grassroots organizing experience in the community, the work place, and the progressive political movement. One such "elder" was Pilipino immigrant labor leader Philip Vera Cruz, then in his sixties. Vera Cruz represented the *manong* generation—the first wave of Pilipinos who came to the United States in the early twentieth century and worked in agricultural fields, canneries, hotels, and restaurants.

Now 88 years old, Vera Cruz continues to educate a new generation of activists. His lifetime of experience in grassroots organizing embodies the historic themes of Asian American activism: devotion to the rights of working people, commitment to democracy and liberation, steadfast solidarity with all who face oppression throughout the world, and the courage to challenge existing institutions of power and to create new institutions as the need arises. These themes have defined his life and shaped his approach to the question of empowerment—an approach that is different from standard definitions in our community today.

Vera Cruz is best known for his role in building the United Farm Workers (UFW), a culmination of his many years of organizing in agricultural fields. In 1965, he was working with the Agricultural Workers Organizing Committee, AFL–CIO, when Pilipino farmworkers sat-down in the Coachella vineyards of central California. This sit-down launched the famous grape strike and boycott, eventually leading to the formation of the UFW. Many books and articles have told the story of the UFW and its leader Cesar Chavez. But until recently, no one has focused on the historic role of Pilipinos in building this movement. Craig Scharlin and Lilia Villanueva have filled that vacuum with their new publication about Vera Cruz's life.

Following the successful grape boycott, Vera Cruz became a UFW vice president and remained with the union until 1977, when he left due to political differences with the leadership. He was critical of the lack of rank-and-file democracy in the union, and the leadership's embrace of the Marcos dictatorship in the Philippines. Since 1979, Vera Cruz has lived in Bakersfield, California, and has continued to devote his life to unionism and social justice, and to the education of a new generation of Asian American youth.

Vera Cruz's life experiences have shaped a broad view of empowerment. For Vera Cruz, empowerment is grassroots power: the expansion of democracy for the many. Becoming empowered means gaining the capacity to advocate not only for one's own concerns but for the liberation of all oppressed peoples. Becoming empowered means being able to fundamentally change the relationship of power and oppression in society. Thus, Vera Cruz's vision is very different from that of today's young professionals. For them, empowerment is leadership development for an elite. Becoming empowered means gaining the skills to advocate for the community by gaining access to decisionmakers. Thus, for young professionals, the key leadership quality to develop is assertiveness. Through assertiveness, leaders gain access to policymakers as well as the power to mobilize their followers. In contrast, Vera Cruz stresses the leadership trait of humility. For him, leaders are "only incidental to the movement"—the movement is "the most important thing." For Vera Cruz, empowerment is a process where people join to develop goals and ideas to create a larger movement—a movement "that the leadership can then build on."

Vera Cruz's understanding of empowerment has evolved from his own social practice. Through his experiences in the UFW and the AFL-CIO, Vera Cruz learned about the empty democracy of bureaucratic unions and the limitations of the charismatic leadership style of Cesar Chavez. Through his years of toil as a farmworker, he recognized the importance of worker solidarity and militancy and the capacity of common people to create alternative institutions of grassroots power. Through his work with Pilipino and Mexican immigrants, he saw the necessity of coalition-building and worker unity that crossed ethnic and racial boundaries. He has shared these lessons with several generations of Asian American activists.

But aside from sharing a concept of empowerment, Vera Cruz has also promoted a larger moral vision, placing his lifetime of political struggle in the framework of the movement for liberation. Three keywords distinguish his moral vision: "compassion," "solidarity," and "commitment." Vera Cruz's lifetime of action represents compassion for all victims of oppression, solidarity with all fighting for liberation, and commitment to the ideals of democracy and social justice.

Activists today need to learn from Vera Cruz's compassion, solidarity, commitment, and humility to create a new moral vision for our community. In our grassroots organizing, we need a vision that can redefine empowerment—that can bring questions of power, domination, and liberation to the forefront of our work. We need a vision that can help us respond to the challenge of conservatives and neo-conservatives, and sharpen dialogue with young professionals. We need a new moral vision that can help fill the ideological vacuum in today's community.

Nowhere is this ideological challenge greater than in the current debate over the model minority stereotype. The stereotype has become the dominant image of Asian Americans for mainstream society, and has generated intense debate among all sectors of our community. This debate provides an opportunity for activists to expand political awareness and, in the process, redefine the Asian American experience for the 1990s.

In the current controversy, however, activists criticize the model minority stereotype politically but not ideologically. Activists correctly target how the concept fails to deal with Asian American realities: the growing population of poor and working poor, the large numbers of youth who are not excelling in school, and the hardships and family problems of small-business people who are not "making it" in U.S. society. Activists also correctly point out the political ramifications of the model minority stereotype: the pitting of minority groups against each other, and growing inter-ethnic tensions in U.S. society. In contrast, conservative and neo-conservative proponents of the model minority concept argue from the standpoint of both political realities and a larger moral vision. They highlight Asian American accomplishments: "whiz kids" in elementary schools; growing numbers of Asian Americans in business, politics, and the professions; and the record enrollment of youth in colleges and universities. Conservatives and neo-conservatives attribute these accomplishments to Asian culture and tradition, respect for authority, family cohesion, sacrifice and toil, rugged individualism, and self-reliance—moral values that they root in conservative thinking. Conservatives and neo-conservatives recognize that "facts" gain power from attachment to ideologies. As a result, they appropriate Asian culture and values to promote their arguments.

But is Asian culture inherently conservative—or does it also have a tradition of militancy and liberation? Do sacrifice, toil, and family values comprise a conservative moral vision only—or do these qualities also constitute the core of radical and revolutionary thinking? By asking these questions, activists can push the debate over the model minority concept to a new, ideological level. Moreover, by focusing on ideology, activists can delve into the stereotype's deeper meaning. They can help others understand the stereotype's origins and why it has become the dominant image for Asian Americans today.

Historically, the model minority stereotype first arose in the late 1950s—the creation of sociologists attempting to explain low levels of juvenile delinquency among Chinese and Japanese Americans.[41] The stereotype remained a social-science construct until the 1960s when a few conservative political commentators began to use it to contrast Asian Americans' "respect for law and order" to African Americans' involvement in civil rights marches, rallies, and sit-ins. By the late 1970s, the stereotype moved into the political mainstream, coinciding with the influx of new Asian immigrants into all parts of the United States. But the widespread acceptance of the stereotype was not simply due to the increase in the Asian American population or the new attention focused on our community from mainstream institutions. More importantly, it coincided with the rise of the New Right and the corporate offensive against the poor. As discussed earlier, this offensive economically devastated poor communities and stripped away hard-won political gains. This offensive also included an ideological campaign designed to restore trust in capitalism and values associated with free enterprise. Meanwhile, conservatives and neo-conservatives fought to redefine the language of civil rights by attacking federal government "entitlement" programs while criticizing the African American "liberal establishment."

In this political climate, the model minority stereotype flourished. It symbolized the moral vision of capitalism in the 1980s: a celebration of traditional values, an emphasis on hard work and self-reliance, a respect for authority, and an attack on prevailing civil rights thinking associated with the African American community. Thus, the stereotype took on an ideological importance above and beyond the Asian American community. The hard-working immigrant merchant and the refugee student winning the local spelling bee have become the symbols for the resurrection of capitalist values in the last part of the twentieth century.

Yet, we know a gap exists between symbol and reality. Today, capitalism in America is not about small-business activities; it is about powerful transnational corporations and their intricate links to nation-states and the world capitalist system. Capitalist values no longer revolve around hard work and self-reliance; they deal with wealth and assets, and the capacity of the rich to invest, speculate, and obtain government contracts. And the fruits of capitalism in the last part of the twentieth century are not immigrant entrepreneurship and the revival of urban areas; they are more likely to be low-paying jobs, unemployment, bankruptcies, and homelessness.

However, as corporations, banks, and other institutions abandon the inner city, the immigrant merchant—especially the Korean small business—emerges as the main symbol of capitalism in these neighborhoods. For inner city residents, the Asian immigrant becomes the target for their wrath against corporate devastation of their neighborhoods. Moreover, as this symbol merges with other historical stereotypes of Asians, the result is highly charged imagery, which perhaps underlies the ferocity of anti-Asian violence in this period, such as the destruction of Korean small businesses during the Los Angeles uprisings. The Asian immigrant becomes a symbol of wealth—and also greed; a symbol of hard work—and also materialism; a symbol of intelligence—and also arrogance; a symbol of self-reliance—and also selfishness and lack of community concern. Thus, today the model minority stereotype has become a complex symbol through the confluence of many images imposed on us by social scientists, the New Right, and the urban policies of corporate and political elites.

Pioneer Korean immigrant journalist K. W. Lee—another of our Asian American "elders"—worries about how the melding of symbols, images, and stereotypes is shaping the perception of our community, especially among other people of color. "We are not seen as a compassionate people," states Lee. "Others see us as smart, hard-working, and good at making money—but not as sharing with others. We are not seen as a people who march at the forefront of the struggle for civil rights or the campaign to end poverty."[42] Like Philip Vera Cruz, Lee believes that Asian Americans must retrieve a heritage of compassion and solidarity from our past and use these values to construct a new moral vision for our future. Asian Americans must cast off the images imposed on us by others.

Thus, as we approach the end of the twentieth century, activists are confronted with a task similar to that confronting activists in the late 1960s: the need to redefine the Asian American experience. And as an earlier generation discovered, redefining means more than ethnic awakening. It means confronting the fundamental questions of power and domination in U.S. society. It means expanding democracy and community consciousness. It means liberating ourselves from the prisons still surrounding our lives.

In our efforts to redefine the Asian American experience, activists will have the guidance and help of elders like K. W. Lee and Philip Vera Cruz. And we can also draw from the rich legacy of struggle of other liberation movements.

Thus, in closing this chapter, I want to quote from two great teachers from the 1960s: Malcolm X and Martin Luther King, Jr. Their words and actions galvanized the consciousness of one generation of youth, and their message of compassion continues to speak to a new generations in the 1990s.

Since their assassinations in the mid-1960s, however, mainstream commentators have stereotyped the two men and often pitted one against the other. They portray Malcolm X as the angry black separatist who advocated violence and hatred against white people. Meanwhile, they make Martin Luther King, Jr., the messenger of love and nonviolence. In the minds of most Americans, both men—in the words of historian Manning Marable—are "frozen in time."[43]

But as Marable and other African American historians note, both King and Malcolm evolved, and became very different men in the years before their assassinations. Both men came to see the African American struggle in the United States in a worldwide context, as part of the revolutionary stirrings and mass uprisings happening across the globe. Both men became internationalists, strongly condemning U.S. exploitation of Third World nations and urging solidarity among all oppressed peoples. Finally, both men called for a redefinition of human values; they believed that people in the United States, especially, needed to move away from materialism and embrace a more compassionate worldview.

If we, too, as Asian Americans, are to evolve in our political and ideological understanding, we need to learn from the wisdom of both men. As we work for our own empowerment, we must ask ourselves a series of questions. Will we fight only for ourselves, or will we embrace the concerns of all oppressed peoples? Will we overcome our own oppression and help to create a new society, or will we become a new exploiter group in the present American hierarchy of inequality? Will we define our goal of empowerment solely in terms of individual advancement for a few, or as the collective liberation for all peoples?

> These are revolutionary times. All over the globe men are revolting against old systems of exploitation and oppression, and out of the wombs of a frail world, new systems of justice and equality are being born. The shirtless and barefoot people of the land are rising up as never before. "The people who sat in the darkness have seen a great light." We in the West must support these revolutions. It is a sad fact that, because of comfort, complacency, a morbid fear of communism, and our proneness to adjust to injustice, the Western nations that initiated so much of the revolutionary spirit of the modern world have now become the arch anti-revolutionaries ... Our only hope today lies in our ability to recapture the revolutionary spirit and go out into a sometimes hostile world declaring eternal hostility to poverty, racism, and militarism.[44]
>
> —Martin Luther King, Jr.
>
> I believe that there will ultimately be a clash between the oppressed and those who do the oppressing. I believe that there will be a clash between those who want

freedom, justice and equality for everyone and those who want to continue the system of exploitation. I believe that there will be that kind of clash, but I don't think it will be based on the color of the skin.[45]

—Malcolm X

Notes

1. Iranian philosopher Ali Shariati's four prisons analysis was shared with me by a member of the Iranian Students Union, Confederation of Iranian Students, San Francisco, 1977.
2. Allan Bloom, *The Closing of the American Mind,* New York: Simon & Schuster, 1987.
3. Winifred Breines, "Whose New Left?" *Journal of American History,* Vol. 75, No. 2, September 1988.
4. Ibid., p. 543.
5. Sheila D. Collins, *The Rainbow Challenge: The Jackson Campaign and the Future of U.S. Politics,* New York: Monthly Review Press, 1986.
6. Ibid., p. 16.
7. Ronald Fraser, *1968: A Student Generation in Revolt,* New York: Pantheon Books, pp. 354-355.
8. Karen Umemoto, " 'On Strike!' San Francisco State College Strike, 1968-69: The Role of Asian American Students," *Amerasia Journal,* Vol. 15, No. 1, 1989.
9. "Statement of the Philippine-American Collegiate Endeavor (PACE) Philosophy and Goals," mimeograph: quoted in Umemoto, p. 15.
10. Mo Nishida, "A Revolutionary Nationalist Perspective of the San Francisco State Strike," *Amerasia Journal,* Vol. 15, No. 1, 1989, p. 75.
11. George Lipsitz, "Grassroots Activists and Social Change: The Story of Ivory Perry," *CAAS Newsletter,* UCLA Center for Afro-American Studies, 1986. See also, George Lipsitz, *A Life in the Struggle: Ivory Perry and the Culture of Opposition,* Philadelphia: Temple University Press, 1988.
12. Russell C. Leong, "Poetry Within Earshot: Notes of an Asian American Generation, 1968-1978," *Amerasia Journal,* Vol. 15, No. 1, 1989, pp. 166-167.
13. Al Robles, "Hanging on to the Carabao's Tail," *Amerasia Journal,* Vol. 15, No. 1, 1989, p. 205.
14. Warren J. Susman, *Culture as History: The Transformation of American Society in the Twentieth Century,* New York: Pantheon Books, 1973; and Raymond Williams, *Keywords: A Vocabulary of Culture and Society,* revised edition, New York: Oxford University Press, 1976.
15. John M. Liu and Lucie Cheng, "A Dialogue on Race and Class: Asian American Studies and Marxism," *The Left Academy,* Vol. 3, eds. Bertell Ollman and Edward Vernoff, Westport, CT: Praeger, 1986.

16. See Mary Kao, compiler, "Public Record, 1989: What Have We Learned from the 60s and 70s?" *Amerasia Journal,* Vol. 15, No. 1, 1989, pp. 95-158.
17. Institute for Labor Education and Research, *What's Wrong with the U.S. Economy? A Popular Guide for the Rest of Us,* Boston: South End Press, 1982. See especially chapters 1 and 19.
18. Samuel Huntington, "The United States," *The Crisis of Democracy: Report on the Governability of Democracies to the Trilateral Commission,* ed. Michel Crozier, New York: New York University Press, 1975.
19. Center on Budget and Policy Priorities, *Still Far from the Dream: Recent Developments in Black Income, Employment and Poverty,* Washington, D.C., 1988.
20. Center for the Study of Social Policy, *Kids Count: State Profiles of Child Well-Being,* Washington, D.C., 1992.
21. Manning Marable, *How Capitalism Underdeveloped Black America,* Boston: South End Press, 1983, pp. 252-253.
22. Vincent Harding, *The Other American Revolution,* Los Angeles: UCLA Center for Afro-American Studies, and Atlanta: Institute of the Black World, 1980, p. 224.
23. For analyses of the changing status of Asian Americans, see Lucie Cheng and Edna Bonacich, eds., *Labor Immigration Under Capitalism: Asian Workers in the United States Before World War II,* Berkeley: University of California Press, 1984; Paul Ong, Edna Bonacich, and Lucie Cheng, eds., *Struggles for a Place: The New Asian Immigrants in the Restructuring Political Economy,* Philadelphia: Temple University Press, 1993; and Sucheng Chan, *Asian Americans: An Interpretive History,* Boston: Twayne Publishers, 1991.
24. For an analysis of the growing power of Asian American young professionals, see Yen Espiritu and Paul Ong, "Class Constraints on Racial Solidarity among Asian Americans," *Struggles for a Place,* Philadelphia: Temple University Press, 1993.
25. Arthur Hu, "AIDS and Race," *Asian Week,* December 13, 1991.
26. Marable, *How Capitalism Underdeveloped Black America,* p. 182.
27. William McGurn, "The Silent Minority," *National Review,* June 24, 1991.
28. Ibid., p. 19.
29. C.L.R. James, *Beyond a Boundary,* New York: Pantheon Books, 1983, pp. 116-117.
30. LEAP Asian Pacific American Public Policy Institute and UCLA Asian American Studies Center, *The State of Asian Pacific America: Policy Issues to the Year 2020,* Los Angeles: LEAP and UCLA Asian American Studies Center, 1993.
31. Mao Zedong, "Where Do Correct Ideas Come From?" *Four Essays on Philosophy,* Beijing: Foreign Languages Press, 1966, p. 134.
32. See "Asian Pacific American Workers: Contemporary Issues in the Labor Movement," eds. Glenn Omatsu and Edna Bonacich, *Amerasia Journal,* Vol. 18, No. 1, 1992.

33. Edna Bonacich, "The Social Costs of Immigrant Entrepreneurship," *Amerasia Journal,* Vol. 14, No. 1, 1988.
34. Dean S. Toji and James H. Johnson, Jr., "Asian and Pacific Islander American Poverty: The Working Poor and the Jobless Poor," *Amerasia Journal,* Vol. 18, No. 1, 1992, p. 85.
35. Miriam Ching Louie, "Immigrant Asian Women in Bay Area Garment Sweatshops: 'After Sewing, Laundry, Cleaning and Cooking, I Have No Breath Left to Sing,'" *Amerasia Journal,* Vol. 18, No. 1, p. 12.
36. Miriam Ching Louie, "Asian and Latina Women Take On the Garment Giants," *CrossRoads,* March 1993.
37. Peter N. Kiang and Man Chak Ng, "Through Strength and Struggle: Boston's Asian American Student/Community/Labor Solidarity," *Amerasia Journal,* Vol. 15, No. 1, 1989.
38. Lydia Lowe, "Paving the Way: Chinese Immigrant Workers and Community-based Labor Organizing in Boston," *Amerasia Journal,* Vol. 18, No. 1, 1992, p. 41.
39. Namju Cho, "Check Out, Not In: Koreana Wilshire/Hyatt Take-over and the Los Angeles Korean Community," *Amerasia Journal,* Vol. 18, No. 1, 1992.
40. Craig Scharlin and Lilia V. Villanueva, *Philip Vera Cruz: A Personal History of Filipino Immigrants and the Farmworkers Movement,* Los Angeles: UCLA Labor Center and UCLA Asian American Studies Center, 1992, p. 104.
41. For an overview of the evolution of the "model minority" stereotype in the social sciences, see Shirley Hune, *Pacific Migration to the United States: Trends and Themes in Historical and Sociological Literature,* New York: Research Institute on Immigration and Ethnic Studies of the Smithsonian Institution, 1977 (reprinted in *Asian American Studies: An Annotated Bibliography and Research Guide,* ed. Hyung-chan Kim, Westport, CT: Greenwood Press, 1989). For comparisons of the "model minority" stereotype in two different decades, see "Success Story of One Minority Group in U.S.," *U.S. News and World Report,* December 26, 1966 (reprinted in *Roots: An Asian American Reader,* ed. Amy Tachiki et al., Los Angeles: UCLA Asian American Studies Center, 1971); and the essay by William McGurn, "The Silent Minority," *National Review,* June 24, 1991.
42. Author's interview with K.W. Lee, Los Angeles, California, October 1991.
43. Manning Marable, "On Malcolm X: His Message & Meaning," Westfield, NJ: Open Magazine Pamphlet Series, 1992.
44. Martin Luther King, Jr., "Beyond Vietnam" speech, Riverside Church, New York, April 1967.
45. Malcolm X, interview on Pierre Breton Show, January 19, 1965, in *Malcolm X Speaks,* ed. George Breitman, New York: Grove Press, 1966, p. 216.

Korean merchants watch a demonstration supporting the boycott of their store in the mostly black Flatbush neighborhood. © 1990 by Andrew Lichenstein, Impact Visuals.

2

BETWEEN BLACK AND WHITE

An Interview with Bong Hwan Kim

ELAINE H. KIM

Introduction

This is a narrative about Bong Hwan Kim, former director of the Korean Community Center in Oakland and current director of the Korean Youth and Community Center in Los Angeles. The story is based on interviews conducted after the April 1992 civil disaster in Los Angeles, which resulted in extensive material loss and incalculable psychic damage to the Korean American community Kim serves. At the same time, the disaster has helped stimulate among Korean Americans a mood of reflection and questioning that may ultimately strengthen the social and political consciousness we need for a more self-determined future.

It is difficult to describe how disempowered and frustrated many Korean Americans felt during and after the *sa-i-ku p'ok-dong* [the April 29 "riots"]. Korean Americans across the country shared the anguish and despair of the Los Angeles *tongp'o* [community], which everyone seemed to have abandoned—the police and fire departments, black and white political leaders, the Asian and

Pacific American advocates who tried to dissociate themselves from us because our tragedy disrupted their narrow and risk-free focus on white violence against Asians. At the same time, while the Korean Americans at the center of the storm were mostly voiceless and all but invisible (except when stereotyped as hysterically inarticulate, and mostly female, ruined shopkeepers or as gun-wielding male merchants on rooftops concerned only about their property), we repeatedly witnessed Americans of African, European and, to a slightly lesser extent, Chinese and Japanese descent discussing publicly the significance of what was happening.

Within a week or two after April 29, 1992, the mainstream news media began a feverish and short-lived search for "spokespersons" from the Korean American community. Naturally, they seized upon whatever U.S.-born English-speaking Korean American educators and attorneys they could find, creating "representatives" several times removed from the people most affected by the disaster: limited-English-speaking immigrants of modest means, people who had spent the last decade or more working 12 to 14 hours a day, six or seven days a week, in pursuit of brave and often humble dreams that others had reduced to ashes in the space of a few hours. When public attention shifted to sexier and more current issues a few months later, the media all but forgot both the spokespersons and the ruined families.

Elsewhere, I hope to help give voice and visibility to these ruined families. Here I would like to pay tribute to the unsung heroes left "holding the bag" after the television cameras turned their lenses elsewhere and the sound and fury died down. These are the community workers faced with trying to solve the long-term and day-to-day problems of the decimated Los Angeles Korean American community. By interviewing one such person, I hope to bring to light some of the general issues Korean American communities are pondering, especially the tensions between generations, social classes, and genders; between Korean Americans and other ethnic and racial groups; between South Korea and Korean American communities; and between the "American dream" and Korean American realities. I also hope to celebrate the work of community activists, which is not often recorded for posterity. Beyond the limelight and rarely rewarded with money or glory, their unglamorous activities help move us all toward racial equality and social justice.

The psychic and material violence Los Angeles Korean Americans suffered during the *sa-i-ku p'ok-dong* has often been referred to as a "wake-up call" about what the "American dream" means in the 1990s. Perhaps we are paying for believing in the myth that we could survive and flourish by working hard, minding our own business, and putting our faith in institutions like the police and politicians who are charged with protecting and representing us. We need to develop new models of citizenship. We also need to nurture the kind of leadership willing to go against the grain, as one must if one is to fight injustice and work to benefit the disenfranchised.

Until now, the mainstream media has valued Korean American experiences only for what they say about race in a black/white paradigm of U.S. race relations. Korean Americans need to create a new space for ourselves beyond the black/white binary and the hierarchy of values it implies as we struggle to "become American" in a self-determined way. I hope that Kim's story, which is but one of many stories we must tell, will help retrieve Korean Americans from the periphery, centering us as subjects of a history we create.

Korean Americans know themselves to be individuals with roots and context, people with rich and complex histories, thoughts, feelings, and flamboyant dreams. But most Americans see us primarily through the lens of race; they see us as all alike and caring only about ourselves. There is an urgent need for us to inscribe our narratives wherever and whenever we can. Thus, while I want this portrait to be a celebration of community service and advocacy, I also want readers to experience the intensely idiosyncratic aspects of an individual Korean American's personality and experiences. The views that Kim expresses shift with changing circumstances, and they will undoubtedly change substantially as he continues to work with Los Angeles' stricken Korean American community. At the same time, it is apparent he did not arrive at these views hastily, but instead, rooted them in his evolving personal sense of Korean American identity as well as his cumulative experiences during a decade of community work.

I. My Childhood

I came to the United States in 1962, when I was three or four years old. My father had come before us to get a Ph.D. in chemistry. He had planned to return to Korea afterwards, but it was hard for him to support three children in Korea while he was studying in the United States, and he wasn't happy alone, so he brought the family over. He got a job at a photographic chemicals manufacturing company in New Jersey, where he still works after almost 30 years. He never made it past the "glass ceiling." I view him as a simple person who must have been overwhelmed by the flip side of the American dream they never tell you about. There was never a place for him in America except at home with the family or maybe at the Korean church. Both of my parents were perpetual outsiders, never quite comfortable with American life.

The Bergenfield, New Jersey, community where I grew up was a blue-collar town of about 40,000 people, mostly Irish and Italian Americans. I lived a schizophrenic existence. I had one life in the family, where I felt warmth, closeness, love, and protection, and another life outside—school, friends, television, the feeling that I was on my own. I accepted that my parents would not be able to help me much.

I can remember clearly my first childhood memory about difference. I had been in this country for maybe a year. It was the first day of kindergarten, and I was very excited about having lunch at school. All morning, I could think only of the lunch that was waiting for me in my desk. My mother had made *kimpahp* [rice balls rolled up in dried seaweed] and wrapped it all up in aluminum foil. I was eagerly looking forward to that special treat. I could hardly wait. When lunch bell rang, I happily took out my foil-wrapped *kimpahp*. But all the other kids pointed and gawked. "What is *that*? How could you eat *that*?" they shrieked. I don't remember whether I ate my lunch or not, but I told my mother I would only bring tuna or peanut butter sandwiches for lunch after that.

I have always liked Korean food, but I had to like it secretly, at home. There are things you don't show to your non-Korean friends. At various times when I was growing up, I felt ashamed of the food in the refrigerator, but only when friends would come over and wonder what it was. They'd see a jar of garlic and say, "You don't *eat* that stuff, do you?" I would say, "I don't eat it, but my parents do; they do a lot of weird stuff like that."

My father spelled his name "Kim Hong Zoon." The kids at school made fun of his name. "Zoon?" they would laugh. They called me "Bong" because "Bong Hwan" was too hard to pronounce.

As a child you are sensitive; you don't want to be different. You want to be like the other kids. They made fun of my face. They called me "flat face." When I got older, they called me "Chink" or "Jap" or said "remember Pearl Harbor." In all cases, it made me feel terrible. I would get angry and get into fights. Even in high school, even the guys I hung around with on a regular basis, would say, "You're just a Chink" when they got angry. Later, they would say they didn't mean it, but that was not much consolation. When you are angry, your true perceptions and emotions come out. The rest is a façade.

They used to say, "We consider you to be just like us. You don't *seem* Korean." That would give rise to such mixed feelings in me. I wanted to believe that I was no different from my white classmates. It was painful to be reminded that I was different, which people did when they wanted to put me in my place, as if I should be grateful to them for allowing me to be their friend.

I wanted to be as American as possible—playing football, dating cheerleaders. I drank a lot and tried to be cool. I had convinced myself that I was "American," whatever that meant, all the while knowing underneath that I'd have to reconcile myself, to try to figure out where I would fit in a society that never sanctioned that identity as a public possibility. Part of growing up in America meant denying my cultural and ethnic identity, and part of that meant negating my parents. I still loved them, but I knew they could not help me outside the home. Once when I was small and had fought with a kid who called me a "Chink," I ran to my mother. She said, "Just tell them to *shut up*." My parents would say that the people who did things like that were just "uneducated." "You have to study hard to become an educated person so that you will rise above all that," they would advise. I didn't really study hard. Maybe I knew somehow that studying hard alone does not take anyone "above all that." I have lost contact with everyone from my East Coast life except for a few Korean American friends from the Korean church our family attended.

I am the second oldest and the only male of four children. My family treated me as special, especially because I am the first and only son in the Kim line for two generations. My mother had lost two boys before me—one was stillborn and the other died at two after drinking *yangjetmul* [a caustic soda commonly used in Korea to whiten laundry]. She was very thankful to have me. My sisters became aware of how our parents, especially our mother, felt toward me, and they grew to feel the same. They concluded that I was special to the family. Unlike them, I was encouraged to go out and explore the world outside our home.

I was a natural athlete, and I enjoyed every kind of sport. My parents encouraged my interest in sports, indulging and nurturing all my boyish and manly enthusiasms by sparing no expense whenever I needed equipment. Probably sports saved me from complete lack of self-esteem as an Asian growing up in New Jersey in the early and mid-1960s. Through sports, I got lots of positive feedback and was able to make friends with white boys, who respected my athletic abilities even though I was Asian. In high school, I was elected captain of the football team, and my girlfriend was captain of the cheerleaders. I was not particularly good in school. My parents were upset, but I didn't pay much attention to them.

When I got to college, I experienced an identity crisis. Because I was no longer involved in sports and because I was away from home, I no longer felt special or worthwhile, and I became very depressed. I hated even getting up in the mornings. Finally, I dropped out of school.

I decided to go to Korea, hoping to find something to make me feel more whole. Being in Korea somehow gave me a sense of freedom I had never really felt in America. It also made me love my parents even more. I could imagine where they came from and what they experienced. I began to understand and appreciate their sacrifice and love and what parental support means. Visiting Korea didn't provide answers about the meaning of life, but it gave me a sense of comfort and belonging, the feeling that there was somewhere in this world that validated that part of me that I knew was real but few others outside my immediate family ever recognized.

After spending a year in Korea, I returned to finish college, and then I packed up and headed for California. I had always wanted to go to the West Coast, not only because of the mystique of California "freedom," but also because I heard that Asian Americans had a stronger presence there. I wasn't much into career planning; I still have trouble planning my life over five-year time spans. I wasn't looking forward to getting a job in the mainstream labor market, but I was anxious to find out what the "real world" was like.

II. Working for the Community

I had heard that the Korean Community Center of the East Bay (KCCEB) in Oakland was doing good work, so I went there and offered my services as a volunteer. Before I knew it, I was immersed in the social network of the people who had created and helped sustain the center. I was impressed by them, by their social beliefs and their commitment to change. These were people who had been able to create something where nothing had existed before, creating community and carving out a space for Korean Americans. And they made me feel I belonged somewhere.

I became the director of KCCEB in 1982. During the five years I served there, we expanded the programs and activities and increased the financial base. I learned about progressive politics and coalition building through working with other Asian American organizations and people who had come up through the civil rights era of the late 1960s and early 1970s. These are things I had missed in my white suburban existence, and the people at KCCEB helped put things in perspective for me, in terms the histories of people of color and the political, social, and economic implications of racism. At KCCEB, I also acquired certain skills; I learned about leveraging American resources, fundraising strategies, proposal writing, meeting the payroll, balancing budgets, developing commercial real estate for non-profit organizations, and generally about building and maintaining an organization.

The most rewarding part of the work at KCCEB was experiencing opportunities to transform dreams and abstract ideas into concrete realities. We designed the Koryo Village Center, a non-profit economic development project to create small business opportunities for recent immigrants and raise revenues to develop KCCEB's self-sufficiency at the same time. We purchased and renovated a building to house senior citizens' programs. We also did advocacy work on a wide range of issues, working to establish and support programs for disadvantaged people in Oakland.

In 1988, I was contacted by the outgoing director of the Los Angeles Korean Youth Center (KYC), which was re-named Korean Youth and Community Center (KYCC) in 1992. The agency was looking for a new director. At the time, I was in the midst of planning and raising funds for the Koryo Village Center, so I didn't think about leaving KCCEB. But a member of the board of directors who had mentored me advised me to take the job in Los Angeles as an opportunity develop my skills and widen my range of activities. She said that I probably should not remain in a job for more than five years if it seemed that I had little more to learn from it.

When I settled into my new job, I was surprised to find that there were no sizable Korean American organizations in Los Angeles, even though the Korean community there was the largest in the country.

KYC was renting a crowded and dilapidated space on South Oxford Street. It was unbearably hot in the summer. About $200,000 had been raised, through donations and fund-raisers, for a new building. I found and arranged for the purchase of our current site on Ingraham Avenue, where we relocated in 1989. Because I was always concerned about the dearth of affordable housing in California cities, I had the idea of constructing low-cost housing units on our lot with office space for our agency. I worked with a member of our board who worked for a community redevelopment agency to create a plan to leverage what we already owned to attract funds for this new project, and it worked. In the summer of 1992, we tore down our old building and began construction on our new 19-unit edifice, which will have spacious first-floor offices for KYCC, for our 55 staff members.

Working with staff and board members, I was able to increase the organization's funding base from $250,000 to $500,000 during my first year with the agency. The size and political potential of the Korean American community was obvious to people in the public sectors in the city and county, and I was able to use the proposal writing skills I had acquired in Oakland to apply for support from many different funding sources. Within four years, I was able to increase the annual budget from $300,000 to $1,500,000 and the number of funding sources from six to twenty. Our funding now comes from federal, state, county, and city sources as well as from foundations, corporations, private donations, and service fees.

Building KYCC was challenging and fun. I also enjoyed trying to establish links between our agency and other Asian Pacific American organizations. I joined the Asian Pacific Planning Council, an organization of human services organization heads, which I was elected president of in 1990. Although I was working for a Korean American social services agency, I saw my work as being much broader than social services. I am interested in community empowerment, fighting racism, and working with others to create real equality of opportunities. I had been trying to figure out how to reach out to Chicano, Latino, and African American community organizations when a 15-year-old African American girl, Latasha Harlins, was shot and killed by a Korean shopkeeper, Soon Ja Du, in 1991.

III. Working with the African American Community

When I first moved to Oakland in June, 1982, I had had no experience to speak of working with African Americans. In fact, I was traumatized by my first experience with African Americans in California. I had gone looking for a good basketball game, and the best one I found happened to be in an all-black neighborhood in East Oakland. I joined right in, and one of the men on the court started pushing me and calling me a "Chink." Finally I slugged him, and he fell to the ground, bleeding. He slugged me back, ripping open my lower lip, so I slugged him again and knocked him down. When he got up and started going toward his car, the other men on the court warned me that he was going to get his gun and that I should take off as quickly as possible. I went home alone to nurse my injuries. I remember washing rice over and over again; somehow, that was very therapeutic. Later, my friends from KCCEB told me that contrary to what I had thought, African Americans in Oakland did not necessarily think of Asians as "brothers under the skin." I had assumed that we were all people of color who would naturally get along. Nor had I realized that many African Americans don't know the difference between Koreans and other Asians, like Chinese or Japanese who, unlike Koreans, usually try to avoid physical confrontations. "Obviously," they said, "the man on the basketball court pushed you around because he thought you were Chinese or Japanese and would not fight back."

Thanks to what I learned from my friends at KCCEB, I came to understand that as people of color Korean Americans had much to share with African Americans. I was interested in educating Korean immigrants about Korean American racism and about what it means to be people of color in the United States.

Immediately after the Harlins killing, I joined the Black-Korean Alliance, which had been organized through the city of Los Angeles' Human Relations Commission in 1986 after four Korean shopkeepers were killed by African Americans during one month. From 1986 to 1991, Alliance members had been trying to develop channels of communication between Korean American merchants and residents in South-Central. They held monthly meetings of merchants and community organization representatives. They operated according to what is called the "dispute resolution model," which emphasizes increasing mutual knowledge and understanding through talking, but this only works when both parties are interested in resolution.

The first meeting I attended was held on the day after Latasha Harlins had been killed. Some black leaders organized to condemn the killing and appeared on the visual media making strong statements with racial overtones. Danny Bakewell of the Brotherhood Crusade appeared in front of Soon Ja Du's store to hang a sign on the door that read, "This store is closed for murder and disrespect of African Americans."

Trying to head off open conflict, I worked with a group of Korean community people to organize a press conference. The first-generation immigrants did not know how to talk to the media. They could not speak English. We worked together to issue a statement, expressing sympathy to the Harlins family and asking for peaceful resolution of the negative after-effects of the killing.

It was apparent that the fragile Black-Korean Alliance was not really a coalition. It was a motley group of individuals representing only themselves. There were no recognized community organizations backing the Alliance. The majority of Koreatown leadership expressed little interest in forming alliances with African Americans. Nor were we ever able to get recognized African American leadership to the table. The director of the Los Angeles NAACP, Joe Duff, and Mark Ridley Thomas, then director of Southern Christian Leadership Conference, made it clear that "this black-Korean thing" was not high on their list of priorities. Many African American political leaders were concerned lest ground be lost relative to Latino and Asian immigrant newcomers. Instead, there was a visibly organized constituency led by Danny Bakewell, who was speaking on behalf of Latasha Harlins' family and heading a campaign to get Korean businesses out of black communities in South-Central. His argument was that Korean merchants were the barriers to African American economic development and were thus responsible for the creation of the African American underclass. He never mentioned that Korean immigrants had bought their stores from African American owners, who had bought them from Jews after Watts in 1965.

The Korean members of the Black-Korean Alliance were forced into acting on behalf of Koreans to balance the Brotherhood Crusade's aggression and anti-Korean rhetoric. A media-driven

81

leader, Bakewell would say inflammatory and generalizing things about Koreans being rude and disrespectful to African Americans He would reiterate that a black teenager's life was worth less to Korean store-owners than a $1.79 bottle of orange juice. The media were attracted to Bakewell's sensational rhetoric; in every article printed about the case, the *Los Angeles Times* would refer to the $1.79. We continually sought to locate a middle ground or a meeting point with African American community leaders and organizations, but our invitations were ignored and our telephone calls never returned. We felt powerless, insignificant, and frustrated. The larger Korean community concluded that Bakewell had the support of the African American community, at least on the issue of Koreans.

In hindsight, I see that Bakewell had created a climate that made it almost impossible for any self-respecting African American to oppose him, because he said he was advocating self-determination for African Americans. Opportunistically appealing to xenophobia in the grassroots African American community by scapegoating politically powerless and insignificant Koreans, he was pinpointing an issue that the middle-class African American leadership had been unable to adequately address. Bakewell was not interested in resolution, since he benefitted from continued conflict.

During the summer of 1991, the Black-Korean Alliance organized a meeting at an African American church to promote discussions between Korean merchants and African American community residents. About 100 community people and 50 merchants and a number of Korean immigrant community leaders attended. The event was extensively covered by the media. I arrived just as the meeting was beginning, shortly after Danny Bakewell had condemned the event and staged a walkout. He was trying to close down the meeting, but most of the other African Americans did not leave with him. After a panel presentation, we invited people from the audience to speak. Many African Americans were waiting in the line to speak against the stores' high prices and merchants' rudeness and suspicion that African American customers were going to steal something. They complained about the Korean merchants not hiring employees from the community. There was a sprinkling of African Americans who talked about the larger picture, saying that "kicking Koreans in the butt" would not solve the problems caused by economic neglect and lockout.

The atmosphere was highly charged. No Koreans got up to speak. Finally, a couple of Korean-speaking people tried to say something through interpreters. I got in line to speak, not knowing what to say but knowing I had to say something to ease the tensions. When I got to the microphone, I said that not all Koreans are rude and disrespectful and that Korean Americans were facing many of the same problems with drugs, gangs, and street violence that African Americans were facing. I said that we didn't know each other on a person-to-person or community-to-community basis and that we needed to break down the barriers and mutual ignorance.

In the end, the event was a failure. All we could do was create a forum for people to air their feelings. The Black-Korean Alliance was not set up to do anything about the problems. That's the failure of the human relations approach to community problems and racial tensions: No amount of "human relations" between two disenfranchised groups makes any real difference without a social action agenda that will address the underlying social and economic problems. It's easy to get people to come into a room and talk. What's tough is to get them to work together to solve problems. By bringing those people together, we created the perception that we could try to do something about the problems, when in fact we could not. We didn't have the resources, nor did we have the players. The Korean merchants barely understood what was going on because their English was limited. Overall, the community forum helped further discredit the Black-Korean Alliance as an organization that was unable to relate effectively with grassroots constituencies.

The Korean members of the Black-Korean Alliance were placed in the position of simply reacting with a frenzy to whatever inflammatory remarks Danny Bakewell made through the news media. Bakewell would say something, and the media would call us to fan the flames. Naturally, it was mostly English-speaking

Korean Americans who could respond. Jai Lee Wong of the County Human Relations Commission, Marcia Choo of the Asian Pacific American Dispute Resolution Center, Edward Tae Han Chang of Cal Poly Pomona (see Chapter 3), Jerry Yu of the Korean American Coalition, and I were the individuals the media continually called on to respond. We kept trying to keep the focus on structural problems, emphasizing that Koreans were being caught in the middle and should not be blamed or scapegoated for the economic frustrations of African Americans. Then Jerry Yu pronounced to the news media on his own that he agreed with Judge Joyce Karlin's decision to issue a five-year suspended sentence for Soon Ja Du. This infuriated many African Americans, who concluded that Korean Americans agreed with Soon Ja Du. The black rage was not only at the verdict but also at the thought that Koreans didn't care that a young African American girl was dead. In fact, many Koreans did care, but they were themselves furious at the African American rhetoric directed at them. The situation esca- lated—the killing and the verdict, the boycott and the incidents in front of the store—it was a downward spiral.

Many Korean merchants, concluding that it was "us" against "them," supported Du and the verdict. Some contributed to Judge Karlin's fight against the African American-led recall movement. Many of the merchants felt that there was more public understand- ing of and sympathy for African Americans than for them. They cited that 30 or 40 Korean shopkeepers had been killed by African American robbers in Southern California since the mid-1980s, and complained that even though the mortality rate for Korean grocers was higher than for U.S. soldiers in Vietnam during the Vietnam War, no one seemed to pay attention. The situation escalated when an African American who was robbing a Korean-owned store shot the owner's nine-year-old daughter, purportedly saying, "This is for Latasha." He was never caught. And then Lee Arthur Mitchell, an African American, was shot by Korean grocer Park Tae Sam in a struggle at the cash register.

The police ruled the killing a justifiable homicide, but Danny Bakewell quickly organized a boycott of Park's store. The Korean American members of the Black-Korean Alliance started meeting with first-generation Korean community leaders, most of whom were from the Korean American Grocers' Association (KAGRO) and the Korean Chamber of Commerce. The immigrants were adamant: They believed that giving in to the boycott, which they considered patently unfair because Park had had no choice but to defend himself, would spell disaster for Korean American small businesses all over southern California.

Many Korean immigrants wanted to stop the boycott. Donations were pouring in—bills from impoverished senior citizens and larger amounts from associations of wig dealers and beauty supply retailers. We formed a special fund-raising organization, and within three months we had collected $30,000. We felt we had a Korean community mandate to oppose and counter the boycott. I felt the same way myself; I was angry because I too thought the boycott was wrong.

An African American colleague told me that Park Tae Sam's store was finished the first day of the boycott and advised us to write it off. I didn't believe him, because so many Korean immigrants were enraged over what they thought was an example of being scapegoated for problems not of their making. There were no vehicles for solving the problem, so I went with other Koreans against the boycotts, working with the emergency relief fund to keep the store open. The immigrants entrusted the second-generation Korean Americans with collecting the donations. We started funneling the payments to Park, who believed that everything we were doing was for him as an individual, when in fact we wanted to address a larger problem. To us, his immediate needs were secondary to the organizing potential of the issue. He insisted that he needed $6,000 a month and made up stories to the Korean language press that undermined our integrity, calling our distribution coordinator *sagikun* (thief), and implying that we were stealing the money.

Fueled by the news media, racial tensions were escalating and the positions were becoming more polarized. Just as African Americans would not oppose the boycott, Korean Americans felt they had no choice but to oppose it. In the Korean-speaking community, emotions were running high: People felt that they were being kicked around by white and black Americans, none of whom would run the mom-and-pop stores themselves, because the work hours were too hard and too long and the risk too great.

In this environment, it was difficult for me as a Korean American to register protests against the verdict in the Soon Ja Du case. The Black-Korean Alliance's position was to condemn the appellate courts for upholding Karlin's decision [to suspend Du's sentence]. With Joe Hicks [of the Southern Christian Leadership Conference] and Karen Bass [of the Community Coalition for Substance Abuse Prevention and Treatment], we hammered out a position on the need for reform of the judicial system. We spoke against the leeway in sentencing judges are given in the legal system and called for community involvement in judicial decision-making, especially because of the dramatic impact these legal decisions were having in our communities. There was no mainstream coverage of our position in the media, but the Korean media attacked me vociferously the next morning: "Who is this Kim Bong Hwan anyway, a Korean or a nigger? He is not even a store-owner himself; what does he know about their tragedy [being killed by African American robbers]?" I was barraged with angry telephone calls from irate members of the community. I felt terrible and afraid.

The mistake we made was trying to earn first-generation support and trust, when there was so little support and participation from the African American side. It was almost impossible for any Korean Americans to step in to discuss any middle ground. As someone who had a foot in the Korean community, I struggled for a foothold in the African American community. Although I failed to do this in the end, I was able to establish ongoing relationships with African American leaders, and I may have helped increase African American awareness that there were Koreans with views contrary to their stereotypes of us.

The mistake that most people make is to assume that all African Americans think one way and all Korean Americans think another way, when it's much more complex. I have spoken with many people who think mainly in terms of who are the "haves" and who are the "have-nots," rather than in terms of race. They know that the issue has been defined by the media. On the other extreme, there are people who fall for the generalizations about Korean greed or African American thievery.

Depending on how you choose to look at things, "having" and "not having" is relative. Some might think of Korean Americans as the "haves" if they have their own small businesses, but Korean Americans are not the ones who call the shots in any American institutions, whether in politics, industry, education, or communications. In fact, we have no political clout whatsoever, as evidenced by what happened after the April 1992 civil disaster. We are not even in the loop. People of color, Korean Americans included, are lucky if they get invited to participate in any decision-making about the allocation of power and resources.

African Americans are more politically empowered than Asians or Latinos because they have been here the longest, and the civil rights movement legacy has allowed them to participate more meaningfully than other minorities. The white/black relationship is probably the closest of any political relationship. Perhaps it's because of white guilt from slavery and its repercussions. African American political empowerment has not been completely self-determined: The white power establishment has granted some opportunities, but never enough to allow African Americans to define their own agenda. Thus, the black middle class has token participation, while a disproportionate number of poor African Americans are incarcerated and unemployed. If African Americans are the most politically established community of color, Asians and Latinos don't have much to look forward to.

To be able to participate, you have to have an environment that is welcoming, with concrete opportunities for participation. In fact, racial minorities are told implicitly and outright that they aren't welcome. For Asian Americans, the message is delivered through exclusion, racist immigration and employment restrictions, and through xenophobic hatred and hate crimes, from the internment of Japanese Americans in the past to whites beating up Asians in the present and telling them to "go back to China." The message comes through when Asians and other immigrants of color are exhorted to trade in their language and cultural heritage for uncertain and conditional existence on the fringes of the dominant society. The rhetoric is that the doors are open, that there are equal opportunities. But the reality is still discrimination based on skin color.

Political power relationships haven't changed since the "riots," so the African American political leaders haven't changed their positions. But the common folk are expressing more interest in finding out about each other. There have been many more community-based organization representatives contacting us wanting to do things together. Latasha Harlins' aunt, Denise Harlins, called to suggest that we work together. She said that she was fed up with the African American politicians, who rallied to help after Latasha was killed only to leave her, two years later, with no visible political support or lasting benefit. She wanted to create a program in her niece's memory that would be of long-term community benefit, perhaps by turning Soon Ja Du's empty store, which she had defended during the "riots," into a community center. An "O.G." [Original Gangster] who was once a member of the Crips called me, concerned about potential conflict between gang members and Korean swapmeet owners over some hats he had formed a business to produce. Apparently, he had been cheated by an African American businessman who sold the hats at half price to Korean swapmeet owners. I offered to write a letter in Korean that he could take around explaining what the situation was and ask them not to sell the hats. KYCC has an urban beautification project employing African American, Latino, and Korean American youth. Just recently a group of African Americans called Parents of Watts visited me to say they wanted me to help them organize a social event with the Korean merchants in their neighborhoods so that they could get to know each other. We could establish a model program to avert merchant-resident conflicts.

What some African American political leaders ignore is what people in the grassroots communities know. African American political leaders have to realize that if they continue to cling to the belief that all they have to do is maintain what they have now, their communities will be doomed. The vision and spirit of the civil rights movement was much larger than just African Americans. They have to join with other political "have-nots" to open the door wide open for everyone. During this period of unprecedented demographic shifts, many Americans have uneasy feelings about power shifts. People of color who have been kept back are chomping at the bit, fighting for every scrap that comes their way, arguing over whose crumb it is. What is needed is visionary leadership that speaks to the larger possibilities of empowerment for the many. Ultimately, African American, Latino, and Asian coalitions could become very influential in Los Angeles.

African American communities were politically strong but economically frustrated, Asian American communities were economically stronger and politically invisible, and Latino communities were both politically and economically disenfranchised. It's hard to imagine what happened in April 1992 as a Latino-Korean conflict. Many Korean merchants feel lingering resentment at the role Central Americans played as looters. The traditional Korean love/hate relationship with the poor spills over into attitudes toward Latinos. Like many Latinos, Koreans are immigrants from a homeland decimated by colonial subjugation and U.S. cultural imperialism. As struggling immigrants, they have much to share: I often see working-class Koreans working side-by-side with Latino laborers, speaking a combination of Korean and Spanish, and eating spicy foods together. Adult Koreans understand what it means to be from a poor country village and what it's like to live "like a deaf mute" in a society where power is located in the English language. But the majority of Korean immigrants want desperately to regard themselves as belonging to the middle class, as better than Latinos, whom they believe they have to exploit in a capitalist society.

There is potential for alliances between our community and the Latino communities. The Latino congressman who represents Koreatown has two Korean American staff members and makes himself accessible to the Korean community. Right now I am working to organize neighborhood-based focus groups between Central Americans and Korean Americans, with the goal of putting together a multiracial planning council in Koreatown. KYCC has hired a community organizer who was active in the movement against the military dictatorship in El Salvador to conduct block-by-block canvassing in the neighborhoods. This project will require a delicate balancing of Central American street vendors who might be exiled fighters against fascism in their homelands with Koreatown's richest and most capitalistic developers. I could see myself taking the Central American side in the future on affordable housing, playgrounds, and social services as opposed to high-rise office buildings that would only generate contributions to politicians and fat profits for a few developers. Every issue comes down to a convoluted configuration of class and race.

Someone from MALDEF (Mexican American Legal Defense and Education Fund) pulled me aside during a meeting about re-districting to point out that due to demographic shifts, Asians and Latinos could work together because we never had very much to begin with. "We have little to lose and a lot to gain by working together," he said, "while African Americans stand to lose their hard-won civil rights gains from the 1960s, given their declining numbers."

Ultimately, we need a multiracial coalition that includes European Americans, a coalition that supports true equality and enfranchisement. The toughest part will be convincing those with the most that even if a redistribution of power means no gains for them in the short term, the society as a whole will be better for everyone in the long term.

IV. Toward Social Justice and Equality

I am always amazed at how pervasive this stereotype of Asian Americans as a model minority is. It doesn't benefit us for whites to believe we are smarter or "better" than other people of color. Instead of mutely accepting a designated place in the social hierarchy, we must work toward a completely different social structure based not on hierarchy but on social justice and equality, as espoused in the U.S. Constitution. Immigrant Korean parents often view themselves as sacrificial lambs, believing that even though they go to their graves deaf, dumb, and blind, they are doing it so that their children can achieve the so-called American dream.

Their kids work incredibly hard, knowing that only they can vindicate their parents for their sacrifice. In the end, they may think that as Korean Americans with college degrees they are fulfilling their parents' expectations according to the myth of the American dream. But instead, they become the target of resentment from all sides: white resentment and fear of Asian yellow peril takeover and black and brown resentment because of the perception that Asian Americans are honorary white people unconcerned about social justice issues.

People don't realize that a large percentage of Asian immigrants are from the middle classes of their homelands. When they come to the United States, they suffer socio-economic decline, but ironically this decline is perceived as achievement. The Southeast Asian refugees who didn't come from the middle class share a lot with Spanish-speaking working-class immigrants. Those Asians who don't conform to the model minority stereotype are invisible in mainstream society. There are going to be more and more Korean American high school dropouts and juvenile delinquents succumbing to urban deterioration. There's only so much that the much-touted "family values" can do to defend against these pressures. The family unit can't operate all alone, in a vacuum, indefinitely.

The stereotype of Asians as goody-goody conformists is so pervasive. (We play into it, too.) I don't think Asian America will produce an eloquent spokesperson like Martin Luther King, Malcolm X, Cornel West, or even Al Sharpton or Danny Bakewell in the near future. Even though Korean Americans see preachers every Sunday delivering their oratories, there is no translation into English and the *style* of English. I have been inspired by Harold Washington, Ronald Dellums, and other black speakers I have heard, but never by Korean language speakers. It's more likely that Korean Americans will learn from the African American tradition of oratory style, just as they have been inspired by African American rap. The Korean style would never fly in this country. Or we'd have to create our own U.S.-rooted style. In my own mind, my own experiences with struggles against social injustice come more out of an American than a homeland Korean context. When I look now at racist colonial power relations perpetuated in Korea through U.S. imperialism, I understand the arrogance of power and how it is extended throughout the world, with profound impact on the lives of millions of people no one in America knows or cares about.

V. Acknowledging Diversity in the Community

U.S.-born Chinese and Japanese Americans think they can work with me because they think I am like them, quite different from their stereotype of the aggressive Korean immigrant. But what really is an "Asian Pacific American" anyway? If you look at who hangs out with whom, it's by ethnicity. I recognize the long-term importance of having as many separate ethnicities supporting an Asian Pacific American agenda as possible, but at the same time, there isn't enough substantive attention being paid to the differences. You could almost look at Asian Pacific American political presence as being a "paper tiger." We can't present a cohesive platform across any level of government. Instead, there is a fragile, tentative alliance of mostly Chinese and Japanese Americans with a few Korean and Filipino Americans. Asian Pacific Americans are such a diverse community of color that many ethnicities don't really fit under the umbrella.

There is a huge gap between Asian American civil rights-type activism from the 1960s and 1970s, where there may be a token Korean American among the Chinese and Japanese Americans, and Korean immigrant community leadership. For example, the Asian Law Caucus, which regards itself as the political vanguard of Asian America, took a position on the Soon Ja Du verdict without consulting first-generation Korean-immigrant community leaders. At a time when Asian Pacific American communities have grown faster than at any time in U.S. history, with various communities being composed primarily of first-generation immigrants, we have to ask whom are these Asian American organizations representing, and to whom are they accountable? In fact, as the communities continue to grow, those organizations that call themselves "Asian American" cannot gloss over the fact that they are not rooted deeply enough in each specific ethnic community to have a sanctioned political position or social agenda for "Asian Americans."

Anti-Asian violence is an important issue, but immigrant communities do not understand hate crimes against Asians. Unless those groups who are leading the fight spend at least as much energy interacting with people in the various specific Asian communities as they do talking to white establishment politicians and funding sources, they cannot be viewed as truly representing the interests of our diverse Asian Pacific American communities. If they actually went into the communities, they would be forced to incorporate what the communities' interests are, and these may have less to do with white violence against Asians than with their livelihoods and whether their children will survive the violence in the streets. Many people in our communities never interact with whites anyway. Their experiences with anti-Asian violence is black and brown. You hear almost nothing from Asian American anti-Asian violence coalitions about interracial violence. Depending on how you look at the issue, the targeting of Korean stores during the April "riots" could be called a hate crime.

A few African American leaders still refuse to acknowledge that Korean stores were even targeted. Some just don't want anyone to pay attention to Koreans; they want the focus to remain on African American businesses being burned, African American community people being unable to find places to shop, and the need for African American business opportunities.

Asian American organizations that refuse to consider the possibility of non-white anti-Asian violence keep us trapped in an old black-white paradigm of race relations, which some African American community leaders cling to, to avoid losing ground to Asians and Latinos.

What is needed now is a new kind of Asian Pacific American coalition, a kind that asserts Asian Pacific American identities as political strategy without better established or larger groups controlling the agenda by leveling the differences. Without a doubt, working together is better than working alone. At this moment, KYCC has been working in an Asian Pacific Coalition that emerged after the "riots" to try to ensure fairness to both Korean and African American communities. Responding to the African American community's call to reduce the number of liquor stores while at the same time being mindful that the ruined merchants' need to regain a means of livelihood, we have been trying to help burnt-out Korean and African American liquor merchants to establish other businesses that would serve community needs. For example, we were able to get the City Council to waive costly sewage hookup fees for conversion of liquor stores to laundromats and other businesses. We have also been working through Rebuild L.A. to introduce Korean and other former liquor store owners to larger scale franchising opportunities, such as fast food restaurants and automotive businesses. Significant headway would have been difficult, if not impossible, for Koreans alone or for Asian American groups without central Korean involvement.

VI. Differences in the Korean Community

Koreans in Los Angeles built their own networks: The Korean business directory lists hundreds of civic organizations and associations according to hobby, college, school, and church membership. For the past 15 or 20 years, the community has been very insular, existing beyond the reach of the American mainstream. When I go to Korean community events, I often think about how difficult it must be for the immigrants to live in this society while not being part of it. When I see Korean senior citizens walking toward me on the sidewalk, as if they were deaf, dumb, and blind, it's hard to imagine how they survive day-to-day. I feel a lot of empathy for them. Maybe it's because of my parents. I know what they have had to go through.

I speak Korean well enough to communicate what I need to. Being able to speak Korean helps me remain rooted and sensitive to Korean American needs. As a Korean-speaking person, I want to make political and social issues accessible to speakers of Korean. As an English-speaking person, I can represent Korean needs to the mainstream. It's a complex and schizophrenic existence. I feel pulled in different directions all the time. If I were monolingual in English, I would not have to deal with contesting demands. The fact that I cannot speak Korean as well as a native, born and raised entirely in Korea, has been an advantage for me, because I am not expected to behave exactly the way a Korean monolingual person would. People give me a break when I speak clumsily or commit a *faux pas*. I could not have become a community advocate if I had been thrown into first-generation immigrant politics, which would have made it impossible to focus on the large political context of Los Angeles.

After the debacle, many different groups launched competing efforts to respond to the situation without any coordination. Everyone was proclaiming himself to be the leader of Koreatown. There was no consensus; no one was cooperating. People might argue that donations from South Korea demonstrate how much people in Korea care about overseas Koreans. In my view, the money made everything worse. It wasn't enough to help the victims re-establish their livelihoods—a few million is nothing compared to $400 million losses—but it was enough to fuel dissension and conflict in the already decimated community. At the same time, perhaps the big fanfare the South Korean government tried to make about their paltry donations reinforced black and white views of Koreans as perpetual foreigners who don't need or deserve U.S. public sector support because we get assistance from our homeland. What really infuriates me is that the South Korean government came in as the would-be savior of Koreans in Los Angeles after they'd written us off: it never helped us solve the "black/Korean conflict" because it didn't want to risk its relationship with the U.S. government. It's incredible that opposition party presidential candidate Kim Dae Jung was among the parade of politicians who passed through here. In the end, they did little or nothing for Koreans in Los Angeles. Now, a year after the "riots," only about one-fourth of the Korean American victims are back working. The South Korean government has done no more than the do-nothing city and county of Los Angeles to help them get back on their feet economically, and Korean Americans are as invisible and politically powerless as ever.

I was devastated personally by the *sa-i-ku p'ok-dong*. I had just returned to our agency from a meeting in South-Central when I learned about the King verdict. I was dumbfounded. But more than thoughts about the injustice of the verdict, I thought, "The Korean store owners are in trouble." That night, I went to the First African Methodist Episcopalian Church. The atmosphere was very charged; a feeling of rage was in the air, like electricity. The church was so crowded that I could not get in, so I went home. I heard later that some Korean reporters were attacked in front of the church. The next day, we started getting news of the damage to the Korean American community. Everyone at KYCC was scared and horrified. I couldn't believe what was happening. We tried to pull together a press conference of Asian and Pacific Americans to condemn the verdict, but there was no mainstream media coverage whatsoever. On the way to the press conference, I was driving down Olympic Boulevard, where I could see that there were no cops at all, just looters running across the street in front of my car with their arms full, carrying electronics goods. It was bizarre, surrealistic, a nightmare of anarchy.

I felt terrible. Even a week or two later, I broke down crying while driving by the ruins of a large, two-story commercial building I had passed on the way to work every day. It had been filled with life, and now nothing remained except charred ashes and shell of the concrete walls. I was just overwhelmed by the destruction and the knowledge that it had been done deliberately. It was so unjust; I was filled with rage and a sense of hopelessness because I did not even know who to be angry at. Later, I focused my anger at the Los Angeles Police Department, the City Council, and the Mayor's office. All during the rampage, we had called them, and they kept saying they'd look into it and get back to us. We were as politically well-connected as anyone in Koreatown, and that's how insignificant we and all other Korean Americans really were.

For several months, I suffered from serious depression. I would wake up in the middle of the night, overwhelmed by fear. I could neither sleep nor eat; I lost ten pounds and became haggard and gaunt. I was fortunate because at KYCC there were many things to keep me busy instead of sitting around feeling powerless with rage and frustration. I know that many other Korean Americans, not only in Los Angeles but in other cities across the United States, are still so deeply wounded that a year later they cannot speak about what happened without weeping. I don't know what I actually accomplished, but I worked frantically to stave off feelings of anxiety and depression. Media calls came in to our agency from around the world, and I tried to dispel the notion that "black/Korean conflict caused the riots." The commercial media continued to try to use Korean Americans to sensationalize the situation and to confirm their version of the story, which was about how blacks and Koreans hate each other.

I worked furiously, putting in 15-hour days at home and at the office, talking to the media, calling on people from the African American community, helping to organize victims' assistance and food distribution, and conducting fundraising campaigns. Our agency started working with the Youngnak Church, the Oriental Mission Church, the Korean American Coalition, the Korean Health Education Information and Referral (KHEIR), and some individual Korean American faculty members through the *Korea Times* to get food and money to the victims. We organized the Koreatown Emergency Relief Committee and distributed the first $500 per family. The food distribution went on for months.

Some of the money could have been held and leveraged. For every one dollar, we could have obtained four dollars in federal or private sector funds in the form of flexible loans and investments, with repayment arrangements to be determined by a community-based non-profit investment organization. There are certain types of investment vehicles with creative financing. I didn't even dare to suggest some of the ideas I had, for fear that I would be attacked as being in it for myself. There was just too much fighting and suspicion. Perhaps now that some time has passed, we can start talking about a non-profit small business investment corporation to help victims get back to work. All of Koreatown is suffering from the ripple effect of 2,300 small businesses being suddenly ruined. The community needs to re-establish its small businesses. There are huge problems with the Small Business Administration. Besides just working against the roadblocks being set up in the city's licensing and hearings divisions, our agency might be able to help establish an investment organization.

VII. From Riots to Bridge-Building

The *sa-i-ku p'ok-dong*, like the internment of Japanese Americans and the wholesale lynching and "driving out" of Chinese Americans in the past, is an institutionally sanctioned racist act against Korean Americans. We can't dismiss it as a fluke or an aberration in a social system that is otherwise basically working fine. I will always incorporate the experience of the *sa-i-ku p'ok-dong* in my thinking and my work. And I will continue to remind Korean Americans that such a thing could recur. Next time we must not serve as cannon fodder in a battle over historical problems we did not create.

I hope that the "riots" had a profound impact on Korean American community perceptions of our own needs. There had not been a collective longing for leadership before. People were fighting over credit and titles. It was bad, but the community was doing all right economically, and that's all that seemed to matter. The American dream of Korean immigrants was based on economic rather than political wants. That's the desire that capitalism engenders, both in Korea and in the United States. Korean Americans played by the rules of the game that were already set up. The rhetoric in the United States is about inclusiveness, about everyone, no matter what color, being rewarded for working hard and minding her or his own business. The ideals are great, but the reality is about political powerlessness for people of color in a hostile and racist environment.

What stands between Korean Americans and the promise of the American dream is racism. For immigrants of color, the prerequisite for becoming American has been leaving your culture by the door. But you can give up your culture and still not be accepted. You'll be hated instead, in a society that blames you whether you "succeed" or "fail" in your efforts to attain the American dream.

I can't understand why so many young Korean Americans have conservative values, why they give themselves up to the status quo. It's disheartening that so many of them want to go into the legal profession, which in my view is the upholder *par excellence* of the status quo. It's all about manipulating the rules of the game, which implies accepting the rules of the game and becoming part of a network of colleagues whose power and privileges are dependent on locking lay people out of even knowing the code words or logic that lawyers monopolize.

To many Koreans and Korean Americans, leadership is equated with social status, professional qualifications, and advanced degrees. That's why attorneys and academics with no record of involvement in the community can be so quickly accepted as spokespeople. Many Korean immigrants are only interested in the person's credentials, not in her or his track record. Perhaps it's a holdover from Korean Confucianism, which places so much emphasis on social status.

Another obstacle to the development of community leadership is the Korean cultural bias against women. I agree with the people who criticize Korean American men for being self-centered and individualistic. We have all been raised to believe that men are more valuable than women, and each son is usually convinced by his family that he is God's greatest gift to the world. When you bring together a whole group of individuals who believe that they are the most important and intelligent beings on earth, it is almost impossible for them to cooperate with each other to reach consensus. Also, there are Korean American men who can't deal with the brutal realization that no one out there in the "real world" thinks they are special in any way. There are very few opportunities for women to become genuinely respected community leaders. Women are still expected to function primarily in wife and mother roles; to do otherwise is to risk being labeled a freak worthy only of curiosity mixed with veiled pity. Among the immigrants, men often take credit for ideas offered by women, who are pressured to conform to traditional female roles. Capable second-generation Korean American women, repelled by sexism in Koreatown politics, often withdraw, taking their talents elsewhere. The only other option is for them to try to gain a foothold by trying to play the Korean community's particular brand of patriarchy off against the dominant society's sexism and racism.

We have to create opportunities for women and for younger Korean Americans to become leaders and community builders.

99

While leaders need to be rooted in their communities, they need not blindly obey the "will of the masses." A leader has to be able to identify what benefits all people, which in the end is more than just his or her ethnic group or constituency but the society as a whole. A leader has to have a vision of a better society and has to have enough support and involvement from a critical mass of constituency to move in that direction. If you have a leftist opinion and the majority in the community is rightist, you have to get in there and struggle to bring about a positive outcome. That is the toughest part. Otherwise, you are just casting your opinions around, insisting that you have "the answer," when no one person, organization, or group has "the answer." The situation is too complex, too volatile, and too divided. I agree with Henry Cisneros, who says that leaders of the 1990s will have to be more than inspirational; they will have to be bridge-building problem solvers.

The powerful have to be held accountable. I distrust power, no matter what color or how well-intentioned. What will be the outcome of the decisions of the powerful if those they have power over have no part in the process? I don't buy this American individualism stuff. Individual success stories don't translate into well-being for the Korean community as a whole. If we accept the rules of the game as they are, that capitalist maximization of profits make society work well for everyone—then we are doomed. The game should be about creating a humane and just society, where people can provide their unique perspectives and do their part to build a better world. Korean Americans could be an enrichment instead of a "problem" that needs solving. I want to believe that those who have been on the outside can bring that outsider perspective in and transform America into a place of peace and justice for ordinary people of all races and backgrounds.

3

AMERICA'S FIRST MULTIETHNIC 'RIOTS'

EDWARD T. CHANG

After the first verdict in the Rodney King trial, a Korean merchant was notified by a "regular customer" that if he wanted to live he should leave his store as soon as possible. He immediately closed the store and went home. On the way, he tuned into the Korean radio station and heard of the mayhem in his business area. His store on the corner of Normandie and Florence was being looted and set on fire. Little did he know that by the end of the rioting,[1] his losses combined with those of 2,700 other Korean businesses would total around $460 million—more than half the city's total property damages.[2] Never in their lives did Koreans feel so much rage and injustice at the American system.

The events were a culmination of years of neglect, abandonment, hopelessness, despair, alienation, injustice, isolation, and oppression that exploded in the wake of the King verdict. Suspicion, fear, and distrust between different ethnic and racial groups turned into the massive destruction of the Los Angeles. All of sudden, residents of Los Angeles were forced to confront the myth of Los Angeles as a model multiethnic city. Promoting itself as a "world city" and a shining example of a multiculturalism, Los Angeles is in fact a sad collection of "separate and unequal" communities. In their landmark 1989 study of widening inequality in Los Angeles urban planner Paul Ong and others documented that "to achieve full integration, over three-quarters of all blacks and over half of all Chicanos would have to move into Anglo neighborhoods."[3]

During the riots, I was forced to wear three different hats: a scholar engaged in "objective" research, a community advocate for the Korean victims, and a member of the Black Korean Alliance trying to bridge the gap between the two communities. I soon realized that wearing three hats was an impossible task. I had to choose between scholarly research and assuming a partisan role by serving as a spokesperson for the Korean American community.

Reporters kept my phone busy 15 hours a day for almost two weeks after the riots. They wanted to know if Korean-African American tensions contributed to the riot. They also wanted to hear Korean American reactions to the riot. One of the most common complaints of the reporters was that they could not find Korean American spokespeople who could articulate their feelings in English. I had to play the role of voicing the anger, rage, betrayal, resentment, and abandonment of Korean American victims who lost everything they owned.

The purpose of this chapter is two-fold. First, I analyze the riots from a multiethnic perspective by tracing its causes. To what extent did racial and class inequality contribute to the explosion of the city? Second, I ask what lessons can we learn from the riots, and what are their implications for the Asian American movement?

Beyond Black and White

The 1968 Kerner Commission Report concluded that America was divided into two separate and unequal nations—one black, one white. This is how the experts used to describe race relations in America. In the past, the race problem meant a "black" problem. The demographic composition of urban cities has undergone rapid changes during the past 20 years, however, and that has profoundly altered our ways of life. As a nation, we can no longer define race relations as a black/white issue.[4] Existing race relations theories are no longer viable or relevant since they cannot fully explain our society. There is an urgent need to develop new theories that will adequately reflect the rapidly changing demography of the United States.[5]

The demographic shift of South Central Los Angeles has been even more dramatic during the past two and half decades. In 1965, South Central Los Angeles was largely known as a "black area" with 81 percent African American residents. "Black flight" to the suburbs accelerated during the 1980s changing the face of South Central Los Angeles. The African American population declined 20 percent from 369,504 to 295,312 between 1980 and 1990. At the same time, the African American population in nearby Inland Empire of Riverside and San Bernardino County increased 99 percent and 134 percent.[6] Today, 48 percent of South Central's population is Latino. And in Los Angeles as a whole, whites constituted less than half of the city's population as of 1980 (48 percent).

Such demographic shifts have increased tensions and polarization among different ethnic and racial groups in the United States. The tensions have reached a potentially explosive point. African Americans feel that the increasing numbers of immigrants from Latin America and Asia are squeezing them out. Latin American immigrants often compete with African American residents for affordable housing, jobs, education, health, and social welfare programs. Highly publicized confrontations at South Central Los Angeles construction sites have occurred, including Danny Bakewell and the Brotherhood Crusade chasing away Latino workers and proclaiming, "If black people can't work, nobody works."

African Americans are also worried that they are losing political and economic "gains" they made during the 1960s' civil rights struggle. South Central Los Angeles is now a multiethnic community, and African Americans are concerned that they are losing influence and control in what used to be their "exclusive" domain. They are understandably suspicious of the growing numbers of Latino immigrants and Korean shop-owners in "their" neighborhoods. In fact, fights already have occurred between the

Latino and African American communities over the redistricting for the city council. Latinos are demanding proportional representation to reflect population changes, while African Americans argue that they are entitled to retain their share of gains to compensate for past injustices. And Asian Americans are now beginning to participate in the political process. For example, the Korean American Victims Association staged daily protests at City Hall for a month to demand compensation for Koreans who lost their businesses during the riots.

If this "politics of race" continues to dominate city politics, Los Angeles will suffer from polarization along racial boundaries, pitting one minority group against another. Obviously the system has failed to provide "justice" for all. Where did it go wrong?

Los Angeles Riots: 1965 and 1992

Is there a difference between the Watts riots of 1965 and the Los Angeles "riots" of 1992? What took place in Los Angeles for a few days in April 1992 showed a remarkable resemblance to Watts in 1965. We could easily mistake the following description of the Watts riot for the Los Angeles riots of 1992.

> They looted stores, set fires, beat up white passersby whom they hauled from stopped cars, many of which were turned upside down and burned, exchanged shots with law enforcement officers, and stoned and shot at firemen. The rioter seemed to have been caught up in an insensate rage of destruction.[7]

Gun sales tripled as citizens armed to protect themselves during and shortly after the Los Angeles riots. During the Watts riot of 1965, we witnessed a similar reaction; "some pawnshops and gun stores have been robbed of firearms and gun sales reportedly have tripled since the riots."[8]

Was there a conspiracy to riot before the King verdict? Many believed that gang members organized and planned the civil unrest. However, both the Kerner Commission report of 1968 and the

FBI investigation of the 1992 Los Angeles riots could not find any concrete evidence to support these suspicions. Charles J. Parsons, head of FBI Special Agent in Charge said, "I am not ruling out the possibility that there was pre-rioting plan, but we don't have any hard evidence of that."[9]

The similarities end here however. Several important differences exist between 1965 and 1992. As I discussed earlier, the 1992 Los Angeles riots involved a multiethnic uprising, whereas the Watts riot was primarily an African American revolt against injustice and racism. The Watts riot was confined to geographical areas largely known as South Central Los Angeles, whereas the riots of 1992 spread north of South Central Los Angeles into Koreatown, Hollywood, Pico-Union, and other middle-class neighborhoods.

In the 1960s, the civil rights movement had gained momentum, and many Americans, including whites, were sympathetic to the minority (i.e., black) issues of poverty, racism, unemployment, and injustice. Whites were willing to pay for and provide assistance to improve the quality of life for African Americans and other disadvantaged minorities. As I will discuss later, though, the rise of the neoconservative movement during the late 1970s and 1980s has left white Americans less willing to "pay for" social and economic programs to aid the underprivileged.

In the 1960s, many African Americans felt optimistic. They hoped to improve their lives by actively participating in electoral politics, and they believed they could attain the "American Dream". Today, however, despair, hopelessness, and a sense of abandonment are widespread in the African American community. The gap between the haves and the have-nots widened, and many African Americans lost their "American Dream" as they dropped out of the labor market.[10] "In the 1960s, racial disorder was about rising expectations; today it is about diminishing expectations."[11]

The Los Angeles riots seemed a cry for help. One woman explained that "this was the first time she could get shoes for all six of her children at once." No doubt, the social, economic, and political conditions of South Central Los Angeles, and the ideological shift to the right, were the main causes of the Los Angeles riots.

The "riots" told us that we have ignored these problems for too long.

Deindustrialization and South Central Los Angeles

The restructuring of the economy—plant closings, runaway shops, and domestic disinvestments—has deepened racial and class inequality in U.S. cities. Deindustrialization, or the structural realignment of the American economy during the 1970s and 1980s, was the U.S. corporate response to the economic crisis created by increasing global competition. "Runaway shops" and overseas investment were an aggressive tactic by capitalists to regain competitiveness and increase profits. "By the beginning of the 1980s," wrote economists Barry Bluestone and Bennett Harrison in *The Deindustrialization of America* "every newscast seemed to contain a story about a plant shutting down, another thousand jobs disappearing from a community, or the frustrations of workers unable to find full-time jobs utilizing their skills and providing enough income to support their families."[12] Although some politicians blamed the increase of imports from Asia for the loss of American jobs, the deindustrialization of the U.S. economy caused the plant closures. In fact, during the decade of the 1970s, private disinvestment in plants and equipment probably eliminated at least 32 million jobs in the United States, estimate Bluestone and Harrison.[13]

Suddenly, unemployment was no longer the poor's problem. Many companies simply decided to pick up and move to other areas where wages were lower, unions weaker, and the business climate better. The middle-class workers in traditional manufacturing industries such as steel, rubber, and auto were the hardest hit as they experienced permanent displacement with no prospect of finding equivalent employment. "The lower-middle and middle rungs of the American occupational structure are at risk: the top and the bottom grow," wrote Michael Harrington in *New American Poverty* in 1980.[14] In other words, deindustrialization polarized class inequality in the United States: High-tech industries and low-paying unskilled jobs grew, and traditional middle-class jobs declined. For example, while New York City lost 400,000 jobs between 1970 and 1980, white-collar industries increased their employment by 17 percent[15] and the number of sweatshops rose.

Meanwhile, on the West Coast, deindustrialization also took its toll. General Motors, Goodyear, Firestone, and Bethlehem Steel used to provide jobs and economic security to the residents of South Central Los Angeles, but by the 1980s, they had vanished. In a study of racial inequality in Los Angeles, Ong and other researchers found that "in the late seventies and early eighties alone, Los Angeles lost over 50,000 industrial jobs to plant closures in the auto, tire, steel, and non-defense aircraft industries. Since 1971, South Central Los Angeles, the core of the African American community, itself lost 321 firms."

Despite the warning of the Watts riot of 1965, the socioeconomic conditions of South Central Los Angeles continued to deteriorate. South Central Los Angeles has suffered from chronic poverty, high unemployment, inferior schooling, and soaring high-school drop-out rates. Various studies have found that one in four black men in their 20s is in jail or otherwise involved in the criminal justice system, black men in poor neighborhoods are less likely to live to age 65 than men in Bangladesh, and the majority of black babies are born in single-parent households.[16]

In fact, 1990 census data shows that the status of African Americans has in fact deteriorated since the 1960s. The 1990 poverty rate was over 30 percent, higher than at the time of Watts riot (27 percent). Per capita income of South Central Los Angeles in 1990 was a mere $7,023, compared with $16,149 for Los Angeles County as a whole. More importantly, half of those 16 years and older were unemployed and not looking for a job. These statistics clearly show the failure of "trickle-down" economics; the economic recovery and boom of 1980s did not improve socioeconomic conditions of South Central Los Angeles residents. Instead, African Americans who live in the inner city often must endure the burden of the "black tax"—higher insurance and mortgage rates, abusive police patrols, and lower quality education.

The future prospects are even more gloomy, since African Americans are grossly underrepresented in the growing high-tech related industries. According to Edward Park, high-technology managers are using race and ethnicity to mitigate a class-based consciousness. Rather than hire the "traditional industrial labor force" (i.e. white and black), these managers are fostering ethnic rivalry by employing Asian immigrant workers over African Americans because Asian immigrants are perceived as docile, diligent, and easily exploitable.[17]

1980s: Era of Neo-conservatism

The Los Angeles riots exposed the failure of the 1980s neo-conservative policies. Since the passage of the 1965 Civil Rights Act, the Republican Party has dominated the presidency of the United States through its strong support from white middle-class votes. The only exception came when the Watergate scandal forced former President Nixon to resign. Beginning with the landmark 1975 Bakke decision, (when Allan Bakke, a white applicant to a California medical school, charged the school with "reverse discrimination") the attitudes of white Americans began to shift from progressive (willing to support social and economic programs to aid minorities) to conservative views (emphasis on morality, strong family values, law and order, and lowering taxes).[18]

The resurgence of the neo-conservatism has hurt minority groups during the 1980s as the federal government cut funding for social programs for inner cities. White Americans were willing to spend more tax dollars for a military build-up than to address so-called "black problems." Most white Americans now believe that "blacks have been given more than a fair chance to succeed" with the passage of the Civil Rights Act and the implementation of the affirmative action programs. In fact, many whites believe that liberals and Democrats "gave in" too much to the demands of black Americans at the expense of whites.

The resurgence of neo-conservatism ensured the election of conservative presidential candidate Ronald Reagan in 1980, his landslide reelection in 1984, and the election of George Bush in 1988. These Republican administrations implemented a "politics of race" by blaming victims and scapegoating immigrants and minorities for societal problems. Although no concrete proof exists to suggest that the state has promoted or justified the recent waves of anti-Asian activities, a correlation does seem to exist between the Republican Party's policies of scapegoating and the increase of anti-Asian violence. As a result, during the 1980s, we have witnessed the sudden increase of inter-minority conflicts such as Korean/African American and Latino/African American tensions and the rise of anti-minority violence. By looking back at the history of the majority/minority relationship, we see that the power structure has a way of blaming the victims for social and economic problems in this country.

Police Brutality and the Justice System

Police brutality is nothing new to African Americans living in the inner city. The Los Angeles Police Department (LAPD) has had a reputation for brutalizing African American suspects. In fact, police mistreatment of an African American suspect triggered the Watts riot of 1965. Los Angeles has learned little from its history; little has changed. Although the King videotape shocked most Americans, for African Americans it simply confirmed the reality they face on a daily basis. Young African American men are often stopped just because they fit a "description" or are in the wrong neighborhood. African Americans are often treated as "guilty" until proven innocent, although the Constitution of the United States supposedly guarantees otherwise.

A white appalled and disgusted by the tape of the Rodney King beating probably feels sympathy and compassion for King. In contrast, a black feels threatened and alarmed that "it could have been me." White Americans cannot even begin to grasp what it is like to be harassed by police or denied a job just because of the color of their skin. Many Asian Americans also felt shock and dismay over the brutal beating of King.

The Latasha Harlins and Rodney King verdicts added to the perception that the justice system does not serve the interests of African Americans. A Korean immigrant grocer, Soon Ja Du, shot and killed a 15-year-old African American girl, Latasha Harlins, on March 18, 1991. Mrs. Du was found guilty of voluntary manslaughter and sentenced to five years probation. Such lenience exacerbated tension between Korean American and African American communities and underlined the justice system's racist double standard.

Inter-ethnic Relations: Korea/African American Tensions

The media has continued to portray the 1992 riots as an extention of the ongoing conflict between Korean merchants and African American residents, despite the fact that more than half the looters arrested were Latinos.[19] Indeed, Korean-African American conflict has surfaced as one of the most explosive issues facing many cities in the United States since the early 1980s.[20] Despite many efforts to alleviate tensions, the situation has only worsened.

In January 1990, the Red Apple boycott—which lasted a year-and-half in the Flatbush section of Brooklyn, New York—focused national attention on growing tensions between African Americans and Korean Americans. The relationship between the two communities suffered further when Korean American merchants in Los Angeles shot and killed two African American customers within a three-month period, March to June 1991. Led by Danny Bakewell of the Brotherhood Crusade, African Americans boycotted Korean-owned stores. During the boycotts, Bakewell was seen on TV almost daily making highly charged remarks against Korean Americans. This certainly heightened the tensions and helped further polarize the two communities.

One of the most common complaints by African Americans against Korean Americans focuses on "rudeness." Some merchants are indeed rude to their customers, although the majority are kind and courteous. Korean Americans are exceptionally family-oriented, and that affects their attitudes in dealing with people they don't know. Korean Americans themselves complain that they too have experienced "rudeness" from fellow Korean merchants. In general, Korean Americans are nice to people they know but "rude" to strangers. Part of this "rudeness" is prejudice, but part is misunderstanding. Therefore, while it is wrong for Korean Americans to deny they are prejudiced, it is also wrong for African Americans to accuse all Korean merchants of being "rude."

Inter-ethnic tensions in African American neighborhoods have historical roots. Jewish merchants and African Americans clashed during the 1960s. During the Watts riots, rioters looted and burned down many Jewish-owned stores; they destroyed 80 percent of the furniture stores, 60 percent of the food markets, and 54 percent of the liquor stores.[21] Korean immigrants are perceived as part of "a long line of outsiders who came into African American neighborhoods to exploit the community." First whites, then Jews, Chinese, Japanese, and now Koreans dominate the business interests in the African American community. Although over the years the conflicts in Los Angeles have shifted from one racial group to another, the class-based nature of the struggle has remained consistent. It is not, therefore, a racial issue, but a class issue involving small business and residents.

In the eyes of the underclass who have nothing to lose, the merchant class represents wealth. But Korean Americans perceive themselves as simply trying to make a living. Korean Americans often complain that life in the United States is a life of making payments. Although Korean merchants are able to make some profits from their stores, many can barely keep up with their monthly bills, such as mortgage, car, utility, and merchandise payments. These different perceptions of the status of Korean merchants have exacerbated the tensions and polarized the two communities.

In addition to believing that Korean merchants behave rudely, African Americans believe that they fail to contribute economically to the community. They complain that Korean merchants overcharge for inferior products and do not hire African American workers or contribute profits back to the community.

In any colonial situation, the middleman is inevitably a target of oppressed people. For example, Korean independence fighters saw Koreans who collaborated with the Japanese colonial government as an enemy of Korean people. Japanese-collaborators were protecting the interests of the colonial government in Korea. Therefore, Koreans had to eliminate Japanese-collaborators in order to achieve independence for Korea. That's how some African Americans perceive Korean Americans—as a "layer" that protects the interests of white America and preserves the status quo. Korean Americans have become a "symbol of oppression."

Why are African Americans unable to attain the same level of class power as Jews, WASPs, and Asians? Historically, non-African American merchants have dominated the economy of African American communities. Despite many attempts by African American leaders who advocate economic self-sufficiency and self-help, the African American community still suffers from a lack of African American-owned businesses in their own neighborhoods. Many African American-owned businesses fail because they are often under-capitalized, lack sufficient skills, and face stiff competition from well-financed white-owned corporations. In particular, African American leaders charge that African American capitalism has not materialized because of the discriminatory lending practices by financial and banking institutions.

Lessons for the Asian American Community

What do the Los Angeles riots mean to the Asian American community? Although many Asian American-owned businesses were damaged or destroyed during the "riots," very few people were aware of the extent of this tragedy (see the following table). The riots raised some serious questions about the viability of Asian American coalitions. One *Los Angeles Times* article argued that "Asian Americans had widely diverse reactions to the upheaval in Los Angeles highlighting strains exacerbated in recent decades."[22] Furthermore, the same article claimed that the "Asian American movement has failed to capture the common agenda." Many Asian American activists and community leaders questioned the timing and intention of the *Los Angeles Times* article. Although many condemned it as divisive, I strongly believe that we must show courage and acknowledge our problems, and begin to build "common agendas" to unite Asian American groups.

Historically, Asian American Studies played a critical role defining and uniting Asian American groups. Asian American Studies grew out of student activism and a desire to link students and academics with grassroot communities. During the early stage of its development, Asian American Studies primarily concerned itself with the issue of reclaiming what historian Yuji Ichioka called our "buried past." Issues of identity, history, and racism dominated research topics as Asian Americans felt it important to reaffirm their roots and reestablish an identity.

However, immigration has drastically changed the Asian American community during the past 20 years through immigration. Today, the number of immigrants outnumbers native-born Asian Americans. The real challenge for our community is to truly represent the interests of all Asian Americans, especially the majority of foreign-born. So far, Asian American Studies has failed to bring different communities together by creating common agendas for all Asian American groups. There is an absolute urgency to build networks between Asian American Studies and new immigrant and refugee communities.

For Korean Americans, the riots raised the important question of what it means to be "Korean American." The 1992 riots will be remembered as a turning point in Korean American history, similar to the internment of Japanese Americans. They opened the eyes of Korean immigrants to the problems of institutional racism, social and economic injustice, and the shortcomings of the "American Dream." Some Korean Americans felt a deep sense of disappointment at how other Asian Americans deserted them during and after the riots. Similarly, many in the Southeast Asian community are asking whether Asian American Studies is relevant to the issues of community. How long can we continue to play an advocacy and consciousness-raising role without input from new immigrant and refugee communities? These are important and difficult questions that those in Asian American Studies must addressed as we move to the twenty-first century.

After the riots, we often heard from community advocates including Reverend Cecil Murray, John Mack of the Los Angeles Urban League, and Danny Bakewell of the Brotherhood Crusade

Damage to Asian American-owned Businesses*

Korean American	2,300	$400.0 million
Chinese American	262	$53.0 million
Japanese American	10	$3.2 million
Filipino American	25	$7.5 million
Total	2,597	$463.7 million

Source: Shinyodo Marketing Survey

* Shinyodo survey did not include other Asian Americans, such as Vietnamese, Cambodian, Thai, and Laotian American-owned businesses. If we include these figures, the total damage would be much higher.

that "they can understand why some African Americans have participated in the violent destruction of properties and community. We understand where they are coming from. It does not justify the violence, but we certainly can understand and explain their behaviors." African Americans have suffered from years of racism, poverty, abandonment, betrayal, and racial injustice. Thus, community advocates have shown an extraordinary degree of patience, compassion, sympathy, and understanding toward those who looted and burned down stores.

These same individuals have shown a very little understanding, compassion, and sympathy toward Korean immigrants however. They show impatience with Korean immigrants who are struggling to learn the American language, culture, and customs.

Furthermore, some Asian American activists show a similar lack of compassion, implying that Korean Americans were responsible for their own suffering and that they "deserved" it. I agree that some Korean immigrants were responsible for exacerbating conflict between the Korean American and African American communities, but we cannot blame the majority of Korean Americans for the events of April 1992. Recently, at the National Association for Asian American Studies conference in San Jose, California, I expected the Association to hold a general meeting to discuss the implication of the riots for the Asian American community. But the Association failed to reach out to the Korean American community. If Asian American Studies cared about Korean American and other Asian American victims, they would have shown the same degree of compassion and understanding as many African American academics showed toward their own communities during and after the riots."

The real challenge for Asian American Studies in the decade of 1990 is how to expand our agenda to include immigrant and refugee issues. It is our responsibility to reach out to immigrant and refugee populations whether we agree with their perspective or not. If new members of our community need to be educated about U.S. history, culture, and racism, we should provide educational programs. Many newcomers are naive and ignorant about life in the United States. We must show that we care!

It is important to acknowledge that some in Asian American Studies have sincerely tried to reach out to the immigrant and refugee community. The efforts have not been successful however. The traditional approaches, whatever they may have been, did not work. It is time for change. Fortunately, I see signs of improvement. For the first time, I witnessed inclusion of many panels on refugees, Filipinos, Pacific Islanders, and the Korean American community during the May 1992 Association meetings at San Jose. We are moving in the right direction.

But we must do more. Some Asian American Studies academics have forgotten their roots. During the past 20 years, Asian American Studies has tried to gain legitimacy and acceptance in the university community. In the process, some academics lost their connection to the community they are supposed to represent. Because of the lack of institutional supports, many Studies scholars felt forced to choose between either playing the role of the community activist or engaging in traditional academic research. One way to overcome this institutional barrier is to seek research topics that are relevant to the Asian American community. I strongly believe that relevancy is the key to reestablishing the connection between Asian American Studies and the community.

If Asian American Studies wants to grow, our agenda must broaden to include the concerns of new immigrant and refugee communities.

Conclusion

The 1992 riots were a turning point in Asian American history. They provided us with a unique opportunity to reexamine our ways of life and ideas. It awakened us to the new American reality: the end of the era of black/white relations and the beginning of a multiethnic and multiracial community.

Peaceful coexistence for different racial, ethnic, and national groups cannot be accomplished without more educational, social, and political efforts. How can we promote understanding, harmony, and trust between different racial, ethnic, and religious groups? We must learn to appreciate our differences. I propose an "Ethnic Studies" requirement for all school-age children in the United States. More importantly, our teachers, professors, and corporate executives must learn the real lessons of living in a multiethnic and multiracial community.

Notes

1. In this chapter, I chose to use the term "riots" over other terms, such as upheaval, civil unrest, rebellion, uprising, or insurrection to reflect the view of Korean Americans.
2. *The Korea Times,* July 4, 1992. It is also important to note that 48 percent of victims of the riots were not insured, according to the Department of California Insurance survey.
3. Paul Ong et al., *The Widening Divide: Income Inequality and Poverty in Los Angeles,* Los Angeles: UCLA Urban Planning Department, 1989.
4. *Los Angeles Times,* May 21, 1993 reported that 12,545 arrests were made between 6 p.m. April 29, 1952 and 5 a.m. May 5, 1992—the period of civil disorder. The racial breakdown of those arrested was: Latinos 45.2 percent, blacks 41 percent, and whites 11.5 percent.
5. Edward T. Chang, "New Urban Crisis: Intra-Third World Conflict," Shirley Hune et al., eds., *Asian Americans: Comparative and Global Perspectives,* Pullman: Washington State University Press, 1991: 169-178.

6. *Los Angeles Times,* August 13, 1992. According to the 1980 and 1990 U.S. Census, the African American population increased from 30,088 to 59,966 in Riverside County, and 46,615 to 109,162 in San Bernardino County.
7. *Violence in the City—An End of a Beginning? A Report by the Governor's Commission on the Los Angeles Riots,* December 2, 1965.
8. National Advisory Commission on Civil Disorders, New York: Bantam Books, 1969: 153.
9. *Los Angeles Times,* July 25, 1992.
10. According to the 1990 U.S. Census, 41.8 percent of residents of South Central Los Angeles have dropped out of the labor force.
11. Kevin Phillips, *Politics of Rich and Poor,* New York: Random House, 1991.
12. Barry Bluestone and Bennett Harrison, *The Deindustrialization of America,* New York: Basic Books, Inc., 1982: 4.
13. Ibid, 35.
14. Michael Harrington, *New American Poverty,* New Jersey: Princeton Universtiy Press, 1981: 166.
15. Saskia Sassen-Koob, "Recomposition and Peripheralizaiton at the Core," *New Normads,* San Francisco: Synthesis Publication, 1982.
16. *Los Angeles Times,* August 1, 1992:1.
17. Edward Park, "Asian Immigrants and the High Technology Industry in Silicon Valley," Ph.D. dissertation, Department of Ethnic Studies, U.C. Berkeley, 1992.
18. For more information on the Allen Bakke case, see Nathan Glazer, *Affirmative Discrimination: Ethnic Inequality and Public Policy.* New York: Basic Books, 1975.
19. *Los Angeles Times,* May 21, 1992.
20. Edward T. Chang, "New Urban Crisis: Korean-Black Conflicts in Los Angeles," Ph.D. dissertation, Department of Ethnic Studies, U.C. Berkeley, 1990.
21. Sholmo Katz, ed., *Negro and Jew: An Encounter in America,* London: The MacMillan Company, 1966: 76.
22. *Los Angeles Times,* July 13, 1992.

Cambodian woman with incense and candle for offerings during Katen festival. © 1990 Dan Grzyminski, Impact Visuals.

4

ROSES, RITES, AND RACISM

An Interview with Sophea Mouth

SONIA SHAH

Sophea Mouth is an outspoken Cambodian activist organizing and studying in Madison, Wisconsin. He is a founder of the United Refugees Party, which organizes for Cambodian, Hmong, and Laotian communities in Wisconsin. He is also president of United Refugee Services and a member of the County Office of Commissioners. He has appeared on several television and radio programs to rail against the racism and joblessness plaguing the Southeast Asian community in Madison. In Dane County, Southeast Asians comprise the largest minority group.

I interviewed him over the phone on July 8, 1993. He spoke eloquently and movingly about the travesties of cultural collision afflicting the Southeast Asian refugee community—ravaged on one hand by atrocities and war at home and on the other hand by ignorance, fear, and violence in the adopted land. The following is an excerpt from that interview.

Like most Cambodians in the United States, I come from a large city in Cambodia. I lived through the Khmer Rouge holocaust, and by 1979, I escaped to Thailand with my family. There, we applied for sponsorship, and got sponsored by a Presbyterian church in Lake Geneva, Wisconsin. We worked on a farm there,

119

and I went to high school. There were some problems; I didn't get along with my sponsorship family, they didn't treat me right, they thought I should be subservient to them. I concentrated on going to school, but my father couldn't stay. He moved to Madison, Wisconsin. I stayed to finish high school, then moved to Madison to go to college.

Problems cropped up in Madison. We have a number of Hmong, Laotian, and Cambodian people here. My brother was beaten up by the police. There was a misunderstanding between the white [police] and the Cambodian community. We have survived the Khmer Rouge [and as a result] we don't respond to authority very well. Whenever [government officials] approach us, we run; they don't understand that we are attempting to flee because of our past experiences.

Since then, I've been involved heavily in the community. I am president of United Refugee Services, which provides services to the Hmong and others, by locating public facilities, finding jobs, etc. I'm also a member of the County Office of Commissioners, and there I deal with a lot of minority issues related to housing discrimination, jobs, Indian mascots, you name it.

I requested a police liaison from the City of Madison community to facilitate communications, so they don't respond to us with beating. It didn't work out very well. If the community liaison knew about anything illegal in the community, he had to report it to the police, which was contrary to what we wanted. One Hmong practice is called "early marriages," at 12, 13, 14 years of age. American people think this is a big problem, that this is statutory rape, and it is against the law. To us it is a cultural issue that is important. One of the functions of early marriages is they keep kids away from gangs, and give them responsibility. A friend of mine worked as the liaison to the police, and he couldn't report it. He didn't report it. We're not going to give information that would get our people arrested. The purpose [of the liaison] was to educate the police force to understand our culture better. We educate ourselves about U.S. law and the legal system.

It is their ignorance and fear which lead to discrimination against us and our religion. The Hmong here, they have a tough time getting funeral homes to open up for their [funeral ceremonies]. They think the Hmong are a cult, their ceremonies are evil, because they involve bringing a dead chicken into the funeral home. [People in the Hmong community] wanted to know, can we get the city to do something? I said, I doubt it. You just have to build your own place. But we don't have the credit to get loans.

For the Cambodian people, the main issue is gangs and violence. The school district is not willing to recognize that there is a problem with race. They want to maintain their "standard" that there is no racial problem. Yet there is much racial fighting: white versus Asian, black versus Asian. It's a mess.

We fear our kids are being brainwashed and we could lose our culture ... Cambodian parents feel they can't discipline or control their kids anymore. The children call the police when their parents spank them. They learn this at school. For us, we discipline our kids by giving them a quick whip, because we love them. The Americans see that as abuse. When the kids call the police, they respond aggressively, brutally. The social workers, the school system, give the kids false ideas about freedoms, choices, and all these wrong ideas. The kids don't look up to their parents anymore, they have lost their respect. Only a few graduate from high school. They join gangs, they can't read or write, they can't even read their own language.

A friend of mine works with the youth. He was so upset about this one case. A child came home late, one or two o'clock in the morning. The parents were upset, they whipped her a few times. She called the police. The police are supposed to use their own discretion, whether to arrest or not. There were no marks on the child, but they took the father in anyway. He ended up going to jail, paying $500 in bail, and having to go through some sort of nonsense training. [One parent whom this happened to] was so ashamed, he committed suicide.

We told them, "Educate us. Don't drag us to jail right away and make us lose our face, so we end up killing ourselves." People have other problems: alcoholism, dealing with the kids, the police, the lack of jobs, the language isolation; these are very stressful problems. They are compounded by the families at home, sending letters asking for money you don't have, and the memory of Khmer Rouge atrocities. [In this sense] the problems for the Cambodian people are much worse than for anyone. The mental health group here set up these groups [to deal with some of these problems] but with very little success. They call it "Post Traumatic Stress Syndrome."

But it's more than that. In any Cambodian community, the problems are so severe, there is no way Western medicine has any way of relating to them. We think that building a temple for the elderly would be better treatment than this talking therapy. We are not used to this psychoanalysis. I thought it was silly. People just go because they are required to. There really is no sign of improvement.

Getting education is one of the solutions. But it is difficult to do that. Our young aren't achieving to their potential. You think the parents have problems, the children are affected too. You see a lot of stress in our children. I am probably one of the first to get a college degree in this community, and to be in graduate school now, and I don't know how I did it. During the Khmer Rouge, my family was separated. My mother was shot in front of me. I had to endure a lot of pain, I witnessed many murders and killing. Plus, I didn't have any education at home. I had a couple of years of reading and writing. I had to learn it all here.

The movement here is to countereducate, not to assimilate. Assimilation assumes that there is one right culture. We want to maintain a separate identity and culture, so we can educate our young to not join a gang, to get a good education, to get jobs. When the government promotes cultural diversity, they are not serious about learning about other people's cultures. Their suggestion usually is "just read this book and you'll know everything about it."

A Cambodian social worker from Minnesota came to a conference I was at. It was clear that she didn't really understand. She was into assimilating into the mainstream. She was brainwashed. You go to American school, you accept the system, and you can't think for yourself anymore. You just mimic the system. She was asked to give a suggestion on what to do to help Asians in the community. She said, "Just think of them as roses that have been transplanted to this place. Give them nutrients and watch them grow." I said, "We are not flowers or plants, we are human beings and demand our rights!"

In Cambodia, there was one American pilot who accidently flipped a target switch and killed 127 people. That pilot was fined $700, and the survivors got $100 each. It is very depressing to think about that. That doctor who is supposed to be an expert on Cambodian mental health problems [like PTS] said, "You just have to think of them as one of us, as human." I was shocked—that they were just beginning to think we are human.

It has been very difficult to get jobs around here, blue-collar jobs. Some employers still don't trust us. [For example] in the post office, there are a lot of Vietnam veterans, who can't deal with Asian people. One mailman came to my door and said he couldn't deal with walking around this neighborhood. It reminded him of the war when he had to shoot a lot of these people.

I tried to get a job with the county. They ask you, "How would you do this and that," which is a cultural question. If you are Asian you have a certain way of doing things, but if you don't do it the American way, they penalize you. They asked me, "What is the cause of social problems in this county and Madison especially?" I said, "Many things, political, social, and economic. A differential allocation of resources." The person said we can't hire you, you're too radical, you might create problems here. They thought I am communistic, or socialistic. That is what I grew up with. What can I say? I can't say that people are lazy, they don't want to work, etc. The system is the problem. It is not working for people like us.

Even in education, you have to play a game to get your degree. And then, among people who have, they still are not hired. When before it was the question of qualification, now it isn't qualifications, maybe there aren't enough jobs. You know, we get this runaround. First this and then that. I was invited to a conference on Workforce 2000. I said I didn't want any more empty promises, you have to take action. We are desperately in need of jobs, and we are committed to work.

This Hispanic guy said that Asians are the most discriminated-against people in this county, and I agree with him. I went on a call-in radio show with him to talk about the problem. One person called and asked, "What do you people think about abortion?" This is absurd! We are still trying to put rice on the table, and they are asking us about abortion. We are so far apart, people don't understand what our needs are.

I've been approached by many ministers to convert. I tell them I don't need help, I am not lost. In my community, the church offers Good News clubs for teenage Hmong people. Some of the Hmong didn't know this teen club was teaching Christian scripture. The church thinks "The only way to make them civilized is to make them part of our beliefs."

We have been so divided in this country. We are still being made fun of on TV and news media. We must unite, and work together, whether for political or social goals. We are the largest non-white community in this county, but we only have a couple people working for the government. The blacks and the Latinos are hired more than us, even though their populations are smaller. We have to be represented in every facet of this country, not assimilation, but full participation.

What is important is to help rebuild the community here for the next generation. We need education in the Khmer language, funding, education, and jobs. There is no simple solution to any of our problems. If you try to come up with a simple solution, it only makes the problem worse.

5

WHEN KNOW-NOTHINGS SPEAK ENGLISH ONLY

Analyzing Irish and Cambodian Struggles for Community Development and Educational Equity

PETER NIEN-CHU KIANG

Lowell, Massachusetts, the birthplace of America's industrial revolution and the crucible for many important developments in U.S. immigrant and labor history, has undergone a new period of dramatic demographic change caused by the rapid, recent growth of Latino and Southeast Asian populations.[1] During the 1980s, for example, the number of Cambodians in Lowell grew from less than 100 to between 15,000 and 25,000—totaling one-fifth of the city's population and making Lowell the second largest concentration of Cambodians in the country after Long Beach, California. Rapid demographic change has triggered conflict, particularly around schooling and the new immigrant communities.

This chapter[2] explores recent dynamics of Cambodian community development in light of Lowell's remarkable history during the mid-1800s—a time when rapid demographic change led to the development of the nation's second-largest concentration of Irish in the country. Analyzing the development of the Irish community and its relationship to issues of public education during this earlier historical period reveals themes that situate schools in their social context and that link current struggles for educational equity in Lowell with dynamics of leadership, institution-building, and community empowerment.

We face obvious limitations in applying specific lessons from mid-nineteenth century Lowell to the present. The city's economy and political institutions have changed dramatically during the past 150 years. Furthermore, the social, cultural, racial, class, and religious characteristics of the two immigrant groups are substantially different.[3]

Nevertheless, given the lack of focused research on Cambodian community development as well as continuing debates over larger issues of race, class, and immigrant assimilation in the United States, Lowell provides a useful lens through which we can assess contemporary social conflicts and community strategies for empowerment. As historian Mark Scott Miller asserts in his study analyzing the impact of World War II on Lowell:

> At each step of the city's history, Lowell's citizens experienced the extremes of the advance of American society and its social and economic structures. Because Lowell's life as a city is so dramatic, changes in this archetypical community clarify trends that more moderated experiences in other communities might obscure.[4]

A Brief History of Lowell

The town of Lowell was established in 1826 during the United States' industrial revolution. Seeking to expand their economic base, Boston-based gentry purchased land along the Merrimack River and built a chain of textile mills with an elaborate, interlocking system of canals that powered looms with energy generated by the river's current. As Lowell emerged as the country's textile center, the mills recruited teenage girls from the area's surrounding farms. Paid at half the male wage, yet earning more than they would from farm work, the mill girls lived in dormitory-style housing constructed next to the factories. Harsh working and living conditions led to some of the country's first labor organizing—including mill girl strikes in 1834 and 1836, the birth of the Lowell Female Labor Reform Association in 1844, and a petition to the Massachusetts Legislature for a 10-hour workday in 1845.[5]

With successive waves of European immigrants arriving on the East Coast throughout the 1800s and early 1900s, cheap immigrant labor entered the booming textile industry and replaced the mill girls. The mill girls' dormitories evolved into overcrowded tenement housing for successive waves of Irish, French Canadian, Greek, Polish, and Portuguese immigrants.

As the textile industry reached its height in the 1890s, Lowell became widely recognized as a city built by immigrants. Labor organizing also continued in the city as the Yiddish-speaking Lowell Workingmen's Circle formed in 1900 and Greek immigrants led a city-wide strike in 1903 that set the stage for the well-known Bread and Roses strike of 1912 in the neighboring mill town of Lawrence.

But by the 1920s, the textile industry in Lowell entered a long period of depression and economic decline. By 1945, eight of the city's eleven big mills had closed and unemployment had soared. Foreshadowing the decline of many Midwestern industrial cities during the 1970s, Lowell and other textile mill towns in the area all but died during this period.

In the 1970s, a combination of factors, including emerging of new industries fueled by high-technology research at Massachusetts-based universities and the political muscle of the Massachusetts congressional delegation—which included Speaker of the House "Tip" O'Neill, Senator Edward Kennedy, and Senator Paul Tsongas (who was born and raised in Lowell)—led to a turnaround in the state's economy. A combination of federal dollars and corporate investment revitalized Lowell's economy, enabling the city to move from 13.8 percent unemployment in 1978 to 7 percent in 1982 to less than 3 percent in 1987. After rehabilitating the run-down mill factories, the city's vacant industrial land dropped from 100 acres in 1978 to zero by 1987.[6]

Serving as the backdrop for the launching of Michael Dukakis's presidential campaign in 1988, campaign managers cited Lowell as the model city of the Massachusetts economic miracle, having overcome industrial decline to reemerge as a leading center of the country's high-technology revolution. Lowell's remarkable rebirth generated an optimism within the city that paralleled accounts from the early days of industrialization during the 1830s when Lowell was described as "the focus of all eyes ... a light upon a hill."[7]

Demographic Change and Community Development: The Irish Case

Lowell owes much to Irish immigrants who were among the initial laborers to construct a set of canals and factories in 1822 even before residents formally incorporated the city. By 1830, more than 500 Irish had settled permanently in "paddy camps," later known as "the Acre," on the outskirts of the mill village at the center of town.[8]

During the 1830s, two contrasting trends emerged. The Irish population established a stable community based upon working in the mills in Lowell and the surrounding area, developing ethnic businesses and a small entrepreneurial class, and, most importantly, constructing an Irish Catholic church in the neighborhood. Erected in 1831, St. Patrick's Church served as "a symbol of the Irish presence in Lowell and represented the Irish commitment to order and stability," wrote historian Brian Mitchell. "The church was, in effect, the center of the first stirrings of community among the Irish in Lowell."[9]

However, as the Irish population grew, so did local resentment and anti-Irish Catholic reaction. In May 1831, a general riot left one person dead and many others injured. Street fights and harassment escalated. Lowell city officials reported in 1832 that "a disturbance of the peace is of almost nightly occurrence."[10]

These two trends continued during the next two decades, and intensified with the massive influx of Irish immigrants escaping Ireland's potato famines in the 1840s. By 1840, the Irish population of Lowell had already reached 21,000. By 1850, the arrival of famine Irish increased the number to more than 33,000—roughly 30 percent of the city—making Lowell the second largest concentration of Irish in the country, after Boston.

The growing Irish population created new markets and opportunities for the small Irish entrepreneurial class who owned ethnic neighborhood businesses, rented out tenement apartments, and contracted Irish labor for the mills. With increased support from the Boston-based Irish Catholic church leadership, Lowell's Irish community, which had long since outgrown their 1831 church facility, succeeded in constructing a magnificent new St. Patrick's Church in 1854.

At the same time, rapid demographic change led to growing concerns about public image and order in the city, particularly after the influx of poor, uneducated famine Irish. Anti-Irish sentiment, climaxed in 1854, less than a month after the dedication ceremony of the new St. Patrick's church, when the Know-Nothing party swept into elected office in Lowell and throughout the state on an explicitly anti-Irish campaign platform.[11] Lowell's local Know-Nothing party was founded in 1851 with a call to action against "the swarms of Irish poor who wreaked such havoc upon the moral, economic, and social character of Lowell."[12]

The city's Yankee base then turned to Lowell's educational institutions to resolve some of the growing social conflicts. Like the evolution of common schooling throughout New England, Lowell's grade schools embodied deeply felt goals of assimilating and Americanizing immigrants. Lowell's attention to public schooling reflected strong desires for social order and stability amidst the growing crime, poverty, and health problems that had allegedly accompanied the famine Irish to the city. Long-time Lowell residents saw schooling as the vehicle to preserve and promote their Yankee standards and power. Schooling through the 1840s and 1850s became the process through which Lowell's Irish became employable. Public school certificates of school attendance became standard letters of introduction for Irish children seeking work in the mills.[13]

Of any city institution, the public schools dealt most directly, and perhaps most equitably, with the Irish community. Interestingly, as Mitchell notes, "Of all Irish political activity, participation on the school committee was most significant."[14] A compromise agreement over schooling between the city and the Irish community in 1835 exemplified this relationship. Unlike New York and other cities where the issue of public schooling for Irish Catholic children fueled bitter debate and hostility between school officials and the church, a compromise negotiated between local priests, Boston's Bishop Fenwick, and Lowell city officials allocated public education funds to support parish schools attended by Irish Catholic school children.

The compromise, hailed by all parties, maintained nominal school committee authority, while providing for significant Irish community control. School committee decisions on hiring, curriculum, and textbook selection, for example, were to be based on choices acceptable to the church and its Catholic instructors. The agreement recognized the significance of the Irish Catholic community as a constituent group in the city,[15] and resulted in the incorporation of the majority of Lowell's Irish Catholic school children into the public school system.[16]

The 1835 compromise remained in effect until 1851 when anti-Irish sentiment, harnessed by the Know-Nothing party, removed these public funds for parish schools, forcing them to close.[17] By then, the Irish constituted a majority of the labor force working in the mills. As anti-Irish sentiment grew through the 1840s with the coming of the famine Irish, a new generation of Irish community leadership emerged to respond to the worsening social climate by calling for unity under the banner of the church. Central to their strategy was establishing new Catholic parish schools with their own funding and facilities.

Unlike their predecessors who tried to accommodate community needs with Yankee concerns for order and stability, the emerging generation of Irish leadership in the 1850s advocated fulfilling the community's needs by strengthening the roles of the family and the church. Over time, this approach succeeded in forging a new, working-class, Irish Catholic identity that evolved into a cohesive voting bloc and significant political force in the city—eventually producing Lowell's first Irish mayor in 1882 and dominating city politics from that time to the present.[18]

Demographic Change and Community Development: The Recent Case

More than a century after the Irish had settled the Acre, a small number of Puerto Ricans arrived in Lowell in the late 1950s as part of large-scale Puerto Rican migrations throughout the Northeast industrial states. In the late 1960s, a large group of Puerto Rican workers based at garment factories in New Jersey were transferred to Lowell. Through the 1970s, Puerto Ricans and growing numbers of Dominicans established a more permanent Latino community. By 1987, the Latino community had grown to than 10 percent of the city.[19] In neighboring Lawrence, Massachusetts, the Latino community swelled to 30 percent of the city's population—reflecting significant demographic changes throughout the Merrimack Valley area.

The most dramatic growth in Lowell during the 1980s, however, resulted from Southeast Asian refugee resettlement and secondary migration. The U.S. Census counted 11,493 Asians in Lowell in 1990, compared to only 604 in 1980. Highly critical of undercounting by the U.S. Census, Lowell city and community estimates show a profile of less than 100 Cambodians in 1980 compared to between 15,000 and 20,000 Cambodians in 1990. In addition, city and community leaders estimate an additional 1,000 Lao and 1,000 Vietnamese. During the 1980s, Lowell became home to the largest Cambodian community on the East Coast and the second largest concentration of Cambodians in the United States after Long Beach, California.

The majority of Cambodians in Lowell are secondary migrants—having moved there from other states rather than arriving directly from refugee camps in Southeast Asia. Many settled in Lowell because of the city's well-publicized economic health and availability of jobs. The establishment of one of the few Cambodian Buddhist temples in the country in the mid-1980s drew many, while others came because family members or friends had already established themselves there. Still others came simply because they heard that Lowell was a place where Cambodians live.

As the numbers of Latinos and Southeast Asians expanded rapidly during the 1980s, the city found itself unprepared to address the multiple issues of housing, bilingual services, and civil rights that confront new immigrants. Furthermore, Lowell's economic rejuvenation had failed to refurbish the city's nineteenth century housing stock and public school facilities, particularly in neighborhoods such as the Acre where large numbers of Latinos and Southeast Asians had settled. Educational issues and the schools quickly emerged as a primary concern for Lowell's new immigrant communities.

Schools as Sites of Struggle

Lowell has the sixth largest Hispanic student population and second largest number of Asian students in Massachusetts. In 1975, only 4 percent of Lowell's students were children of color. By 1987, however, students of color made up 40 percent of the school-age population. Half of them had limited English proficiency. As Southeast Asians continued to migrate to Lowell throughout 1987, as many as 35 to 50 new Southeast Asian students arrived and enrolled in school each week. Strains on the public school system quickly reached crisis proportions.

In trying to accommodate state bilingual education mandates, the Lowell School Committee responded to the population influx by establishing makeshift bilingual classrooms. Overcrowded classrooms combined students from grades one to six. Partitions in cafeterias separated bilingual classes in Spanish, Lao, and Khmer. Special compensatory education classes were held in the quieter hallways. Administrators converted the basement boiler room and an auditorium storage area of one school into classrooms. One teacher had to conduct a Lao bilingual class in a converted bathroom that still had a toilet stall in it. School administrators placed other students in non-school facilities, such as the Lowell Boys Club and Lowell YMCA. This process segregated 170 Latino and Southeast Asian elementary-age school children in buildings that lacked libraries and cafeterias as well as on-site principals or supervisory staff.

At a school committee meeting to discuss the crisis on May 6, 1987, 100 Latino and Southeast Asian parents came to voice their concerns about their children's education. After requesting to speak with the assistance of interpreters who accompanied them, the parents were quickly rebuffed by George Kouloheras, senior member of the School Committee, who declared that they were in an English-Only meeting in an English-Only town in an English-Only United States. Kouloheras then walked out—undermining the quorum needed for the meeting to continue. He later castigated the Latino parents as "those bastards who speak Spanish."[20]

During the months from May 1987 through November 1988, Latino and Southeast Asian parents responded by developing a 33-point program of demands for educational reform and by filing a Title VI lawsuit in federal court against the city for unconstitutional segregation and denial of equal educational opportunities to students of limited English proficiency.[21] In the process, they confronted disenfranchisement within the city's political institutions as well as anti-immigrant resentment and racial intolerance.

In June 1987, under pressure from parents and the state board of education, the Lowell School Committee adopted a desegregation plan that Kouloheras and many white residents vehemently opposed because it required mandatory busing to integrate several predominantly white schools. The desegregation plan became the focal point for candidates' campaigns during the fall 1987 School Committee and City Council elections.

Fueled by English-Only rhetoric, anti-immigrant sentiment escalated throughout the summer and climaxed in September with the drowning of Vandy Phorng, a 13-year-old Cambodian boy who was thrown into one of the canals by an 11-year-old white boy who called him racist names. The white child's father was an outspoken advocate for English-Only in Lowell.

In the 1987 School Committee election, Kouloheras and his ally, Kathryn Stoklosa, received the highest tallies of votes. Voters also elected Sean Sullivan, a first-time candidate whose campaign focused exclusively on opposing "forced busing," while defeating George O'Hare, a longtime incumbent who supported the desegregation plan.

For the Southeast Asian and Latino parents, the election reinforced what they had begun to recognize—in spite of their significant and growing numbers, they had no political representation or even influence within the city's institutions. The only Hispanic in City Hall, for example, as many community leaders were quick to point out, was a gardener.[22]

In the months following the city elections, the parents continued to press their case forward with assistance from the advocacy organization, Multicultural Education, Training, and Advocacy (META), Inc. and a statewide Latino parents network, Parents United in the Education and Development of Others (PUEDO). In November 1988, the coalition of Latino and Southeast Asian parents, known affectionately as MAMA, or the Minority Association for Mutual Assistance, won an historic victory as the Lowell School Committee accepted most of the parents' demands for reform and settled the lawsuit out of court.

In spite of their gains, however, anti-immigrant sentiment continued, and culminated in November 1989 when Lowell's electorate voted on a non-binding referendum introduced by George Kouloheras to declare English the official language of the city. The English-Only referendum passed by a wide 72 percent to 28 percent margin with 14,575 votes for and 5,679 votes against.[23]

Not unlike the Know-Nothing electoral sweep of 1854, the three-to-one English-Only referendum vote galvanized nativist opposition to the rapid demographic changes taking place in Lowell. Yet, as Camilo Perez-Bustillo notes, it was ironic that so many European Americans, whose families were themselves victims of exclusion and harassment as immigrants in Lowell, felt so threatened by the population growth of Latinos and Southeast Asians.[24]

Strategies for Cambodian community development and empowerment in Lowell, particularly in relation to schooling and educational issues, are far from clear. However, themes from the historic example of Lowell's Irish community suggest some ways to analyze and participate in the process of contemporary Cambodian community development in Lowell, and perhaps in other cities as well.

The Role of Religious Institutions

As the most important institution within Lowell's Irish community, the Catholic church provided moral, social, and political guidance for all its members. The construction of St. Patrick's Church, first in 1831 and again in 1854, signified major landmarks in the community's development. Church facilities served a variety of roles, including classroom space when public school facilities were inappropriate or inadequate. Local priests, with the sanction of Boston's bishop, handled not only their religious duties, but also functioned as political leaders with the responsibility of representing their community's interests in negotiations with city officials. Their successful brokering of the education compromise of 1835 highlighted this crucial political role of religious leaders.

In the recent case, a majority of the Latino parents are Catholics with strong ties to their own local churches. Furthermore, most of Lowell's Cambodians are Buddhists. Reminiscent of St. Patrick's Church, when community members established a Buddhist temple in 1984 it became the first significant symbol and landmark of the Cambodian community's place in Lowell. Many of the Cambodian secondary migrants who settled in Lowell after 1984 specifically came because of the presence of Cambodian monks and the temple.

Unlike the Irish priests, however, the Cambodian monks have neither sought nor attained recognition by city officials as having a role to play in political affairs, despite the fact that they are the single most important influence on the direction of Cambodian parents. Community advocates have observed, for example, that only a small number of Cambodian parents will go to City Hall or a public school to meet about educational issues, while a large crowd of parents will go to the temple to discuss the same topics.

Examples ranging from Lowell's Irish Catholic church in the mid-nineteenth century to the roles of black churches and Jewish temples in other places at other times suggest that religious institutions are significant in community education and development. The survival and growth of Cambodian Buddhist temples are essential to the maintenance and rebuilding of Cambodian culture and identity in the United States. Can Cambodian monks go beyond that internal community role to participate actively in Lowell city politics and lead the external process of Cambodian community empowerment in ways comparable to Irish Catholic priests? Or, will such a role fundamentally compromise their spiritual and moral legitimacy that rests upon their renunciation of worldly affairs?

In Asia, Buddhist monks have asserted moral leadership within political contexts (including those who self-immolated in Vietnam to protest government policies during the war). The appropriateness of such comparisons to Cambodian monks in the United States, however, is unclear. Nevertheless, a chair of Lowell's Buddhist temple was one of the main community leaders in the 1987 parents' struggle. Though not a monk himself, he has often voiced the need for Cambodians to run for school committee and city council office, and he may do so in the future.

The Influence of Middle-Class Entrepreneurs

During the 1830s, the small number of Irish store-owners and entrepreneurs wielded considerable social, economic, and political influence within the community and played a key role in negotiating the 1835 schools compromise. Mitchell identifies them as a class force because of their relative economic security and their perspective, which he describes as less transient, less clannish, more broad-minded, more independent, and the "most 'American' of the Irish in Lowell."[25]

The strategy for community development articulated by these entrepreneurs, and exemplified in their own lives, was one of accommodating Yankee interests for the sake of peace and stability. In the 1840s, as the numbers of famine Irish multiplied, the middle-class entrepreneurs initially benefitted because of expanded market opportunities. However, their accommodationist strategy proved inadequate or inappropriate for the masses of poor Irish immigrants. By the mid-1840s, a new generation of service-oriented priests who called on community members to unite behind an Irish Catholic working-class identity in order to strengthen the community's own institutions eclipsed their leadership.

Today, a class sector similar to the Irish middle-class entrepreneurs comprises the main public leadership within the Cambodian community. Their approach to city/community relations is also comparable in its accommodationist tendency. While some observers of community dynamics have suggested that the desire for harmony and stability expressed by the Cambodian community leadership is a cultural value, the Irish case suggests that it may also be a class characteristic. An articulated working-class identity or an organization outside the Buddhist temple that can reach the masses of Cambodians in Lowell does not yet exist.[26]

Cambodian experiences, identities, and options for community development in Lowell differ from those of the nineteenth century Irish immigrant community because of racism and other historical as well as structural factors. Nevertheless, class orientation does matter, as the Irish case shows, particularly in framing strategies for community development. Class dynamics and class orientations to leadership[27] within the Cambodian community, then, are important dimensions to examine in the coming years as the Cambodian community matures.[28]

The Economic Context and Role of Industry

While the first two themes from the Irish case refer to internal dimensions in the community, it is also important to locate the processes of demographic change and community development in the context of the local economy. One way of understanding the history of Lowell is to view it through the lens of industry.

The story of Lowell's Irish is simultaneously the story of Lowell's industrialization and urbanization brought about by nineteenth-century capitalist expansion. The need for productive, exploitable labor in the mills propelled Irish settlement, continuing cycles of demographic growth and change, class and ethnic conflict, and expanded public education. The mills dominated Lowell life, providing an external logic for Irish community development within the larger structure and constraints of industrial capitalism.

Similarly, it is impossible to understand why Cambodians came to Lowell in such large numbers in the 1980s without analyzing the city's economic revitalization. Central to the city's rebirth was the decision of An Wang, a Chinese immigrant and chair of Wang Laboratories, Inc., to relocate his company to Lowell in 1976. Wang purchased cheap industrial land, and with the added incentive of $5 million in federal grants, built new electronics assembly plants and corporate office towers. The timing of the move coincided with Wang's take-off as a company. Corporate sales rose from $97 million in 1977 to $2.88 billion in 1986. As the largest employer in Lowell, Wang's payroll in 1986 accounted for $114 million—infusing the city with a significant, new economic base.[29]

Cambodians flocked to Lowell because of the promise of jobs during the early 1980s. Like the Irish and later waves of immigrants who were concentrated in entry-level assembly work, Cambodian immigrant and refugee workers remained vulnerable to shifts in the local and regional economies inherent in the boom and bust cycles of capitalism.

But since 1988, Wang Laboratories has faced steady and severe economic difficulties, leading to lay-offs of thousands of employees, drops in quarterly earnings and stock prices, and resignations of many managers, including An Wang's son, Frederick. Following An Wang's death in April 1990, the company's fortunes continued to deteriorate. Between 1988 and 1992, Wang's work force declined from 31,500 to 8,000. Facing estimated losses of nearly $140 million in fiscal year 1992, Wang Laboratories filed for Chapter 11 bankruptcy in August 1992.[30] In March 1993, the company announced an additional 500 layoffs for Massachusetts-based workers as part of its Chapter 11 plans.[31]

With Wang's decline and the Massachusetts recession in its fifth year, economic scapegoating of Cambodians has continued, reminiscent, to some extent, of the targeting of Irish immigrants during the depression years of the late 1830s. Drastic cuts in school budgets and social services have coincided with increased unemployment, homelessness, small business closings, and youth gang and drug activity among Cambodians in Lowell. Cambodian community leaders have also observed patterns of migration out of Lowell with as much as 15 percent of the population seeking a better living elsewhere.

The Cambodians and Irish each supplied crucial sources of cheap labor for economic growth in Lowell during nineteenth-century industrialization and in the 1980s with the city's high-technology revitalization. Each group faced the consequences of the cycles of capitalism, however, and became targets when social, economic, and political conditions grew more polarized during the periodic and inevitable downturns in the city's business cycle.

While the example of mid-nineteenth century Irish community development highlights the significance of religious institutions and the role of middle-class entrepreneurs in the growth of Lowell's Cambodian community, the case also suggests that such community development efforts—however heroic—are bounded by the logic and larger social context of the economy.

Electing the Know-Nothings Again

Lowell is a city of 100,000 residents, but only 40,000 voters. The overwhelming majority of Southeast Asians and Latinos have not registered to vote, however, and many are not citizens. Yet, they account for roughly 45 percent of the city's population, and are continuing to grow. Successful candidates in Lowell elections typically receive less than 10,000 votes. George Kouloheras, the top vote-getter in the 1987 School Committee race, for example, received only 8,400 votes. Although not a factor in the most recent election, the political potential of both the Latino and Cambodian vote seems exceptional in this context.

It is useful to remember that in 1854, when the city's population was nearly one-third foreign-born, voters elected the mayor based on a "Know-Nothing" anti-Irish, anti-immigrant platform. Later waves of European newcomers continued to face resentment, exclusion, and exploitation characteristic of the immigrant experience in New England.

Eventually, however, each group achieved some measure of representation and political power. As early as 1874, with nearly 40 percent of the population immigrants, Samuel P. Marin became the first French-Canadian to win elected office in Lowell. Under his leadership, the ethnic "Little Canada" community thrived. By the 1950s, most of Lowell's European ethnic groups, including the English, Irish, Greeks, and Polish had succeeded in electing their "favorite sons" mayor and had won basic political representation within the city.

Will the newest immigrant groups of Latinos and Southeast Asians follow this same pattern of European ethnics' structural assimilation into the social, economic, and political mainstream of Lowell? Or alternatively, does the current state of disenfranchisement confronting Latinos and Asians reflect their non-white status in the tradition of the African American experience as much as it does their being new immigrants?

When They Say 'American,' They Don't Mean Us

Prior to the dramatic influx of Latinos and Southeast Asians to Lowell, the city was ethnically diverse but racially homogeneous. Lowell's African American population, according to the 1990 United States Census, comprises less than 3 percent of the city's population.

Noting the implications of this reality during the 1987 parents' struggle with the school committee, a Latina member of the city's Human Rights Commission Planning Committee observed: "People in Lowell talk about it being an ethnic city, but they only embrace that and endorse that as long as they [the various ethnic groups] are white."[32] A Lao community leader involved with the parents' struggle echoed: "When they say 'Americans,' they don't mean us. Look at our eyes and our skin. We are minorities, but we have rights, too. We need to support each other."[33] A Puerto Rican parent leader added:

> They don't want our minority children mixing with their white children ... they are not thinking of the education of all kids, only of their kids. We want to make sure our kids get equal opportunity.[34]

The Southeast Asian and Latino communities must recognize their own minority group membership if they are to strengthen their organizations, develop leadership, promote consciousness, and build coalitions within and between that can lead toward empowerment.

Although we can draw significant and useful comparisons between the Irish and Cambodian community development, particularly in their struggles over schooling, race and racism have also shaped Cambodian experiences and status within the city's social, economic, and political institutions. These have no clear parallels with the Irish case.

For example, at the height of the influx of Southeast Asians to the Lowell schools during 1986-1987, many Cambodians and half of the entire Lao high-school student population dropped out. During the next two years, local media reports, school officials, and police authorities expressed increasing alarm at the growth of Southeast Asian youth gangs in Lowell. While some accounts pandered to stereotypic images of Asians as devious criminals who do not value life, more reasoned explanations for the proliferation of Southeast Asian gangs pointed to the recession and limited job opportunities, lack of family support systems, and academic or social problems, including linguistic and cultural differences experienced by Southeast Asian youth in school.

Some gangs formed specifically and explicitly to defend themselves against racial harassment in school or the neighborhood. A 21-year-old former Cambodian gang member states unambiguously: "Racism has shaped my life, my experience ever since the first day I set foot in this country ... In the gang, I watch your back, you watch my back. We look out for each other."[35] For many youth, the religious institutions and middle-class entrepreneurs have little relevance because they fail to respond meaningfully to the realities of racism that the young people experience in school and on the streets.

In addition to race, the social and political realities of Cambodians as refugees with unresolved relationships to their homeland represent a second important distinction from the Irish case that also confounds predictions about Cambodian community development and the future of Lowell. Many of Lowell's Cambodians have returned as visitors to Cambodia (Kampuchea) since 1992 to see family, to participate in reconstruction, and to develop business enterprises. If peace eventually comes to the country, many more Cambodians are likely to move back permanently. At the same time, future normalization of diplomatic relations between Cambodia and the United States will create new mechanisms for Cambodian immigration to the United States, especially through the family reunification preferences of U.S. immigration policy. The international situation and Cambodia-United States relations will have significant impact on the future of Cambodian community development in Lowell and throughout the country.

Schools have historically served as sites of struggle by immigrants and communities of color for access, equity, and democratic reforms. Schooling and school committee policy represented critical issues for Lowell's Irish throughout the 1800s. Similarly, for contemporary generations of immigrant and refugee parents who have sacrificed their own lives and dreams in order to give their children opportunities for security and social mobility, the schools typically represent their single most important investment in this country.

Historically and currently, as cities have undergone dramatic shifts in their demographic make-up, the schools have quickly emerged as one major arena, and often as the initial battleground, where contradictory agendas unfold based on conflicting relations and responses to population changes. Anti-immigrant sentiment, racial harassment, and English-Only advocacy characterize one set of responses to the challenge of changing demographics currently facing Lowell as well as many other U.S. cities. These reactions, framed by struggles over turf and the interests of a shifting electorate, often lead to divisiveness and segregation as in the case of the Lowell Public Schools, and even violence and tragedy as in the killing of 13-year-old Vandy Phorng.

Like the rise and fall of the Know-Nothing party as the Irish presence grew in Lowell during the 1850s, efforts by the city's Latino and Southeast Asian communities to gain access and equity for their children in the schools have met with resistance, if not overt hostility, and have led directly to their demands for political representation and political power.

For the future, Cambodian strategies for community development and educational equity in Lowell, framed by their experiences as immigrants and workers as well as by their realities as refugees and racial minorities, will link them to historic legacies shared by earlier generations, but will also require that they reshape the city and make history for themselves.

Notes

1. Puerto Ricans comprise the majority of the Latino population along with some Dominicans; Cambodians comprise the majority of the Southeast Asian population, although there are some Lao and Vietnamese.
2. Major portions of this chapter are adapted from: Peter Nien-chu Kiang, "Southeast Asian Parent Empowerment: The Challenge of Changing Demographics in Lowell, Massachusetts," Monograph No. 1, Massachusetts Association for Bilingual Education, 1990; and from: Peter N. Kiang, "Education and Community Development Among Nineteenth Century Irish and Contemporary Cambodians in Lowell, Massachusetts," *New England Journal of Public Policy*, Fall 1993.
3. Thanks to Joel Perlmann for his comment on an earlier draft of this paper.
4. Marc Scott Miller, *The Irony of Victory: World War II and Lowell, Massachusetts*, Urbana: University of Illinois Press, 1988, viii.
5. Kevin Cullen, "Lowell: The Dark Side of the Boom," *Boston Globe*, October 25, 1987. For autobiographical recollections of life among the early mill girls, including a section on education, see Harriet H. Robinson, *Loom and Spindle*, Kailua, HI: Press Pacifica, 1976. Also see Thomas Dublin, *Women at Work: The Transformation of Work and*

Community in Lowell, Massachusetts, 1826-1860, New York: Columbia University Press, 1979.

6. Cullen.

7. Thomas Bender, *Toward an Urban Vision: Ideas and Institutions in Nineteenth Century America*, Lexington, KY: University of Kentucky Press, 1975, 42.

8. For further descriptions, see Bender, 1975; or Brian C. Mitchell, *The Paddy Camps: The Irish of Lowell, 1821-1861,* Urbana University of Illinois Press, 1988.

9. Mitchell, 56.

10. Quoted in Bender, 107.

11. The Know-Nothing Party, a nativist political party initially established as a secret society in New York, dominated Massachusetts politics and controlled the state legislature during the mid-1850s. Millard Fillmore ran for the United States presidency as a Know-Nothing candidate in 1856.

12. Mitchell, 134-135.

13. Mitchell, 114-116.

14. Mitchell, 49.

15. Mitchell, 49-55.

16. The agreement never enabled large numbers of Irish to attend Lowell High School, however. See Bender, 123-126, for more discussion of Irish enrollments and high school attendance.

17. Bender, 123.

18. Mitchell, 142.

19. The 1990 U.S. Census, criticized for undercounting immigrants and people of color in urban areas, counted 10,499 Hispanics in Lowell out of a total population of 103,438.

20. Diego Ribadeneira, "School Panelist in Lowell Accused of Racism," *Boston Globe,* May 8, 1987 and Nancy Costello, "Kouloheras Sparks Racial Clash at Meeting, *Lowell Sun*, May 7, 1987.

21. The legal precedents for this comes from the 1964 Civil Rights Act and the 1974 Equal Educational Opportunities Act.

22. Doris Sue Wong, "Lowell Is Seen Not Fulfilling Its Promise for Many Asians, Hispanics," *Boston Globe*, November 3, 1987.

23. Jules Crittendon, "English Referendum Passes Nearly 3 to 1," *Lowell Sun*, November 8, 1989.

24. Camilo Perez-Bustillo, "What Happens When English-Only Comes to Town? A Case Study of Lowell, Massachusetts," in James Crawford, ed., *Language Loyalties: A Sourcebook on the Official English Controversy*, Chicago: University of Chicago Press, 1992, 194-201.

25. Mitchell, 40-41.

26. Interestingly, the Latino community leadership in Lowell has been more effective in reaching and mobilizing the masses behind a clear agenda. This may reflect their longer residence in Lowell relative to the

Cambodian community and, for Puerto Ricans, the advantage of already having U.S. citizenship status and some voting rights.

27. For a provocative discussion of immigrant leadership, see Victor R. Greene, *American Immigrant Leaders, 1800-1910*, Baltimore: Johns Hopkins University Press, 1987.

28. For discussion of an integrated, multidimensional theoretical framework that analyzes the backgrounds and identities of Southeast Asian refugees in the United States based on culture and ethnicity, refugee status, immigrant status, and race, see: Peter Nien-chu Kiang, *New Roots and Voices: The Education of Southeast Asian Students at an Urban Public University*, Ed.D. dissertation, Harvard University, 1991.

29. John Wilke, "Wang Had Key Role in Lowell's Economic Revival," *Boston Globe*, November 9, 1987.

30. Jonathan Yenkin, "Wang Says '92 Loss May Get Worse," *Boston Globe*, September 25, 1992.

31. Josh Hyatt, "Wang Set to Unveil Ch. 11 Plan Today," *Boston Globe*, March 16, 1993, 1, 42.

32. Quoted in Wong.

33. Sommanee Bounphasaysonh, personal interview, June 11, 1987.

34. Alex Huertas, personal interview, June 11, 1987.

35. Sarovem Phoung, panel presentation, "Facing Asian American Civil Rights Issues in the 1990s," University of Massachusetts, Boston, 1993.

6

PRESENTING THE BLUE GODDESS

Toward a National Pan-Asian Feminist Agenda

SONIA SHAH

We all laughed sheepishly about how we used to dismiss the South Asian women in our lives as doormats irrelevant to our feminist lives. For most of us in that fledgling South Asian American women's group in Boston, either white feminists or black feminists had inspired us to find our Asian feminist heritage. Yet neither movement had really prepared us for actually finding any. The way either group defined feminism did not, could not, define our South Asian feminist heritages. That, for most of us, consisted of feisty immigrant mothers, ball-breaking grandmothers, Kali-worship (Kali is the blue goddess who sprung whole from another woman and who symbolizes "shakti"—Hindi for womanpower), social activist aunts, freedom-fighting/Gandhian great-aunts. In many ways, white feminism, with its "personal is political" maxim and its emphasis on building sisterhood and consciousness raising, had brought us together. Black feminism, on the other hand, had taught us that we could expect more—that feminism can incorporate a race analysis. Yet, while both movements spurred us to organize, neither included our South Asian American agendas—toward battery of immigrant women, the ghettoization of the Indian community, cultural discrimination, bicultural history and identity.

I felt we were starting anew, starting to define a South Asian American feminism that no one had articulated yet. As I began to reach out to other Asian American women's groups over the years and for this chapter, however, that sense faded a bit. Asian American women have been organizing themselves for decades, with much to show for it.

Our shakti hasn't yet expressed itself on a national stage accessible to all of our sisters. But we are entering a moment in our organizing when we will soon be able to create a distinctly Asian American feminism—one that will be able to cross the class and culture lines that currently divide us.

The first wave of Asian women's organizing, born of the women's liberation and civil rights movements of the 1960s, created established groups like Asian Women United in San Francisco, Asian Sisters in Action in Boston, and other more informal networks of primarily professional, East Asian American women. They focused on empowering Asian women economically and socially and accessing political power. Asian Women United, for example, has produced videos, like "Silk Wings," which describes Asian women in non-traditional jobs, and books like *Making Waves,* an anthology of Asian American women's writing.

In contrast, the second wave of organizing, politicized by the 1980s multicultural movements, includes the many ethnically specific women's groups that tend to start out as support networks, some later becoming active in the battered women's movement (like Manavi in New Jersey, Sneha in Hartford, and the New York Asian Women's Center, which offer battery hotlines and shelter for Asian women) and others working in the women-of-color and lesbian/gay liberation movements. Culturally, these groups are Korean, Indian, Cambodian, Filipina, and from other more recently arrived immigrant groups who may not have felt part of the more established, primarily East Asian women's networks. These different groups are divided by generation, by culture, and by geographic location. Anna Rhee, a cofounder of the Washington Alliance of Korean American Women (WAKAW), a group of mostly 1.5 generation (those who emigrated to the United States in early adulthood) and second generation Korean American women, with an average age of 27 to 28, says she felt "we were starting anew, because of the focus on English speaking Korean women, which was different from any other group we had seen." WAKAW, like many similar groups, started as a support group, but has since evolved into activism, with voter registration and other projects.

Talking to different Asian American woman activists, I was inspired by the many projects these activists have undertaken, and impressed with the overwhelming sense women had that the Asian American women's community today stands at a crossroads ripe with possibility. The New York Asian Women's Center, which runs several programs fighting violence against Asian women, just celebrated its 10th birthday. The Pacific Asian American Women's Bay Area Coalition honors Asian American women with Woman Warrior (á là Maxine Hong Kingston's novel) leadership awards, catapulting their honorees on to other accolades. Indian Subcontinent Women's Alliance for Action (ISWAA) in Boston just assembled a grassroots arts exhibit of works by and for South Asian women. Asian Women United, in addition to several other videos, is working on a video of Asian American visual artists. The Washington Alliance for Korean American Women is taking oral histories of Korean mothers and daughters. Everyone has a story of another group starting up, another exciting Asian American woman activist.

So far, Asian American women activists have used two general organizing models. The first is based on the fact that Asian women need each other to overcome the violence, isolation, and powerlessness of their lives; no one else can or will be able to help us but each other. The groups that come together on this basis focus on the immediate needs of the community: housing battered women, finding homes for abandoned women and children, legal advocacy for refugee women, etc.

The second model uses the basis of shared identity and the realization that both Asian and U.S. mainstream cultures make Asian American women invisible as organizing principles. The groups that come together on this basis work on articulating anger about racism and sexism, like other women of color groups, but also on fighting the omniscient and seductive pressure to assimilate, within ourselves and for our sisters.

Today, our numbers are exploding, in our immigrant communities and their children, and subsequently, in our activist communities. Our writers, poets, artists, and filmmakers are coming of age. Our activist voices, against anti-Asian violence, battery, and racism, are gaining legal, political, and social notice. We still have much ground to cover in influencing mainstream culture: we must throw those exoticizing books about Asian women off the shelf and replace them with a slew of works on pan-Asian feminism; women of color putting together collections of radical essays must be able to "find" Asian American feminists; *Ms.* magazine must offer more than a colorful photo of an Indian mother and daughter with less than three lines about them in a related cover article; critics must stop touting Asian American women's fiction as "exotic treasures"; Fifth Avenue advertising executives must stop producing ads that exploit tired stereotypes of Asian female "exotic beauty" and "humble modesty" with images of silky black hair and Asian women demurely tucking tampons into their pockets.

Our movement faces crucial internal challenges as well. Longtime Asian American feminists activists, such as Helen Zia, a contributing editor to *Ms.*, wonder, "What makes us different from white feminists or black feminists? What can we bring to the table?" and complain that "these questions haven't really been developed yet." Others, such as Jackie Church, a Japanese American activist, state that "there just aren't enough Asian American feminists who aren't doing five different things at once."

On the one hand, our national Asian women's groups, while inclusive across Asian ethnicities, haven't yet developed an Asian feminism *different* from black or white feminism. On the other, our ethnically specific groups, while emotionally resonant and culturally specific, are still remote and inaccessible to many of our sisters.

The movements of the 1960s colluded with the mainstream in defining racism in black and white terms; racism is still defined as discrimination based on skin color, i.e. race. They also, to some extent, elevated racism, defined in this way, to the top of layers of oppression. This narrow definition has distorted mainstream perception of anti-Asian racism and even our perception of ourselves—as either non-victims of racism or victims of racism based on skin color. By these assumptions, an Indian assaulted because she "dresses weird" is not a victim of racism; a Chinese shopkeeper harassed because she has a "funny accent" is not a victim of racism. Mainstream culture finds neither of these incidents as disturbing, unacceptable, or even downright "evil" as racism. By this definition, one must either be in the black or white camp to even speak about racism, and we are expected to forget ourselves. Whites try to convince us we are really *more like them;* depending upon our degree of sensitivity toward racist injustice, we try to persuade blacks that we are more like them.

For example, many Asian American women have described Asian women's experience of racism as a result of stereotypes about "exotica" and "china dolls," two stereotypes based on our looking different from white people. But our experiences of racism go far beyond that. Rather than subvert the definition of racism itself, or uncover new layers of oppression just as unacceptable and pernicious as racism but based on what I call cultural discrimination, we have attempted to fit our experience of discrimination into the given definition. We too assume that racism is the worst kind of oppression, by emphasizing that racism against us is based on skin color and racial differences. Indeed, when we forged our first wave of women's movement, solidarity with other people of color whose activism revolved around black/white paradigms of oppression was a matter of survival. And organizing around racially based oppressions served as common ground for all ethnic Asians.

Yet our experiences of oppression are, in many qualitative ways, different from black and white people. For me, the experience of "otherness," the formative discrimination in my life, has resulted from culturally different (not necessarily racially different) people thinking they were culturally central: thinking that *my* house smelled funny, that *my* mother talked weird, that *my* habits were strange. They were normal; I wasn't.

Today, a more sophisticated understanding of oppression is emanating from all people of color groups. The L.A. riots, among other ethnic conflicts, unmasked to belated national attention the reality of an ethnic conflict (between blacks and browns, as well as between the white power structure and oppressed people of color) impossible to explain away simply as white-against-black racism. Multicultural movements and growing internationalism have raised questions about our hierarchy of oppressions. Asian American men and women activists are beginning to create legal and social definitions of cultural discrimination. Our movement can march beyond black/white paradigms that were once useful, and start to highlight cultural discrimination—our peculiar blend of cultural and sexist oppression based on our accents, our clothes, our foods, our values, and our commitments. When we do this successfully, we will have not just laid a common ground for all ethnic Asian women for the practical goal of gaining power, we will have taken an important political step toward understanding and, from there, struggling against the many layers of oppression.

The search for identity that has compelled Asian American women to separate into cultural-, age-, generation-, class-, and geographic-specific groups will ensure that the emerging pan-Asian American feminism retains emotional resonance. Although the very specificity that makes them so useful limits these groups, as their numbers grow, coalition building and networking become not only viable options, but necessary for advancing difficult agendas requiring extensive resources and support. These coalitions and networks must struggle to find common ground that retains emotional resonance while being inclusive.

Our common ground must be more than our simply being "Asian," which encompasses so much diversity as to be practically useless as an ethnic category, particularly since our specific cultural heritages are so much more meaningful. The general "feminist" agenda, commonly understood as that of the mainstream white middle-class women's movement, is also problematic. The racism and classism of the traditional white women's movement, as well as the threat of violence from our community's patriarchy, has sometimes held us back from calling ourselves "feminists." "The whole attitude" of white feminism, says Sunita Mani of Indian Subcontinent Women's Alliance for Action, "is that my strong-mindedness is my American-ness, not my Asian-ness." The heightened demand for specificity that grows out of groups like ISWAA makes the simple grafting of the feminist label onto our organizing untenable: We need something that recognizes our Asian activist heritage and our cultural specificity. As Carol Ito, a board member of the Pacific Asian American Women's Bay Area Coalition in San Francisco says, "We didn't want to be called feminist." "Feminism was seen as a white, middle-class concern," says Korean American Elaine Kim, literary critic and a member of Asian Women United. "Race discrimination was much more vivid than sexism."

Our movement owes much to black feminism. But, while white feminism seemed to ignore race and culture analyses, black feminism, on the other hand, worked under the black/white paradigms and according to a hierarchy of oppressions, which Asian American women can neither accurately nor powerfully organize under. The black/white paradigms of both feminist and civil rights struggles create false divisions and false choices for Asian American women. Recently, a group of 1.5 generation South Asian women who organize against battery held a conference on South Asian women. This group, demographically, having emigrated later than the parents of second-generation South Asian Americans, tends to hail from greater class privilege. Second-generation South Asian American activists boycotted the conference, charging that the organizers, because of their class privilege and their relative newness to the Asian American community, sidelined issues of U.S.-based racism and discrimination.

This is a false division, especially dangerous in such a relatively small activist community. When first faced with American racism and its black/white constructs, immigrants with class privilege, even activist ones, are apt to dismiss racism as "not their problem." (As the mainstream defines it, strictly speaking, it isn't.) Efforts by second-generation activists and beyond, confined as we have been to black/white paradigms, to convince our sisters at other locations on the culture/class continuum that what we suffer is similar to what the black community suffers will necessarily be difficult if not impossible. Yet we are natural allies, given a broader critique of oppression that includes cultural discrimination and an accurate portrayal of our own experiences of racism on a continuum of oppressions linked to imperialism, immigration policy, and sexism: across real divisions of immigration status and class and certainly across the false divisions of black/white race analysis and black/white feminism.

As Asian Americans, Asians in America, Americans of Asian descent, or however we choose to think of ourselves, we all grapple with conflicting signals and oppressions in our lives because we are all situated, to differing degrees, in both Asian and American cultural milieus. As any of these, we not only suffer cultural discrimination as men also do, but our own form of cultural schizophrenia, from the mixed and often contradictory signals about priorities, values, duty, and meaning our families and greater communities convey. We encounter sexist Asian tradition, racist and sexist white culture, anti-racist non-feminist women heroes, racist feminist heroes, strong proud Asian women who told us not to make waves, strong proud non-Asian women who told us *to* make waves, and on and on.

Black/white paradigms have informed the conception of cultural or racial difference as well: White people are all white, black people are all black. No room exists for cultural duality in a world where one is automatically relegated to one camp or another based on biology. Yet the problems of cultural duality as well as the concomitant experience of cultural discrimination are exactly what unite the Asian American women's community across our differences. We all reconcile these tensions and oppressions in different ways, by acting out a model minority myth, for some; by suffering silently, for others; by being activist, for still others. As we grapple with conflicting signals and oppressions in our lives with the support of our sisters, as well as struggle against cultural discrimination, we can reimagine and reinvent ourselves and our priorities. We can politicize the process of cultural reconciliation, and tag it for feminism and liberation.

This broader critique that the Asian American women's community is groping towards does and must continue to include this empowering and activist commonality among Asian American women: Not just the fact and nature of our oppressions, but the nature of our responses to oppression, what I call bicultural feminism.

The plea for bicultural feminism is not simply that Asian American women activists call themselves bicultural feminists. It is a call for an agenda that subverts the black/white paradigms, articulates cultural discrimination and how it illuminates and connects to other processes of oppression, and politicizes the process of cultural reconciliation for feminism and liberation.

A poor immigrant Asian woman follows an abusive husband to the United States; she doesn't speak English and is cut off from the women who supported her in her home country; she is beaten nearly to death by her one contact to the outside world. This woman needs a bicultural feminism. Within black/white constructs of racism, she cannot name the threats to her with the authority that racism carries. Within narrow white feminist paradigms and essentialist notions of cultural difference, she is presented with false choices for liberation: Either become a prototypical "American" woman, with all the alien cultural cues that implies, or go back to Asia. She needs an activism that struggles against the danger she encounters as a non-English speaking Asian woman in America; she needs an activism that empowers her to liberate herself in this country (with money, legal services, shelter, and support) while recognizing and politicizing the cultural reconciliation she must undergo to liberate herself (by reimagining her duty as an Asian wife as a duty to herself, for example).

When my little sister, who is just beginning to see herself as a sexual person, thinks she is a "slut" for wearing tight jeans, she needs this bicultural feminism. Not a mainstream white feminism, which might suggest she throw away her tight jeans because she is objectifying herself, nor one that simply suggests she revert to the dress of her "homeland" and wear a revealing sari—but one that would affirm that she doesn't have to abandon Indian values or filial respect of whatever it is that makes her fear appearing "slutty."

It is possible that first-generation Indians reject the trappings of American sexuality, such as tight jeans, as culturally alien. The subsequent interpretation by their children and their greater American communities, however, that they are anti-sexuality stems from the dominant paradigm of a monoculture: white culture and black culture, which is simply the poor, darker version of the white culture. An Asian American feminism that emphasized cultural duality and reconciliation would subvert this notion. There are many cultures, many sexualities, and many trappings of such. My sister needs to name the cultural conflicts she is involved in for what they are, and reconcile her visions of sexuality and empowerment within the cultural confines of white patriarchy and Indian patriarchy. A bicultural feminism would ensure that she does this in a feminist, liberated way.

As bicultural feminists, we are empowered to enter the broader discussion and struggles around us with something more substantial than identity politics and our slightly different take on racism within the black/white dichotomy. As we approach the concept and practice of the extended family, for example, we can apply our critical reinventions to the struggle for accessible child care, by shifting the turgid debate away from paid care and toward building cooperative care centers and work-sharing. As we approach social and linguistic difference within Asian American families, we can apply our insights to the current debates about gay parents raising potentially straight chilren, or to white families raising children of color, for example, by advocating for the fitness of the child's cultural community rather than for the "fitness" of the parent. As we remember our histories as Asian women, we can apply our sense of outrage, over the internment, the brain drain, and the treatment of refugees, to the struggle for just immigration policy. We can reinterpret Asian paradigms of filial and familial duty as social responsibility. We can use anti-materialism as a basis for building an ecological society.

I remember, in that South Asian American women's group, we were all looking forward to Mira Nair's film, "Mississippi

Masala." We took Nair as a kind of model—a seemingly progressive Indian woman filmmaker who had gained the kind of financial backing necessary for reaching wide sectors of the South Asian community. "Masala" was the first film we knew of that would portray an Indian American woman in her cultural milieau as the protagonist.

I don't know what Nair's intentions were, but her Indian American protagonist was little more than a standard Western-defined beauty, her biculturalism little more than occasional bare feet and a chureedar thrown over her shoulder. Although a refugee from Uganda living in Mississippi with Indian parents, she was phenomenally unconcerned with issues of race, history, culture, and gender. Given the dearth of accessible activist commentary on biculturalism and feminism beyond the black/white divide, even a sympathetic "opinion-maker" like Nair can hurt our movement by portraying us as little more than exotic, browner versions of white women, who by virtue of a little color can bridge the gap between black and white (not through activism, of course, just romantic love). If Asian American women's movements can effectively unite within bicultural feminist agendas, we can snatch that power away from those willing to trivialize us, and "Masala" and our less sympathetic foes beware.

Resources

- Washington Alliance of Korean American Women, 1623-J Carriage House Terrace, Silver Spring, MD 20904-5681.

- Pacific Asian American Women's Bay Area Coalition, 450 Taraval, Suite 283, San Francisco, CA 94116.

- Indian Subcontinent Women's Alliance for Action, call Riti Sachdeva in Boston, MA, (617) 232-5165.

- Asian Women United, c/o Lilia Villanueva, 1218 Spruce Street, Berkeley, CA 94704.

- Asian Sisters in Action. PO Box 38-0331, Cambridge, MA 02238

- New York Asian Women's Center, 39 Bowery, Box 375, New York, NY 10002.

- Manavi, PO Box 614, Bloomfield, NJ 07003.

- Sneha, c/o Hansa Shah, 100 Woodpond Rd., Glastonbury, CT 06033.

II

Where Are You From?
When Are You Going Back?

Exploring Race and Identity

7

SEEING YELLOW

Asian Identities in Film and Video

RICHARD FUNG

Up until the nineteenth century, Chinese people imagined themselves at the center of the world. They saw their country occupying the space between heaven and earth: the Middle Kingdom. As an imperialist, colonizing power they developed what is now politely referred to as "Han chauvinism," which categorized all non-Han people—Mongolians, Miao, Tibetans ... and white people—as barbarians. In popular speech Chinese speakers still often refer to non-Chinese as ghosts.

But when the Chinese—most of them peasants—began to immigrate to the Americas in the last century, they came under another form of racism. They lost—to the extent that peasants can possess it—their power to define others, and instead became the defined, the circumscribed. They were told who could come, where they could live and work (for smaller wages) ... and in Canada and the United States they were charged a head tax for all these privileges.

The Japanese, who believed they were descended from the sun goddess, suffered a similar fate. Their ancestors had repelled the Chinese in the twelfth century when the wind of the gods, the *kamikaze*, rose up to destroy the invading ships of Kublai Khan.

They had dominated Korea and received tribute from Okinawa—that is, to the extent that ordinary people receive the benefits of tribute. But when they came here, they too found that they were told where to live and work.

While the Chinese, the Japanese, the Koreans, the Filipinos, and the Vietnamese had fought each other in their old countries, and sometimes continued to do battle in the new, they had one thing in common. Here, they were all branded with the mark "oriental." Before, they had just seen themselves as east or west of a given mountain, a town or an island. In this new land, they were collectively and permanently east of something ... or someone. And while one group was occasionally singled out for praise or hostility—so that was seen as being too rich and buying up all the land, or too poor and working below market value, or owing allegiance to a threatening foreign power, or flooding the land with refugees and street gangs—the makers of laws and decisions really couldn't tell one from the other, and could only see the yellow in their skins. In World War II, the Canadian government issued buttons that marked the wearer as Chinese, to distinguish him or her from the Japanese Canadian "enemy." There are rare stories of buttons being lent to friends so they could pass. To the East and Southeast Asians, their skin had of course just been skin: coarse with work, pale from a life of privilege, hairy or smooth. But then, even some of them began to look at their own hands and see them as yellow. Soon, rather than different shades of human, they began to notice that the hands of others were white, brown, red, and black. It's not that they hadn't noticed differences before, or that they didn't have their own conceptions of beauty or worth, but this particular coding and hierarchy of "races" was new.

"Asian" consciousness only begins to eclipse national consciousness in the context of white racism, and particularly as experienced here in the diaspora. It is premised on a shared sense of visibility, and less on any common cultural, aesthetic, or religious roots: What does Filipino Catholicism have to do with Japanese Buddhism or the Islam of Malaysia? In North America, "Asian" is often used simply as an acceptable replacement for "oriental." Referring to an actual geographical origin, the term

162

seems to carry less colonial baggage. Yet it is worth remembering that Asia is not in fact a natural entity but exists only in relation to notions of Europe and Africa developed in the West. These are political and economic demarcations closely tied to the colonial project. Even today, when we witness the shuffle of states in the former Eastern Bloc, there is anxiety in Western Europe as to where to draw the line for possible inclusion in the European Economic Community. Where does Asia start and Europe leave off, and in whose interests are these borders drawn?

Another problem exists with the term "Asian." Asia, as it has been defined, covers a large portion of the globe: from Turkey to Korea and from Siberia to India. Whereas in North America, East and Southeast Asians have claimed the term, in Britain, "Asian" is commonly taken to refer to people whose ancestry lies in the Indian subcontinent and Sri Lanka. People of Indian, Pakistani, Bangladeshi, and Sri Lankan descent are rooted in a variety of cultural and religious traditions but share a similar history of British colonialism. More importantly, no matter whether they are born in North America, come from the subcontinent or from the Indian diaspora in Africa, Southeast Asia, the Pacific, or the Caribbean, they occupy comparable places within the North American racial configuration: They are seen to look alike.

Both South Asians and East/Southeast Asians are rightly Asian. Yet because we are *seen* to constitute distinct groups, our experiences of racism and our resulting politics of resistance tend to follow different lines. Hence, organizing under the banner "Asian" leads to many logistical problems: Around whose terms are discussions of Asian identity framed? Who gets included and who tokenized? In the United States and particularly in Canada, many have chosen to organize explicitly as "South Asians," while "Asian" groups continue to draw predominantly from East and Southeast Asian communities ... with the occasional South Asian member. Some endeavors have consciously attempted a "pan-Asian" basis of unity, but this works only when organizers take difference and equity into account and plan them right from the start. Resolving this issue, however, is only partly a matter of finding more accurate names, as people will always fall out of attempts to carve up and categorize the continuity and fluidity that actually exists in the world. At the same time, we draw strength from using our socially constructed identities (with all of the problems I've described) as a lever for organizing and challenging racism. In describing and problematizing our own (albeit shifting) locations, we can move out to understand a system from which we share common oppression. It's in this way that I choose to work within a "yellow" experience of race. This I call "Asian," but with the full recognition that Asian is not only this experience.

Given that the form of racism we encounter in North America is that of white superiority, it isn't surprising that the struggle for Asians to reclaim our subjecthood (or to shed our otherness) has been phrased as a tug of war between yellow and white. But something is wrong with this binary opposition of white oppressor and yellow oppressed. Whereas racism privileges whiteness and targets a somewhat shifting body of "others," anyone, no matter their status or color, can engage its discourses. There is a way that power is fluid and shifting *at the same time* that it is concentrated at the top. We tread on dangerous ground if we lose sight of either aspect.

Let me give you three examples. First, when I leave my home and walk to the subway, I pass a man who is young, white, anglophone, "able-bodied," and (I'm presuming) heterosexual. He asks me for money. He lives on the street and is economically poorer than I am. But he's also a skinhead, and if I don't give him money, I am aware he may resort to racist harassment. Second, this summer when I walked over to my corner store, I overheard a black kid and a white kid mimicking aloud the language of the Vietnamese children playing on the street. I revisited all those conflicted emotions of my childhood: anger and embarrassment mixed with an attempt to "contextualize" what I had witnessed. Finally, after returning home from a recent trip to Chinatown, my mother perused her bills because, she says, "You can't trust those Chinese merchants." By citing these three examples I by no means want to suggest that a white street person, a black child, and my mother have the same social powers, or the same exercise of racism as an immigration official, a police officer, a university professor, a government minister or a corporate head. However, to me, the power of racism is generated in an endless multiplicity of sites, including the self. The children and the young man have no power to deny me education or employment, yet these incidents continuously reassert my social place and my sense of my own (limited) possibilities.

Given the historical misrepresentations of mainstream media, I am not surprised that most independent films and videotapes produced by North American men and women of Asian descent seek redress from white supremacy. They perform the important tasks of correcting histories, voicing common but seldom represented experiences, engaging audiences used to being spoken about but never addressed, and actively constructing a politics of resistance to racism. In her comprehensive article, "Moving the Image: Asian American Independent Filmmaking, 1970-1990," filmmaker-critic Renee Tajima chronicles the myriad strategies Asian Americans have employed in identifying and exposing white and Eurocentric assumptions both on the screen and behind the camera. Consider, for example, Valerie Soe's two-minute epigram of a videotape, *All Orientals Look the Same* (1985), in which the title phrase forms a continuous chant beneath a ceaseless procession of different Asian faces; the juxtaposition is all she needs to expose the lie of the stereotype. *Who Killed Vincent Chin?* (1989) by Christine Choy and Renee Tajima, on the other hand, demonstrates the consequence of that stereotype—Vincent Chin was killed in Detroit by white unemployed autoworkers who thought he was Japanese—and thereby articulates a basis of unity for Asians on this continent, if only for self-protection.

But in this chapter I want to turn my attention to a small but important body of work that addresses issues of identity and politics beyond an axis of white and yellow. Here I am not primarily interested in those pieces that place Asians alongside other people of color in positions of solidarity or equivalence, such as Pratibha Parmar's *Emergence* (1986), Shu Lea Cheang's *Color Schemes* (1989), or Michelle Mohabeer's *Exposure* (1990). These are impor-

165

tant works. I want, however, to focus on films and tapes that explore differences *among* Asians, as well as between Asians and other non-white peoples.

North American popular politics has developed the term "people of color." This formulation has the advantage of drawing connections between people and avoiding slippage into a discourse of racial purity. But while it is true that non-white peoples are all casualties of white supremacy, the term "people of color," like "Asian," draws a line that collapses racial difference and assumes unity of purpose. From the early 1990s, a number of incidents began to fracture this illusion. In Los Angeles and New York, we have seen increasing hostility between African and Asian Americans. In Toronto, we have witnessed the scapegoating of Vietnamese youth and recent immigrants from the People's Republic of China for increasing violence in Chinatown. The police and the mainstream media point these fingers for sure, but they do so with the collusion of the Chinatown business class.

Two documentary films—*Bittersweet Survival* (1982) by Christine Choy and Orinne J.T. Takagi and *Mississippi Triangle* (1984) by Christine Choy, Worth Long, and Allan Siegel—uncover the socio-political and economic roots of interracial tension. This is a critical undertaking because it undermines the notion that racism is simply a question of attitude, or worse, of some ingrained, quasi-genetic antipathy ascribed to "human nature." *Mississippi Triangle* examines the interplay of class and race in the American South, focusing on the fabric of interactions between whites, blacks, and Chinese. In this cotton-growing region, categorization according to race is a crucial aspect of social organization. *Bittersweet Survival* looks at more recent immigrants: Southeast Asian refugees. Having escaped the dangers of war in their home countries—war made devastating through American involvement—families arriving in the United States face racist policies and resentment. Often resettled in the poorest of inner-city neighborhoods, they find themselves pitted against existing black communities for limited resources.

Juxta (1989) ponders the fallout from another earlier war. Directed by Hiroko Yamazaki, this short drama follows the relationship between two children, both born of U.S. servicemen in Japan after World War II. The mothers of the children are best friends and Kate and Ted grow up almost as brother and sister. However, this closeness changes radically when the families are reunited with their fathers in the United States. Kate's father is white and Ted's black and the whole social organization of racism—including the prejudices of Kate's white grandmother—pulls the two children and their families apart, leading to pain and tragedy. As adults, Kate and Ted try to rebuild the intimacy they once shared.

Juxta concentrates primarily on white bigotry. But though Asians have often suffered for not being white, their relationship to other groups of people of color has not necessarily been easy. In Spike Lee's *Do the Right Thing* (1989), after the angry crowd has demolished Sal's Pizzeria, they turn to the other symbol of external exploitation, the Korean grocery store. In the heat of confrontation, the owner anxiously defends his business by sputtering "Me no white. Me no white. Me black. Me black. Me black." In a world divided into black and white, the Asian is asked to choose on which side of the fence he sits. In this film, the Korean shop owner's claim to black identity seems fuelled mainly by expediency and immediate self-interest. Yet it (enigmatically) works and the crowd reluctantly moves on ... for the time being. The film suspends judgement. *Do the Right Thing* presents a vivid portrait of racism in action. Yet, unlike *Bittersweet Survival*, its exclusive focus on a single neighborhood means that we see only the effects of power. The political and economic factors and decisions that produce that picture escape analysis.

With the ingenious use of a mole, *Sally's Beauty Spot* (1990) similarly interrogates the place of Asians in a black-white matrix. In Helen Lee's short experimental film, an Asian woman's obsessive attempt to erase a mark from her breast becomes a metaphor for a struggle with identity and racialized notions of beauty. Lee juxtaposes this narrative with a meditation on spectatorship, as the off-screen voices of Asian women (and quotes from theorist Homi K. Bhabha) interrogate the 1960 Hollywood film *The World of Suzy Wong*, unleashing a multiplicity of readings and positions in relation to the film. As Sally rethinks her mole from blemish to beauty mark, the metaphor is literalized on-screen as a kiss with a black man. Her cover-all make-up spills onto the floor as the words "black is" are typed onto a sheet of paper.

From the 1960s we know that the missing word is "beautiful." But what about yellow? *Sally's Beauty Spot* is densely packed with metaphor and does not lend itself to a literal reading. Yet it leaves itself open to an interpretation that suggests our struggle as Asians involves locating ourselves within black politics. The use of the same framing for Sally's kiss with the black man at the end of the film and a white man earlier underlines the white-black binarism.

For Asians to show solidarity with people of African descent, we should not have to claim blackness. Indeed, I would argue that we can only work toward unity by speaking from where we actually are. Obviously, all Asians are not the same, and our various locations will always shift. In any case, this location is not black or white or some position "in between." The struggle against racism is not one of finding a convenient or seemingly correct drawer to fit in. It first involves the traumatic but ultimately liberating task of seeing that the boundaries, and indeed the contemporary conception, of race are not natural, but socially constructed and specific to the times in which we live. For while the early use of "race" in English referred to the French race, the British race and so on, the division of humanity into white, black, red and yellow was only codified and popularized in the eighteenth century, through the work of Enlightenment scientists such as Swedish botanist, Charles Linnaeus. Struggling against racism also entails working with race not simply as one autonomous piece of the mantra of race, class, gender and sexuality. We must recognize that the experience of racism is gendered, classed, and sexualized: My experience of racism as a middle-class, gay Chinese man is different from that of a middle-class, heterosexual Chinese man or a working-class, Chinese lesbian.

Beyond implications of its metaphors, the yellow-black sexuality in *Sally's Beauty Spot*—and in *Juxta*—is rare and highly charged. Miscegenation is the ultimate fear for many Asian parents, especially if the "outsider" is other than white. The scarcity

of representations of interracial sexuality among the "others"—
further rare examples include *Mississippi Masala* (1991) by Mira
Nair and the lesbians in *Sammy and Rosie Get Laid* (1987) directed
by Stephen Frears from a script by Hanif Kureishi—bespeaks a
situation in which producers are not interested in touching an
issue that is so taboo as to be repressed. Or else it reveals the subtle
work of racist assumptions in the economics of funding and distribution: on whose terms is it decided what is important, interesting,
and viable?

But while *Sally's Beauty Spot* is ground-breaking for trans-
gressing the white-centeredness that even informs our anger, the
fact that Sally never kisses an Asian unfortunately reflects the
absence of Asian men from Western sexual representation. For
while white males have traditionally fetishized Asian women as
sexual objects *par excellence*—and they are still not ubiquitous
even within these terms—Hollywood and television have cast
Asian men either as villains with a threatening but unspoken/un-
speakable sexuality, or more commonly, they have infantilized
them into pre-pubescent grown men such as *Bonanza*'s Hop Sing.
Given this context, it isn't surprising that many North American-
born Asians do not think of other Asians in sexual terms.

Wayne Wang's *Eat a Bowl of Tea* (1988) addresses the question of impotence in an historical setting of the fifties and in the
context of community cultural pressures. It describes the often
ignored personal fallout from the clash of values of different
generations. The issue is also addressed obliquely in Pam Tom's
Two Lies (1990), a short narrative film about beauty and self-
image, in which a Chinese American teenager reflects on her
mother's pending operation to enlarge her eyes. In Helen Lee's *My
Niagara* (1992), however, a short drama co-written with Kerri
Sakamoto, the sexual relationship between two Asians becomes
the film's focus. Julie Kumagai is a young *sansei* woman who lives
alone with her father, her mother having drowned off the coast of
Japan when Julie was just a girl. Since her mother's body was
never found, Julie remains obsessed with the death and with
Japan. At the start of the film, Julie breaks off with her white
boyfriend and later meets Tetsuro, a handsome Korean, born and

raised in Japan. Julie's fascination with a Japan she has never visited is counterposed to Tetsuro's captivation by North American pop culture, his memories of Japan being of either boredom or oppression.

The brief spectacle of Julie and Tetsuro making love is a rare occasion of intra-racial Asian sexuality in a North American production. But this is not a nationalist treatise. While Mr. Kumagai's bewilderment that Julie would leave her (white) boyfriend for "a Korean who wants to be Japanese" hints at the social significance of her choice—both the chauvinism that has informed Japan's relationship with Korea and Koreans living in Japan, and the fact that over 90 percent of *sansei* in Canada marry non-Japanese—the film happily avoids political prescriptiveness on "correct" sexual partners. Julie's and Tetsuro's mutual involvement does not resolve the internal conflicts of identity for either character.

Apart from its nuanced treatment of the question of sex and race, *My Niagara* also upsets an unproblematic notion of home. For Julie, home is a perpetually elusive search for the mother. For Tetsuro, home is equally unreal—neither Korea, Japan, nor Canada—and to be eluded at any cost. Being fourth-generation Trinidadian Chinese and living in Canada, I feel doubly displaced. Canada is not my home in the sense of being my cultural or spiritual source. But while my dreams are invariably set in my childhood house in Trinidad, home is no longer there either. It is certainly not in China, which I've visited only once and then briefly. For me, this is the allure of "Asian" identity, one in which home is somewhere but nowhere. "Asian" consciousness both describes and produces a sense of self not rooted in the old nationalities with their attendant chauvinisms, but in a common experience of being yellow and brown in a world defined by whiteness. It is an identity born of resistance and solidarity.

At the same time, "Asian-ness" can easily mask real power differences, not only of class, gender and sexuality, but of ethnicity itself. In researching this chapter, for instance, it was striking to me how many working Asian American and Asian Canadian film and video makers come from those Asian communities, not necessarily with the longest history here, but certainly with the most economic clout. While there has been work by Filipino, Vietnamese, Thai, and Malay directors, film and video makers of Japanese and Chinese heritage continue to dominate the offerings at "Asian" showcases and festivals. And many Asian groups have not yet had access to production.

I am aware that my sense of priorities, and even my experience of racism, is rooted in being *both* an indistinguishable yellow-skin and specifically Chinese. So that while I may feel solidarity, neither internment nor refugee camps—nor the head tax for that matter—is my own specific history. Even as an Asian producer myself, I cannot speak from these experiences, but I can assist in opening a space in which others can see and hear these visions and voices.

8

THE EXILE WITHIN/ THE QUESTION OF IDENTITY

JESSICA HAGEDORN

with a Postscript/Interview by Karin Aguilar-San Juan

There are questions that come to mind when exploring or attempting to define "Asian American culture" and my own influences as a writer and artist. Should the question actually be *"What is American culture?"* And is the solution inevitably, "Multiculturalism"?

"Your universe is shrinking!" The white man in Salman Rushdie's controversial novel, *The Satanic Verses,* warns the actor Saladin Chamcha (one of the novel's main characters) before Chamcha turns into a goat-like devil. Rushdie's white man is a successful TV producer, and the universe he is referring to is a racial universe. "Aliens," as the quintessential white man calls people of color, are no longer in. Aliens aren't even in among other aliens. Everyone in this shrinking universe seems to clamor for the same things (i.e., Gorbachev's dilemma). Everyone wants to watch "Dynasty," everyone desires the same point of reference. Or do we?

Or is this another brazen example of Western culture's ongoing media hype?

I was born in Manila, Philippines 40 years ago; my upbringing was typically colonial and Catholic. All that was expected of me was that I finish my education and marry well, perhaps even to a non-Filipino. My mother was raised in even stricter circumstances; she longed to be a dancer, but ended up marrying at a young age, bearing three children, and taking up painting on the side. Her painting became another passion, and fortunately for me, she passed this passion for art in all its media down to me at an early age. My maternal grandfather was a writer and an accomplished political cartoonist and teacher, and so my family was not surprised when I decided at age eight that writing and theater were my life's work. No one tried to suppress my ambitions; I'm just not sure how seriously I was taken. The main thing, as in most families with female children, was that I marry a nice man and not embarrass anyone with my "art."

The implication was to make "nice" art, and not take any risks.

I was taught to look outside the indigenous culture for inspiration, taught that the label "Made in the USA" meant automatic superiority; in other words, like most colonized individuals, I was taught a negative image of myself. In school, classes were taught in English, Tagalog was taught as a foreign language (shouldn't this have been the other way around?), and the ways of the West were endlessly paraded and promoted. I sought escape in Tagalog melodramas and radio serials—especially our own lurid and wonderful Tagalog "Komiks"—but I was nevertheless drawn to Hollywood movies and the classics of Western literature. My lopsided education in Anglo ways was sophisticated; by the age of nine or ten, while enjoying the cheap thrills provided by adolescent Nancy Drew mysteries, I was already reading Walt Whitman, Emily and Charlotte Brontë, Honore de Balzac, Edgar Allen Poe, Charles Dickens, and Jane Austen.

I spent my adolescent years in California, and studied theater arts at the American Conservatory Theater in San Francisco. The impact of finally moving to this environment was felt immediately.

I was fourteen when I arrived, and I realized that, in spite of being female, it was perfectly all right for me to explore the city by myself. I started tentatively venturing out—long walks alone!—and to my mother's horror, made it a habit. For those of you born and raised in America, this probably sounds ludicrous. I've seen children as young as ten or eleven (even younger) on public buses by themselves or with their friends. But in Manila, I was always protected and surrounded by older relatives or paid chaperones. It was unthinkable for a young girl to go to the movies by herself. It was a sin.

Perhaps what I value most in Western culture has been this profound sense of "freedom" as a woman—a freedom of movement and choice that is essential to any human being, and certainly essential for any writer. Freedom, of course, has its price.

While I have gotten used to this way of life in America, I straddle both worlds, like most urban Filipinos. When I speak of "home" even now, I refer to life *before* America, in that magical place of my childhood, the Philippines. Being of mixed parentage, I have family in Manila and the provinces, in California and the Midwest, and on my paternal side, family in Spain. In speaking of the Filipino American then, one also has to consider Hispanic roots, Chinese roots, etc. It is this hereditary mosaic that makes up the complex, unique, and dizzying Filipino culture. It is also this "elegant chaos" that definitely informs my work in style and the recurring themes of loss, yearning, alienation, rage, passion, and rebellion.

The actress Ching Valdes/Aran, herself a Filipina now living in New York, once said to me: "It took coming to America to actively Philippinize me." It is a sentiment probably many of us share.

The process of finding a writing "voice" that is true to one's self is often painful, but exhilarating and exciting as well. In the late 1960s and early 1970s, when I began publishing as a poet in San Francisco, I found empathy and revelation in the works of other Filipino writers who had settled in America (Carlos Bulosan, Bienvenido Santos, N.V.M. Gonzalez), as well as Filipino American writers who were born and/or raised in America (Serafin Syquia, Lou Syquia, Oscar Peñaranda, Al Robles, Jocelyn Ignacio, Cyn

Zarco, Norman Jayo, and others). I also discovered the poetic possibilities inherent in everyday speech and musical lyrics by reading and listening to Amiri Baraka, Ishmael Reed, Jayne Cortez, Al Young, Sonia Sanchez, The Last Poets, and my own colleagues, Thulani Davis and Ntozake Shange. Another peer who has really influenced my work is the Puerto Rican poet Victor Hernandez Cruz. Through his innovations, I freed myself to "dance" with my words.

Because I was always interested in writing fiction, I found solace and inspiration in the works of the South American masters: Gabriel García Márquez, Manuel Puig, Luisa Valenzuela, and Guillermo Cabrera Infante. Their dark humor, poetic ironies, bilingual sophistication, pop culture references, surreal images, and fatalism were, for me, much closer to a Filipino sensibility than the contemporary writers I was also reading from other Asian cultures. Japanese writers can be very cool and restrained, whereas the Philippine and Latin American cultures share a more earthy "hothouse" sensibility.

Most urban Filipinos and Filipino Americans probably suffer from cultural schizophrenia, like I do. Hopefully, we will use this affliction to our advantage, for this post-colonial condition has its positive aspects. We need to turn the negative inside out, use it to enrich ourselves and our visions—for where would our extraordinary voices be without the outlaw rhythms of rock 'n' roll, the fractured lyricisms of jazz, the joyous gravity of salsa, the perverse fantasies of Hollywood, and our own epic melodramas?

Is there an Asian American aesthetic? Perhaps one exists insofar as influences that extend from the mother country (place of birth) and merge/clash with the influences of a pop culture that is universally perceived as "American" (i.e., North American). Some of these pop culture clichés include fashion and hence, dictate our self-image (jeans/black leather jackets/baseball caps); music (rock 'n' roll, black rap), which dictates the rhythms in our speech; TV ("The Cosby Show"), our notions of the model "minority."[1] But in this shrinking universe, where white media appropriates black rappers, Asian ethnic fashion, and technology, and pretentious Zen car commercials find their way to television, who can really say Who is influencing Whom?

As Asian Americans, as writers and people of color in a world still dominated by Western thinking, it is vital that we straddle both cultures (East/West) and maintain our diversity and integrity. Writers and scholars have emerged in recent times (some familiar, some new) to continue to challenge the notion of a literature that encompasses the world—and reaffirms our existence in it. It is a multicultural vision that embraces and includes our shrinking universe; it is a multicultural vision that the white man fears and a vision that the rest of us can celebrate.

In the dark and futuristic movie "Blade Runner," the image of a shrinking universe is shocking in its resemblance to society as we already know it. Los Angeles may be the capital in this version, but Japanese ads blink off and on, lighting up awesome electronic billboards, and street signs are posted in languages other than English. Where is the ubiquitous English language? Nowhere to be found. Nevertheless, this being Hollywood, everything is still run by the white man. In this movie, people of color belong to the underground, where they scurry and skulk in the rain, forever powerless, forever bit players in the big picture.

The difference in the art and literature that we are discussing is that it belongs to us. In the constant process of creating our work and recreating ourselves, we acknowledge our roots as well as acknowledge the transformation that occurs living in the shadow of the dominant culture known as white America. Because of the racism that prevails, our work cannot afford to remain "small" or exclusive. If it is to survive and make a positive impact in a constantly evolving society, our work must address a universe as colored, confusing, magical, and terrifying as the one presented in Salman Rushdie's *The Satanic Verses*. I refer to this novel in particular because of the scope of its ambition, and because it confronts head-on a society of immigrants, aliens, others, natives, spirits, racists, angels, devils, and other sacred cows with courage, compassion, humor, and breathtaking genius. It may cost Salman Rushdie his life.

And the list of writers is growing (in no particular order): Bharati Mukherjee, Timothy Mo, Hanif Kureishi (who is British, but whose work accomplishes similar goals), Cynthia Kadohata, Fae Ng, Ninotchka Rosca, Shawn Wong, Amy Tan, Momoko Iko, Maxine Hong Kingston, Marilyn Chin, Garrett Hongo, Lawson Inada, Presco Tabios, Jeff Tagami and Shirley Ancheta, Kimiko Hahn, David Mura, Han Ong, Walter Lew, Laureen Mar, Alfred Yuson, David Henry Hwang, Philip Gotanda, Daryl Chin, Trinh Minh-ha, Ko Won, Cathy Song, David Wong Louie, Nellie Wong, Wing Tek Lum, and so many others!

My novel *Dogeaters* was my attempt to make peace with the past and portray the beauty and richness of Philippine culture even in perilous times. I will probably write about the culture of exile and homesickness in one form of another until the day I die; it is my personal obsession, and it fuels my work.

In response to a recent interview on the question of Asian American identity and how it applies to my work in both literature and the theater, I described my writing (in poetry, theater, fiction, and film) as being populated by edgy characters who superficially seem to belong nowhere, but actually belong everywhere. It's my version of the "human" story.

It really doesn't matter if you're an immigrant or native-born, "F.O.B." or "A.B.C.,"[2] you're discovering who, what, and where you are all the time.

Another question I ask myself over and over again in my work: In what language do we dream?

Identity for me is not only racial, but sexual. I cannot think of myself as addressing the multicultural issue without including gender culture within the framework. We must respect the diversity of ethnic *and* sexual identity; for just as the Spanish version of guilt-ridden Christianity has influenced my psyche, and black and Latin music influences the rhythms of my characters' speech, then I happily acknowledge the wit and black-net veil of lyricism and doom which I have acquired from the works of homosexual writers like Tennessee Williams, Manuel Puig, and even Truman Capote.

JESSICA HAGEDORN

It was a deliberate choice on my part to have one of my central characters in *Dogeaters* be a male prostitute who is half-black, half-Filipino—what one critic has called a "mongrel" child of the streets. My personal vision is very definitely a mongrel one, and I say this with pride.

In a recent essay on multiculturalism published in *Teachers & Writers' Collaborative* magazine, Christian McEwen refers to the distinguished novelist, scholar, and diplomat, Carlos Fuentes: "For someone like Fuentes, skeptical, cosmopolitan, a Mexican national raised and educated in the United States, multiculturalism is more than an aesthetic or theoretical choice. It is a fierce personal necessity, a matter of political and cultural survival." This fierce personal necessity applies to our roles as Asian Americans, as writers, social thinkers, and people of color, and as citizens of the world.

Postscript/Interview by Karin Aguilar-San Juan

Q: Throughout this anthology, contributors try to answer the question: What is the Asian American model of resistance? Would you say more about the Asian American "aesthetic" as a form of resisting the "norms" of white society?

A: In my chapter, I explore questions of identity from my personal experience, and not from some general "Asian American point of view." Is there even one perspective that unites us? I'm not so sure. Well, perhaps food. Love of food, and a certain sensibility regarding beauty. And I do think our cultures are steeped in traditions of grace and hospitality—we share that with other Asian Americans.

Q: What I love about your writing is that it has so many different levels to it, demonstrating over and over again that nobody can ever be reduced to parts—that is, race and gender, or race and profession, or gender and medium, or gender and generation. Your way of addressing the issues of necessity opens up 10 million other questions, because that is the nature of the beast we are confronting. How do writings by different Asian American writers affect you?

A: When I read a Filipino writer like Ben Santos, for example, it's like coming home—like listening to the voices of uncles and *lolos* (grandfathers). It's a familiar, melancholy haunt—the sweet, wistful voice of an old Pinoy man. A very different experience than when I read Louis Chu or Hisaye Yamamoto, who are probably the same generation as Ben but who don't affect me in the same way.

Writers like Santos, poets like Serafin Syquia, were important to me as a young writer because they gave "face" to my life, rage, and cultural alienation. Perhaps Serafin, who died very young, was closer to me personally because we shared many experiences—life in San Francisco, the chaos of the 1960s, an awakening of "nationalistic" pride inspired by African American struggles. Serafin was also only a few years older than me, and his younger brother Lou (also a poet) is a very good friend to this day.

Q: What is this "multicultural vision that the white man fears"?

A: It is still being created, and no one particular writer comes to mind who has already addressed it. Salman Rushdie sort of does, as background landscape to *The Satanic Verses,* but not really. Hanif Kureishi does in his two screenplays, *My Beautiful Launderette* and *Sammy and Rosie Get Laid.* Everyone else seems to be more *ethnocentric* than anything else.

Q: Would you explain why multiculturalism is a matter of survival for you? Do you mean that publishers and the media respond positively to you because you claim a multicultural identity, as a "mongrel child of the streets"? Or do you mean that you cannot avoid producing "multicultural" art because you yourself are the product of a multicultural universe?

A: I claim a multicultural identity because it's the truth for me. My world as a child, my world now is influenced by many other cultures. African American music, the rituals of Catholicism, Hollywood movies, MTV jump-cuts, the precision of English, the playfulness of Spanish, the frugality of the Chinese, the aggression and wit of New York ... It goes back to an earlier point I was trying to make about my particular colonized imagination ... Some of the results have been negative, but some of the results have also meant strength and adaptability. Even North America has got to stop kidding itself—this has never been a homogenous society. The minute the white man stepped on to the Native American and Mexican landscape, the minute the white man started claiming all this as his own, then in some way the white man was also claiming part of those indigenous cultures in order to survive and move on. As far as the media and the publishing industry goes—you should ask them about it. My new novel takes place in America, but also parts of it keep going back to the Philippines. Perhaps the two countries are inextricably linked in my mind. I can't help it. I go to Detroit, New York, San Francisco, but I'm not interested in just writing "an American novel." I'm incapable of it. Though I've been living in America for 30 years now, my roots remain elsewhere…back there.

Q. I appreciate your mention of sexual identity as one of the facets of multiculturalism. You cite Puig, Capote, and other gay male writers, but what about the lesbian writers who in the 1960s, 1970s, and 1980s were so important in paving the way for U.S. women writers of all sexual orientations? I'm thinking of Lorraine Hansberry, Kate Millett, Rita Mae Brown, Jill Johnston, Adrienne Rich, Audre Lorde, Cherríe Moraga, Gloria Anzaldúa, June Jordan, Merle Woo, Helen Zia …

A. I think you misunderstood my references to Capote and Puig. When I was flailing around trying to find myself as a writer (something I think I am still doing), I had to "educate" myself. I did not attend an established creative writing program or go the academic rout—I simply devoured books. In the 1960s and early 1970s, the works of gay Asian American writers simply did not exist for me—especially *gay Asian American women!* I had to reconstruct, deconstruct, and decode for myself as a Filipino American, as a woman, and as a writer—using the works of Puig, Capote, Tennessee Williams, etc. This is my *unrevised* literary history.

Q: Is there a particular literary work you have in mind that exemplifies a multicultural vision, one you think we should be celebrating? I ask only because I think there is a huge difference between the work of, for example, Bharati Mukherjee and Maxine Hong Kingston, in terms of their implicit messages about Asian women in U.S. society.

A: There really haven't been that many novels yet—I think they are still being written. But the one thing that always comes to mind is a stunning poem by Guillermo Gomez-Peña entitled "Califas." I quoted it in my keynote address to the graduating students in ethnic studies at UC Berkeley in 1989, and here's some of it:

> I see a whole generation
> freefalling toward a borderless future
> incredible mixtures beyond sci-fi
> cholo punks, pachuco krishnas
> Irish concheros, high-tech mariachis
> Indian rockers & Anglosandinistas
> I see them all
> wandering around
> a continent without a name…"

It ends with:

> I toast to a borderless future
> with our Alaskan hair
> our Canadian head
> our U.S. torso
> our Mexican genitalia
> our Central American cojones
> our Caribbean sperm
> our South American legs
> our Patagonian feet
> jumping borders at ease
> amen, hey man…"

You get the point, right?

Notes

1. There is no such thing as a "minority" in this culture. The first thing to remember is "minority" is a white concept, and a negative one at that.
2. The phrases "Fresh off the boat" and "American-born Chinese" can be pejorative in certain contexts, but here I'm simply being descriptive.

9

A SHIFT IN POWER, A SEA CHANGE IN THE ARTS

Asian American Constructions

DAVID MURA

I feel at a certain point everything changed. I don't know
   when that point was.
I know there are many things I no longer believe in.
God. Thomas Jefferson. Superman. Ward Cleaver. Aesthetic
   standards. Liberal pluralism.
So many objects of disbelief I don't know where to begin.
The melting pot. The temple of art. Communism. (Commu-
   nism, not the writings of Marx.)
My mother. My father. The escape of Japanese Americans
   from the quagmire of race.
A Ph.D. An MFA. The classics. Intellectual rigor. Liberal guilt.
What else don't I believe in? My life as a case study in clinical
   depression.
My need for wild and abandoned promiscuous sex. My incom-
   petence before fatherhood.

My inability to remain faithful. My isolation. My solitude. My private self.

*

I grew up as an artist with a model of the artist as an elite species, as a superior craftsman, as cultivator and connoisseur of subtleties and beauties too fine for others to perceive.
I saw myself in revolt against bourgeois society, bourgeois comforts, as an alien,
a rebel, one who worshipped chaos, an entropy of emotion, the sources of great art.
I saw myself as one who was certain what great art was. Who had no need,
nor desire, nor obligation to the mundane matters of any social organization,
whether a museum, a theater, a university, or a writing center.
(In short, I inherited the detritus of the nineteenth century view of the artist.
The artist in isolation. The artist as cultural—as opposed to political—rebel.)

*

And I became a writer so I could sit in my room and write. So I didn't have to face an audience,
so I could be alone, with my thoughts, my books, my poems, my words.
So I could abandon myself to quietude and contemplation.
So I could perceive and create beauty and complexity.
So I could live the life of a superior being.

*

Of course, this being had no color. Or sex.
Of course, this being was a white male.
Of course, I was not a white male. (What does it mean to be a white male?)

Of course, I tried very hard to forget this fact.
Of course, I almost succeeded.
Of course, I almost killed myself in succeeding.

*

Something broke. Something opened.
I discovered I was, after all, surprise of surprises, a Japanese
　　American.
I saw in the mirror of my relations that I was, after all, sur-
　　prise of surprises, a person of color.
I saw that these terms themselves were constructions. Which
　　I could alter.
I saw that in altering my present consciousness I was altering
　　my relationship to the past.
I saw that the internment camps were, after all, in my life. In
　　my bedroom. In my body.
I saw other people of color. That there was, indeed, a war
　　going on.
I saw there was a choice. That all my life I had been choosing.
　　That I could choose again.

II

　　I am a Japanese American poet, critic, and non-fiction writer,
and recently, I published a memoir, *Turning Japanese: Memoirs
of a Sansei*. An account of a year I spent in Japan, the book explores
my Japanese American identity in light of that experience. At
various points in the narrative, events in Japan cause me to reflect
on my identity; there are periodic flashbacks concerning my own
life, the life of my parents and grandparents, and the history of
Japanese Americans. I focus on how the internment of Japanese
Americans was occluded in my schooling and in my family, and
how the process of assimilation in a racist culture exacts a terrific
price, one many Americans, including my own family, do not want
to examine.
　　Whenever I describe the book to people, I stress how it centers
on my going to Japan as a Japanese American, how my vision of

Japan is intimately tied to my position as a *sansei* (third-generation Japanese American). In contrast, certain white reviewers focused almost entirely on the book as a travelogue and generally ignored the sections on my Japanese American identity. A couple of critics found the sections on identity self-conscious, and intimated that this self-consciousness intruded on the book's picture of Japan. In a generally favorable review for *Condé Nast Traveler,* Simon Winchester writes:

> On one level, Mura's story presents an illuminating essay about the confusing nature of modern Japanese society ... On the other, it is an engagingly honest diary of an understandably confused young man, a Japanese American ... While it would be impolite to indicate a lack of real interest in Mura and his trials...it is his notes on the society that temporarily surrounds and ultimately (in his opinion) rejects him and prevents him from really 'turning Japanese' that are the more valuable.

I should note that Mr. Winchester's belief that I felt Japan rejected me is more his own projection than what's in my book. Recently, I received a letter about my book from someone who appears to have lived in Japan for some time: "I read it not as a '*sansei*'s memoirs' but as a '*gaijin*'s encounter' with Japan. Because—Japanese ancestry aside—your encounter is in many ways like all first-time coming-to-grips-with-Japan type experiences. And therein lies its universal appeal." Implicit in such remarks is an assumption that a "*sansei*'s memoirs" cannot be as important as a book about encountering Japan. This, of course, is an assumption that no Asian American critic has made; all of them have chosen to use the focus of the memoir on identity as their prime starting point. There is also an assumption here that we can only achieve universality by ignoring questions of identity that a white American does not feel are substantial. If I write as a generic American, that's okay, but if I write as a third-generation Japanese American, that's being self-conscious, that's less than universal.

Part of the problem is the assumption that ignoring differences of identity is the road to the universal. One reason for this assumption is that the differences between my experience of Japan and that of white Americans brings up uncomfortable questions about race and American identity. Many white Americans don't want to deal with these questions and, through much of their lives, have not had to deal with them. In contrast, my memoir explores how, up until my late twenties, I mainly attempted to avoid dealing with my *sansei* identity, and tended to think of myself as a middle-class white person. The result of such an identification, as my memoir makes clear, was self-hatred and self-abuse, a long string of depression, promiscuity, and failed relationships. If I had not become self-conscious about my identity, I might have destroyed myself. What appears to certain white readers as either negligible or a flaw in the book is actually its very lifeline.

My experience with the differences between the perceptions of white reviewers and Asian American reviewers is not atypical for many writers of color. As I have had similar experiences with the reception of my work, I've come to view the question of audience in new ways and to question how cultural contexts affect the uses and effectiveness of art. This in turn has led me to question much of what I've learned about standards, quality, community, objectivity, and the purpose of art.

III

At the center of the most vital new art in our culture is the creation of a new audience.

Or, the recognition of an audience that was always there. Which has been ignored.

Particularly for artists of color, for women, for gays and lesbians, this new audience has been a source of sustenance and energy. This new audience is made up of the communities they live in, and their art comes out of those communities.

For many of these artists, the strength and vitality of their art depends upon the strength and vitality of their communities.

This is why for many artist the distinction between the work of the artist and the work of the social activist has broken down.

This breakdown needs to take place also in the temples of art.

The discovery of the new audience is the discovery of community. That the community exists, and that the community is a continual process of creation.

Where does the community exist? It exists in structures beyond the temples of art that the temples have ignored.

It exists in other temples called churches. Schools. Community centers. Community organizations. Service organizations. Block parties. Reading groups. Sports leagues. Bars. Neighborhood and ethnic papers. Ethnic days of celebration.

Does the community exist in businesses? Civic groups? Unions? Professional organizations? Corporations? Banks? Political parties?

Where does growth come from? Contradiction.

Put an artist in a corporation. There is contradiction.

Put an artist in a church. Contradiction?

Put an artist in a sports bar. Contradiction.

Put an artist before a group of small business people. Contradiction.

Will that change the artist and the art? Will that change the audience?

What artists perform in the temples? What class are they? What race? What sex? What sexual preference? What language do they speak?

Who makes decisions in the temples? What class are they? What race? What sex? What sexual preference? What language do they speak?

Who makes up the audience in the temples? What class are they? What race? What sex? What preference? What language do they speak?

What would happen if the artists, the decision-makers, and the audience were different? Who owns the temples?

IV

As we approach the next millennium, the presence of multiculturalism in the arts will only increase. This increasing presence is caused by changing demographics and various historical forces too numerous and complex to go into here. Of course, we have seen a huge wave of backlash recently against multiculturalism; the forces behind this backlash hold much of the power in this country, whether that power is political, economic, or cultural. These conservative forces arrayed against multiculturalism are terrified about its deeper implications, the possibilities it opens up for a more democratic vision of America.

In the end, despite their power, these conservative forces will lose out. It's not simply that the demographics are against them; as someone remarked to me the other day, "Multiculturalism isn't an option, it's a fact." No, my optimistic outlook is based on what I see going on in the arts: The center of creativity has shifted to the margins; that's where the energy is, where the cutting edge starts.

Over the past few years, I've come to believe we are witnessing a large shift in the way we practice and receive art in this culture. For instance, in the coming years, the question of who holds the power within the world of art will become crucial. Previously marginalized artists and their audiences will become more and more visible. Both these artists and their audiences will challenge established art institutions and arbiters of judgement. This will in turn increase an investigation of who decides which artworks are recognized, praised, and funded in our society and how those decisions are made. To accomplish a shift in cultural power, there will be a greater need for organizations and institutions for and by people of color. In other words, the creation of artists of color depends not merely on the development of artists, but also on the development of editors, curators, teachers, funders, and arts administrators of color.

This increasing visibility and power of multicultural artists and cultural workers will complicate and challenge previous aesthetic standards. For example, such artists often draw on aesthetic traditions that are not derived from a European sense of aesthetics (see for example John Yau's "Please Wait by the Coatroom" where Yau argues that MOMA curator William Rubin misjudges and misrepresents the work of Wilfredo Lam by choosing to view Lam's work solely within the context of European art history rather than in the context of Latin American and African art). At the same time, new works will cause reevaluations of the existing canon. If you add Toni Morrison, Maxine Hong Kingston, and Louise Erdrich at the end of twentieth-century American fiction, Faulkner becomes a more prominent figure than Fitzgerald. On a global scale, amid a list of Third World writers—Chinua Achebe, Ama Ata Aidoo, García Márquez, Nadine Gordimer, Derek Walcott, Isabelle Allende, Salman Rushdie—Toni Morrison fits in a way John Updike does not. One reason for this, of course, is that we come to see racial issues as central rather than peripheral concerns. But even more importantly, many writers of color in this country and in the Third World tend to question traditional European assumptions about the separation of politics and literature, colonialism, our relationship to history, the relationship between the individual and the group, and realism or the nature of spiritual reality.

As these aesthetic shifts take place, the relationship between the artist and the community will change. Many multicultural artists derive their art from the experiences of communities who have not had access to traditional arts institutions. These multicultural artists do not necessarily define their relationship to the community according to certain European concepts of the artist— that is, they often do not view themselves as isolated or alienated from their community; instead they view themselves as representative members of that community. As a result many find more links between art and community organizing. They also see their art as part of their community's struggle to survive and obtain an equal distribution of society's economic and political power. The multicultural artist may therefore perform a number of roles in the community in addition to the creation of his or her own work. Arts programs need to be aware both of the ways in which such activity feeds the creativity of multicultural artists and, at other times, overwhelms these artists, leaving them little time to do their own work.

Because of multiculturalism's base in marginalized populations and because of a changing relationship between the artist and the community, art and artists will be more directly engaged with political issues. This means that art may have an increasing role in shaping debate on public policy and that artists will participate in that debate in new ways. The multicultural artist may be called upon to be a spokesperson for the interests of his or her community, rather than simply an individual artist. (This brings up tricky questions of whether any one individual can represent a community. The obvious answer is no. Yet this does not mean that the artist or any member of the community should not attempt to voice their perception of the community's concerns. The solution is more voices, not fewer.)

All of these changes in the art world will bring new audiences for art, audiences that will represent a wider cross section of U.S. society than previous audiences. These new audiences may respond to and require a different form of arts criticism than the traditional European model. To reach these audiences, artists will have to present their work in non-traditional sites. Through contact with new audiences, artists will begin to produce new and different work, to expand or go beyond the boundaries of their art form. At the same time, certain artists may find that the new audiences accept their work more enthusiastically than traditional mainstream audiences. This happened to me when I began reading to multicultural and Asian American audiences. Such responses may cause artists to reexamine their standards and question who they are writing for. At the same time, if audiences do not respond positively, this may make artists aware of gaps and shortcomings in their work that previously went unnoticed. They may have to confront the fact that their art is less universal than they may have hoped or believed.

Not surprisingly these new audiences from previously marginalized communities are part of a greater shift in the distribution of cultural and political power in this country. What is at stake is who holds power in this country, who determines what our history and our future will be. This is what frightens many conservatives. If the doors are not barred quickly and with a resounding slam in the faces of the new "barbarians," the old patrician order is in trouble. The numbers will soon be with the newcomers.

As multiculturalism takes hold, definitions of what it means to be an artist, how an artist lives and defines his or herself, will change. Many of these artistic changes stem from the previously mentioned shift in the relationship between the artist and his or her community. In *Postmodernism, or The Cultural Logic of Late Capitalism,* Fredric Jameson argues that the modernist conception of the artist as isolated genius has become increasingly rare, and that this is due in part to the more group-based and media-oriented nature of postmodern culture. I think Jameson's point is probably correct, but I also think the artist of color and his or her audience occupy a different relationship to mass culture than mainstream artists or their audience. Asian Americans, for instance, know that within mass culture they generally do not exist; there are no images that reflect who they are. Rather than turning toward mass culture, they must look towards works of literature or theater, performance artists, and smaller scale projects to find their own stories and images. The more they do this, the more they grasp the political ramifications of their cultural marginalization, the more they counter status quo power relationships in this country. Conversely, it's becoming increasingly clear to me that my audience starts with Japanese Americans, then Asian Americans, then multicultural audiences, and then the mainstream "white" audience. For this reason, my work as an artist, my ability to survive as an artist, depends upon the existence of a Japanese American and Asian American community. If this community did not exist, my work would be even more marginalized than it is (for me, "assimilation" means the death of Japanese American art). In contrast to the "art for art's sake" attitude I was taught in English graduate school and the MFA workshop, I now see a symbiotic relationship between art and community, and I find my time occupied more and more with a balance between issues of art and issues of the community. On a day-to-day level, this means that in my thinking the world view of the Academy of American Poets is balanced against what's happening at the local YWCA or at the Japanese American Citizens League or the Hmong Youth Leadership; this sort of balance would have been unthinkable to me a few years ago.

I predict that this conjunction of art and community will draw more and more multicultural artists towards theater and film, towards collaborations and mixtures of genres, precisely because of the social—as opposed to individual—basis of these art forms. Not surprisingly, this will bring about a renewed interest in the artistic traditions of our different ethnic backgrounds, traditions that do not find their bearings in the European Enlightenment or the Romantic era. Thus, the postmodern dissolution of genres becomes the rediscovery of a buried tradition, and the artist's purpose becomes more the preservation and health of the community rather than his or her own individual glory or achievement. This may mean that the view of "high culture," which emphasizes a singular and/or abstract standard of excellence, will be more and more balanced by a view of art as craft, and by a valuing of art for its use value.

V

A very different sense of purpose, one more aligned with community, can restore meaning and energy to our sense of what it means to work as an artist. Thus, one of the most significant aspects of my life as an artist in the past couple years has been working with local Asian Americans in forming an Asian American arts group, the Asian American Renaissance.

The Asian American Renaissance was started early in 1991, when a grassroots group of Asian Americans began meeting to plan an Asian American arts conference. This event, the Asian American Cultural Renaissance Conference, took place on April 24 and 30, and May 1-3, 1992. The participants in the conference included fiction writers, poets, creative non-fiction writers, performance artists, playwrights, visual artists, filmmakers, jazz musicians, rock musicians, and scholars. Such a gathering represented an unprecedented cultural event for Asian Americans in Minnesota and the Upper Midwest.

The members of the Asian American Renaissance include Asian Americans from the arts, social services, business, education, health, and community organizations. We are Hmong American, Japanese American, Chinese American, Korean American, Vietnamese American, Cambodian American, Filipino American,

Laotian American, and Thai American. All of us simply wanted to see and hear art that reflected our concerns and the concerns of our community. The idea for the conference arose when a number of us met at various multicultural events and started talking about Asian American arts. When we began working together, I had no idea what I was committing myself to. At first, I saw the conference mainly as a vehicle to present the work of Asian American artists. As our group worked together, though, I came to see the conference as both a cultural event and as a tool for community organizing. The group felt strongly that the art and its issues would establish the first steps toward social action, and this connection was seen not as a step away from the "real" purpose of art, but a tribute to the power of art. Also, because the idea of the conference originated within the Asian American community, it had an organic life that a conference organized by an established arts institution might not possess; we felt an ownership that we otherwise might not have felt.

In recent years, the influx of immigrants has enlarged, enlivened, and energized the Asian American population in Minnesota. The Asian American community there is relatively young, one that is, for example, just beginning to take an active role in local politics. In order for effective Asian American community action to take place, individuals must be able to view their own individual concerns and needs within the context of a group. Culture and cultural events are a logical starting place for this collective vision. As one of our board members has remarked, "Social change starts in the imagination." Art is a central process through which community members find the symbols and language that can help them achieve unity amidst their opposition to each other and those outside the community. I feel it is through Asian American art that the many different Asian American communities can both explore their own diversity and formulate their own identities, both as communities and as individuals. Moreover, Asian American arts can help people see how the term Asian American designates a collective experience; it points to shared problems, questions, and goals that go beyond the confines of any one Asian ethnic group, such as Hmong American or Japanese American.

The process of collective action must start then within the community, with education and self-definition. Such activities lead to the work outside the community to change the social and political structures that affect the community. Keeping this in mind, we have designed many of our programs to deal with the questions of Asian American identity—how to combine our Asian heritage with the heritage from the West; how to deal with the questions of our history in United States, with our place in the new multicultural vision we are helping create; how to deal with stereotypes that not only harm us psychologically and spiritually but also economically; how to understand and combat racism. Without Asian American art, the members of the Asian American community cannot understand who they have been and who they are. And if we do not know who we are, how can we begin to articulate our economic or political needs in a way that others will be hear? Obviously, we need to go beyond the "model minority" myth and other stereotypes used to caricature our communities. As Mark Tang, a board member and local artist, has noted, "It is important for Asian Americans to present our own image, to tell others how we see ourselves."

In many ways, the members of the Asian American Renaissance feel that the model we're constructing of an arts organization differs from many of the traditional mainstream models. We do not want to construct a temple for art. We do not want to present art as an elitist activity that needs to be "explained" to the community. We do not see the artist as delivering a monologue to the audience or the "uninformed." Instead, we feel that the need for art arises out of the community. We believe that art and the community are created by each other through a constant dialogue with each other. For this reason, we want to give more and more opportunities for various members of the community to create their own art, to give voice to their own desires and sense of the world. We want to build our programs around a spirit of communal participation and dialogue. We are also committed to a multigenerational approach to art, an approach that sees art as an integral human activity at every age. Finally, we want to break down the barriers between services that are seen as involving cultural needs and those which are seen as involving social or political needs. In approaching any program or problem, we want to remember that by helping the community to become aware of itself, the arts can help transform the community and generate community action.

VI

We are post-colonials. Because of history, we are Americans. By race we are Asians. That is a complicated identity, not only racially, but historically. Yeats may be considered the greatest poet in English in the 20th century, but the Irish say that he is a great Irish poet and Yeats thought of himself as an Irishman. His poetry...comes from a different way of speaking the language, the imagery, the mythology, the cultural values, the politics, wishing for an Irish free state. He even became a senator. He was Irish. But does that LESSEN his poetry because he was Irish? Does it diminish the fact that he is a great poet? Does it diminish me to be an Asian American poet? No! That might be the problem of the critic, but that is not my problem. I am happy to be called Asian American or not. People constantly tell me, "Garrett, I'm so happy you didn't go that ethnic route, you became a poet in your own right." People with Pulitzer Prizes would say this to me at cocktail parties. "You are just a poet." Or other people say, "You know Garrett, you really inspired me a long time. Nobody has been up there like you from the beginning with Asian American writing and words." So what is going on here? What's going on here is that society impinges its values on the individual constantly and reinterprets what interaction you have on its own terms.

—Garrett Hongo,
Asian American Renaissance Conference
St. Paul, MN, May 1992

Perhaps the key issue of the Asian American Renaissance Conference centered on the term Asian American and its relationship to the arts. The discussion of this issue indicated that both Asian American art and the Asian American community are, in certain senses, just beginning. As the poet Garrett Hongo once remarked to me, "We [Asian American artists] may be very sophisticated as individuals, but as a culture, there's a lot to be done."

Certainly, the conference planners recognized that the term Asian American is problematic. For instance, there are over 30 ethnic groups brought together under the umbrella of the Council for Asian-Pacific Minnesotans. As Valerie Lee, the director of the conference, asked, "What do we have in common except for racism and rice?"

The idea of unity through diversity, while useful, has by now become almost a cliché. Moreover, within the context of art, such an idea creates certain questions. Art, as we all know, resists categories, recognizes in the attempt to define a desire to confine, to shun complexity, mystery, singularity. We see in categories the inaccuracy of language and a mental lassitude. We see in it a refusal to contemplate, to open ourselves up to what is truly other.

At a conference panel, "Asian American Literature: The Canon and Community," the poet Li-Young Lee argued that the label Asian American represents a type of confinement: "I wouldn't even bother calling myself Asian American...I was writing for a long time, then all of a sudden I would see this little label on the horizon. I step to the left and it steps to the left with me, I step to my right and it moves with me. I am stepping toward my future, my life, and that fucking label keeps coming with me. It has nothing to do with me. Somebody else invented it...it's like a Social Security number."

In the same panel, the poet Garrett Hongo remarked, "Though the world may see me as an Asian American, or a Jap, that is not the way I see myself...So a category, or an anthology, or a panel that is called Asian American literature or identity is a training session for the dismantling of the idea that you can characterize people in a category, not a reasserting of that category."

After hearing the poets speak, a white male immediately stood up and asked Hongo, "You're editing an Asian American poetry anthology. Does what you just said mean that some time in the future we'll get to a point where we no longer need such a thing as an Asian American poetry anthology?"

Hongo replied gruffly, "No," and said nothing else.

A white poet and friend later told me she was baffled by this interchange. She felt she'd come to learn about the Asian American canon; after all, this was what the panel had been titled. She didn't understand why Hongo had answered so abruptly; she felt this was a message that she, as a white person, was probably not there to ask questions, but simply to listen. She didn't say that she was offended by this, but I know she felt put off. Certainly, by Minnesota standards, Hongo had been decidedly rude. The white male had asked the question in good faith.

As the question-and-answer period progressed, Asian Americans began to ask questions. One young man said, "I am a Korean adoptee. I came over here when I was three months and I was raised by a Caucasian family. Am I Asian American?" From the audience, Nellie Wong spoke eloquently of the political implications of our writing and her work in social activism. I felt a sense of intimacy and safety, of different members of the community talking among ourselves.

And yet, despite the need for Asian Americans to concentrate our attention on each other, I do feel we need to examine the interchange between Hongo and his questioner. For this interchange was charged with racial overtones that people don't always understand. In such instances, the misunderstanding and anger are a result of two very different sets of experiences and perspectives. It is here that the term Asian American can be useful: The term acknowledges these different sets of experiences and perspectives.

On one level, Hongo was angry because when we opened up the panel for questions, the first two people I called on were white males. He reminded me that a Chinese American moderator had done the same thing at a panel Hongo and I were on in New York.

But they were the only ones raising their hands, I protested.

"Then you wait until some Buddhahead raises their hand," said Hongo.

In part, Hongo resented the unconscious presumption of the white males that they were free to ask questions and speak. In an ideal world, we might all feel this presumption, but in the real world, this is not the case. In the real world, Asian Americans, whether male or female, are generally more reluctant to speak up in a question-and-answer period than a white male. (Am I generalizing here? Stereotyping? Yes. Do I know the phenomenon I've just described has a good deal of truth? Yes. Are these positions contradictory? Yes and no.)

The white male's presumption to speak is based on a real social power. The Asian American's reluctance to speak is based perhaps on cultural mores—though this certainly depends in part on one's generation and ethnic background—but it also is based on the marginalization of Asian Americans, no matter what their generation or ethnicity. (There are individual exceptions, but those exceptions do not disprove the general tendency.) Hongo's anger was directed at the disparity in power between whites and Asian Americans. This disparity was evidenced by the fact that, even at an Asian American panel, the first two questioners were white male. My friend's bewilderment at Hongo's reaction had much to do with her ignorance of the marginalization Hongo has experienced, his awareness of the mainstream culture's desire to diminish him.

Which brings me to a second source of Hongo's anger. True, categories can be used to diminish the singularity of any one person, particularly a member of a marginalized group, and this diminishment can be a way of robbing that person of power. But this does not mean that the absence of categories in referring to a member of a marginalized group will always be empowering. In fact, it can be just the opposite. The attacks against affirmative action and the desire for a "color blind" judgement, a judgement beyond racial categories, deny the ways such judgements, over the long run, work for the advantage of whites. The reasons for this ought to be obvious: Whites are generally the ones who exercise such judgements and are the ones who create the criteria for such judgements; they have more of the resources to ensure that they will perform well according to such judgements. In other words, the denial of race in such an instance is a denial of an inequality of power.

Hongo sensed in his white male questioner a desire to get beyond ethnicity, beyond color or race. He also sensed that this desire has arisen in a time when Asian American artists are declaring a certain independence from the white mainstream, when we are beginning to examine and own the particularities of our experience. Did the questioner consciously feel a desire to deny the issues of race, or did he feel his was a genuine, unbiased intellectual query? It's hard to tell. What is clear is that many whites, particularly white males, make purported attempts to erase or transcend the categories of race in order to ignore the privileges they have enjoyed and exercised because of those categories. Some of these privileges may not be things they actively desire or want, yet they are present nonetheless. After being a moderator for several panels, I've come to notice how much easier it seems for me to recognize the hands of white males in the audience. Why is this? Did all these white males ask for this privilege? But there it is, embedded in my brain, and I have to work consciously not to call on these individuals first.

There is one more underlying premise to Hongo's reaction. In his critique of the term Asian American, Hongo was addressing certain social constructions within the Asian American community, particularly in ethnic studies departments. These constructions would limit the artist to some party line that designates a "true" Asian American art as opposed to a "false" Asian American art, or which tends to look at art solely through the lens of social realism. One example of such a construction occurs in the introductory editorial essays of the *Big Aiiieeeee!!!*, where a binary opposition is used to divide Asian American writers into the "real" and the "fake." Such constructions simplify both the work of individual Asian American writers and the field as a whole; moreover, they mirror the hierarchical models of the dominant culture and posit a questionable opposition between the center and margins within Asian American writing and within Asian culture. As

Trinh T. Minh-ha has observed, there are centers within the margins and margins within the center. Asian or even Chinese or Japanese culture is not a monolith, is not one solid unity. How can we therefore designate a true or central Asian American culture? Finally, as Li-Young Lee suggests, terms such as Asian American, with their heavily sociological baggage, can function like a Social Security number and cause us to ignore the singularities and spiritual aspects of our experience, can simplify our examinations and depictions of our existence.

And yet, our thinking about these matters must take place on many levels and ought to entertain, I think, a range of contradictory stances. Despite his critique of an Asian American essentialism, Hongo also objected to the way a critique of the social constructions of the Asian American community could become, in the mind of the white questioner, a way of dismantling the notion of an Asian American community or an Asian American writer. Similarly, when I hear certain Asian American writers expressing a desire to be considered "just a writer," I sometimes sense that the underlying desire is to be considered "just like a white writer." When such an Asian American writer says this, who pops into his or her head when he or she hears the word writer—John Updike or Toni Morrison? Virginia Woolf or Zora Neale Hurston? In this way, the attempt to move beyond categories tends to reinforce a submersion of questions of power and cultural indoctrination.

Even if the category of Asian American is, in many ways, a fictive construct, it still has its uses, and it can function as a needed, if imperfect, tool in speaking of our experiences. As Marilyn Chin said on the panel: "We can't erase our difference, we look a certain way, and the world responds." At the same time, in protest against this response, something else arises, a different way of looking at ourselves. "We are from different classes, we come to America," she said to Li-Young Lee, "and...we were born again. These are Japanese Americans and just five decades ago, the Japanese oppressed us [the Chinese]. The fact that Asian American is part of our vocabulary...means we are born again as something wonderful, we are brought together. We transcended our parents or the problems of our parents and our ancestors."

One can say that we, as Asian Americans, are bound together by a common history. But what is that history? Certainly, the Asian immigration laws or other racist phenomena do not recognize our ethnic differences. But beyond that, our common history becomes something we define and learn about, something in the making. If we reject that history, we have little to bind us together. The less we know about other Asian American ethnic groups, the less we are bound together. In other words, the term and the cohesion it fosters are things we create.

At the same time, Asian America is something that exists, which we are just beginning to define. I know that when I sit with a mixed group of Asian Americans it feels differently from when I am the sole Asian American in a group of whites. I know that when I sit with Japanese Americans it feels differently than if I'm with a mixed group of Asian Americans. And I know that when I'm with a group of people of color it feels differently from being with any of these other groups. And as an artist, I know that when I read my work to an Asian American audience the response is different than from a white audience. There is less bewilderment and more empathetic understanding. From other poets, less jealousy or inattention and more camaraderie and encouragement.

I don't feel I have found a language to express these differences. I don't have ways of categorizing them. I know all this comes out of the experiences of racism I share with other Asian Americans or other people of color, and that this experience is not merely one of insults or prejudice, but also entails a search for a place where I feel safe to own and express my own experience and alienation from this culture. I know, too, these differences involve a particular relationship to history. When I get together with Japanese American friends, our discussion of the impact of the internment camps can be more detailed, more exploratory. I know that in an Asian American or Japanese American group I suddenly become aware of my own singularity in a new way, that my own experience is revealed with a new depth of understanding, a depth I don't think those who aren't Asian American or Japanese American can quite see. In such encounters, I feel myself plunging beyond the social imagination and the societal conceptions of ourselves, moving into a realm beyond categories or labels, where a new language must be invented. And yet, at the same time, through a label like Japanese American, I can name a certain feeling of togetherness I am encountering with others in the group.

Certainly, this was my experience spending time together with the other poets on the panel, Marilyn Chin, Garrett Hongo, and Li-Young Lee. And I think it was their experience too. When I first saw Garrett Hongo on the Bill Moyers program on contemporary poetry, I had the sense of seeing a Doppelgänger of myself. I had never seen nor heard a Japanese American man talk about literature on television. The experience was so unprecedented that I almost could not process it; there was no language to encompass it. As I've gotten to know Garrett, I've come to understand how different we are—in temperament, in family and class background, in our sexuality, in our relationship to the community of Japanese Americans. For instance, I grew up in an all-white mainly Jewish suburb; Hongo grew up in Japanese American communities in Volcano, Hawaii, and Gardena, California, and possesses a deeper knowledge of Japanese American history than I do. From the beginning, our friendship has helped me move toward articulating the possibilities of being a Japanese American. Similarly, during the conference, Marilyn Chin read a poem that mentioned in a disparaging way, Ren Xu Kai, a warlord who was the first president of China. When Li-Young Lee told her that Ren Xu Kai was Li-Young Lee's grandfather, she kidded Lee about the fact that she was from the peasant class with "big feet" while he was from the aristocracy. Later, Lee said that listening to Chin's poems, he suddenly realized that their irony and humor gave a breadth and life to her poetry that was absent in his own, that his own pursuit of "high seriousness" was based on a literary convention, was part of a European conception. As we talked, I sensed we all felt more free to explore our own experiences and, at the same time, to alter our directions, to begin anew; this freedom came from a sense of safety and acceptance we did not always feel, especially among white poets.

In one sense, the process we are undergoing is not new. It has taken place elsewhere, at other times. I think of those points where the colonized, educated in the lore of the colonizer, reverencing the colonizer as master, suddenly sees the colonizer not as something to be aspired to or emulated, as a superior being or the center of attention, but as a human being, a product of history, someone whose power is temporary and unjustly held. What happens then is a turning inward, a discovery and a creation, as well as a retrieval, of a new set of myths, heroes, and gods, and a history that has been occluded or ignored.

10

THE PREDICAMENT OF FILIPINOS IN THE UNITED STATES

'Where are you from? When are you going back?'

E. SAN JUAN, Jr.

We live in a racist society, a racial formation called "the United States of America," where—and this is not news at this late day—people of color suffer daily from racial, national, and class oppression. And in the same breath we Filipinos, together with others, struggle daily to survive and affirm our human dignity. Jamil Abdullah Al-Amin (formerly H. Rap Brown) stated in 1987 that in the United States "Racism is to America what Catholicism is to the Vatican. Racism is the religion, and violence is its liturgy to carry it out." [1] Signs of the times—like Willie Horton and Rodney King, not to mention thousands of everyday incidents in university campuses

---

This chapter is based on a lecture delivered at the University of Colorado, Boulder on April 26, 1992.

and urban battlegrounds like Bensonhurst, Miami, Milwaukee, Detroit, and recently Los Angeles, where the unprecedented rebellion sent tremors through the boardrooms of the ruling class. Or in places such as Jersey City and Detroit, where hatred of Asians and Arabs is peaking. All these indicate that Al-Amin's observation, instead of being rendered obsolete, is being confirmed in ways that frighten some and paradoxically elicit the homage of its victims in others.

By the year 2000 the Filipino body count will surpass the two million mark. We are rapidly becoming the majority (21 percent of the total in 1992) of the Asian American population of nearly 10 million. More than half-a-million (664,938 to be exact) entered the country between 1965 and 1984. This third (even fourth) wave of immigration comprised mostly professionals and technical workers, unlike their predecessors, the farmworkers of Hawaii and California and Alaskan cannery hands memorialized in Carlos Bulosan's *America Is in the Heart* (1948). Over 170,000 Filipinos enter the country legally every year. This doesn't include about 25,000 Filipinos serving in the U.S. Navy (chiefly as stewards and mess boys), a number greater than those serving in the Philippine Navy itself—an anomalous phenomenon where Filipino citizens function as mercenaries eager to serve their former colonial master. [2]

Because of this demographic change, and for other reasons, now is an opportune time to assert our autonomy from the sweeping rubric of "Asian American," even as we continue to unite with other Asians in coalitions for common political demands. There is a specific reason why the Filipino nationality in the United States (even though the majority of U.S. citizens still cannot distinguish us from the Asian Others) needs to confront its own destiny as a dislocated and "transported" people: that reason is of course the fact that the Philippines was a colony of the United States for over half a century and persists as a neo-colony of the nation-state in whose territory we find ourselves today.

The reality of U.S. colonial subjugation and its profoundly enduring effects—something most people cannot even begin to fathom, let alone acknowledge—distinguish Filipinos from the Chinese, Japanese, Koreans, and others from the Asian continent.

To understand what this means is already to resolve halfway the predicament and crisis of dislocation, fragmentation, uprooting, loss of traditions, exclusion, and alienation—tremendous spiritual and physical ordeals that people of color are forced to undergo when Western powers fight and divide the world into spheres of domination for the sake of capital accumulation, when populations are expediently shuffled around the global chessboard of warring interests.

We see this crisis of deracination and exile (permanent or temporary) in the phenomenon of the "brain drain," a factor that partly explains the continuing underdevelopment of the Third World. It is no joke that the Philippines, now an economic basket case in Asia, every year produces thousands of doctors, nurses, scientists, and engineers for the world market. As exchangeable commodities, many of them immediately head for the United States—in addition, more than a million "warm body exports" now inhabit the Middle East and Europe—while in the Philippines, where 80 percent of the people are poor and 30 percent of the children malnourished, most towns and villages don't have any decent medical/health care (not to mention other vital social services) to sustain a decent quality of life for all their citizens.

All studies of the 1980 and the 1990 census show that Filipinos, despite being highly educated, enjoy the lowest average income among Asians. We are historically denied access to occupations in management and other prestigious careers. According to sociologists Victor Nee and Jimy Sanders, Filipinos remain a "disadvantaged minority group," concentrated in low-skilled and low-status jobs with low mean income. I am not referring to those Filipino doctors and a handful of corporate consultants each earning a quarter of a million dollars every year. But despite this picture of structural disadvantage, we find ourselves astonished at the celebratory thrust of the impressions and responses of Filipinos recorded by Ronald Takaki in his instructive history of Asian Americans, *Strangers from a Different Shore*. Takaki cites the following testimonies from recent Filipino immigrants:

"In the United States, hard work is rewarded. In the Philippines, it is part of the struggle to survive." Images of American abundance, carried home by the *Balikbayans,* or immigrants returning to their homeland for visits, have pulled frustrated Filipinos to this country. When Carlos Patalinghug went back for a visit in 1981 after working in the United States for 10 years, he told his friends: "If you work, you'll get milk and honey in America." Other Balikbayans described the United States as a "paradise."[3]

We all know that comparisons are always made to what the person would have earned in the Philippines assuming she was employed—the exchange rate of dollars to pesos, ignoring cost of living disparities, indeed works miracles. Isn't this mutable exchange rate—index of the unequal relations of power between North and South—the opium of the masses, not religion?

Incredible is the story of Maria Ofalsa who came in 1926 and two years after was hospitalized "from overwork and exhaustion"; her family experienced horrendous prejudice, harassment, eviction which they quietly bore throughout the Depression and up to the fifties. Finally, after getting her citizenship in 1952 and still aware of the racism around her, she tells her compatriots: "When you come here to the United States remember this is not our country, so you try to be nice and don't lose your temper and try to be friendly and don't put on a sour face."[4] Frankly I don't know whether we should consider Maria a saint or a fool. Some of us know that Filipinos, faced with rampant paralegal violence in Watsonville, California and other places in the late twenties and thirties, did not act nicely when they initiated militant actions, like those by the Filipino Labor Union in 1933 as it tried to organize 30,000 compatriots. Or those by the Agricultural Workers Organizing Committee in 1959, which led to the historic Grape Strike of 1965 and laid the immediate foundation for the establishment of the United Farm Workers of America. The epochal inter-ethnic union struggles of Filipinos and Japanese workers in Hawaii in 1920 and 1924 also deserve tribute and commemoration. Philip

Vera Cruz, a distinguished veteran union leader, declared in the sixties: "I think the only way to change things is to break up the corporations and weaken the enemy... Agribusiness is built on the exploitation of farmworkers ... It's the same struggle all over the world, many fronts of the same struggle."

Contemporaries of Maria Ofalsa, Manuel Buaken, and Carlos Bulosan probably lost their temper then. Buaken wrote in 1940:

> Where is the heart of America? I am one of the many thousands of young men born under the American Flag, raised as loyal idealistic Americans under your promise of equality for all ... Once here we are met by exploiters, shunted into slums, greeted by gamblers and prostitutes, taught only the worst in your civilization.[5]

Bulosan also lost his temper when he summed up his experiences in the thirties and forties: "I came to know afterward that in many ways it was a crime to be a Filipino in California."

It might be instructive to recall that although over 175,000 Filipinos in the United States in the thirties were officially designated "nationals," wards under American "tutelage" and without the rights of citizens, in 1934 with the passage of the Tydings-McDuffie Act, Buaken and Bulosan and their compatriots suddenly became aliens. They were "birds of passage" trapped in the promised land. Earlier they had been forbidden to marry Caucasians; during the Depression, they were barred from owning land and receiving public assistance. In 1940, they were subjected to another humiliation: All Filipinos had to register and be fingerprinted like ordinary criminals.

Not altogether unprecedented, the sisters of Maria Ofalsa today have turned out to be "troublemakers." In another continent, amid the utter indifference of the Philippine government to the plight of thousands of domestics in the Middle East, we recently learned that one of these brutalized Filipinas, a certain Lourana Crow Rafael, 44, is accused of killing a member of the Kuwaiti royal family, Sheika Latifa Abdullah Al-Jaber Al-Sabah, after the Sheika refused the domestic's request to travel to her home country in the wake of the enormous terrors before and after the Gulf War.[6]

Talk of losing one's temper under those circumstances! How can we even begin to imagine that scenario (even assuming that our domestic is not being framed) without lapsing into another mystery-filled Hollywood banality! Recently, two planeloads of Filipina domestics arrived in Manila from Kuwait bearing tales of cruel and inhumane treatment, rape, horrible physical and psychic tortures, which some Westerners find incredible and fantastic.

With the formal independence of the Philippines in 1946, and the coordinated resistance of Filipino workers here in the late forties and fifties—in particular among Alaskan cannery workers—to racist violence and persecution, a new sensibility emerged among the second generation of Filipinos. Most of those who came of age in the great civil rights struggles of the sixties and the anti-war movement of the early seventies articulated the Filipino protest against racial and national oppression in sympathy with the resurgent anti-imperialist movement in the Philippines against the U.S.-Marcos dictatorship. Many Filipinos born here in the United States matured during the "Great Transformation" of the sixties and linked their struggles with the heroic ordeals of the *manongs*—in such mass coalitions around the International Hotel in San Francisco and union organizing of farm workers. (There's a whole history still to be written about these not-yet-forgotten struggles.) When the eighties arrived, the impulse of opposition and criticism seemed to subside. I quote from a letter written by a Filipina immigrant to the *Hartford Courant* at the time of Aquino's assassination in 1983:

> For me, the killing hit home in more ways than one.
> I was born a Filipino. That may seem like an easy statement to make, but even as I write it, I am amazed at the embarrassment I used to feel. Ever since my parents brought me to the United States, I had been ashamed of who I am and ashamed of my nation.
> When friends at school said it was disgusting to see my mother serve fish with the head still intact, or for my father to eat rice with his hands, or to learn that stewed dogs and goats were some examples of Filipino

delicacies, I took their side. I accused my own of being unsanitary in their eating habits...

And when Marcos flaunted his tyranny and declared martial law in 1972, and my aunt said that it was the best thing that ever happened to the Philippines, as long as you kept your mouth shut, I accused Filipinos of lacking the guts to fight for themselves...

But everything changed for me when that man [Benigno Aquino] I had laughed at landed in my homeland and died on the airport tarmac.

For the first time I accused myself of not having enough faith in, and hope for, my own people. Maybe because I'm older now, maybe because of the assassination, I see things differently.

In the past I felt that I had no right to be proud of my people. Now, with the cruel Marcos regime tottering, I have finally awakened. Filipinos all over the world need the strength that comes with pride, now more than ever. It is time for all of us to speak up, regardless of the consequences.[7]

This woman refused to follow Maria Ofalsa's advice to keep her mouth shut and behave nicely. Unfortunately we have few like her. Understandably enough, most Filipinos are busy making money to survive and support relatives in the Philippines. They don't want to have anything to do with what's going on politically in their country of origin (or even here, for that matter) even though every American who encounters them will connect them to those islands—are they still "our colonies in the Caribbean"? How many Filipinos have we heard confessing to their American "hosts" how "my country [of origin] is shit!" and how I am so happy and proud to finally be an American citizen? These aliens—who have renounced their homeland but are not accepted anywhere else—hang in the limbo of what Franz Fanon, in *The Wretched of the Earth,* designates as the symbolic violence of the self-denying colonized.

As to be expected, these Filipinos have dutifully internalized the ethos of bureaucratic individualism, the ABCs of vulgar utilitarianism, inculcated by the media and other ideological apparatuses in the Philippines and reproduced here in the practices of everyday life. Although some still pay homage to the rituals of the traditional Filipino family, many have now transformed themselves into the living exemplars of neo-social Darwinism during a recession. They believe they are adapting to the mores of their adopted country and are making themselves "true" Americans, "the genuine Stateside articles."

We know that in instances where hospital strikes occur in any big city, planeloads of nurses from the Philippines are ordered by the cost-cutting management to function as "scabs," a title they surely do not deserve. (Note that the 50,000 Filipino nurses in the United States send back home over $100 million annually, more than the earnings from Philippine gold exports; and that the taxes on the remittance of Filipinos in the Middle East and domestics in Canada, Japan, Hong Kong, and elsewhere, is the number one dollar earner for the Philippine government.) In one major case in 1946, 7,000 Filipino workers and their families were recruited by the Hawaii Sugar Planters Association to break The Great Sugar Workers Strike. In due time, however, they quickly realized that their exploiters were using them and so joined the strikers organized by the International Longshoremen and Warehousemen's Union.[8]

In the eighties, despite the fact that a larger proportion of recent Filipino immigrants possess superior technical and professional skills, we still found a pattern of consistent downgrading and underemployment. How is this to be explained or justified? Pharmacists, lawyers, teachers, dentists, engineers, and medical technicians who have logged years of experience are often forced to engage in sales, clerical, and wage labor. The evidence shows that Euro-Americans still think Filipinos are good only at manual work in the fields. (One brilliant Filipino lawyer I know was so humiliated by Euro-Americans who nourished such racist attitudes that even his children experienced psychic damage in witnessing their father's suffering.) In the past, Filipinos were considered merchandise listed next to "fertilizer" or "manure" by farm proprietors. Today, the demand for Filipino nurses and domestics—contract labor avidly promoted by the Philippine government—may represent for certain government bureaucrats an improvement in our international status as supplier of cheap labor and other resources to the industrialized metropoles.

In the racially stratified and ethnically segmented labor market of the United States, as well as in the rest of the world, Filipinos occupy the lower strata, primarily in service occupations such as food, health, and cleaning; because of this, Filipino men earn only about two-thirds of the average income of white men. Despite these problems of discrimination in the labor market and underemployment, Filipinos as a group (for various reasons not entirely cultural) have not developed entrepreneurial skills for small ethnic enterprises such as those Koreans and Indians in the big cities undertake.

How can we explain the persisting neo-colonial subjugation of Filipino bodies and psyches, so many "manacled minds" impoverished by learned self-denigration? Why is it that unlike other racial minorities Filipinos are unable to resolve the crisis of expatriation and uprooting, of alienation and national marginalization, through strong and enduring commitment to promoting the larger good of one community? Why is it that this community is non-existent, and if there, at best fragmented and inutile? Why is it that Filipinos in the diaspora don't feel or understand their subjugation as a race and nationality? Perhaps I am asking rhetorical questions. One wonders whether forming an identity-based community is the answer. Recall the notorious Hilario Moncado whose Filipino Federation of America (founded in 1925 in Los Angeles and fueled by supposed ethnic pride) opposed the unionization efforts of Filipinos in Hawaii. One more proof that pursuing liberation via ethnicity alone is suicidal!

Various U.S. experts have ventured answers to explain the continuing "invisibility" or "forgottenness" of the Filipinos in the United States and its corollary, the underdevelopment of the homeland. Theodore Friend for one blames the historic legacy of Spain fostered by Marcos and Aquino, a legacy that plagues Latin American countries as manifested in such markers of dysfunctionality as "autocracy, gross corruption, bloated debt, a deprofessionalized military, private armies, death squads." Remarking on Aquino's charisma as "Mother of Sorrows" unable to clean up "the patronage ridden" civil service and "the anarchy of ruling families" which define Philippine politics, Friend urges Filipinos to "shake free of Hispanic tradition."[9] But what happened to the period of U.S. tutelage, from 1898 to 1946 and thereafter, the asymmetrical power relations between "the bastion of the Free World" and its erstwhile colony? (This is also the message of Stanley Karnow in his lengthy apologia for American imperialism, *In Our Image*.[10] Nowhere does Friend even mention U.S. violence and its manipulation of the landed and comprador elite in its colonial conquest and domination of the Philippines for almost 50 years! For his part, historian Peter Stanley does mention this, but only to praise it as "the relatively libertarian character of U.S. rule" over Taft's "little brown brothers." The much-touted U.S. legacy of schools, roads, public health programs, artesian wells, "democratic" politicians, and "the most gregariously informal, backslapping imperialist rulers known to history" serves to explain, for Stanley, why Filipinos cherish a "deferential friendship" for Americans.[11] Does this then explain why Fred Cordova, in his pictorial essay *Filipinos: Forgotten Asian Americans* boasts that "An estimated one million innocent Filipino men, women and children died while defending Americanism during World War II from 1941 to 1945"?[12] Indeed isn't the appropriate question: Are so many Filipinos really so screwed up that they would make such a sacrifice? Think of it: one million natives defending the cause of Lone Ranger and Charlie Chan. One million dark-skinned natives sacrificing their lives for Americanism. As for celebrating Filipino "firsts" in order to generate ethnic pride, what does it signify if we learn that Filipinos were the first this and that, to wit, the first Asians to cross the Pacific Ocean for the North American continent or that their descendants in New Orleans, Louisiana, fought with the pirate Jean Lafitte and the Americans during the War of 1812? Would such knowledge relieve the pathos of a situation bewailed so often by Bienvenido Santos, inventor of the myth of Filipinos as "lovely people": "Think of the impotence of Filipino exiles in America who are displaced and uprooted wandering in strange cities."[13]

To return to our American mentors: Stanley suggests that Filipinos who come from different regions of the islands form fraternal groups based on localities of origin because they find it "difficult to conceive of each other as sharing a national identity." While such a proposition is flawed by a functionalist bias in blaming the victims for the inadequacy of their culture, it nevertheless prompts one to reflect on the following: We Filipinos don't have any real identification of ourselves as belonging to a nation because that nation of all the classes and sectors in the Philippines is non-existent; that organic embodiment of the national-popular will has not yet come into being, and has in fact been aborted and suppressed by U.S. military power when it was being born during the revolution of 1896-1898, a culmination of three centuries of revolts against Spanish rule. We don't have a popular-democratic nation to serve as the matrix and locus of authentic sharing and belonging—that nation is still emerging, a manifold complex of antagonisms and struggles still in the agony of unfolding. What we call the Philippines today, a society where state power is controlled by a comprador-oligarchic elite whose interests center on the preservation of an unjust and unequal status quo, is for all practical purposes still a dependent formation, virtually an appendage of the United States ruling class, notwithstanding substantial gains in decolonization during the last 20 years climaxing in the Philippine Senate's decision to remove the U.S. bases, thanks to the prodding of Mt. Pinatubo.

Consequently, according to the Filipinologist H. Brett Melendy, Filipinos up to the fifties were perceived as a social problem in the United States, because of their "cultural backgrounds and value systems" that pivot around the family and indigenous kinship structure.[14] Melendy blames the Filipinos for their sojourner mentality, not the racializing apparatuses of the U.S. state or the racially hierarchic institutions of civil society, for their exclusion, their exploitation, their abject poverty. Apparently, Filipinos are miraculously able to retain and assert their cultural values despite a legacy of colonialism and imperialism at home and abject poverty and discrimination stateside. Ironically, had Filipinos retained these "cultural values," we would be better positioned to unite and construct our community in symbolic rituals of autonomy and integrity, to represent it as a coherent, resourceful, sustainable locus of meaning and value.

This is the predicament we Filipinos face as we enter the threshold of a new century. In the crisis of dislocation and fragmentation that we continue to experience in a racist polity, how can we reconstitute a unified if heterogenous community here that can generate a discourse and practice of collective resistance, of autonomy and integrity?

In 1989, I sent a letter to *Philippine News* in San Francisco posing questions that elaborate possible stages of our ethnogenesis, questions such as the following: What really distinguishes the Filipino community here in its historical formation? How is it tied to the history of the Philippines as a colony of Western powers? What specific elements of immigrant history, the suffering and resistance of various waves, should we select and emphasize that will mobilize and unify Filipinos? What struggles should we engage in to forge a dynamic and cohesive identity, struggles that will actualize the substance of civil and human rights? What political and moral education should we undertake to develop and heighten the consciousness of a distinct Filipino identity and political presence in the United States? Finally, on what moral or ethical principles (superior and alternative to the bureaucratic individualism of "free market" capitalism) should we ground this Filipino community?

This is not just a question of what do I want? and with whom shall I cooperate to acquire what I want?—the pragmatic rationality of means-ends. The question of what we are going to do cannot be answered unless we answer a prior question: In what events—or narratives, if you will—that are now proceeding in contemporary world history shall we participate? Is it a narrative of assimilation and integration, or a narrative of emancipation and national self-determination? Is there a universalizing or transcendent multiracial narrative, a global narrative that subsumes and guarantees our self-empowering, if long-delayed, ethnogenesis?

Some historians entertain the belief that the reason Americans had the notion that Filipinos were dog-eating savages can be traced to the widely publicized ethnographic exhibit of primitive tribesmen that the U.S. colonial government in the Philippines helped to organize for the Louisiana Purchase Exposition at St. Louis in 1904. But I think it is misleading to ascribe to this minor spectacle an exorbitant power that might even overshadow the now mythical stature of the Iron Butterfly's (Imelda Marcos) shoe fetish—a relatively innocuous instance of conspicuous consumption that nonetheless gave the Philippines a niche in the American consumerist imagination: "Don't those little brown savages usually go barefoot?" Whatever the narcotic power of these media spectacles may be, if we continue to delude ourselves that we are not objects of racist interpellations—that we are in fact on the way to successful incorporation into the U.S. nation-state—then history might repeat itself: We shall for the moment be paraded again as dutiful little brown brothers and sisters civilized by American tutelage, a hybrid subspecies soon to be made extinct in some proverbial melting-pot, a quaint cross between the comic-strip icon of the Mexican *bandido* and those "inscrutable Orientals" who should be shipped back as soon as possible—"go back where you came from" is the taunt I often hear—thus restoring the purity of the body politic. A mythical purity as an obsession, the myth of purity feeding on and nourishing white racism.

What we need to do, the agenda for constituting the Filipino community as an agent of historic change in a racist society, cannot of course be prescribed by one individual. The mapping and execution of such a project can only be the product of a collective effort by every one who claims to be a Filipino in the process of engaging in actual, concrete struggles, in conjunction with the efforts of other people of color in the United States to rid society of the material conditions that beget and reproduce class, gender, and racial oppression. The future in the twenty-first century is there for us to shape—if we dare to struggle, dare to sacrifice and win!

Notes

1. *Time,* February 2, 1987.
2. Catholic Institute for International Relations, *The Labour Trade* (London: CIIR, 1987), 42.
3. Ronald Takaki, *Strangers from A Different Shore* (Boston: Little, Brown & Co., 1989), 433.
4. Quoted in Lawrence Johnson, "Filipinos," *Rice,* July 1988.
5. Buaken quoted in Carey McWilliams, *Brothers Under the Skin* (Boston, MA: Little, Brown & Co., 1964), 248.
6. "Kuwaitis are 'treating us like animals,'" *USA Today,* February 21, 1992.
7. *Hartford Courant,* September 12, 1983.
8. *The Labour Trade,* 30 and 36.
9. Theodore Friend, "Latin Ghosts Haunt An Asian Nation," *Heritage,* December 1989, 4.
10. Stanley Karnow, *In Our Image,* (New York: Random House, 1989.)
11. Peter Stanley, "The *Manongs* of California," *Philippines-U.S. Free Press,* November 1985, 4.
12. Fred Cordova, *Filipino: Forgotten Asian Americans,* (Iowa: Kendall/Hunt, 1983), 221.
13. Quoted in Leonor Aurens Briscoe, "PAJ Interview: Bienvenido N. Santos," *Philippine American Journal* (Summer/Fall 1990), 13.
14. H. Brett Melendy, "Filipinos," *Harvard Encyclopedia of American Ethnic Groups* (Cambridge, MA: Harvard University Press, 1980), 362.

11

IS THE ETHNIC 'AUTHENTIC' IN THE DIASPORA?

R. RADHAKRISHNAN

My 11-year-old son asks me, "Am I Indian or American?" The question excites me and I think of the not-too-distant future when we will discuss the works of Salman Rushdie, Toni Morrison, Amitav Ghosh, Jamaica Kincaid, Bessie Head, Amy Tan, Maxine Hong Kingston, and many others who have agonized over the question of identity through their multivalent narratives. I tell him he is both and offer him brief and down-to-earth definitions of ethnicity and how it relates to nationality and citizenship. He follows me closely and says, "Yeah, Dad (or he might have said Appa), I am both," and a slight inflection in his voice underscores the word "both," as his two hands make a symmetrical gesture on either side of his body. I am persuaded, for I have seen him express deep indignation and frustration when friends, peers, teachers, and coaches mispronounce his name in cavalier fashion. He pursues the matter with a passion bordering on the pedagogical, until his name comes out correctly on

My thanks to Henry Finder for permission to reprint this essay, parts of which were originally published in *Transitions 54*. I also wish to thank Karin Aguilar-San Juan and Sonia Shah for inviting me to think through some of these issues. This essay is dedicated to my son Surya, and to Naina, Sayantini, and their heterogenous generation.

alien lips. I have also heard him narrate to his "mainstream" friends stories from the *Ramayana* and the *Mahabharatha* with an infectious enthusiasm for local detail, and negotiate nuances of place and time with great sensitivity.

My son comes back to me and asks, "But you and Amma (or did he say Mom?) are not U.S. citizens?" I tell him that we are Indian citizens who live here as resident aliens. "Oh, yes, I remember we have different passports," he says and walks away.

At a recent Deepavali (a significant Hindu religious festival) get-together of the local India Association (well before the horrendous destruction of the *Babri masjid* by Hindu zealots), I listen to an elderly Indian man explain to a group of young first-generation Indian American children the festival's significance. He goes on and on about the contemporary significance of Lord Krishna, who has promised to return to the world in human form during times of crisis to punish the wicked and protect the good. During this lecture, I hear not a word to distinguish Hindu identity from Indian identity, not a word about present day communal violence in India in the name of Hindu fundamentalism, and not even an oblique mention of the ongoing crisis in Ayodhya. In a sense, these egregious oversights and omissions do not matter, for the first-generation American kids, the intended recipients of this ethnic lesson, hardly pay attention: They sleep, run around, or chatter among themselves, their mouths full of popcorn. I do not know whether I am more angry with the elderly gentleman for his disingenuous ethnic narrative or with the younger generation, who in their putative assimilation do not seem to care about ethnic origins.

I begin with these two episodes because they exemplify a number of issues and tensions that inform ethnicity. I imagine that the main problem that intrigued my son was this: How could some*one* be both *one* and something *other*? How could the unity of identity have more than one face or name? If my son is both Indian and American, which *one* is he *really*? Which is the real self and which the other? How do these two selves coexist and how do they weld into one identity? How is ethnic identity related to national identity? Is this relationship hierarchically structured, such that the "national" is supposed to subsume and transcend ethnic identity, or does this relationship produce a hyphenated identity, such as African-American, Asian-American, and so forth, where the hyphen marks a dialogic and non-hierarchic conjuncture? What if identity is exclusively ethnic and not national at all? Could such an identity survive (during these days of bloody "ethnic cleansing") and be legitimate, or would society construe this as a non-viable "difference," that is, experientially authentic but not deserving of hegemony?

The Indian gentleman's address to his audience of first-generation Indian Americans raises several insidious and potentially harmful conflicts. First it uses religious (Hindu) identity to empower Indian ethnicity in the United States, which then masquerades as Indian nationalism. More on this later. What does the appeal to "roots and origins" mean in this context, and what is it intended to achieve? Is ethnicity a mere flavor, an ancient smell to be relived as nostalgia? Is it a kind of superficial blanket to be worn over the substantive U.S. identity? Or is *Indianness* being advocated as a basic immutable form of being that triumphs over changes, travels, and dislocations?

The narrative of ethnicity in the United States might run like this. During the initial phase, immigrants suppress ethnicity in the name of pragmatism and opportunism. To be successful in the New World, they must actively assimilate, and therefore, hide their distinct ethnicity. This phase, similar to the Booker T. Washington-era in African American history, gives way to a Du Boisian-period that refuses to subsume political, civil, and moral revolutions under mere strategies of economic betterment. In the call for total revolution that follows, immigrants reassert ethnicity in all its autonomy. The third phase seeks the hyphenated integration of ethnic identity with national identity under conditions that do not privilege the "national" at the expense of the "ethnic." We must keep in mind that in the United States the renaming of ethnic identity in national terms produces a preposterous effect. Take the case of the Indian immigrant. Her naturalization into American citizenship simultaneously minoritizes her identity. She is now reborn as an ethnic minority American citizen.

Is this empowerment, or marginalization? This new American citizen must think of her Indian self as an ethnic self that defers to her nationalized American status. The culturally and politically hegemonic Indian identity is now a mere qualifier: "ethnic." Does this transformation suggest that identities and ethnicities are not a matter of fixed and stable selves but rather the results and products of fortuitous travels and recon-textualizations? Could this mean that how identity relates to place is itself the expression of a shifting equilibrium? If ethnic identity is a strategic response to a shifting sense of time and place, how is it possible to have a theory of ethnic identity posited on the principle of a natural and native self? Is ethnicity nothing but, to use the familiar formula, what ethnicity does? Is ethnic selfhood an end in itself, or is it a necessary but determinate phase to be left behind when the time is right to inaugurate the "post-ethnic"? With some of these general concerns in mind, I would now like to address the Indian diaspora in the United States.

This chapter began with a scenario both filial and pedagogic. The child asks a question or expresses some doubt or anxiety and the parent resolves the problem. The parent brings together two kinds of authority: the authority of a parent to transmit and sustain a certain pattern generationally and the authority of a teacher based on knowledge and information. Thus, in my response to my son, "You are both," I was articulating myself as teacher as well as parent. But how do I (as a parent) know that I know? Do I have an answer by virtue of my parenthood, or does the answer have a pedagogic authority that has nothing to do with being a parent? In other words, how is my act of speaking for my daughter or son different from a teacher speaking for a student? What about the ancient Indian *gurukula* system (characterized by male privilege) that insisted that society should wean the child away from the parents for purposes of knowledge and learning? Is knowledge *natural,* or is it a questioning of origins? In either case, is there room for the student's own self-expression? How are we to decide whether or not the "conscious" knowledge of the teacher and the "natural" knowledge of the parent are relevant in the historical instance of the child/student?

Let's look at yet another episode as a counterpoint to my teacherly episode with my son. During the last few years, I have talked and listened to a number of young, gifted Indian children of the diaspora who, like my son, were born here and are thus "natural" American citizens. I was startled when they told me that they had grown up with a strong sense of being exclusively Indian, and the reason was that they had experienced little during their growing years that held out promise of first-class American citizenship. Most of them felt they could not escape being *marked* as different by virtue of their skin color, their family background, and other ethnic and unassimilated traits. Many of them recited the reality of a double-life, the ethnic private life and the "American" public life, with very little mediation between the two. For example, they talked about being the targets of racial slurs and racialized sexist slurs, and they remembered not receiving the total understanding of their parents who did not quite "get it." Sure, the parents understood the situation in an academic and abstract way and would respond with the fierce rhetoric of civil rights and anti-racism, but the fact was that the parents had not gone through similar experiences during their childhoods. Although the home country is indeed replete with its own divisions, phobias, and complexes, the racial line of color is not one of them. Thus, if the formulaic justification of parental wisdom is that the parent "has been there before," the formula does not apply here. Is the prescriptive wisdom of "you are both" relevant?

Within the diaspora, how should the two generations address each other? I would suggest for starters that we candidly admit that learning and knowledge, particularly in the diaspora, can only be a two-way street. The problem here is more acute than the unavoidable "generation gap" between students/young adults and teachers/parents. The tensions between the old and new homes create the problem of divided allegiances the two generations experience differently. The very organicity of the family and the community, displaced by travel and relocation, must be renegotiated and redefined. The two generations have different starting points and different givens. This phenomenon of historical rupture within the "same" community demands careful and rigorous analysis. The older generation cannot afford to invoke India in an authoritarian mode to resolve problems in the diaspora, and the younger generation would be ill-advised to indulge in a spree of forgetfulness about "where they have come from." It is vital that the two generations empathize and desire to understand and appreciate patterns of experience not their own.

What does "being Indian" mean in the United States? How can one be and live Indian without losing clout and leverage as Americans? How can one transform the so-called mainstream American identity into the image of the many ethnicities that constitute it? We should not pretend we are living in some idealized "little India" and not in the United States. As Maxine Hong Kingston demonstrates painfully in *Woman Warrior,* both the home country and the country of residence could become mere "ghostly" locations and the result can only be a double depoliticization. For example, the anguish in this book is *relational*; it is not exclusively about China or the United States. The home country is not "real" in its own terms and yet it is real enough to impede Americanization, and the "present home" is materially real and yet not real enough to feel authentic. Whereas at home, one could be just Indian or Chinese, here one is constrained to become Chinese-, Indian-, or Asian American. This leads us to the question: Is the "Indian" in Indian and the "Indian" in Indian American the same and therefore interchangeable? Which of the two is authentic, and which merely strategic or reactive? To what extent does the "old country" function as a framework and regulate our transplanted identities within the diaspora? Should the old country be revered as a pre-given absolute, or is it all right to invent the old country itself in response to our contemporary location? Furthermore, whose interpretation of India is correct: the older generation's or that of the younger; the insider's version or the diasporan?

These questions emphasize the reality that when people move, identities, perspectives, and definitions change. If the category "Indian" *seemed* secure, positive, and affirmative within India, the same term takes on a reactive, strategic character when it is pried loose from its nativity. The issue then is not just "being Indian" in some natural and self-evident way ("being Indian" naturally is itself a highly questionable premise given the debacle of nationalism, but that is not my present concern), but "cultivating

Indian-ness" self-consciously for certain reasons; for example, the reason could be one does not want to lose one's past or does not want to be homogenized namelessly, or one could desire to combat mainstream racism with a politicized deployment of one's own "difference." To put it simply, one's very being becomes polemical. Is there a true and authentic identity, more lasting than mere polemics and deeper than strategies?

Before I get into an analysis of this problem, I wish to sketch briefly a few responses to the home country that I consider wrong and quite dangerous. First, from the point of view of the assimilated generation, it is all too easy to want to forget the past and forfeit community in the name of the "free individual,"a path open to first-generation citizens. As Malcolm X, Du Bois, and others have argued, it is in the nature of a racist capitalist society to isolate and privatize the individual, and foster the myth of the equal and free individual unencumbered by either a sense of community or a critical sense of the past. As the Clarence Thomas nomination has amply demonstrated, the theme of "individual success" is a poisoned candy manufactured by capitalist greed in active complicity with a racist disregard for history. We cannot afford to forget that we live in a society that is profoundly anti-historical, and leaders represent us who believe that we have buried the memories of Vietnam in the sands of the Gulf War, which itself is remembered primarily as a high-tech game intended for visual pleasure. We must not underestimate the capacity of capitalism, superbly assisted by technology, to produce a phenomenology of the present so alluring in its immediacy as to seduce the consumer to forget the past and bracket the future.

The second path is the way of "Mississippi Masala," revelling uncritically in the commodification of hybridity. The two young lovers walk away into the rain in a Hollywood resolution of the agonies of history. Having found each other as "hybrids" in the here and now of the United States, the two young adults just walk out of their "prehistories" into the innocence of physical, heterosexual love. The past *sucks,* parents *suck,* Mississippi *sucks,* as do India and Uganda, and the only thing that matters is the bonding between two bodies that step off the pages of history, secure in their

225

"sanctioned ignorance," to use Gayatri Chakravorty Spivak's ring-ing phrase. What is disturbing about the "masala" resolution is that it seems to take on the question of history, but actually trivializes histories (there is more than one implicated here) and celebrates a causeless rebellion in the epiphany of the present. Just think of the racism awaiting the two lovers. In invoking the term "masala" superficially, the movie begs us to consume it as exotica and make light of the historical ingredients that go into making "masala." My point here is that individualized escapes (and corre-spondingly, the notion of the "history of the present" as a total break from the messy past) may serve an emotional need, but they do not provide an understanding of the histories of India, Uganda, or the racialized South.

What about the options open to the generation emotionally committed to India? First, it is important to make a distinction between *information about and knowledge of India* and an *emo-tional investment in India.* What can be shared cognitively between the two generations is the former. It would be foolish of me to expect that India will move my son the same way it moves me. It would be equally outrageous of me to claim that somehow my India is more real than his; my India is as much an invention or production as his. There is more than enough room for multiple versions of the same reality. But here again, our inventions and interpretations are themselves products of history and not subjective substitutes for history. The discovery of an "authentic" India cannot rule over the reality of multiple perspectives, and, moreover, we can not legislate or hand down authenticity from a position of untested moral or political high ground.

Second, my generation has to actively learn to find "Indian-ness" within and in conjunction with the minority-ethnic continuum in the United States. To go back to my conversations with the younger generation, it is important to understand that many of them confess to finding their "ethnic-Indian" identity (as distinct from the "Indian" identity experienced at home) not in isolation but in a coalition with other minorities. It is heartening to see that a number of students identify themselves under the Third World umbrella and have gone so far as to relate the "Third World out there" and "the there" and "the Third World within." (I am aware that the term "Third World" is deeply problematic and often promotes an insensitive de-differentiation of the many histories that comprise the Third World, but this term *when used by the groups that constitute it* has the potential to resist the dominant groups' divide-and-rule strategies.)

My generation is prone, as it ages, to take recourse to some mythic India as a way of dealing with the contemporary crises of fragmentation and racialization in the United States. Instead, we could learn from first-generation Indians who have developed solidarity and community by joining together in political struggle. The crucial issue for the older generation here is to think through the politics of why we are here and to deliberate carefully about which America they want to identify with: the white, male, corporate America, or the America of the "rainbow coalition." In cases where economic betterment is the primary motivation for immigration into the United States, and especially when these cases are successful, it is easy to deny the reality of our racially and *color*fully marked American citizenship. Even as I write, communities are targeting school teachers with "foreign" accents for dismissal.

Third, it is disingenuous of my generation to behave as though one India exists "out there" and our *interpretation of India* is it. This is a generation both of and distant from India, therefore the politics of proximity has to negotiate dialectically and critically with the politics of distance. We may not like this, but it is our responsibility to take our daughters and sons seriously when they ask us: Why then did you leave India? I believe with Amitav Ghosh (I refer here to his novel *The Shadow Lines)* that places are both real and imagined, that we can know places that are distant as much as we can misunderstand and misrepresent places we inhabit. As Arjun Appadurai, among others, has argued, neither distance nor proximity guarantees truth or alienation. One could live within India, and one can not care to discover India and live "abroad" and acquire a nuanced historical appreciation of the home-country, and vice versa. During times when the demographic flows of peoples across territorial boundaries have become more the norm than the exception, it is counter-productive to maintain that one can only understand a place when one is in it. It is quite customary for citizens who have emigrated to experience distance as a form of critical enlightenment or a healthy "estrangement" from their birthland, and to experience another culture or location as a reprieve from the orthodoxies of their own "given" cultures. It is also quite normal for the same people, who now have lived a number of years in their adopted country, to return through critical negotiation to aspects of their culture that they had not really studied before and to develop criticisms of their chosen world. Each place or culture gains when we open it to new standards.

In saying this I am not conceding to individuals the right to rewrite collective histories that determine individual histories in the first place, nor am I invoking diasporan cultural politics as a facile answer to the structural problem of asymmetry and inequality between "developed" and "underdeveloped" nations. My point is that the diaspora has created rich possibilities of understanding different histories. And these histories have taught us that identities, selves, traditions, and natures do change with travel (and there is nothing decadent or deplorable about mutability) and that we can achieve such changes in identity intentionally. In other words, we need to make substantive distinctions between "change as default or as the path of least resistance" and "change as conscious and directed self-fashioning."

Among these mutable, changing traditions and natures, who are we to ourselves? Is the identity question so hopelessly politicized that it cannot step beyond the history of strategies and counterstrategies? Do I know in some abstract, ontological, transhistorical way what "being Indian" is all about and on that basis devise strategies to hold on to that ideal identity, or do I—when faced by the circumstances of history—strategically practice Indian identity to maintain my uniqueness and resist anonymity through homogenization? For that matter, why can't I be "Indian" without having to be "authentically Indian"? What is the difference and how does it matter? In the diasporan context in the United States, ethnicity is often forced to take on the discourse of authenticity just to protect and maintain its space and history. Does "black" have to be authentic except as pressured by "white"? It becomes difficult to determine if the drive toward authenticity comes from within the group as a spontaneous self-affirming act, or if authenticity is nothing but a paranoid reaction to the "naturalness" of dominant groups? Why should "black" be authentic when "white" is hardly even seen as a color, let alone pressured to demonstrate its authenticity?

Let us ask the following question: If a minority group were left in peace with itself and not dominated or forced into a relationship with the dominant world or national order, would the group still find the term "authentic" meaningful or necessary? The group would continue being what it is without having to authenticate itself. My point is simply this: When we say "authenticate," we also have to ask "authenticate to whom and for what purpose?" Who and by what authority is checking our credentials? Is "authenticity" a home we build for ourselves or a ghetto we inhabit to satisfy the dominant world?

I do understand and appreciate the need for authenticity especially in First World advanced capitalism where the marketplace and commodities are the norm. But the rhetoric of authenticity tends to degenerate into essentialism. I would much rather situate the problem of authenticity alongside the phenomenon of relationality and the politics of representation. How does authenticity speak for itself: as one voice, or as many related voices, as monolithic identity or as identity hyphenated by difference? When someone speaks as an Asian American, who exactly is speaking? If we dwell in the hyphen, who represents the hyphen: the Asian or the American, or can the hyphen speak for itself without creating an imbalance between the Asian and the American components? What is the appropriate narrative to represent relationality?

Back to my son's question again: True, both components have status, but which has the power and the potential to read and interpret the other on its terms? If the Asian is to be Americanized, will the American submit to Asianization? Will there be a reciprocity of influence whereby American identity itself will be seen as a form of openness to the many ingredients that constitute it, or will "Americanness" function merely as a category of marketplace pluralism?

Very often it is when we feel deeply dissatisfied with marketplace pluralism and its unwillingness to confront and correct the injustices of dominant racism that we turn our diasporan gaze back to the home country. Often, the gaze is uncritical and nostalgic. Often, we cultivate the home country with a vengeance. Several dangers exist here. We can cultivate India in total diasporan ignorance of the realities of the home country. By this token, anything and everything is India according to our parched imagination: half truths, stereotypes, so called traditions, rituals, and so forth. Or we can cultivate an idealized India that has nothing to do with contemporary history. Then again, we can visualize the India we remember as an antidote to the maladies both here and there and pretend that India hasn't changed since we left its shores. These options are harmful projections of individual psychological needs that have little to do with history. As diasporan citizens doing double duty (with accountability both here and there), we need to understand as rigorously as we can the political crises in India, both because they concern us and also because we have a duty to represent India to ourselves and to the United States as truthfully as we can.

Our ability to speak for India is a direct function of our knowledge about India. The crisis of secular nationalism in India, the ascendancy of Hindu fundamentalism and violence, the systematic persecution of Muslims, the incapacity of the Indian national government to speak on behalf of the entire nation, the opportunistic playing up of the opposition between secularism and religious identity both by the government and the opposition, the lack of success of a number of progressive local grassroots movements to influence electoral politics—these and many other such issues we need to study with great care and attention. Similarly, we need to make distinctions between left-wing movements in India that are engaged in critiquing secularism responsibly with the intention of opening up a range of indigenous alternatives, and right-wing groups whose only intention is to kindle a politics of hatred. Diasporan Indians should not use distance as an excuse for ignoring happenings in India. It is heartening to know that an alliance for a secular and democratic South Asia has recently been established in Cambridge, Massachusetts.

The diasporan hunger for knowledge about and intimacy with the home country should not turn into a transhistorical and mystic quest for origins. It is precisely this obsession with the sacredness of one's origins that leads peoples to disrespect the history of other people and to exalt one's own. Feeling deracinated in the diaspora can be painful, but the politics of origins cannot be the remedy.

Time now for one final episode. Watching Peter Brooks' production of the Hindu epic *Mahabharatha* with a mixed audience, I was quite surprised by the different reactions. We were viewing this film after we had all seen the homegrown TV serials *The Ramayana* and the *Mahabharatha*. By and large, initially my son's generation was disturbed by the international cast that seemed to falsify the Hindu/the Indian (again, a dangerous conflation) epic. How could an Ethiopian play the role of Bheeshma, and a white European (I think Dutch) represent Lord Krishna? And all this so soon after they had been subjected to the "authentic version" from India? But soon they began enjoying the film for what it was. Still, it deeply upset a number of adults of my generation. To many of them, this was not the real thing, this could not have been the real Krishna. My own response was divided. I appreciated and enjoyed humanizing and demystifying Krishna, endorsed *in principle* globalizing a specific cultural product, approved the production for not attempting to be an extravaganza. On the other hand, I was critical of some of its modernist irony and cerebral posturing, its shallow United Nations-style internationalism, its casting of an African American male in a manner that endorsed certain black male stereotypes, and finally of a certain western/Eurocentric arrogance that commodifies the work of a different culture and decontextualizes it in the name of a highly skewed and uneven globalism.

Which is the true version? What did my friend mean when he said that this was not the real thing? Does he have some sacred and unmediated access to the real thing? Is his image any less an ideological fabrication (or the result of Hindu-brahminical canonization) than that of Peter Brooks? Did his chagrin have to do with the fact that a great epic had been produced critically, or with the fact that the producer was an outsider? What if an Indian feminist group had produced a revisionist version? Isn't the insider's truth as much an invention and an interpretation as that of the outsider? How do we distinguish an insider's critique from that of the outsider? If a Hindu director had undertaken globalizing the Hindu epic would the project have been different/more acceptable/more responsive to the work's origins? But on the other hand, would a Western audience tolerate the Indianization of Homer, Virgil, or Shakespeare? Questions, more questions. I would rather proliferate questions than seek ready-made and ideologically over-determined answers. And in a way, the diaspora is an excellent opportunity to think through some of these vexed questions: solidarity and criticism, belonging and distance, insider spaces and outsider spaces, identity as invention and identity as natural, location-subject positionality and the politics of representation, rootedness and rootlessness.

When my son wonders who he *is,* he is also asking a question about the future. For my part, I hope that his future and that of his generation will have many roots and many pasts. I hope, especially, that it will be a future where his identity will be a matter of rich and complex negotiation and not the result of some blind and official decree.

References

Ahmad, Aijaz. *In Theory.* London: Verso, 1992.

Amin, Samir. *Eurocentrism.* New York: Monthly Review Press, 1989.

Anderson, Benedict. *Imagined Communities: Reflections on the Origin and Spread of Nationalism.* London: Verso, 1983.

Anzaldúa, Gloria. *Borderlands/La Frontera.* San Francisco: Aunt Lute Books, 1987.

Appadurai, Arjun. "Disjuncture and Difference in the Global Cultural Economy." *Public Culture* 2.2 (1990):1-24.

Bhabha, Homi K., ed. *Nation and Narration.* New York: Routledge, 1990.

Chatterjee, Partha. *Nationalist Thought and the Colonial World: A Derivative Discourse.* Delhi: Oxford Univeristy Press, 1986.

Chow, Rey. *Woman and Chinese Modernity: The Politics of Reading Between East and West.* Minnesota: University of Minnesota Press, 1991.

Dasgupta, Sayantini. "Glass Shawls and Long Hair: South Asian Women Talk Sexual Politics." *Ms.* Vol. 3-5, (March-April) 1993: 76-77.

Dhareshwar, Vivek, and James, Clifford, eds. *Inscriptions, Vol.* 5 (1989).

Ghosh, Amitav. *The Shadow Lines.* New York: Penguin, 1988.

hooks, bell. *Black Looks: Race and Representation.* Boston: South End Press, 1992.

Jayawardena, Kumari. *Feminism and Nationalism in the Third World.* New Delhi: Kali for Women, 1986.

Kingston, Maxine Hong. *The Woman Warrior.* New York: Knopf, 1976.

Kishwar, Madhu. "Why I Do Not Call Myself a Feminist." *Manushi,* Vol. 62 (1990): 2-8.

Lloyd, David and Abdul, JanMohamed, ed. *The Nature and Context of Minority Discourse.* New York: Oxford University Press, 1990.

Manushi 74-75, double issues, January-February, March-April, 1993.

Mohanty, Chandra Talpade. "On Race and Voice: Challenges for Liberal Education in the 1990s." *Cultural Critique,* Winter 1989-90: 179-208.

——, ed. *Third World Women and the Politics of Feminism.* Bloomington: Indiana University Press, 1992.

Morrison, Toni, ed. *Race-ing, Justice, En-gendering Power.* New York: Pantheon, 1992.

Aamir, Mufti and McClure, John, eds. *Special issue on postcoloniality, Social Text* 31/32.

Mahmut, Mutman and Yegenoglu, Meyda, eds. *Inscriptions Vol.* 6: "Orientalism and Cultural Differences."

Nandy, Ashis, ed. *Science, Hegemony and Violence: A Requiem for Modernity.* Oxford: Oxford University Press, 1988.

Radhakrishnan, R. "Culture as Common Ground: Ethnicity and Beyond." *MELUS, Vol.* 14, No. 2 (Summer 1987): 5-19.

——. "Postcoloniality and the Boundaries of Identity." Forthcoming, *Callaloo,* (Fall 1993).

Rosaldo, Renato. *Culture & Truth: The Remaking of Social Analysis.* Boston: Beacon Press, 1989.

Rushdie, Salman. *Imaginary Homelands.* New York: Penguin, 1992.

Said, Edward W. *Culture and Imperialism.* New York: Knopf, 1993.

——. *Orientalism.* New York: Vintage Books, 1978.

Kumkum, Sangari and Vaid, Sudesh, eds. *Recasting Women: Essays in Indian Colonial History.* New Brunswick: Rutgers University Press, 1990.

Shiva, Vandana. *Staying Alive: Women, Ecology and Development.* New Jersey: Zed Books, 1989.

Sunder Rajan, Rajeswari, ed. *The Lie of the Land: English Literary Studies in India.* Oxford: Oxford University Press, 1992.

Photo © 1993 by Corky Lee, used with permission.

12

SMELLS LIKE RACISM

A Plan For Mobilizing Against
Anti-Asian Bias

RITA CHAUDHRY SETHI

When I started my first job after college, Steve Riley, an African American activist, asked me: "So, how do you feel being black?" I confessed, "I am not black." "In America," Steve responded, "if you're not white, you're black."

U.S. discourse on racism is generally framed in these simplistic terms: the stark polarity of black/white conflict. As it is propagated, it embraces none of the true complexities of racist behavior. Media sensationalism, political expedience, intellectual laziness, and legal constraints conspire to narrow the scope of cognizable racism. What remains is a pared-down image of racism, one that delimits the definition of its forms, its perpetrators, and, especially, its victims. Divergent experiences are only included in the hierarchy of racial crimes when they sufficiently resemble the caricature. Race-based offenses that do not conform to this model are permitted to exist and fester without remedy by legal recourse, collective retribution, or even moral indignation.

Asians' experiences exist in the penumbra of actionable racial affronts. Our cultural, linguistic, religious, national, and color differences do not, as one might imagine, form the basis for a modified paradigm of racism; rather, they exist on the periphery of offensiveness. The racial insults we suffer are usually trivialized; our reactions are dismissed as hypersensitivity or regarded as a source of amusement. The response to a scene where a Korean-owned store is being destroyed with a bat in the 1993 film, *Falling Down* (a xenophobic and racist diatribe on urban life)[1] reflects how mainstream America/American culture responds to the phenomenon of anti-Asian violence:

> There was, in the theater where I saw the film, a good deal of appreciative laughter and a smattering of applause during this scene, which of course flunks the most obvious test of comparative racism: imagine a black or an Orthodox Jew, say, in that Korean's place and you imagine the theater's screen being ripped from the walls. Asians, like Arabs, remain safe targets for the movies' casual racism.[2]

The perpetuation of the caricature of racism is attributable to several complex and symbiotic causes. First, Asians often do not ascribe racist motivation to the discrimination they suffer, or they have felt that they could suffer the injustice of racial intolerance, in return for being later compensated by the fruits of economic success. Second, many Asians do not identify with other people of color. Sucheta Mazumdar posits that South Asians exclude themselves from efforts at political mobilization because of their rigid self-perception as Aryan, not as people of color.[3]

The final and most determinative factor, however, is the perspective that excludes the experiences of Asians (and other people of color) from the rubric of racism. Whites would deny us our right to speak out against majority prejudice, partially because it tarnishes their image of Asians as "model" minorities; other people of color would deny us the same because of monopolistic sentiments that they alone endure real racism.

For example, a poll conducted by *The Wall Street Journal* and NBC News revealed that "most American voters thought that Asian Americans did not suffer discrimination" but in fact received too many "special advantages."[4] Similarly, when crimes against

Asians were on the rise in housing projects in San Francisco, the Housing Authority was loathe to label the crimes as racially motivated, despite the clear racial bias involved.[5] The Deputy Director of the Oakland Housing Authority's response to the issue was: "There may be some issues of race in it, but it's largely an issue of people who don't speak English feeling very isolated and not having a support structure to deal with what's happening to them."[6]

Other minorities reject Asian claims of racial victimization by pointing to economic privilege or perceived whiteness.[7] Such rejections even occur among different Asian groups. Chinese Americans in San Francisco attempted to classify Indians as white for the purposes of the California Minority Business Enterprise Statute: "If you are a white, male buyer in the City, all else being equal, would you buy from another Caucasian [i.e. Indian] or from a person of the Mongolian race?"[8]

The perspective of some people of color that there is a monopoly on oppression is debilitating to an effort at cross-ethnic coalition building. Our experiences are truly distinct, and our battles will in turn be unique; but if we are to achieve a community, we must begin to educate ourselves about our common denominator as well as our different histories and struggles. Ranking and diminishing relative subjugation and discrimination will only subvert our goal of unity. Naheed Islam expresses this sentiment in part of a poem addressed to African American women:

> Ah Sister! What have they done to us! Separated, segregated, unable to love one another, to cross the color line. I am not trying to cash in on your chains. I have my own. The rape, plunder, pain of dislocation is not yours alone. We have different histories, different voices, different ways of expressing our anger, but they used the same bullets to reach us all.[9]

The combination of white America refusing to acknowledge anti-Asian discrimination, and minority America minimizing anti-Asian discrimination foists a formidable burden upon Asians: to combat our own internalized racial alienation, and to fight extrinsic racial classifications by both whites and other minority groups. It also renders overly simplistic those suggestions that if South Asians simply became "sufficiently politicized" they could over-come fragmentation in the struggle by people of color.[11]

As activists, a narrow-minded construct of racism impairs our political initiatives to use racism as a banner that unites all people of color in a common struggle.[10] The mainstream use of the word "racism" does not embrace Asian experiences, and we are not able to include ourselves in a definition that minimizes our encounters with racism. Participation in an anti-racism campaign, therefore, is necessarily limited to those involved in a battle against racism that fits within the confines of the black/white paradigm, and conversely relegates anti-Asian racism to a lesser realm in terms of both exposure and horribleness.

We need to be more sophisticated in our analysis of racism, and less equivocal in our condemnation. In doing so, we will expand the base of opposition against anti-Asian racism, and forge an alliance against all its myriad forms. The first step in this process is for Asians to apply a racial analysis to our lives. This involves developing a greater understanding of how racism has operated socially and institutionally in this country against ourselves and other people of color, as well as acknowledging our own complicity; and secondly, accepting ourselves as people of color, with a shared history of being targeted as visibly Other. Only then can we act in solidarity with other efforts at ending racism.

Anti-Asian Racism: Fashioning a More Inclusive Paradigm

Racism takes on manifold creative and insidious expressions. Intra-racism, racism among different racial communities, and internalized racism all complicate an easy understanding of the phenomenon. My project here is to uncover shrouded racism per-petrated against Asians, particularly South Asians, in an attempt to broaden the use of the term.

Accent

It is only since 1992 that the Courts have begun to realize the legitimacy of discrimination based upon accent.[12] Immigrants, primarily those not of European descent,[13] suffer heightened racism because of their accents, including job discrimination and perpetual taunting and caricaturization. This is a severe and pervasive form of racism that is often not acknowledged as racist, or even offensive. Even among Asians there is a high degree of denial about the accent discrimination that is attributable to race. In a letter to *The New York Times,* an Asian man blithely encouraged immigrants to maintain their accents, without acknowledging the potential discrimination that we face, though he personally was "linguistically gifted" with an "American accent." The man wrote, "Fellow immigrants, don't worry about the way you speak until Peter Jennings eliminates his Canadian accent."[14]

Accent discrimination is linked directly to American jingoism, and its accompanying virulently anti-immigrant undertones. In the aforementioned movie "Falling Down," the protagonist has the following exchange with a Korean grocer:

Mr. Lee: Drink eighty-five cent. You pay or go.

Foster: This "fie," I don't understand a "fie." There's a "v" in the word. It's "fie-vah." You don't got "v's" in China?

Mr. Lee: Not Chinese. I'm Korean.

Foster: Whatever. You come to my country, you take my money, you don't even have the grace to learn my language?[15]

A person's accent is yet another symbol of otherness, but it is one that even U.S.-born minorities do not regard as a target for race-based discrimination. Language is implicitly linked with race, and must be treated as such.

Subversive Stereotyping

The myths that are built based on the commonality of race are meant to depersonalize and simplify people. To many, the Indian Persona is that of a greedy, unethical, cheap immigrant. This stereotype is reflected in popular culture, where its appearance gives it credibility, thereby reinforcing the image. In the television comedy, *The Simpsons,* a purportedly politically sensitive program, one of the characters is a South Asian owner of a convenience store. In one episode, in an effort to make a sale, he says, "I'll sell you expired baby food for a nickel off." Similarly, in the program, *Star Trek: Deep Space Nine,* an alien race called the Firengi (Hindi for Foreigner) are proprietors and sleazy entrepreneurs who take advantage of any opportunity for wealth, regardless of the moral cost.[16]

These constructs are reified in everyday life as people respond to Indians as if they have certain inherent qualities. Indian physicians, for example, are perceived as shoddy practitioners, who are greedy and disinterested in the health of their patients. In successful medical malpractice suits, Indian doctors are routinely required to pay higher penalties.[17] Similarly, in the now-famous "East Side Butcher" case, where an Indian doctor was convicted of performing illegal abortions, there was no racial analysis despite the fact that no one had been prosecuted for that crime in New York State since the early 1980s despite the fact that hundreds of illegal abortions are performed annually.[18] Another Indian doctor, less than two weeks later, was found guilty of violations in her mammography practice and fined the largest amount in New York State history in such a case. One can not help but wonder if these convictions were, at least in part, motivated by the stereotype of the Indian immigrant.[19]

The Onus

A white, liberal woman once asked my friend Ritu if she wasn't being overly sensitive for taking offense when people put their feet near her face (a high insult in Indian culture), when she could not fairly expect people to understand her culture. The onus is always on us, as outsiders, to explain and justify our culture while also being expected to know and understand majority culture.[20] Constant cultural slights about cows, bindis and Gandhi are deemed appropriate by the majority while we are expected to subjugate expression of our culture to an understanding and acceptance of American culture. As another example, the swastika is an extremely common, ancient Hindu symbol. However, Hindus cannot wear or display the swastika in America because of Hitler's appropriation of it, and the expectation that we suppress our cultural symbols in an attempt to understand the affront to Jewish Americans. The assumption that it is our normative responsibility to make our culture secondary is racist because it suggests that one culture should be more free to express itself than another.

Religious Fanaticism

Eastern religions are commonly perceived as fraudulent, cultish, and fanatical; they are rarely perceived as equally legitimate as the spiritual doctrines of the Judeo-Christian tradition. The story of immaculate conception is accepted as plausible, while the multi-armed, multi-headed God is an impossible fantasy. Hinduism is portrayed as Hare Krishnas chanting with shaved heads and orange robes; and Islam is characterized as a rigid, violent, military religion. These hyperbolic characterizations are responsible for the fear of religion that causes local communities to refuse to permit places of worship in their neighborhoods.[21]

Western appropriation of Hindu terms reflects the perception of religion as charlatanical; the words have been reshaped through their use in the English language with an edge of irreverence or disbelief.

	Hindi Meaning	English Use
1. Guru	Religious teacher	Purported head; self-designated leader
2. Nirvana	Freedom from endless cycle of rebirth	Psychedelic ecstasy; drug-induced high
3. Pundit	Religious scholar	One with claimed knowledge
4. Mantra	A meditative tool; repetition of word or phrase	Mindless chant

Similarly, during times of political crisis (the 1991 Persian Gulf War; the February 1993 World Trade Center bombing), Islam has been the object of derision as a dangerous and destructive religion. After the suspects from the World Trade Center bombing were identified as Muslims, the media, the FBI and mainstream America responded with gross anti-Muslim rhetoric. A Professor in Virginia pointed out the ignorant conflation of the entire Muslim population into one extremist monolith:

> Not all Islamic revivalists are Islamic fundamentalists, and not all Islamic fundamentalists are political activists, and not all Islamic political activists are radical and prone to violence.[22]

Muslims have linked these characterizations of their religion to racial demonization.[23] *The Post* carried a headline entitled "The Face of Hate" with the face of a dark-skinned, bearded man of South Asian or Middle Eastern descent (the accused bomber). Similarly, the *New York Times* described the work of courtroom artists: "the defendant's beakish nose, hollow cheeks, cropped beard and the sideways tilt of his head."[24] In an Op-Ed piece in the *New York Times,* one Muslim responded to this description: "Such racial stereotyping serves nothing except to feed an existing hate and fear."[25]

Indicia of Culturalness

Indicia that identify us as other are generally used as vehicles for discrimination; with East Asians, eye-shape provides the target for racial harassment. South Asians' unique attributes are warped for use as racist artillery: attire (we are towel heads and wear loin cloths and sheets); costume (we are dot-heads); and odor (we are unclean and smelly). Nila Gupta has written about the power of smell, and its identification of South Asians as targets for racist behavior:[26]

> it is spring
> she walks a strong walk
> but they are waiting
> for her in the air
> they can't smell curry and oil poori and dahl for breakfast
> scents they are trained to hate
> confusion
> like hunting dogs after prey
> enraged
> thrown off the scent
> by a river
> enraged
> was she trying to pass?

Gupta's poem recounts a moment of racial discrimination as it is manifested in the degradation of cultural characteristics. When we explore racism, and its effect upon different ethnic and cultural groups, we must also examine the unique ways that specific groups experience racism, and the more neutral proxies and buzzwords used to signify race.

Class Conflicts/Economic Envy

Racism and economic tension are inextricable because race discrimination against Asians has often been manifested as class competition, and vice versa. Since the early 1800s, when Asians became a source of cheap labor for the railroads, we have been an economic threat. As Asians have more recently been portrayed as the prosperous minority, the favored child of America, there has inevitably been sibling rivalry. When auto workers beat up Vincent Chin, was it Japanese competition in the auto industry or unbridled racism that motivated the murderers? When African Americans targeted Korean-owned stores in the riots in Los Angeles after the Rodney King verdict, was it the economic hardship of the inner city and perceived Asian advantages or was it simply racism? The answer is that race and class are inseparable because of the inherent difficulty in identifying the primary or motivating factor; any racial analysis must consider economic scapegoating as an avenue for racial harassment and racial victimization as an excuse for expressing economic tensions.

Conceptual and Perspective Differences

When an immigrant perspective clashes with a white American perspective, the conflict should be considered a racial one. Values such as individuality, privacy, confrontation, competition, and challenging the status quo are considered positive and healthy; however, these components of the liberal state are not necessarily virtues elsewhere. When Hawaiian children do not respond to competitive models of teaching, but thrive in group activities; and when Punjabi children defer to authority, rather than challenge their teachers out of intellectual "curiosity," they are harmed by their inability to function in an essentially and uniquely "American" world. Identifying the differences in perspective and lifestyle between Asian immigrants and Americans will help in recognizing arenas in which we will be at a cultural/racial disadvantage.[27]

A Case Study in Anti-Asian Racism: The Dotbusters of Jersey City

In early fall of 1986, Asian Indians in New Jersey were the targets of racial terrorism. Houses and businesses were vandalized, and graffitied with racial slurs, women had their saris pulled, Indians on the street were harassed and assaulted, and a 28-year-old man was beaten into a coma. The *Jersey Journal* received and printed a letter from a group calling themselves the Dotbusters threatening all Asian Indians in Jersey City, and promising to drive them out of Jersey City. Teenagers in Dickinson High School were found with Dotbuster IDs. In spite of the obvious danger to the community, the police were unresponsive and denied that any Indians should truly be concerned.

The most heinous incident was the murder of Navroze Mody, a 30-year-old Citicorp executive. Navroze was bludgeoned to death with bricks by a group of young Latinos. Long after he had lost consciousness, he was repeatedly propped up and beaten further. His white companion was not touched. Four of the eleven attackers were indicted for manslaughter; two of the indicted were also accused of assaulting two Indian students two weeks before killing Navroze.

Despite the context in which the murder occurred, the incident was not generally perceived as racist in motive by the mainstream, the press, or the Indian community. The ways that Indians were targeted made it convenient to try to find other names for their encounters with racism. Their experiences were unrecognizable as the caricature of racism, and there was a collective refusal to be expansive and open-minded in interpreting what was happening.

The tone for the general characterization of the crime as not racially motivated was set by Hudson County Prosecutor, Paul DePascale, assigned to Mody's case. Although he conceded that: "There was no apparent motive for the assault other than the fact that the victim was an Asian American,"[28] he refused to pursue criminal charges for racial bias.[29]

The press, a reflection of mainstream sentiment, was reluctant to label the crime as racial in nature. Even *The Village Voice*, a liberal newspaper, carried a story asking above the headline: "Was his [Navroze Mody's] murder racially motivated?[30] One newspaper accepted the racial motive by qualifying it as a "new" racism/ "new" bigotry. The defendants' supporters saw no racial animus against Indians in the crime, inquiring instead: "Do you think there would be justice if it was the other way around? If the Indian were alive and the Puerto Rican dead?"[31]

Indians-at-large were mystified about the source of the anti-Asian wave of violence and found it difficult to accept as pure racism. People looked for other potential justifications and alternative labels.[32] One community leader remarked, "We pay our taxes," and characterized the Indian community as "faultless immigrants" in an effort to distinguish Asian Indians from African Americans and Latinos.[33] A second-generation Indian lawyer characterized such attacks as "national origin" discrimination, rather than racism.[34] Such denial prevented Asian Indians from making the obvious connection to other groups victimized because of their race.

The uncommonness of the anti-Indian discrimination obfuscated the real racism that rested at its core. Economic envy was the most obvious non-racial analysis proffered for escalating crimes against Asians. One Jersey City resident commented: "I've been in this country all my life and they come here and plop down $200,000 for a house."[35] Part of the infamous Dotbuster letter contained similar comments to journalist Ronald Leir: "You say that Indians are good businessmen. Well I suppose if I had 15 people living in my apartment I'd be able to save money too."[36]

Another major source of attack was traditional Indian attire. According to one community leader: "The number two factor for racism is that we look different."[37] Similarly, the hate group, the Dotbusters, takes its name from the cosmetic dot, or bindi, worn by many Indian women on their foreheads.

Finally, Indian languages and residential clustering create a sense of exclusive cohesiveness that threaten Jersey City's non-Asian communities. Anything that represented the insular-seeming culture was the object of harassment and hatred. Indian religion and cuisine were mocked, and Indians were repeatedly characterized as smelly (due to the lingering scents of cooking spice).

Despite the heinousness of the crime, the Mody case, and anti-Indian violence, did not receive sufficient public attention or outrage. During the same time that the case was being tried, the

RITA CHAUDHRY SETHI

Howard Beach case[38] was in the headlines of all major newspapers. Of the four Howard Beach attackers, three received manslaughter convictions; of the eleven attackers in the Mody case, three were convicted of aggravated assault, and one of simple assault. Perhaps it was because Asian Indians did not know how to employ the political system that the verdicts returned did not fit the crimes committed. Perhaps it was because the attackers were also minorities. But the main reason why justice was not served was because the racism that Indians were enduring did not fit the neat, American paradigm for racial violence.

In 1993, we can no longer see the world in black and white, where "those who don't fit the color scheme become shadows."[39] Lessons from our battles with bigotry should convince us that our understanding of it and the machinery we have built to fight it are hopelessly obsolete. Denying the richness of our community of people of color ultimately undermines the objective of unity, and hampers our political work combatting racism. During the late '80s, the left fought to find a common ground for people of color to coalesce; however, it is now the time to refine our collective mission to truly encompass the range of diversity among us. Any movement forged upon the principles of equality and tolerance can only be legitimate if it represents its margins.

Notes

1. While the film generated much debate about the possible ironic intent of its stereotyping, the reactions of moviegoers showed that the irony was lost on most audiences.
2. Godfrey Cheshire, complete citation for article not available.
3. Mazumdar, Sucheta, "Race and Racism: South Asians in the United States" *Frontiers of Asian American Studies.*
4. Polner, Murray, "Asian-Americans Say They Are Treated Like Foreigners," *The New York Times,* March 7, 1993, Section B, p. 1.
5. Racial slurs were rampant (including "Go home, Chinaman" and accent harassment) and tension between the Asian and African American community was worsening. The fact that the perpetrators were African American might have contributed to the general reluctance to characterize these crimes as racially motivated. Again, this reflects an inability, or an unwillingness, to intellectually digest racism between non-white races, as it falls outside of the narrow black/white paradigm.

6. Chin, Steven, A. "Asians Terrorized in Housing Projects" *San Francisco Examiner.* January 17, 1993, B1.

7. Witness this morsel of divisiveness: In Miami, where large Latino and African American populations coexist, a Cuban woman was sworn in as State Attorney General. Many in the African American community were dismayed by this decision, and responded by stripping Cubans of their "rank" as a minority. One black lawyer commented: "Cubans are really 'white people whose native language is Spanish' and others agreed that Cuban Americans should be "disqualified because they have higher income levels than other minorities." Certainly there is complexity in this conflict; however, the net result is that people who could be in alliance based on race are divided. Rohter, Larry. "Black-Cuban Rift Extends to Florida Law School" The New York Times; March 19, 1993; B16L.

8. Transcript of San Francisco Board of Supervisors Special Session of Economic and Social Policy Committee April 30, 1991.

9. Islam, Naheed. "Untitled" from *Smell This,* an official publication of The Center for Racial Education, Berkeley, CA 1991.

10. Here, and throughout my chapter, I am operating within the constructs of our existing political reality. I am not addressing the normative question of whether people of color should be in coalition against racism, but given that it has been our primary organizing principle, how can we be more effective and inclusive?

11. Mazumdar, *supra* at p. 36.

12. Interestingly, the case was brought by the EEOC while under the tenure of Joy Cherian, a naturalized Indian. The Commission's 1980 guidelines covering this type of discrimination were written by an Indian, and the case was brought by an Indian plaintiff. Is that what it takes to obtain recognition of the racism that we experience?

13. The Executive Assistant for the Commissioner noted: "If an employer has an applicant who speaks with a French accent…or with an English accent, they say, 'How cute.' But if he speaks with a Hispanic accent they say, 'What's wrong with this guy?'"

14. Letter to the editor from Yan Hong Krompacky. "Immigrants, Don't Be In Such a Hurry to Shed Your Accents," *The New York Times* March 4, 1993.

15. Foster then proceeds to demolish Mr. Lee's grocery store with a bat, in much the same way that Japanese cars were hatefully demolished just before Vincent Chin's death.

16. That such stereotypes exist in two programs that are perceived as being among the more progressive on television is itself indicative of the continuing denial that anti-Asian racism exists.

17. According to several medical malpractice attorneys.

18. This was exacerbated further by the fact that Dr. Hayat's sentence was so severe that even the District Attorney's Office had expected less and was "pleasantly surprised." Perez-Pena, Richard, "Prison Term for

Doctor Convicted in Abortions" The New York Times, June 15, 1993, p. B1.

19. These stereotypes find expression everywhere. I was haggling for a pair of earrings in Times Square, and the vendor asked me if I was Indian. When I replied that I was, he responded, "Oh, I should have guessed. Indians don't want to take anything out of their pockets."

20. In an effort to better integrate into America culture, and mend relations with ethnic groups in New York City, Korean grocers are taking seminars to learn to smile more frequently, supposedly rare in their culture. *The York Times,* March 22, 1993

21. "It's the Hindus! Circle the Zoning Laws." Viewpoint by Bob Weiner, *Newsday,* April 26, 1993, p. 40.

22. Steinfeld, Peter. "Many Varieties of Fundamentalism." *The New York Times* no date! An even better response was: [the World Trade bomber suspect's] "variety of fundamentalism was not any more representative of Islam than the people in Waco are representative of [mainstream] Christianity." *Id.*

23. Op Ed Letter to Editor "Don't Let Trade Center Blast Ignite Witch Hunt," March 23, 1993

24. "Surprises In A Crowded Courtroom," Moustafa Bayami March 5, 1993

25. *Ibid.*

26. Gupta, Nila. "So She Could Walk" from *The Best of Fireweed;* Women's Press, Canada (1986).

27. Many Asians find themselves in low-ranking jobs in the corporate world because their skills have little application in the old boy cultural network. This is due in part to different concepts of authority and competition, as much as it is pure racial bigotry. My point is that the two should be viewed together to truly understand the full flourish of racism.

28. Vicente, Raul Jr., "Cops Arrest Two As Dotbusters." *Gold Coast,* March 24-March 31, 1988, p. 4.

29. His failure to label this as a racially-motivated crime may in fact be racially motivated. In March of 1988 there was opposition by Inter Departmental Minority Police Action Council in Jersey City to his appointment as city's acting police director because of alleged discrimination against a black woman officer. "Minority Cops Blast Director," Gold Coast March 31, 1988, p. 7.

30. "Racial Terror on The Gold Coast" *The Village Voice* January 26, 1988.

31. Jersey Journal 3/1/88

32. The collective denial precluded group solutions. Around the same time in Elmhurst 25 African American and Indian families were "preyed" upon in Queens. However, Indians were uninterested in forging an alliance with the African American community to fight ongoing racial harassment. Pais, Arthur, "Long Island Families Were Apathetic and Tearful When Harassed," India Abroad July 31, 1987, p. 1.

33. Walt, Vivienne, "A New Racism Gets Violent in New Jersey," *Newsday,* 4/6/88, p. 5.
34. Spoken at the Strategy Session for the case of Dr. Kaushal Sharan, March 28, 1993, by a representative of the *Indian American Magazine.*
35. Walt, Vivienne, "A New Racism Gets Violent in New Jersey," *Newsday,* 4/6/88, p. 5.
36. Letter to *Jersey Journal* on August 5, 1987.
37. Walt, Vivienne, "A New Racism Gets Violent in New Jersey," *Newsday,* 4/6/88, p. 5.
38. 1986 attack by white youths in Queens where a group of African Americans were stranded; one person died when he was chased onto a highway by the mob.
39. Zia, Helen, "Another American Racism," *The New York Times* letter to the editor.

III

**The
Heat
Is
On**

**Asian Americans on the Road
to Empowerment**

13

Overcoming our Legacy as Cheap Labor, Scabs, and Model Minorities

Asian Activists Fight for Community Empowerment

MILYOUNG CHO

The ground is red, garish with the paper shrapnel through which we wade and trample. Explosions of firecrackers pepper the air, and for a flash, I think of Molotov cocktails and what it would be like if people were lobbing these incendiary devices instead of firecrackers this New Year's Eve. Either way, Chinatown, New York City, is a battlefield. And while many celebrate, and many others work (as they do each and every day and night of the year—ever productive, laboring in substandard buildings, churning out piles of clothing), a boisterous crew of 40 are out tonight fighting the good fight.

For four consecutive years, restaurant workers and elder employees, labor organizers, activists, and construction workers of color shut out of the industry's racist unions and denied access to jobs, have gathered in front of the Silver Palace Restaurant on the

Bowery for what has become our annual New Year's protest. Every year the Chinese American Planning Council (CPC) hosts a New Year's banquet fundraiser which is attended by the organization's wealthy supporters and some of the city's political figures and celebrities.

The CPC is the largest Asian American social-service agency in New York City, if not east of the Rockies, providing what they describe as a "variety of services ... (including) employment and training, economic and housing development, cultural arts, day care services, multisocial services, senior citizen services and youth services." The CPC claims, through service provision, "to improve the quality of life among both immigrants and established Asian Americans."

The protesters contend otherwise. The CPC has a record of underpaying its older workers at one-third to one-half the going rate for younger, less experienced workers. Meanwhile, senior workers have filed a class-action suit citing age discrimination. Ever since workers at the Hong Ning housing project and Phoenix Food Services attempted to join a union in December 1992, the CPC has harassed, transferred, threatened to fire, and has even beaten one of the workers. Moreover, CPC is in contempt of two federal injunctions for underpaying construction workers. Two hundred construction workers who participated in CPC's Intercity Remodeling and Apartment Repair (IRAR) have been waiting for CPC to pay them the $2 million the U.S. Labor Department says they are owed. The CPC also owes $1 million to 30 IRAR workers whom it illegally fired when the workers formed a union in 1988.

Although some of the money raised by the agency's New Year's Eve fundraiser will inevitably wind up in the hands of the lawyers who defend the CPC from the numerous suits its employees file against it for discrimination, labor violations, and robbery, it is the protesters, and their supporters, whom the city criminalizes this evening. Five demonstrators are forcefully seized by the cops and then hauled off: arrested, handcuffed, and packed in a police van for exercising their First Amendment rights. The rest continue picketing, calling for a boycott of the fundraiser to CPC supporters who arrive in limousines, nestled in flouncing silver fox and mink coats. As we wage our protest, hemmed in by a line of restless, heaving cops and their barricades, we are not thinking about the racial unity that others so often herald as the decisive ingredient for overcoming the oppression we face as people of color. We, as workers and activists, are more concerned about justice—and getting paid.

Although the fact that a publicly supported social-services organization is exploiting its own workers makes the CPC labor dispute particularly outrageous, such illegal and unfair labor practices are standard fare in Chinatown. As Chinatown historian Peter Kwong summarizes, "Chinese employers maintain a virtual monopoly over the Chinatown work force. They can get away with abuses of all kinds."[1] He describes the brutal conditions of the garment sweat shops and Chinatown restaurants where workers put in a 70-hour week for less than minimum wage, under hazardous working conditions and without job security. According to Kwong, the underground economy in which Chinatown's restaurants, garment factories, and other businesses participate is beyond the control of government regulation in terms of taxes (due to a tacit agreement between government officials and Chinatown owners), and worse, the high productivity of this enclave is based on low wages and exploitation: "The central premise for economic development in Chinatown is cheap labor."[2] These industries are cloistered in an underground Chinatown economy where Chinese immigrants work for Chinese bosses who operate outside the mainstream U.S. economy and labor market. Here, prevailing minimum wage and labor laws, regulations, and safety standards, do not apply.

Chinatown is the oldest and most entrenched underground enclave among New York's Asian communities, but immigrants of the different Asian ethnic groups are caught in similar plights.[3] The suspension of labor laws, miserable working conditions, long hours, and extremely low wages prevail for workers who are employed by, for example, the family-owned and operated Bangladeshi construction outfits, Japanese restaurants, and Korean beauty salons, dry cleaners, and groceries.

Thousands of Filipinas work for white families as domestics in an underground industry in which they are particularly vulnerable to sexual abuse and the threat of deportation, in addition to all the other work-related abuses. New York's yellow cab industry, although regulated by the City's Taxi and Limousine Commission, is not subject to labor laws. A network of white owners of large fleets of cabs control the industry, taking advantage of the generous leeway they have to maximize their enormous profits due to the lack of labor regulations that might otherwise require them to provide, for instance, minimum wages, safety features, and the right to unionize. Instead, thousands of Pakistani, Bangladeshi, and Indian drivers (who comprise well over 40 percent of the industry's work force) work 12-hour shifts, six to seven shifts a week, for an average of $45 in unsafe vehicles that are highly prone to robberies and violent crimes.[4]

Unlike white European immigrants, Asians and other immigrants from the Third World are shut out of the mainstream U.S. economy. Language barriers and the racist and exclusionary nature of industries that supply better jobs (labor economists describe these "primary sector" industries as "large corporations, often monopolies, where workers are unionized, have job security, earn high wages"),[5] trap most Asian immigrants in highly stressful, exploitative jobs where their bosses are often of their own nationality/ethnicity.[6] As Kwong found, "The racial segmentation of the U.S. labor market effectively excludes the Chinese (Asian) immigrants from taking [that] path."[7]

The history surrounding the Exclusion Acts of a century ago—when employers lured Asians to this country to fill undesirable jobs and then used them as strikebreakers against white unionists—foreshadowed the social and economic situation today: Asians are shut out of decent jobs at the same time others scapegoat them for "stealing" jobs from "Americans." Recent demonstrations against the construction of federal buildings at the edge of Chinatown have highlighted the exclusionary nature of the more attractive blue-collar union jobs. In this ongoing struggle, construction workers, residents, and Chinatown laborers have protested against the federal government building a federal court house in Chinatown (the supposed seat of U.S. "justice") without hiring any Chinese workers.

If large sectors of the Asian communities are working in Asian-owned and operated underground economies, how can racism affect them? Part of the answer lies in the fact that discriminatory unions and old-boy network hiring systems shut Asians and other immigrants of color out of jobs with liveable wages and reasonable conditions outside of their communities. They are therefore forced to take the exploitative and undesirable jobs with employers often of their own ethnic group or nationality. "Fellow countrymen" though they may be, their bosses are entrepreneurs and capitalists first in extremely competitive industries. And, as has become apparent, they will stop at nothing to maximize profits even if it means exploiting their "own people." This capitalist drive fits neatly into a larger economic framework. Asian owners ghettoize immigrants (Asian and otherwise) in the worst jobs while at the same time maintaining a larger racially diverse and segregated work force, and by underpaying most workers, they help drive down the cost of labor in general.

As writer Manning Marable cautions in an article entitled "The New Black America," we "must recognize the subtle ways in which political, economic, and social institutions are assuming a non-racialist form, but nevertheless perpetuate the prerogatives of domination."[8] The U.S. Supreme Court's confirmation of Clarence Thomas is a recent example that reveals both the subtle and insidious nature of racism. It is a lesson for the nation that even people of color, *depending on what they stand for* (and in this case specifically a black man when black men are typically considered "criminals" in the U.S. "justice" system), can be viewed as tolerable, even useful, and therefore desirable to a racist, sexist institution. Clarence Thomas personifies for black communities in this country what the model minority myth and its legacy does to working Asians. The idea that a single black man can achieve economic and social status, all the while rejecting "hand-outs" and affirmative action, alleviates the government from any responsibility to a third of the country's population that continues to toil in deprivation. Similarly, when a few Asians successfully climb the social and economic ladder, the powers that be use their accomplishments as proof that the system works, that racism must not be operative, that if the "model minority" can do it, anyone can.

Racism is sophisticated, adopting chameleon-like qualities to ensure its survival. While mass movements and legal battles have delegitimized Jim Crow institutions and given all citizens the right to vote, racism, like a virus, evolves and naturally selects itself to take on new more resistant strains to evade civil rights laws and even social dictates, such as the necessity to be politically "correct."

Community is dynamic, ever changing, defined by both internal and external conditions, and based on how its members respond, adapt, and relate to a fluid reality. As communities (not to mention the larger social and political framework) change, so must our organizing strategies. When it is our Asian "brothers" who don't pay us, who sell us down the river for personal gain and political expedience, who participate in building rifts, alienating us from other communities of color that share our class interests, who perpetrate the silence and domination of straight women, lesbians, and gay men, we need strategies to challenge these abuses of power and refuse to participate in reinforcing them.

This chapter is based on observations of community struggles I have been involved in either tangentially or directly. In November 1992, I interviewed seven Asian American activists, organizers, and community workers, some who have been active since the 1970s, with whom I have worked in one capacity or another. Some of their voices appear in this piece as quotes.

Reframing the Debate on Racial Equality

In 1991, New York City was embroiled in a battle over redefining City Council district lines. The Federal Supreme Court had determined that the structure of the City of New York's government was unconstitutional, violated the Voters' Rights Act, and mandated establishing a new charter to reorganize the Council. As a result of the new charter, the city created the N.Y.C. Districting Commission. The Commission was to oversee the rearrangement of City Council districts to maximize the voting strength of underrepresented communities, namely, communities of color. The city would create 51 new districts from the original 35, a development that would purportedly enhance the chance for communities of color being fairly represented on the City Council.

Political groups, developers, politicians, and other interest groups inserted themselves into the turf war to redraw boundaries, each battling to stretch the borders to their advantage. Politicians in particular took advantage of the free-for-all gerrymandering and drafted proposals that shaped boundaries to accommodate their voting blocks, defining districts of impossibly illogical shapes and dubious common sense. One of the main proponents of a so-called "Asian District" was Chinese American City Council candidate Margaret Chin. Chin's organization, the Asian Americans for Equality (AAFE), was once a self-defined Marxist-Leninist organization that more recently has been jockeying to place its members into the mainstream of City politics and has colluded with the forces of gentrification through its real estate speculation and development activities.

The Asian American Union for Political Action (AAUPA), a collective of Asian American activists, labor organizers and community workers committed to economic justice, and political empowerment of Asian communities in the New York area, was at the forefront of vocalizing the Asian American community's strong objection to Chin's redistricting plan.[9] AAUPA vehemently denounced Chin and AAFE's "Asian District" on the grounds that the plan isolated Chinatown, a poor and working-class community, from the neighboring, predominantly Latino Lower East Side with which it shares many interests and needs. Instead, Chin's plan attached Chinatown to the white, upper-middle-class Battery Park area. Moreover, because the residents of Battery Park (incidentally, Chin's neighborhood of residency) comprise a larger more influential voting block than the residents of Chinatown, this would translate politically into the opposing voice of the Battery Park residents overshadowing any agenda reflecting the needs of the vast majority of Chinatown's residents. According to AAUPA, "This plan … split Chinatown from the rest of the Latino, African American, and low-income white community of the Lower East

Side, and cast Chinatown into a district composed of a majority of affluent, white voters. Yet Chin and the Districting Commission argued this plan was tailor-made to ensure that an Asian candidate, i.e. Chin, would triumph."[10] And, as the prevailing logic goes, Chin's "Asian District" would therefore benefit all Chinese residents. At the same time that Chinatown's district borders were being disputed, a district plan presented by another City Council candidate, Antonio Pagan, was lumping the Lower East Side onto the West Village, which like Battery Park, is also an affluent white area.

Although commercial and luxury real estate developers have for years encroached upon Chinatown, threatening the industry and low-income residential base, the neighborhood has remained, nonetheless, a ghetto for poor and working-class Chinese. The key issues are preserving and developing jobs and housing as well as providing more services such as bilingual education, affordable health care, and job training and eliminating police and racist violence. At the same time that Chin claimed she represented the Chinatown community, she unabashedly pandered to the white affluent residents of Battery Park. Chin, according to the AAUPA *News*,

> appealed to nationalist desires for Asian representation, while in reality, her political strategy banked on an alliance with affluent whites. While attempting to maintain a progressive veneer of supporting low-cost housing and increased social services for the poor, Chin concealed a history of anti-worker positions and alliances with developers.[11]

Chin's recent track record includes supporting garment shop owners in a crucial labor struggle, crossing workers' picket lines (such as demonstrations against the CPC), and aligning with Chinatown realtors.

In response to the different racially divisive district plans that Chin and Pagan put forth, several groups united to define district boundaries and propose a plan that combined Chinatown and the predominantly Latino Lower East Side into the "Unity

District." The group that formed, Lower East Side Coalition for a Multiracial District, included AAUPA, Good Old Lower East Side, Joint Planning Council, Charas, It's Time, and the Chinese Construction Workers' Association. The logic was that the two poor and working-class, immigrant communities of color have more in common with each other than either did with white, middle-class Battery Park (Chin's plan) or white, middle-class West Village (Pagan's plan). Unfortunately, the Redistricting Commission adopted a district plan similar to the one Chin and AAFE proposed.

Although the Unity District lost, AAUPA put forward a progressive platform for the November 1991 City Council elections, that "addressed key community issues for Chinatown and the Lower East Side residents—the need to preserve manufacturing zoning and jobs for workers in lower Manhattan, commercial and rent control and protection of lease renewals, increasing affordable housing for the poor, and effective delivery of city services."[12] Katherine Freed, a white woman, adopted this platform. This development effectively shifted the debate from "simply issues of representation based on color, to crucial economic issues facing residents of Chinatown and the Lower East Side," said the AAUPA News.[13] Initially, however, several AAUPA members were reluctant to rally behind Katherine Freed precisely because her whiteness represented an all-too-familiar relationship to power. As a result of personal histories and experience, some people assumed that as a white woman, Freed was likely to use and abuse the community, misrepresent, or at best maintain a traditional relationship characterized by "benevolent" patriarchy that white politicians tend to have with marginalized groups. Nonetheless, in good faith, AAUPA supported Freed over Chin with the understanding that the community might have to hold Freed accountable to her commitment to economic development for working people.

The battle over Council district lines and Chin's candidacy for City Council alerted progressive members of the Asian community of the danger of equating racial/ethnic representation with community empowerment. As Peter Kwong points out, "There is no guarantee that a Chinese candidate is necessarily better for the community."[14] Margaret Chin was not the first candidate who ran in Chinatown on her ethnicity, defining the debate in terms that are, as AAUPA describes, "a narrow, ultimately self-defeating view of community empowerment."[15] In 1985, Virginia Kee, the current president of CPC, also ran for a post, and like Chin, she too ran on her Chinese ethnicity.

No Asian sits on the 51-seat Council, in a city where a steadily growing 8 percent of the population is Asian. For this reason alone, there is a psychological, if not political, urgency to elect Asian Americans. Had Margaret Chin won the seat, however, given her history with the community and the interests she represents, her election would have been a hollow victory to the vast majority of the Asians in her district and throughout the city. As AAUPA cautions: "In light of the renewed drive to transform Chinatown into a high-rent commercial and luxury residential area, an Asian City Council member willing and eager to provide an Asian face to front for the plans of developers is precisely what Chinatown does not need. The election of Chin would have been a disaster for Chinatown."[16]

The phenomenon of playing the race card and milking racial and ethnic loyalty for support is by no means restricted to Asian communities. As Marable explains, "victories" that are defined by the color of our elected officials skin

> are presented to working-class and poor blacks as their symbolic victories, direct proof that racism has declined in significance. Their election can be viewed as a psychological triumph for African Americans, but they represent no qualitative resolution to the crises of black poverty, educational inequality, crime, and unemployment.[17]

When we vote strictly according to race, we may overlook the most crucial issues that truly affect our lives, such as access to decent jobs and affordable housing. Instead of empowering our communities, we may actually be furthering the ascendence of the very individuals who use their race as a means to further personal political aspirations at the expense of the community they claim to serve. Kwong comments on some of the major fallacies of race representation:

> Backing candidates on the basis of their ethnicity is a game almost everybody is playing. It is a losing game. Worst of all, it leaves the power relations within the Chinese community unchanged. Those holding power in traditional organizations are not challenged. Furthermore, so-called community leaders with money and organizational backing could easily become politicians representing the community in the electoral process.[18]

Just as some politicians use racial and ethnic loyalty against us in the political arena, exploitative Asian bosses use it as a tool to keep us trapped, immobilized, and docile in the work place. In the next section, I present a struggle waged by Asian and Latino workers of the Shinwa Restaurant challenging the unfair labor practices and racial discrimination of their Japanese bosses.

Worker Organizing Crosses Racial Lines at Pricey Japanese Eatery

In the fall of 1990, a group of immigrant Korean and Chinese waitresses and waiters approached the Chinese Staff and Workers Association (CSWA), a Chinatown-based workers' and labor rights organization, and exposed the unfair labor practices of their employer, the Shinwa Restaurant. The waitresses and waiters told CSWA that the restaurant takes a significant portion of their tips (17 to 40 percent), an illegal practice. By that point, the restaurant had stolen approximately $200,000 in tips. CSWA notified the Local 318 Restaurant Workers' Union and called a team of Asian American activists to further investigate the situation and support the workers. They discovered that Shinwa not only steals tips, but has organized its work force and the pay scale according to a highly suspect racial hierarchy.

Shinwa Restaurant, a pricey Japanese eatery located on 5th Avenue, the heart of New York City's most exclusive shopping

THE STATE OF ASIAN AMERICA

district, is a subsidiary of Shinwa, Inc., a multinational corporation based in Japan whose primary business is construction. The management is composed exclusively of Japanese individuals who maintain tight connections with their country of origin and the multinational's headquarters. Shinwa, Inc. exported these individuals to oversee their U.S. venture.

The management enjoys decent salaries and full benefits. One step down in pay scale and status are the bartenders—all of them white. In fact, a Japanese American with 15 years of bartending experience applied for the job and was rejected on the basis of not being "American." When he maintained that he was indeed American, having been born in the United States, the employer again stressed, "No, this job is only for *Americans!*" obviously equating "American" with white. Bartenders also receive decent pay, benefits, and are allowed to keep 100 percent of their tips. The cooks, who are considered very close to management, are all Japanese. The waitresses and waiters are all immigrants from at least six different Asian countries. They receive salaries as low as two dollars an hour, no benefits, and are denied a significant portion of their tips. The kitchen help, busboys, and dishwashers are all Latino, mostly from Mexico and Central America. They receive no tips and a pittance for wages, in most cases less than minimum wage, and no benefits. Most of the Latino workers began working at Shinwa when it opened in 1987 and typically work over 60 hours a week. They have all been systematically restricted to the lowest paying, most menial jobs in the restaurant and none of them has ever received a raise or been promoted to waiter. Some of Shinwa's workers are sponsored by the restaurant and have received work permits through the restaurant. The cooks as well as the management have their employment status legitimized under this arrangement. And, although most of Shinwa's wait staff, busboys, dishwashers, and kitchen help are undocumented, it is only the Japanese waitresses and waiters who have received work permits from Shinwa. Shinwa, which maintains a work force of over 40, has never hired a black person.

In the winter of 1991, the waitresses and waiters of Shinwa began to organize, first among themselves primarily around the tips issue, and then along with the Latinos to form a union as a means to negotiate better wages and job security. Shinwa responded to the workers' activities with harassment and intimidation. Within three months it fired two workers, and then, four of the waitresses and waiters quit due to the intense intimidation. Shinwa immediately replaced them with Japanese workers who proved to be very loyal to management. The crackdown polarized the workers. Fearful that they would lose their jobs and the work permits they received through Shinwa's sponsorship, some of the Japanese workers began to side with the management. The other Asian workers and the Latinos continued their organizing efforts, demanding the right to join the union and negotiations to get their tips back and decent pay.

Having failed to adequately purge the work force through its initial series of intimidations, Shinwa resorted to other tactics. Pro-management workers physically assaulted two of the Latino workers and management cut back the shifts of the leaders of the pro-union workers, in some cases to one-forth the hours they had initially worked. In addition, after repeatedly threatening to turn workers in to the Immigration and Naturalization Service (INS), Shinwa ordered all workers to turn in their immigration documents to prove they were "legally" working and residing in the United States. The Asian and Latino pro-union workers, at this point 20 or so individuals, collectively decided to refuse to pass in documents of any kind regardless of whether they were "legal" or not. By uniting to resist Shinwa's manipulative entrapment, they effectively outwitted and temporarily staved off the restaurant's ability to use the INS against them.

In an interview, Stan Mark, a lawyer with the Asian American Legal Defense and Education Fund, remarked:

> Race and ethnicity are really social, political definitions that the culture/society which adapts that kind of racism forces on people. We need to figure out another way to break out of [the racial ethnic definitions that confine us]. The common ground that people have regardless of

their background is really economic issues that break across those lines.

Even though Shinwa was using race and the racial and ethnic diversity of the work force to pit worker against worker, and even though it was relying on the ethnic, nationalist loyalty of the Japanese workers to drive a wedge into the efforts of the pro-union workers, the workers overcame these divisive tactics. Through their focus on the economic issues uniting them, the Shinwa Restaurant workers' campaign successfully transcended racial lines. The workers' struggle, in fact, inspired progressives to form the Shinwa Workers' Support Committee. This multiracial ad-hoc support group has been working together to educate and mobilize different communities to participate in solidarity demonstrations and sit-ins against Shinwa.

As of recently, the workers at Shinwa continue to push for negotiations, pressuring management with regular pickets and demonstrations and a media smear campaign.[19] Although the workers have yet to win better wages and their back tips, the recognition of their union, and an end to the discriminatory and unfair practices, the campaign is a model for multiracial organizing. The workers simultaneously challenged their boss's racism and racist policies by confronting the economic and anti-immigrant exploitation that Asians and Latinos share.

Challenging Narrow Nationalism and Media Pigeon Holes Key to Overcoming Racial Divisions

Commenting on the fragmented Asian American movement, Chinatown labor organizer Wing Lam observed,

> Some Asians are into self-promotion, they want to be a part of the mainstream, and are unhappy because they are not a part of it ... Professional organizations pop up because people are frustrated by the existing order, [they are] squeezed out because of racism. They come

together to fight for better representation; feel that they
have been discriminated against, [they] react to racism.

This need to fight racism because it prevents individuals from
entering into the mainstream (the glass ceiling complex) applies
to the many highly nationalistic business groups that have sprung
up over the past decade. Most notably are the numerous Korean
American business associations organized according to trade or
profession.

Beginning with the year-long boycott waged by members of
the black community against the Red Apple grocery in the
Flatbush section of Brooklyn, Korean communities have become
the public center of a controversy surrounding their problematic
relation to black communities and capital. Without diverting into
a long discussion about Korean and black relations, I want to
present a troublesome dynamic that is a direct off-shoot of this
situation: The Korean community has been stereotyped as playing
the role of a puppet for a racist system; the actions of some
members of the Korean community directly fuel perceptions that
Koreans are in league with white racist institutions.

In the fall of 1990, during the time that blacks were boycotting
Red Apple because one of workers, the owner's brother, attacked
a black customer, a largely unpublicized yet highly disturbing
situation unfolded. One of the many Korean grocers located on
125th Street in Harlem contacted the Korean American Business
Association in Flushing, New York. The owner of the store claimed
that an unlicensed fruit vendor, located near the front of his store,
was taking away his business. The Business Association promptly
called the cops and instructed them to have the sidewalk vendor
removed. Within a day, the police arrived and trashed the Latino
vendor's stand and produce without first checking to see if he had
a vendor's license which, in fact, he did.

This unquestioning allegiance that members of the Korean
business association networks have with each other, and the
reliance on a racist law enforcement system to protect and further
its business interests, justifiably raises questions about where
some of these Korean individuals align themselves in relation to

communities of color working against racist oppression. While many Flatbush residents were boycotting the Red Apple, grocers and members of numerous Korean business associations demonstrated this same loyalty to their peer, Bong Jae Jong, owner of the Red Apple, by raising thousands of dollars for him without knowing whether his brother was guilty of the alleged racist attack. In this situation as well, the store owner and his supporters approached the police. The police amassed a blockade of cops, stationing up to 50 officers, sometimes in riot gear, during the year-long boycott. An injunction by the city prevented any demonstrator from going within 15 feet of the store, which found itself in the middle of a maze of police barricades.

If we neglect to openly challenge the tyranny of the more visible and organized elements of the "community," we allow ourselves to be pigeon-holed as an ethnic group, or even an entire race, and then used as puppets or mouthpieces for someone else's agenda. The employment of racial pigeon-holing is a divisive tactic. This couldn't have been illustrated more graphically to me than in the summer of 1992 during the aftermath of the Rodney King verdict.

TV delivered to living rooms across the nation images of blacks "wilding," looting, pulverizing bystanders, setting South Central Los Angeles aflame with their unleashed fury; TV juxtaposed this onslaught with flashes of Korean men standing atop their stores, armed with rifles; then cut to anguished and besieged hard-working Korean moms and pops spouting off that blacks were savages and criminals. It was one thing to be assaulted by a barrage of these contextless, inflammatory images every time I turned on the television. It was another thing to be directly used, to be seized by ubiquitous forces of media, to participate in a word-splicing, image-mangling melee as reporters tried to wrest their own creation out of a diverse and complicated community and give life to a Korean proto/stereotype.

At the time, I was on the staff of the Committee Against Anti-Asian Violence (CAAAV), a New York City-based organization that has embraced a multipronged approach to combat racist violence and police brutality. It has begun to address issues of other types of violent oppression, such as economic injustice, through community organizing, education, and public-policy advocacy. Teams of mainly second-generation, college-educated Asian Americans comprise the core of the active members who work with immigrant communities on these issues. In our work, the media often approach us for a few-seconds-long sound bite to make some pat statement about the magnitude and horrors of anti-Asian violence. We get these calls every week, sometimes several a day. Given that the level of visibility of progressive Asians is virtually non-existent in the mainstream media (or even left-wing media for that matter), we feel compelled to oblige pushy reporters. We talk to them. We spend a good deal of time carefully outlining the reality—the roots, the history of our struggle—only to find the next day that the reporter has twisted our words or has not even mentioned our organization and work in the article. Indeed the media manipulates us, but what happened that summer was beyond word-splicing and sentence omissions. During the course of less than a week following the verdict, while the streets were still smoking, I must have received a dozen calls, from the most obscure monthly magazine to New York City's most prominent rag.[20] I will recount to you just one example of an interview that I gave during this period.

The first question Rick, of Ft. Lauderdale's WFTL radio station, asked for his over-the-phone, live interview went something like this: "What do Koreans think of the riots, the burning down of Korean stores by Blacks in LA?"

I took a stab at reframing the question, dodging his hysteria-provoking question by making a disclaimer: "First of all, I want it on the record that although I am Korean, I am very removed from Koreatown and South Central LA and even from the particular merchant class of Koreans in New York City that might have a very different reaction from me. I want to caution that although Koreans are often lumped together, we are not a homogeneous monolithic group ..."

Before I could finish my sentence, he irritably interjected: "But what do you *think* about stores being *looted, fire bombed, burned* to the ground, people losing all they had, their entire lifetime investments ..."

I could sense his intense agitation. Remaining calm, I said, "I think we need to take a step back and look at some of the roots of the tension. It's a tragedy for the Korean families whose lives and businesses have been shattered, but before we just react and feed into the ongoing hysteria, we must look at the history and specific incidents surrounding the rage and the black/Korean rela—"

He cut me off: "Are you telling me that you don't believe in individual responsibility?" He snarled at me with a venomous rage that betrayed the depth of his investment in my answer. Had I been prepared to rise to the occasion and be equally on the offensive, I would have shot his own question right back to him on the spot. When WFTL initially contacted CAAAV to ask someone from the organization, preferably someone Korean, to be on the show, they presented the discussion topic as anti-Asian violence and the work of CAAAV. Having agreed to do the interview, what I had failed to anticipate was that Rick was planning to use me (or whatever Korean he could get, *as if our ethnic background implies a particular political leaning*) to showcase the reactions of a Korean American to the events in Los Angeles. (I happen to be an East Coast second-generation Korean who spent exactly two days in Los Angeles in 1990 during a layover on an east-bound flight).

The interview escalated into a screaming match. He accused me of being a traitor to my people: "I can't believe you call yourself *Korean*. How can you be a spokesperson for your people? You work for a group called the Committee Against Anti-Asian Violence and you're defending *black* people! You should be a spokesperson for some *black* organization!"

He spat, outraged, personally and profoundly insulted—as if being Korean and black were so completely mutually exclusive to the point of being virulently opposing entities. I can't remember what more erupted, not to mention what I actually ended up saying before I hung up in the middle of the show. He didn't let me talk, he continued to scream above my voice, insult me and reprimand me. He intended his screaming to silence me. It was effective because it was impossible for me to finish my original point, which suggested that we should examine the reasons for the backlash before universally condemning "black people" and jumping to the conclusion that Koreans living in the United States should officially declare war against an entire race. He wanted me to react like the many young second-generation children of merchants who are memorialized for their declarations that they are scared for their lives every time a black customer walks into their parents store, that they don't like black people. On one major network news show, one young Korean American stated that she is so hateful of black people that if a black person appears on television, she changes the channel or turns it off.

In a recent article entitled, "Remembering Latasha: Blacks, Immigrants, and America," Wanda Coleman describes the prerogative of a racist system: "When merchants like Soon Ja Du mimic whites' fear of blacks, their behavior is condoned, if not rewarded by our society."[21] Because Rick, the radio interviewer, was unsuccessful in his attempt to wrangle from me an anti-black statement, despite his force-feeding, he had to condemn and denounce me and declare that I was not Korean.

People of color share a collective experience of constantly being told who and what we are, of having our experiences and histories distorted and erased. When we refuse to play the role of the loyal Uncle Tom or the upstanding Model Minority, we also deny Rick and people of his ilk a valuable mouthpiece to be used to front for and exhonorate a racist United States.

Conclusion

The annual New Year demonstrations against CPC are becoming an icon for New York City's Asian American movement culture. We tromp on the picket line to the urban hip-hop beat of our chants, to the campy Cantonese-English/English-Cantonese slogans:

"CPC sucks the blood of the community!" rails an outraged protester.

"Blood-sucking vampires!" hurls another.

"Blood-sucking vampires!" echoes the rest of the picket line.

"No cheap labor!" someone shouts and then, bullhorn in hand, commences a speech: "Chinese are not slaves! The Chinese community refuse to be used as cheap coolie labor. When we cheap labor, we drive the wages down for all workers—black, Latino workers. Boss won't hire anyone but us. But when we say, 'No cheap labor!' we fight for all communities, not just Chinese community!"

It is a high standard we must hold ourselves to and it takes a lot of self-respect to not be used as de facto scabs or as puppets to defend the abuses of white racism, to reject a role that has historically been carved out for us as strikebreakers and model minorities. The country is approaching a turning point when the "minority" will become the "majority." For this reason, in order to maintain the current world order, there is an increasingly high premium placed on the political and class identification of Asians in this country. Community and workers' struggles are pointing to new approaches to build true relationships with other communities of color to resist a divide-and-conquer strategy that is as operative as ever.

Notes

1. Kwong, Peter, *The New Chinatown*. New York, Hill & Wong, 1987, p. 66.
2. Ibid., p. 64.
3. New York City's Chinatown has become the haven not only for Chinese immigrants seeking work but for many other Asian Americans as well. Malaysian and Vietnamese workers (including many who are ethnically Chinese), for instance, work in Chinatown's many garment shops as well as Chinese-owned shops located in surrounding areas, such as Brooklyn.
4. According to the New York Police Department, driving a cab is the second most hazardous and deadly occupation in New York City. The reported average for robberies is three a day; up to a dozen drivers of yellow cabs are killed each year. The most dangerous job in the city in terms of robberies and homicides is tending small retail businesses, which is, incidentally, the occupation of countless numbers of Asian immigrants of all ethnicities/nationalities.
5. Kwong, p. 62.

6. Although the lack of skills is often cited as a reason for why immigrants of color are unable to get decent jobs, immigrants with professional degrees, credentials, and years of experience seem to be caught up in the same service-sector jobs as compatriots who have less than a secondary education. Ironically, where provisions of the McCarran Walter Immigration and Nationality Act of 1952 and the Immigration Act of 1965 once favored the immigration of skilled and educated foreign professional, given the current split economy, where middle-level jobs have all but disappeared, credentialed and "skilled" immigrants are now more threatening than "acceptable." A discriminatory credentials system in the fields of law, medicine, business, and academia, that generally does not recognize credentials obtained in Third World countries, effectively bars immigrants from entering professional occupations.

7. Kwong, p. 67.

8. Marable, Manning, "A New Black Politics," *The Progressive.* August 1990, p. 22.

9. Asian American Union for Political Action (AAUPA), *News.* Winter 1992.

10. Ibid.

11. Ibid.

12. Ibid.

13. Ibid.

14. Kwong, p. 169.

15. AAUPA.

16. Ibid.

17. Marable, p. 21.

18. Kwong, p. 169-170.

19. Still pending is the workers' case with National Labor Relations Board which, having already determined the workers' right to form a union at Shinwa, will bring charges against the restaurant for its labor violations. Also, the workers brought a civil suit against Shinwa for the stolen back wages.

20. Listed are some of the press that contacted CAAAV for quotes and interviews within a three-day period during the first week of May 1992: *Crime Beat, a national magazine covering crime,* asked CAAAV to comment on the "Korean issue" for a feature entitled "Victim's Voice"; *Crain's New York Business,* a weekly journal, asked CAAAV how the Korean community in New York is affected by the Los Angeles situation and wanted lyrics from Ice Cube's overtly anti-Korean/anti-Asian "Black Korea"; "Now It Can Be Told," WNBC's prime-time news magazine, wanted the story on black and Korean relations, *The New York Post* called for a phone interview and actually ended up writing a praiseworthy article on CAAAV's perspective on the crisis in Los Angeles.

21. Coleman, Wanda, "Remembering Latasha: Blacks, Immigrants, and America," *The Nation,* February 15, 1993, p. 189.

273

Photo © by Corky Lee

14

THE HEAT IS ON
MISS SAIGON COALITION

Organizing Across Race and Sexuality

YOKO YOSHIKAWA

> The heat is on in Saigon
> The girls are hotter 'n hell
> One of these slits here
> Will be Miss Saigon
> God, the tension is high
> Not to mention the smell
> —opening lyrics to *Miss Saigon*[1]

Demonstration #1, April 6, 1991

Someone up there was rooting for us. It was perfect weather for a demo—cool, caressing, fresh—as good as spring evenings get in New York City. Moving toward the theater, we were a huge, motley mass of 500 or so, waving signs, chanting—loud, formidable, tough. This was *the* place to be seen and to see if you were a lesbian or gay man of color politically active in the local gay and lesbian community, a white gay man or lesbian committed to fighting racism and sexism, or a leftist Asian or Pacific Islander anywhere along the sexual continuum. We, the organizers, were ecstatic. Not until that moment did we know how much support we would gather in our protest of the Lambda Legal Defense and Education Fund's *Miss Saigon* benefit.

Months before, members of the Asian Lesbians of the East Coast (ALOEC) and of Gay Asian and Pacific Islander Men of New York (GAPIMNY) had learned that two major lesbian and gay community institutions were planning to use *Miss Saigon,* Cameron Mackintosh's Broadway musical, as their annual fundraiser extravaganzas. One of them was the Lambda Legal Defense and Education Fund (LLDEF), a national law organization that champions lesbian and gay rights. The other was New York City's Lesbian and Gay Community Services Center. We felt outraged at these plans, as we saw *Miss Saigon* as the latest in a long line of Western misrepresentations of Asians, perpetuating a damaging fantasy of submissive "Orientals," self-erasing women, and asexual, contemptible men. As Asians and Pacific Islanders who experience the racism and sexism showcased in *Miss Saigon,* we called upon Lambda to drop the fundraiser. Lambda, however, citing its fiscal bottom line, refused to do so. Undaunted, we formed a coalition and organized two demonstrations, the first on April 6, 1991 against the Lambda fundraiser, and the second on April 11, the opening night of the show.

On April 6, a block or so before the theater, we were stopped by police, intent on keeping us where we could not fully see or be seen by the theater-goers. The rumor was that Tom Stoddard, LLDEF's then-executive director, had warned the police that he expected a large demonstration—and possibly violence. While we moved, amoeba-like, across the street to face the theater, the cops closed in. They hauled away six men, two of whom were monitors and active coalition organizers.[2]

The arrests infuriated us. We considered them an excessive exercise in intimidation. In effect, Stoddard drew a line between "law and order"—Lambda's well-dressed, overwhelmingly white, mainly male donors—and us, mostly yellow and brown-skinned, kept at bay by the cops.

Just minutes before 8 p.m., two donors gave their $100 tickets to us. A quick huddle, and Milyoung Cho (also a contributor to this book) and I decided to use the tickets for an impromptu act of civil disobedience. We took off into the enemy zone. Whispering in a deserted bathroom, we hastily planned our action.

The opening number was dazzling—and loud. The musical opens in a brothel in Saigon, where prostitutes vie for the title, *Miss Saigon*. U.S. soldiers buy raffle tickets; Miss Saigon will be the prize. But I was not following the songs—this lusty dance of glistening legs and dark breasts, of ogling eyes and lathered lips in uniform mesmerized me. It pulled me in, as soft porn will. But I also felt sickened and alienated. The show was designed to seduce, flooding the senses with a 3-D fantasy—specifically targeted at a heterosexual western man's pleasure center.

Rumor had it that Jonathan Pryce, a Caucasian British man and leading actor, was close to a nervous breakdown, unnerved by all the controversy and criticism of his role as a Vietnamese pimp. We sat and nervously waited specifically for him. As Pryce entered the set and launched into song, we blasted into ours—deliberate discord, whistling, yelling at the top of our lungs: "This play is racist and sexist, Lambda is racist and sexist!"

Kicked out and back on our side of the street, Milyoung addressed the crowd via bullhorn, saying that what we did in there was only possible because of everyone out here—our demonstration moved two donors to rethink their support of Lambda. With their tickets we brought the coalition's rage from the streets into the theater. It was as though Milyoung and I had acted as the claws of a large, potent animal, infiltrating the theater's inner sanctum and ripping away all illusions of innocence. The roar that swept over us as we, unscathed and exultant, emerged from the theater, was a roar of sheer power, concentrated and raw.

Setting the Stage, December 1990

Aluminum pans were half-filled with pad thai, kim chee, chirashi-zushi, egg rolls. When I walked in to my first coalition meeting, about two dozen people were on the futon couch and all over the floor, eating, talking, digesting. I felt shy, and intimidated. Most of the women were members of Asian Lesbians of the East Coast (ALOEC), the men from Gay Asian and Pacific Islander Men of New York (GAPIMNY). The men were mostly young, good-looking, and physically entangled—arms flung around shoulders, legs entwined, one man leaning back into another's embrace, and someone's hands playing idly in another's long hair. This easy physical intimacy between Asian and Pacific Islander men moved me: I had seen men on the streets of Shanghai leaning into each other, close, but never here, in this country.

By then, *Miss Saigon* was already notorious for casting Pryce in a role that called for an Asian or Eurasian actor. In London, Pryce had been acting in yellow-face, with prosthetically altered eyelids and tinted make-up. In the summer of 1990, as advance sales for the show's Broadway run were racking up millions of dollars, Actors' Equity, the U.S. actors' union, called for the "engineer" to be recast with an Asian American when the show moved to New York. The media labelled the union's demand "artistic censorship," and rallied to support Mackintosh, the producer. When Mackintosh threatened to keep *Miss Saigon* off Broadway entirely, Actors' Equity backed down, unwilling to endanger the profits and jobs *Miss Saigon* would offer.

Our discussion after that first meeting centered on the show's theme and lyrics. Our faces were somber as Gene Nakajima summarized the plot and quoted some of the words used to describe Asians: "greasy Chinks" and "slits." *Miss Saigon* is the opera *Madame Butterfly* created by Giacomo Puccini in 1904, updated and reworked for post-Vietnam War popular consumption. In *Madame Butterfly,* a U.S. naval officer settles in Nagasaki, Japan, with a lovely courtesan known as Madame Butterfly (Chocho-san). Promising to return soon, he sets sail, and she scans the harbor daily, rejecting all other suitors while she waits. Years go by. One day his ship sails in, and he disembarks with his new, white wife on his arm. Madame Butterfly cannot bear the sight, and kills herself.

In a memo submitted in late February 1991, Angelo Ragaza, then a former temporary worker at Lambda, urged his co-workers to examine the "orientalist" significance of both the opera and the musical:

> Westerners, bent on expanding their empires until there remained no territory left to expand into, were particularly interested in complex, centrally controlled Asian societies. These societies tended to be more tricky to infiltrate, politically and commercially. Among them, Japan was, and remains, perhaps the most notorious....
>
> Butterfly is a woman who can only exist for a man, not for or by herself. She symbolizes a Japan who cannot join the modern world without America's "help," and an "East" which has no identity without the benediction of the West. Everything about Butterfly's demise sublimates Western frustration about Eastern impenetrability. From her defloration by an American military official to her ritual suicide with a dagger, Butterfly's tragic death reasserts the primacy of Western virility and, in the mind of the spectator, erases the challenges to that virility posed by the East. Put another way, "Madame Butterfly" is constructed on wishful thinking.[3]

Miss Saigon portrays the doomed romance of a U.S. soldier, Chris, and a Vietnamese prostitute, Kim. In Saigon, Chris meets Kim at a brothel. They spend one night together and fall in love. The next day, U.S. forces abruptly pull out of Vietnam and Chris is forced to leave without her. He returns three years later with his white, U.S. wife, Ellen, to look for Kim and the son Chris conceived with her. Kim, meanwhile, ever faithful to Chris, was forced to flee Vietnam after killing a loathsome government official who was pressing her to marry him. Kim finally is reunited with Chris in Bangkok, only to die in his arms, having killed herself so that Chris and Ellen will raise her son in the United States.

Virtually the entire twentieth century—and its myriad assaults on the cult of white male supremacy—separates *Madame Butterfly* from *Miss Saigon*. During that period, East Asian nations have forced Western nations to contend with them as military and economic peers: with North Korea and North Vietnam (and the dreaded shadow of Communist China) as Cold War enemies, and with Japan, former Axis aggressor, recently refashioned as a global financial heavyweight. In this post-colonial era, the West is no longer unquestionably supreme. These developments have led to a nostalgia for white European racial and cultural supremacy. *Miss Saigon* resurrects a myth that serves the Western empire in the late twentieth century: Abandoned by the white man, the "oriental" woman will voluntarily self-destruct.

True, *Miss Saigon* is only a night's entertainment. A few hours of froth—at $100 a pop—will not a racist make. With the proper dose of irony and detachment, a viewer could perhaps be humored by this show. But is it harmless? Hardly. "Miss Saigon" is yet another name to add to the roster of pop culture stereotypes: Suzy Wong, Charlie Chan, Fu Manchu, "Chink," and "Gook." *Miss Saigon* contributes to an entrenched system of racist and sexist images that straitjackets relationships between Asians and Westerners. This system is backdrop to increasing incidents of violence against Asians and Asian Americans across the United States, and paves the way for exploitation in massage parlors, mail-order bride businesses, and Asia-based tourist industries where women, children, and sometimes men are sold as commodities.

At stake in *Miss Saigon* is how those who control the means of representation and reproduction choose to define people of color and non-Western cultures, and to what ends. *Miss Saigon* rewrites the Vietnam War, pulling a sentimental love story from the carnage of carpet bombing, My Lai, and Agent Orange like a rabbit from a hat. Vietnam becomes just another exotic backdrop, good for a shot of nightclub sleaze and a real live helicopter lift-off. Mackintosh and company spiced the racism of "Madame Butterfly"—a white man's wet dream—with the endorphin-pumping antics of Rambo and came up with a new version of an old story of exploitation to feed into the money-making machines of Broadway. The bottom line is profit, and in a racist and patriarchal society, pliant, self-effacing geisha girls and despicable Asian pimps and traitors sell quite profitably.

While we organized against *Miss Saigon* that winter, the United States, led by President George Bush, invaded Iraq. The rhetoric employed by Bush and company to drum up support for the war sheds light on how *Miss Saigon* falls in with a national syndrome: Simplistic beliefs about other cultures and non-Christian "natives" rationalize imperialism and aggression. Via mass media, Operation Desert Storm sold us glory and glitz, yellow ribbons and "smart" bombs, of an "all-American" winning team, out in the desert, fighting the good fight against the dark, ungodly, and upstart Saddam Hussein. Similarly, by serving up racist images of Asian servility, powerlessness, and depravity, *Miss Saigon* prepares the palate for the neo-imperialist policies advocated by former President Bush. Racist pop culture stifles the possibilities of understanding or compassion across racial or national lines.

The Coalition's Organizational Roots

Dozens of other groups no doubt discussed organizing initiatives against *Miss Saigon* in other overheated apartments all over the city that December 1990. A good number probably never saw the light of day. Our effort, however, weathered the winter, took root, and burst into bloom in spring. The Broadway production of *Miss Saigon* certainly merited public criticism and debate. It was our organizing that brought the problematic themes of the play itself to the public eye.

That first potluck heralded a new political alliance between a number of mostly young New York City Asian lesbians and gay men. Before GAPIMNY's inception, a year or so before, there had been no organization of politically active gay men to match and work with ALOEC. The GAPIMNY-plus-ALOEC combination had vigor: We knew we were pushing open a new and unique space, making community for those who have been marginalized as queers in a straight world, and Asians in a white one. As we came together across gender, we developed an openness toward difference and a flexible negotiating style that served us in good stead as we built our coalition.

A key factor was that we had enough lead time (from December to February) to develop cohesion and strength as a core group.

By no means was that easy. After the first couple meetings, Mini Liu, Milyoung, and I would rush through the cold streets of China-town, heading for the subway back to Brooklyn, and kvetch about "those men": how fractious and immature "they" were, how "they" did not know how to conduct themselves in a meeting.

As time went by, relations improved. Our meetings became more efficient, although they were always long and frequent. We began to work as a team, and to take on organizational roles. James Lee, for example, was archivist and point-person for all flyers, press releases, and our expanding database. I facilitated meetings. Those among us with long histories as activists in the New York Asian American community provided much needed level-headed-ness and pragmatic knowledge. A number of the "younger" mem-bers had been influenced by queer activism generated in response to the AIDS epidemic. There was an in-your-face, no-shit style to our confrontations and organizing that has always been a charac-teristic of ACT UP.

Right up until early March, we focused on convincing Lambda and the Community Services Center to cancel their use of *Miss Saigon* as a fundraiser, not on protesting the play itself. We called on the gay and lesbian community to deal with its institutional racism, and those who responded were men and women, mostly of color, committed to creating a community in which all lesbians and gay men, regardless of color, could find safe haven. They gave our struggle breadth and force. The core group pulled on various threads of friendships and working relationships in the commu-nity, and our coalition grew strong at the center of those tangled skeins.

From our base in the lesbian and gay community, we gath-ered the force and momentum to make our issue visible. We did not go beyond that community until late February, when we decided to take on *Miss Saigon*'s official opening. Only after we were sure that we wanted to make our position on *Miss Saigon* known to the general public, did we actively reach out to Asian and Pacific Islander communities in New York.

I flung myself into this undertaking. It fed a deep hunger in me for community and challenge. All of us in the core group had to deal with the question of how, and in what, do we ground ourselves as the coalition and its goals grew. We learned that we could depend on each other, and find our strength there. We recognized in one another a stubborn, outlaw cunning and resilience, knotted ourselves a rope of sometimes grudging but usually wry affection, and tied ourselves in. It was when my grip on that rope loosened that I most likely found myself drowning.

Confronting Lambda, February 19, 1991

As Lambda's fundraiser was scheduled for April, and the Center's was not until October, our first goal was to persuade Lambda to cancel its benefit. In December, we wrote a letter to Lambda in which we set forth our concerns about *Miss Saigon,* and called upon it to discontinue the fundraiser. The organization responded with a civil but unequivocal no. We arranged a meeting to discuss the issue further.

On February 19, seven people from Lambda's board, staff, and management met with about a dozen of us, at a long table. Encircling us, along the walls, sat people that we had invited to attend: friends, lovers, and allies from lesbian and gay men of color organizations, and progressive Asian groups.

We stated our position in an opening statement:

> What does it mean for Lambda, a civil rights organization that claims to represent *all* Gay men and Lesbian women, to meet its annual budget with images of us as prostitutes and pimps, "greasy Chinks" and "slits"?...
>
> We call upon you to recognize that Lambda's use of a racist and sexist play is blatantly hypocritical and unprincipled. The monies you raise from *Miss Saigon* will disappear by the end of your fiscal year, but we contend every day with the exploitative and dehumanizing stereotypes and violence perpetuated by *Miss Saigon.*
>
> We call upon Lambda to recognize its responsibility as an organization of cutting-edge civil rights litiga-

tion, to put itself on the line for anti-sexist, anti-racist activism, in solidarity with all of us committed to social change.[4]

The meeting was contentious. Tom Stoddard, Lambda's executive director, explained that it was difficult to pull out as Lambda had already invested in the fundraiser, and it was counting on the proceeds, which would be 10 percent of its annual budget. We countered that *Miss Saigon* could ultimately cost Lambda far more in terms of its standing in the gay community. One (white male) board member, volunteered his opinion that *Miss Saigon* is not racist—a (white) friend saw it in London and said so. Carol Buell, another board member, began a sentence with: "Well, when *Miss Saigon* is dead and buried..." and Milyoung interrupted, "Men yell "Suzy Wong" at me in the streets now and that came out 20 years ago!" Ron Johnson, an African American board member, spoke soothingly, sympathetically, of "your pain," and proposed awareness-raising forums on racism for Lambda's donors, to be offered in conjunction with the fundraiser. Tsuhyang Chen, a member of our group, shouted the words "Faggot!" "Dyke!" and asked, in the shocked silence, how would they feel if people were paying money to hear those words used to describe gay men and lesbians. Why, then, is it so hard for you to understand our position vis-à-vis a play in which Asians are called "greasy Chinks" and "slits"?

The meeting was the galvanizing kick we needed to move our campaign up to the next level. Lambda refused to cancel, and we began planning our demonstration for its fundraiser. Those members of the community who participated in that first meeting with Lambda became the first and most stalwart members of our multiracial coalition. Coming face-to-face with Lambda's resistance and creating a forum for our anger pulled the core group of Asian and Pacific Islander lesbians and gay men together as nothing had before.

It was as though all the reasons anyone ever participates in political organizing were made evident during that meeting. We formed a group that we could trust, solidly knit in our understanding of the issues and goals, but loose and diverse enough to allow a range in tactics (some people on our side of the table were more confrontational than others). I felt that I could step out, and risk speaking beyond what I would ever have been able to say alone, because I was with allies who would hear me and be there to back me up if I could not go on. Many of us who are marginalized by virtue of our color and sexual orientation must silently swallow racist or homophobic remarks, institutionalized bigotry, violence and the threat of violence, almost daily. What we swallow twists our bowels, poisons our bodies, affects our loves and lives. Collectively, for once, we set up a situation in which we could say, *directly* to the people who angered and hurt us, what they were doing and how they were accountable.

A few days after our meeting, Stoddard let us know by fax that Lambda would not cancel its fundraiser. The core group of Asians met to discuss our next step, and, hot with anger, we decided to storm Stoddard's office. We marched in, about a dozen strong, and crowded around his desk. The discussion was angry, polarizing, intense. That half-hour had a totemic significance for me; it was as though, talking to and facing that red-faced, loud-voiced figure across the desk, I was standing up to all the white male authority I had ever bowed to in silence before. Stoddard's face metamorphosed to my father's face, as I broke the taboos instilled so well in me as eldest daughter of immigrant Japanese: Do not disobey; do not talk back.

Building a Coalition Within the Lesbian and Gay Community, February to March 1991

Lambda attempted to address our concerns by sending its donors a copy of the statement we had presented at the first meeting and offering to refund those who wished to return their tickets. This did not satisfy us, and we launched a two-pronged strategy: Continue pressuring Lambda to cancel, and greet its theatergoers with a demonstration if it did not.

Our meetings and committees became multiracial. Members of ACT UP, Brooklyn Women's Martial Arts, Gay Men of African

Descent, Kambal sa Lusog, Las Buenas Amigas, Latino Gay Men of New York, Men of All Colors Together, Other Countries, Queer Nation, Salsa Soul Sisters, South Asian Lesbians and Gay Men, We Wah and Bar Chee Ampe, among others, joined.

We had meetings and phone conversations with the staff at Lambda. Seven staffpersons, all women, signed a letter to the board and management urging them to reconsider canceling and offering to take salary cuts to offset any loss of funds that doing so could incur. Lambda's public education coordinator, a Latina activist named Mariana Romo-Carmona, resigned in protest.

On the other coast, California's Gay Asian and Pacific Alliance and Asian Pacifica Sisters put pressure on Lambda's Los Angeles office.

In support of our struggle, Audre Lorde, an African American lesbian feminist poet who has since passed away, refused to accept the Liberty Award from Lambda and did not attend the presentation ceremony. Her response to Lambda's decision to use *Miss Saigon* was:

> ...it was a damned foolish, naive, insensitive thing for Lambda to have done, and again, since I understand why it was done, it makes me furious, it makes me furious!
>
> Until the real nugget of what racism and sexism is all about comes through to the white lesbian and gay community, this thing is going to keep happening all over again. Until every single person in every single organization realizes that people of color, gay or straight, are constantly being misnamed, are constantly being misidentified, and that if you are going to deal with any piece of culture with people of color, you must go to that community and ask: What do you think of this? And that goes from *Dances with Wolves* to *Miss Saigon*.[5]

In March, coalition members met with the board and management from the Lesbian and Gay Community Services Center. This meeting, unlike the one with Lambda, was amicable and productive. The Center is a truly New York City-based organization, with stronger ties and commitment to the local gay and lesbian community. We had more lead time, as the Center's benefit was not until October. The Center witnessed the community's anger in response to Lambda's refusal to cancel and decided to pull out.

Our position stirred strong feelings. At our forum on *Miss Saigon* at the Center on March 29, a stack of anonymous flyers was found outside, accusing the coalition of being homophobic. *The Village Voice's* only mention of this issue echoed that accusation:

> Aren't you tired of hearing about a show that hasn't opened yet? Tough. The latest on [*Miss Saigon*], which finally begins previews March 23, is that two gay Asian groups—Asian Lesbians of the East Coast and Gay Asian and Pacific Islander Men of New York—are up in arms over the show's racism and sexism. Are they pick- eting the authors, the directors, the producer, the the- ater? No, they're criticizing Lambda Legal Defense and Education Fund and the Lesbian and Gay Community Services Center, two of the 250 nonprofit organizations (including the Pearl S. Buck Foundation) selling benefit tickets to *Miss Saigon.* Sounds like sophisticated, more p.c.-than-thou gay-bashing to me...[6]

These comments uncovered a disturbing assumption: When les- bian and gay people of color criticize the white gay male establish- ment, they are "gay-bashing." This implies that one must be white to be gay. And that Asian lesbians and gay men are close kin to skinheads, cruising the Village, looking for "faggots" and "dykes" to beat up.

The divided feelings of the community found outlet in the letters section of *Outweek,* a weekly magazine that ceased publica- tion that summer. Our message was helped by the sharp exchange: The issue was hot, and one way or the other, people gave it thought. *Outweek's* editors and commentator Michelangelo Signorile lam- basted Lambda for its position on *Miss Saigon,* but a number of their readers did not. Some challenged our analysis of *Miss Saigon,* saying that the show actually criticizes U.S. involvement in Vietnam. Others were frustrated or saddened by what they termed infighting, asking why we should do this to Lambda, when it has done so much for all of us in the realm of civil rights.

We found support among lesbian and gay activists of color and white people committed to fighting racism and sexism because the issue spoke to the unequal distribution of power and privilege within the lesbian and gay community. As they do in mainstream society, white men hold a disproportionate amount of institutional power in the queer community. Gay white men sit on boards or head up a number of community organizations, and often help determine priorities and programs. In the allocation of resources such as AIDS funding, or the absence of programs that battle breast cancer, people of color and lesbians have found that their concerns and needs are not automatically given equal shrift.

In calling upon Lambda to withdraw from its benefit, we drew our line: Will you claim as your own our concerns as Asians who, like you, belong to this community? In a larger sense, this is what happens in the United States every time a minority group demands a withheld right, or attacks the discriminatory status quo. But when members of a marginalized group accuse other members within the same group of marginalizing them, they hit a land mine. Some members of the community may rush to its defense, sounding the alarm that they have been betrayed from within. They fear the community will splinter into ineffectual fragments, or that others will pounce upon this weak link. What, they ask, will happen to the real issue—our struggle for recognition and equal rights in society-at-large?

The core group broke a taboo: We rocked the boat, hard. We would not wait until the larger struggle was won. What use are future gains to us if we are not full members in the community that exists now? What is this "community" anyhow? We transgressed—derailed "the struggle," aired dirty laundry—because we were staking a claim to a community of our making. Those who saw that joined us. Fifteen activists, of color and white, described this undertaking in a letter addressed to Lambda in *Outweek:*

We repeat our message to you and all other groups where white men dominate: We can no longer give our time and energy and spirit and lives to those who support our oppression by their racism and sexism. We want a movement where we can bring our whole selves—all of our concerns for freedom—to the organizing table.

There is no tyranny of the oppressed; there is simply the strong call for justice and equality from those who increasingly understand that all oppressions are connected and single issue/single oppression approaches will never bring lasting social change.

... You are left with many years of work ahead of you to try to figure out how to overcome your current reputation for upholding a white heterosexual male view of the world, while we are marching toward a new kind of organizing, a deep and true movement of social change for all of us.[7]

Within the Asian and Pacific Islander Community, March to April 1991

The second demonstration piggy-backed the first. We began organizing for it in late February, when we decided that by supplementing our original coalition with members of New York's Asian and Pacific Islander communities, we could ensure a respectable turnout against the show on opening night. Our plan was to use opening night as the forum to publicly register our opposition to the show itself, proving that we were not just gunning for Lambda.

Our first new ally in this initiative was the Asian Pacific Alliance for Creative Equality (APACE), an organization of Asian theater artists who organized against *Miss Saigon* in 1990 over the casting issue. We were soon joined by others, including Youth for Philippine Action (YPA), the Coalition Against Anti-Asian Violence, the Japanese American Citizen's League, the Pan Asian Repertory Theater, the Chinese Progressive Association, and college students' associations.

They pitched in. Veena Cabreros-Sud read an extraordinarily powerful speech which she and other YPA members wrote for our forum at the Center. Ding Pajaron launched her own fight to educate other parents and administrators at her daughter's private school about *Miss Saigon,* to convince them to cancel their own *Miss Saigon* fundraiser. (In the end, the Bank School went ahead with it.) Lawyers from Asian and Pacific Islander organizations negotiated with the police at the demonstrations and provided counsel.

The Asians and Pacific Islanders we recruited looked to our coalition and saw leaders who were Asian, as they were. They saw a struggle that affected them as Asian and Pacific Islander peoples, and joined it. It should have been that simple. But it was not. We felt threatened. In the lesbian and gay community, Asians and Pacific Islanders had naturally led the opposition against a show that was racist towards Asians. But now, that role was up for grabs—after all, they were Asians, too.

We in the core group were quick to suspect the new members of attempting to erase or dismiss the coalition's lesbian and gay origins and membership. We all, as lesbians and gay men, had directly experienced the conservatism and homophobia of our own Asian and Pacific Islander communities. Simultaneously, we felt a fierce loyalty toward our multiracial gay and lesbian allies, and needed to assert the lesbian and gay roots of the coalition even as we moved away from it.

The closer we came to opening night, the more we were deluged with media requests for interviews. Yet we were divided on the thorny question of who should represent the coalition. There were a few Asians and Pacific Islanders, such as Peter Chow from Asian Cinevision, who were more experienced in presenting a historical and critical perspective on productions such as *Miss Saigon* to the media. However, we were not prepared to give the fleeting space our organizing had wedged in the public eye to people who had not been integral to the organizing since the beginning.

Would they have assuaged our distrust if we had clearly articulated it? Perhaps. On occasion, some of the Asians and Pacific Islanders were impatient with our relative inexperience with the media and decentralized process. There were also those who may have wished to exploit the coalition for their own organization's interests or personal gains. But I recall no outright instances of homophobia.

Our coalition-building in the Asian and Pacific Islander community stumbled over sexual identity. They were not gay, and, therefore, they could not belong. We framed our organizing such that there was in essence two separate groups: gay and lesbian, Asian and Pacific Islander—moving toward two distinct demonstrations. Only in the last week and at the demonstrations, when we were all caught up in the power of what we had wrought, did the coalition become truly one.

Demonstration #2, April 11, 1991

The April 11 demo was less tightly organized and attended. It was less multiracial, more Asian, and more sober. We in the core group were still recovering from the first demonstration and found this one anti-climactic. Opening night was on a weekday, and started early—6:30 p.m. People straggled in late, having been tied up at work or assuming that the show would start at 8 p.m. The police cordoned off small pieces of pavement, and herded us into small pens, effectively diminishing our collective force. NYPD were around the corner in full regalia, mounted on horses, waiting for their cue to burst onto the scene. As the demonstration was smaller than that of April 6, the show of police was overkill.

But how the media swarmed! It was a feeding frenzy of cameras and microphones. All the major networks slotted us as their top story on the evening news that night. And then there were CNN, the *Post,* the *Daily News,* the *New York Times* non-local edition, National Public Radio, etc.

Our two minutes of fame consisted of an Asian talking head mouthing a rapid analysis: *Miss Saigon* is racist and sexist in the stereotypes it parades of Asian women and men as either self-sacrificing geishas or slimy pimps. And yes, we are concerned that Cameron Mackintosh hired a white actor for an Asian role, but, to go further still, we call for challenging and three-dimensional roles for Asian actors in the entertainment and theater industry today.

The primary significance of the second demonstration was that we transmitted the collective voices and faces of Asians and Pacific Islanders, contorted with anger, to society at large. We broke through the ceiling that separates the concerns of sub-communities from mainstream awareness, and gave those who were watching a glimpse—of just the tip—of an iceberg.

What we managed to say was certainly not untrue, nor insignificant. It is just that so much was not said. TV framed the event: The Asian community, monolithic, united, rises up to denounce the injuries of Broadway. No mention was made of our organizing process, no questions were asked about who we were. Why should they? They saw our Asian faces.

The further our organizing took us from the lesbian and gay community, the more asserting our sexuality became a political act. To be a lesbian or gay man in a society that is as homophobic and violent as the United States is to fight for your right to live and love when people might want you dead. To be "out" as lesbians and gay men on an issue that affected us as Asians and Pacific Islanders would show others that we *are* everywhere.

But the media was not interested in tackling that aspect of our coalition. At one point an exasperated TV reporter asked James Lee off the air, "What do lesbians and gay men have to do with protesting *Miss Saigon?*" A link between two such groups was too farfetched for them. Only one piece about the lesbian and gay leadership was ever published in a mainstream paper. Written by Ying Chan, it was buried deep in the *New York Daily News,* and came out days after the demonstration. Peter Kwong wrote an article about our organizing for *The Village Voice* that never saw publication. Both reporters are Asian, and have written extensively about New York City's Asian and Pacific Islander communities.

What we were flew directly in the face of mainstream assumptions about Asians. That Korean grocers are racist, that Asians always excel in math, that Oriental women make good wives, for example—those things are known. But nowhere in their roster of stereotypes was a place for angry, articulate, *queer* Asians. It was too much of a stretch for mainstream society to understand that we could be more than their cardboard cut-out Asians, that we could instead be complex individuals with divergent sexualities and multiple allegiances—just like them.

Conclusion

What, in the end, did we really do? *Miss Saigon* is still on Broadway. We never seriously thought we could close it down, although some of us certainly fantasized about a few well-placed stinkbombs. Lambda vowed to be more sensitive regarding issues that affect people of color. But when Tom Stoddard resigned from his position as executive director, they hired another white man, despite our lobbying efforts for a person of color or a woman.

The coalition, pared down to its lesbian and gay constituency, plowed on for about a year following the demonstrations, pressing various community organizations to actively address the needs and concerns of people of color and women in their decision-making, hiring policies, and programmatic emphases. Finally, it just fizzled out. People left town, or became involved in other consuming issues: HIV and AIDS, violence against Asians and Pacific Islanders, relationships, their own physical survival.

Our coalition pointed the way to a possible future: where a complex identity is not only valued, but becomes a foundation for unity. We who occupy the interstices—whose very lives contain disparate selves—are, of necessity, at home among groups that know little of each other. We know what others do not about reconciling differences in our own lives, and the mutable nature of borders. We have a deep hunger for a place in which we can be, at one and the same time, whole, and part of something larger than ourselves. Our knowledge and desire may at times bring us to action: We push the parameters of existing communities wide open, and cause the struggles of different communities to overlap and meld. In the tangle that ensues, we may also be midwives of vital coalitions.

This can be done only by claiming all of ourselves, with integrity, in community. At the first demonstration, James Lee taped a neon pink triangle to his leather jacket, emblazoned with the words: "San Francisco-born Gay Man of Korean Descent." On any other night, he could have been bashed for that. But that night, his back was covered. Gray-haired Japanese American wives and mothers and brash young white men from Queer Nation marched side-by-side. Dykes in dreads, campy queens, leftists of all persuasions: We owned Broadway.

Finally, a note of acknowledgement: I have not mentioned many people who were important to the coalition. Among them are: Bill Burns, June Chan, John Chin, Lei Chou, Sally Covington, Charlie Fernandez, Ben Geboe, Manolo Guzman, Curtis Harris, Scott Hirose, David Housel, Bert Hunter, Marla Kamiya, Don Kao, Ann Kwong, Mini Liu, Ming Ma, John Albert Manzon, Lance McCready, Gene Nakajima, Alice Ro, Robert Vazquez Pacheco, Vondora Wilson-Corzen, and Lisa Yi.

Notes

1. Lyrics are quoted from the libretto accompanying the *Miss Saigon* compact disc, produced by Alain Boublil and Claude-Michel Schöenberg, 1988.
2. Monitors Haftan Eckholdt and Joe Pressley, as well as activists Chris Hansen, Simon Howard-Stewart, Karl Jagbundhansingh, John Kusakabe were charged with disorderly conduct. The police beat both Kusakabe and Pressley, who are men of color.
3. Open memo to Lambda from Angelo Ragaza, dated February 21, 1991, pp. 6 and 7.
4. From the February 19, 1991 statement by members of ALOEC and GAPIMNY, read by John Manzon and Yoko Yoshikawa.
5. Audre Lorde, quoted from personal interview with June Chan and Mariana Romo-Carmona, recorded on video April 26, 1991.
6. Don Shewey, "Playing Around," *The Village Voice,* March 12, 1991.
7. "Letter to Lambda", *Outweek,* May 1, 1991, p. 5. Signed by Beth Richie, Suzanne Pharr, Val Kanuha, Chris Hansen, Helen Zia, Rebecca Cole, Kelly Kuwabara, Sally Cooper, Dion Thompson, Stephanie Roth, Robert Reid-Pharr, Rick O'Keefe, Tony Glover, Manuel Guzman, and Ann Kochman.

15

IDENTITY IN ACTION

A Filipino American's Perspective

STEVEN DE CASTRO

Identity is cool, but identity without action is masturbation. Some Filipino Americans claim to be down with finding their identity, but they turn away from the struggles of their brothers and sisters, remain aloof to the U.S. government's support of death squads in the Philippines, and remain silent about racism and male domination in America. Some of us other Filipinos see things differently. We are against white supremacy, male domination, imperialism, and police violence. We are for our pride, our beauty, unity, and the future. We always say: *Paghahanap, pagtuklas, at pagbawi:* search, discover, and reclaim. We search for our true story, our collective story, and our story teaches us our duty. Our identity leads us to action.

This chapter is about breaking down Filipino American identity from a youth activist perspective. A lot of this chapter is based on my two years with an organization called Youth for Philippine Action (YPA) in New York City. I quit the group a couple of months ago, and later the group folded. I still agree with the principles and vision of YPA, and I write this as a tribute to that vision, to help carry it forward, even after the organization itself was destroyed.

Last year I checked out this youth forum at the Philippine Consulate in Manhattan. The theme: "Assimilation: How Much is Too Much?" (My answer is that you have to be pretty damn assimilated to even have a title like that.) It was held in the lavish Kalayaan Hall, with cherry oak paneling and twenty-foot ceilings and big fucking glass chandeliers. It's a perfect place for some *ilustrados*[1] to sit around and talk bullshit. On the side wall is a huge gold-framed painting depicting some "happy" Filipina peasants working in the fields. I walked in and thought, man, those peasants are going to be working a long time to pay off the bank loan that built this room.

At that forum you heard stuff like, "It's hard for us because we are minorities, but if you work hard you can make it." "We all come to the United States for economic advancement, so let's fit into the mainstream." "I like hanging out with Americans, they don't see me as different."

But there are other Filipino voices, and the moderator from United Filipino Youth Council lets those voices be heard. One asks, "You say you like hanging out with Americans, and that they don't see you as different. But if you are not different, why don't you refer to yourself as American?" Another sister from a community college says: "We people of color are the majority of the United States, and I am offended when you refer to people of color as minorities."

A young Filipino "banker" on the panel tried to say that he was a living example that we can make it in America, and a young Filipino in the audience said, "I don't care how much money you make. That's not helping our people. And remember Rodney King: next time it might be you who gets beaten by a white cop, my brother!" A shouting argument followed, leading nowhere.

Another young conservatively dressed Filipino from the audience stands up and says: "I did an internship in Washington, D.C. And I know that when one of us goes to a congressman to ask for something, they always smile and appear to be listening, but really they don't see us as equals. They treat us like their little brown brothers. So I think that the only way we are going to get results is if we stop arguing with each other and unite amongst ourselves."

Little brown brothers. The words used by President McKinley when he sought to take over the Philippines with over 100,000 U.S. troops in 1898, except that the Filipinos resisted the big white daddy and fought for four years in the little known Philippine-American War. At the end of the war, the Philippines was a commonwealth of the United States and one-sixth of the little brown brothers and sisters living in the Philippines had been killed. It chokes me up to hear those words, "little brown brothers." It is what white America calls us, it is how they think of us. It is how some of us think of ourselves.

The Filipinos continued arguing with each other, some folks sounding like that night was the first time they ever considered that Filipinos are not white, other folks sounding like the Filipino Malcolm X. I don't think the discussion really went anywhere, but we all learned to ask some fundamental why's.

- Why is it hard for us, and should we call people of color "minorities"?

- Why is the United States the place for getting ahead? Have you ever asked yourself why the Philippines isn't getting ahead?

- What is the mainstream in your mind except white? Did Vincent Chin, at the moment he was about to die, have the choice to suddenly join mainstream America?

- Does "assimilate" mean to become white, or to serve the white?

Everyone could see that the question of *who we are* can't be answered by arguing at each other over how white we should be (or could be). The answer lies in *paghahanap,* the search for our collective story.

We must get back to our collective story, without any lies, omissions, or distortions. We must link up the collective story with our personal story, understanding that Filipinos have unceasingly resisted oppression, but that we have also brought that oppression on ourselves by absorbing the attitudes of the colonizer.

Junior coconuts, like some of those folks at the forum, don't want to check the story. They think they can pick and choose which parts of the story they want to read. They refuse to see that their identity compels them to resist white male-dominated society. Instead, these *burgis Flips* [2] want to fashion a convenient identity that will be edible to the white man, to their white friends, to their white boss. Since their identity isn't based on the full story, their identity is weak and shaky and their life choices are based on insecurity and fear.

Pulling together the fragments of our story takes work. You can't do it alone; that would just be individualistic bullshit. We Filipinos have to work on our identity together, the Tagalog speakers and the non-Tagalog speakers, the 16-year-olds, the drop-outs, and the Columbia graduates. We work it a lot by just hanging out. We share music, we share stories, we share books. It looks a little unorganized, but what's going on is a process of Filipinos learning to stick together in a white world, and putting out a strong message of resistance. It's amazing to see young Filipinos checking out a *barkada* [3] working on identity, and in the beginning they just chill with the group and take in the discussion, without being pushed to accept a certain dogma. Eventually they hook up some experiences they have had in their personal lives with our collective past, and suddenly, you see them wake up! It's liberating.

Anti-Colonial Struggle

A big part of our collective story is the fight against colonization, which means all those fucking Europeans coming into our turf, treating us as inferior, and trying to run our lives. Colonization started in the sixteenth Century when some white guy named Legaspi came to settle the Philippines and extract work from the people, thinking he can make some money that way. Among other things, we were forced to work on the Manila shipyards, fashioning the galleons of Spain's Pacific fleet out of Philippine lumber. Today our colonizers are the U.S. government and the American and

Japanese corporations. The Philippines is the sixth largest gold producer and the ninth largest copper producer in the world. We are the fourteenth largest food producer in the world. And yet it is the foreign corporations who get rich and fat and who make sure that the Philippine people are hungry and poor.

When we talk about colonization it's not because we like to get negative. We do it because we believe in ourselves, that we can de-colonize the situation. But we've first got to stop thinking like the colonizer wants us to think, we've got to do away with what Filipino historian Renato Constantino calls the "colonial mentality." We've got to start doubting the bullshit that white America is trying to feed us in the schools and on TV. We have to stop seeing ourselves as inferior and stop seeing white America as an all-powerful symbol of everything good. Then we can come to a deeper understanding of our collective story. This is how we de-colonize our mentality.

The Philippine Independence Day Parade

One way that Youth for Philippine Action tried to educate the Filipino youth about our collective story was by joining the so-called Philippine Independence Day Parade of 1992. Across the United States, Philippine Independence Day is the largest event for Filipinos. We had a lot of reservations about being part of this parade. As an organization, we thought it was pretty dumb for some Filipinos to be celebrating so-called independence when most Filipinos are forced to live in poverty while big foreign corporations get rich from our land and labor and Filipinos can't speak their mind without the risk of being killed by death squads controlled by rich Flips and armed by U.S. tax money. Still, most of the thousands of Filipinos in New York go to the Philippine Independence Day Parade not to hear the Philippine Consul General congratulate himself. Most go to be with other Flips and to eat some good food. Also, some of the organizers are pretty down with the people's movement.

The thing that everyone forgot while they were putting this whole parade together was that 1992 was the 100th anniversary of the founding of the Katipunan, the first nationalist revolutionary organization of the Philippines. In 1892, Andres Bonifacio and Tandang Sora got with a whole posse of Flips and launched the revolution by tearing up the I.D. cards that the Spanish made them carry. This is called the Cry of Balintawak. After a bloody revolution, the Cry of Balintawak led to the Spanish getting kicked out of the Philippines. And today, we're still crying the Cry of Balintawak, and we're going to keep crying until our brothers and sisters get their land back from greedy landowners and some political prisoners get freed, and the United States gets all the military out of there and all the useless elites and army generals are out of the fucking government. And we're going to keep crying until we get a community center going and the white men no longer order Filipina sisters from a catalog like they were pieces of merchandise and we stop dying of AIDS and white immigration lawyers stop ripping us off of our hard-earned money. And when we get a hold of those white exploiters and the coconuts who help them out, they are the ones who will be crying.

So to us, that's what the Cry of Balintawak and this whole independence thing is all about. YPA built this fourteen-foot parade float, and we got some folks who knew some serious guerilla theater stuff from the Philippines and we re-enacted the founding of the Katipunan, and we all dressed as revolutionaries from 1892, carrying bolos and displaying signs and banners with the messages of today, chanting "Makibaka! Dare to Struggle!"

And we marched with Kambal sa Lusog, the Filipino lesbian and gay organization which does a lot of great AIDS work in New York City and which promotes Filipino American lesbian and gay identity and pride. It takes a lot of guts for pinoy lesbians, gays, and bisexuals to march in our community, which can be so fucking closed-minded that it ignores Filipino AIDS victims, and parents can't even talk to their children about AIDS or about their sexual orientation. And yet we Filipinos were also taught that Jesus said, "Comfort the sick," and that's exactly what Kambal sa Lusag is doing.

The homophobic attitudes we hold demonstrate centuries of colonial Catholic brainwashing whose only purpose is to keep us divided. Unless we can confront this mentality, we will never unite as a people. For instance, why is a Filipino family jumping for joy when the daughter brings home a white man, and yet the family is grossed out that two Filipino men love each other?

Both YPA and Kambal sa Lusog were received pretty well during the parade, and I think both organizations gained a few members that day. But that isn't the end of it. When the new YPA members joined up, we later told them about the next chapter of the story, which is how the Katipunan revolution ended:

After the Spanish colonizers got kicked out, the American colonizers decided that they were going to take over. The Flips weren't having it, so that's how the Philippine-American War began. Filipinos defended their homeland against over 200,000 American troops. The Americans loved to kill. One soldier wrote home, "This is just like shooting niggers." The Americans resorted to water torture. Then they started strategic hamletting and relocation of civilians; a quarter of the population of Luzon lost their lives. They finally pacified us by sending American school-teachers to spoonfeed us American "values" and respect for American institutions—the same bullshit we get now.

They tried to kill our revolutionary feelings by bringing the so-called "Thomasite teachers" to the Philippines in the early 1900s. These white teachers were on a mission to corrupt our young with a worship of American values, so that when our children grew up they wouldn't listen to the revolutionary leaders of the Katipunan, but instead would just worship America. A lot of experts say that the Filipinos in the Philippine-American War weren't ultimately defeated by guns, they were defeated by these schoolteachers feeding our children America's lies. That's colonial mentality.

We've had five centuries of that colonization shit. We've been colonized so many different ways that it's hard to figure out what about us is not colonized. Don't even waste your time trying to figure it out; in truth, the mind of the colonizer lives in all of us. Who we are is born from the relationship between the colonizer and the native in our consciousness. The colonizer and the native are in a tug of war inside us.

Miss Saigon

The colonial mentality is not just fostered in the history books: It is backed up by fucked up images of us in white culture, art, and religious institutions. Every time we promote the truth we are saying that something the white man taught us is a lie. We must protest these lies.

In the winter of 1991 Asian American activists formed the Heat is On *Miss Saigon* Coalition and held a protest at the opening night of the Broadway musical *Miss Saigon*. Three hundred Asian protesters were standing across the street from the debut chanting, "Racist, Sexist Broadway Hit—Why do you pay to see this shit?" On the side, TV crews were interviewing the press liaisons, who represented our position to the media. Me, I was just there to stand and hold a sign.

(Lea Geronimo, a Filipina sister, saw the performance that year. She said, "Back then I wasn't even too political. But when I saw *Miss Saigon,* I felt insulted as an Asian woman.")

Miss Saigon is a Broadway production about a Vietnamese prostitute who falls in love with a white American soldier. The starring role in the debut was played by a prominent Filipina actress named Lea Salonga, who is hailed by the Filipino American community for her achievement of being cast as the prostitute.

During the fall of Saigon the soldier takes off on a helicopter and returns many years later, with his white wife. The Vietnamese woman had been taking care of the Eurasian child that she had with the guy, and the guy takes the child to America and the Vietnamese woman stays behind and kills herself because she can't have the white man.

Now, this is more than just a stupid plot. It's about white people writing about white people, and in an effort to feel good about the injustices and the mistakes they have made in the Vietnam war, they made up this bullshit story. Think about it: If a modern day prostitute in Ermita district were writing the story, what kind of story do you think she would write? Do you think she would portray her experience with American soldiers as romantic?

Do you think she would congratulate white soldiers for being in Southeast Asia? Not.

Is there a conspiracy? Hell no. Powerful white people know how to stick together, they don't need a conspiracy. Check out the movies and see if what I am saying is right. Check out *Year of the Dragon* on video and see if what I'm saying is right. Write a musical about an Asian man and an Asian woman loving each other and working together to get the American troops out of Vietnam, and try to get it on Broadway, and see if what I'm saying is right.

You may think, so what if white folks want to watch this stupid shit? Maybe you're right, maybe it doesn't make a difference. But culture is powerful. Just like the Spanish invader kissed a cardinal's ring before sailing across the Pacific to drive a cross into the sands of a Philippine beach, America has needed to send itself cultural signals to go ahead and invade Vietnam, drop bombs on Arab people, exploit the Philippines, and whatever other bullshit it tries to pull on people of color all over the world.

Our first duty is to de-colonize our own heads. That doesn't mean we should become some type of thought police. It means we got to reflect on things with a critical mind, an open mind, and be smart enough to ask why white society creates these images of us, and what types of images they create for themselves. Then we can oppose these colonial images, because that is our way of tearing at the white man's shining image of himself.

Racism

The young Filipinos I know don't have to do any heavy analysis to understand racism. We understand racism through our eyes and our ears, and that becomes the starting point for our journey backwards and outwards into the collective story, where all other aspects of colonization are revealed, and the will to resist is born. Our raw experience is the beginning of the journey, but just learning about ourselves isn't the end of it. The goal of understanding racism in our lives is not so that we may go, "look how oppressed I am!" or so I think that white people owe me all the time (they don't). We do it so that we can sympathize with all who struggle against racial injustice.

"What's up, monkey?" "Hey Ching Chong! Hey eggroll!" "Here comes the gook!" If you are Filipino in America, that is what you grow up hearing in the schoolyard. All you want to do is belong, but white and black classmates never let you forget that you will never belong in their America.

When you get out of high school, these racist insults seem to get fewer, and come from farther away, usually from a passing car or from a bunch of rednecks walking by. But then, you have to put up with more sophisticated insults. A white man will say to you, "Oh, you're Filipino? I love your women!" or he will smile and start off a story, "I remember when I was in the navy..." Every Filipino knows how the white man's story goes: how he went whoring out of Subic Bay, and fucked some underage sister, and he thinks that proves what a man he is, and he never for one minute thought about the misery of our sister's life that forces her to sell her dignity to some dumb drunk piece of shit like him. And that's the first indignity. The second indignity is that this guy is telling this dumb story to you and is saying, "I love your women!"

The white media largely ignores you and the other one-and-a-half million Filipinos who live in America. When they do mention you, they group you together with the Chinese and Japanese. And when they do mention Filipinos, whether it's Imelda's shoes or about how corrupt our elections are, you wish they hadn't.

On September 22, 1992, this message was broadcast by eight radio stations across the country:

> Filipinos are cheaters and they think playing baseball is the greatest accomplishment of all and not knowing the value of the sport or the purpose of the game.
>
> The Philippines is a very strange country. I always recommend everybody not to go there, unless you want to get laid.
>
> The Philippines is a country where fathers sell their own daughters for sex. That's how desperate they are over there.

I think they eat their young over there.

—*Philippine News,* October 14, 1992

That was Howard Stern, a radio talk show host who makes his living by knowing what Americans will think is funny. And after hundreds of thousands of Americans have had a good laugh on their way to work, listening to the car radio, they get to work and meet you. They work with you, or you work for them. They decide whether to invite you to lunch. They decide whether to promote you, to hire you or fire you. And you thought that you left racism behind when you left the schoolyard.

And if you ever happen to start talking to them about how the U.S. bases should leave the Philippines, their first reaction is, "But what else could the Filipinos do for a living?"

So you try to be white. You try to pretend you don't know what's being said about you. You try to act like they aren't seeing you this way. If you can't beat them, join them. You try to think like them, look like them, be like them. You might even tell racist jokes (even against your own people!) to show how much of a COCONUT you are.

But it doesn't work. Instead of being a true coconut—white inside with a brown shell— it's really the other way around. You may put up a white shell, but deep inside your heart you are a beautiful Filipino. You can't hide it, even if your parents hid your native tongue to shut you off from your Filipino-ness, it's still there. By putting up that white shell you might try to hide your Filipino identity, but you can't. Because you ain't white.

Once you've figured that out you might react in anger. You hate white people. You sneer at Asian-white couples holding hands in the street. You try to purge yourself of your white ways, your white friends, your white album collection, your white foods.

You start looking for your enemies. You lash out at TV commercials that are being racist, at other Filipinos who are ignorant, and at white liberals who just don't understand. You see your pain as part of the social injustice we have to put up with as Filipinos, as Asians, and as people of color. You want to do something about it. Maybe you find others who are just as pissed. You start signing petitions, writing poems, going to meetings. But getting mad and wanting to do something about racism isn't enough. If all you are is mad, you'll soon get bitter, and activists who are bitter aren't worth shit. The reason you are bitter is because you feel powerless against racism and imperialism and sexism, and you start to turn the frustration against the people you organize with, or even against yourself. That purging-your-whiteness thing goes too far, and you start bitching at other Filipinos over every little thing they say or do, as if it's their fault that society is fucked up.

Then it's time to chill out. You aren't the only one who suffers in the world, so don't be so fucking bitter! You don't understand racism, sexism, and imperialism if you only care about how it affects you.

When you learn compassion for others in the world who struggle for justice, you will never be alone. And once you understand the debt you owe to the people who have come before us, you will never be bitter. You will get more effective, more committed. You realize that not all whites are enemies. More important: not all our enemies are white.

Our enemy is not a person, it is a mentality, the colonial racist mentality that people of color are inferior.

Police Brutality in Jersey City

In 1989, Rodin and Minerva Rodriguez, a Filipino couple in Jersey City, heard a large explosion outside their store. When Rodin rushed out front he was carrying a machete, but he relaxed when he saw a cop already out there. Suddenly the white cop started hassling Rodin about the machete. Rodin gave the machete to the officer, who put it in the police car. As the officer was walking back from his car, Rodin wrote down the officer's badge number, and I guess that pissed him off. The cop then beat and kicked Rodin to the ground. He handcuffed the storeowner and dragged him to the police car. Rodin was hospitalized, and to this day suffers from nerve damage in his wrists from being dragged across the ground by his handcuffs.

When the officer saw the wife, Minerva Rodriguez, run into the store to call the police headquarters, he ran into the store after her, beat her up and smashed the phone into pieces. He took both of them to the police station.

The Rodriguez's filed a complaint with the city and pressed charges against the cop, Officer John Chisulo. But the city wouldn't listen to an isolated Filipino. Although there are 11,000 Filipinos in Jersey City, Filipinos have no political pull and there are no Filipinos on the City Council. Rodin felt powerless.

Rodin approached the leaders of every Fil-Am association in Jersey City, and not one of these so-called Filipino community leaders spoke out for justice. The city didn't do anything. The cop got promoted.

This story ain't over. Two years later the same cop was giving a Puerto Rican man named Maximino Cintron Ortiz a parking ticket for tinting the windows of his car while it was parked on the street (which is apparently a crime). Ortiz ripped up the ticket. The cop punched Ortiz and Ortiz hit back. Then Officer Chisulo pulled his handgun and shot Ortiz in the stomach. Ortiz laid on the sidewalk on Manila Boulevard and bled to death.

If Jersey City punished violent racist cops instead of promoting them, Maximino Cintron Ortiz would be alive today. If the Filipinos had united and taken a stand in 1989, there would have been one less funeral in the Puerto Rican community. That's the kind of shit we should be worrying about. While Asian American students packed classrooms, bullshitting about interracial dating, there was a Filipino couple in Jersey City who were demanding justice and a violent police officer who was carrying a gun and patrolling the streets. How could we let this injustice slip by? Because of our silence, Ortiz lost his life.

Despite what happened in Jersey City, times are changing. Young Filipino brothers and sisters are waking up. Every time young Filipinos hear someone on the street call us "chink" or "eggroll," they are less ready to bow their heads. They are more ready to take some heads. That's the way it should be. If the

Filipino is going to get respect in America, we have to refuse to take bullshit.

In Jersey City, we are finally pulling together. Activists are still quietly working with city officials on strategies to prevent and punish police brutality. But Officer Chisulo is still on the police force, and he never served a day in jail. Someday, we will make it harder for cops to get away with beating people of color.

Black/White America

The Jersey City story shows that we people of color have got to pull together if we are going to get some power, and the first job is to clean up our own act. Filipinos and Puerto Ricans can't be dissing each other. We must admit that people of color can be racist, and this racism is an idiotic mindless support of a system that beats us down. We have to commit to stop being racist against each other. Because by being racist against each other, we bring racism on ourselves.

Filipinos know that people of color can be racist, because we can see it in our own family. It's damn painful to be a kid coming back from school when some racist-in-training has just made chink eyes at you, and then you come home and your brothers and sisters and your parents are going "nigger" this and "spic" that, and they are watching TV and cheering on America as some Arabs are getting napalmed. One big reason is that the only images of blacks and latinos shown to folks in the Philippines are those that Hollywood allows them to see. Rene, a Filipino brother, said, "When I came to the United States, I was freaked out by black people. In the Philippines the only image I had of black people was Huggy Bear on *Starsky and Hutch*."

We have to own up to racism in our community even if it is just from ignorance. It doesn't make sense for people of color to be racist. But who says racism makes sense?

Like most Asian Americans, being called a monkey or a chink carries a sting that makes me want to slap the shit out of somebody.

Being called a monkey by an African American person does not lessen the sting. It simply makes me ashamed for that sister's coconut attitude.

Racism, no matter who does it, is white supremacy. Some Asian brothers and sisters think that an African American calling them "eggroll" is black supremacy. But it's not. If that brother beats down Asians all day, is he going to profit? Is he uplifting the African race? If you put down people of color and you are not white, you are just doing the white man's job without getting paid.

White people support this type of racism through their silence, and by refusing to see it as racism but as "inter-ethnic conflict." That's the new bullshit out on the street. By calling people of color's racist attacks against each other "inter-ethnic conflict," white people make like they are passive observers who shouldn't get involved, when actually they are the ones who will profit in the end from the divisions among us.

In 1990 a Korean American storeowner in Los Angeles, Soon Ja Du, shoots an African American girl, Latasha Harlins, in the back. If a white had killed that girl, it would be hard to say it wasn't a racist act. But since it was a Korean American who did the killing, whites can feel they are off the hook, so they can condone the racist killing. So the white judge sentences the so-called model-minority Korean American to probation. And that judge can reject the accusation that she is a racist, because after all, the killing of the black girl wasn't racism, it was "inter-ethnic conflict."

African Americans are pissed off at the sentence, and all the Korean American stores are the target of looting and burning. The enemy is no longer one Korean American, but all of them. If one Korean American hates blacks, then they all hate them. If one Korean American is nasty to me, that's because they are all nasty. In the L.A. riots, 80 percent of the burned stores were Korean American. As if they were all the same, one Korean American has to take the rap for something another Korean American did, and the racists think they should be burned and looted until they "all go back where they came from." But when whites see this on TV, they don't say it's racism. They don't see it as a white judge turning her head from a racist act committed by a Korean American, provoking a violent racist reaction from some African Americans. It's just "inter-ethnic conflict."

African American racists are experts at pushing all the buttons when they make racist speeches and rap songs about Korean Americans, because they can draw on their own experience as victims of racism. And when I see them getting TV time on the white media, I think to myself, "Oh shit. I'm going to have to deal with this out on the street tommorrow." Because we don't have to be Korean American to catch hell. The racist doesn't care whether you are a Filipino, Korean, Japanese, or Chinese. When racists want to beat our asses, they aren't into finding out our cultural differences. To them, Asians are all the same. And while we are getting beat, don't expect any help from the whites. Because as far as they are concerned, it's "inter-ethnic conflict." I had a white progressive friend in school. We were talking one time when I said to her that a black man we knew wrote something that I thought was racist. I'll never forget what she said. She said, "As a white person, I find it difficult to call a black person racist."

Now wait a minute. Does that mean that if a black man calls me a chink, you aren't going to help me tell that brother to go fuck himself? Instead you're going to stand around and let this "inter-ethnic conflict" play itself out. And while that black racist is beating my ass, will you be able to overcome your "difficulties" in calling out racism? What really pissed me off is that she didn't say that the black guy wasn't racist. She said that she just found it "difficult" to call him a racist, as if it's cool for her to be silent about racism when it comes from a black man against a Filipino, because she is white and the racist is black. But what about us: We're not white and we're not black, so what happens when we need backup?

Since we don't fit into the scheme of black/white America, we Asian Americans get very annoyed at some white activists, especially the sycophantic white progressives who—based on their limited experience with people of color—equate fighting racism with never questioning what black folks say or do. Since white progressives don't see me as a legitimate victim of racism, my perspective as an Asian American is ignored and their racism against me is unchecked. That's how you can tell when people are motivated by guilt and not by a sense of justice. In order to assuage their guilt, the guilt-motivated white activist is always kissing the black activist's ass, and latinos and Asians get ignored, because kissing the asses of the folks with the darkest skin is the fastest way to throw off the guilt of a life of white supremacy. We are in a Catch-22: since we are not black, we are too low on the dark skin hierarchy to merit attention. But since we are not white, we are not really listened to as much as the other white activists who sound like they have all their neat little theories down. That's why most of the white friends I have aren't even political. I can count on those white friends more because they don't have white guilt.

We shouldn't want to get our asses kissed by white people! Black folks know that sycophantic white progressives are really not listening to them, that black folks could say, "Let's go blow up St. Patrick's Cathedral" and these white folks would still be nodding their heads. In their frantic mission to purge themselves of their whiteness—which is not what anti-racist struggle is about—these white progressives are treating all people of color in a dehumanizing way, by either ignoring us completely or putting us up on a fucking pedestal. The Filipino American shouldn't be ignored and shouldn't want to be put up on a pedestal. I can be just as racist as a white person sometimes, and if a white person hears it I would hope that they have something to say about it. But at the same time I expect some backup when the time comes.

To the modern-day Filipino American, fighting racism means that we are not going to take bullshit from anybody, whether it is from blacks or from whites or from Puerto Ricans or from anybody else, and we expect support. No one in black/white America is used to seeing Asian Americans getting hardline against racism. But they are going to have to get used to it. We so-called model minorities are not supposed to be into conflict. We are supposed to be all quiet and shit. We're supposed to say, "Let's all live in harmony." But that's not the voice of today's young Filipino American women and men, at least not the ones I know. I think that more young Filipinos are like, "Let's be friends. If you got a problem, let's talk about it. But if you don't give us respect, we'll take off your fucking head!"

The Sisters

Miss Saigon brings out the male domination nature of colonization. This is what most folks fighting imperialism leave out. Colonization is not just about race, but it's also about male domination: Just look at the Filipina woman's story. First of all the colonizer puts up economic barriers to Filipina women. Filipina sisters who have been forced off their land by large corporations must feed their children by becoming prostitutes, signing up with employment agencies for menial jobs abroad where they are the target of labor exploitation and sexual abuse, or trying to become the wife of an American or European man, who orders her from a catalog.

Male domination has not just been another way to strengthen colonial rule. The Spanish destroyed women's power in the Philippines because they were afraid that word of Filipina women would get back to folks in Spain, and that would mess up the hierarchy over there. While Filipina women ruled kingdoms, a Spanish woman couldn't even own a horse or a piece of land. There are legends of great women rulers and warriors, such as Queen Urduja of Pangasinan, whose kingdom traded with Java, China, and India. In fact Manila was invaded and conquered by the woman ruler of Sulu, Lelamen Chanei, only a century before the Spanish discovered the Philippines. In an unpublished essay, A.F. Santos quotes Geronimo J. Pecson as saying, "Centuries before Magellan arrived in the Philippines in 1521, foreign visitors … had written accounts which showed that the Filipino women enjoyed high social esteem and leadership … (But) when Spanish rules and laws were established, the women's rights were curtailed to those of the Spanish women then." Our resistance as a people includes Filipina women finding new power and dignity which had been denied them by the colonizers. And the duty of Filipino men struggling against colonization is that we must struggle to free ourselves from that male domination mindset which is the product of colonialism, or else we are just captive to the coconut mentality, and we are no different from the colonizer.

The Filipino man must not cooperate in any way with the oppression of Filipina women, on the political level, the economic level, the social level, or any level. In fact, Filipino men have the duty to join with Filipina women in the fight against male domination, and in their absence we have a duty to actively defend the rights of the sisters.

In Youth for Philippine Action, we tried our best to demonstrate, through practice, that Filipino men and women can work together in an atmosphere oriented against male domination. We followed a principle of engaging in reflection concerning the ways in which we as individuals perpetuate the oppressions that we are supposed to be against. We were not always successful. Many times women members had left in disgust at what they perceived to be the lack of progress we men had made. Other women had stayed and were working with the men.

As Filipino American activists, it is inevitable that we will progress, we will dissappoint each other, we will progress again. We confront male domination together, as we do all aspects of colonization. Women and men often modify our views. And we change.

Letter from the Philippines
Kamuning District, Quezon City
September 7, 1992

Whenever young Filipino Americans speak at a forum in New York City, the event wouldn't be complete if an older Filipino didn't stand up and say, at least once, "If you feel so strongly about (whatever it is), why don't you go back to the Philippines and see things for yourself?"

Well, here I am, sitting in the office of the Leandro Alejandro Foundation, in the land of my mother and my father. I am in the Philippines for the first time in my life.

National leader Liddy Nacpil-Alejandro introduces me: "This is my friend Steven De Castro. He was born in the States. He doesn't speak Tagalog. But he is truly Filipino." The friend is shocked. Liddy and I smile at each other. Most people greet me with a mix of courtesy and bewilderment.

Right now the people's movement is busting on the new president, Fidel Ramos, who was Marcos' chief of staff and is thinking up new ways to sell us out to the colonizers. Ramos is begging the United States for an increase in military aid so that he can expand the strategic hamletting and the paramilitary death squads. These death squads, called "CAFGU's" (Citizen's Armed Forces Geographical Units), continue to kill movement leaders in the countryside. The United States gives them M-16's so they can do the dirty work of the army. So far the United States is keeping the cash flow steady. And Filipino students and workers are starting to march in the streets against the "U.S.-Ramos regime."

My new Filipino friends and I are trying to figure each other out. Of course, I've had my share of surprises. Like, I can't believe how hard it is to be an activist in a town with no fucking subway. Folks have to take a packed jeepney sputtering black clouds, then they change over to a teenager driving a beat-up little Kawazaki bike with a rumble seat, and at the end of an hour on the streets of Manila you have to wipe the carbon monoxide soot off your skin. Ughhh! The League of Filipino Students officers all sleep packed into one room on a *banig* on the floor. They bathe out of a bucket of water. Even though they are so overcrowded, they don't go out in the morning looking like a bunch of hippies; when they leave the house they are scrubbed clean, hair in place, clothes crisp.

These folks in LFS don't play. The printer fucks up, the phones go down, the food runs out, the cops swing truncheons, the father kicks and beats them for being *aktibista,* they get expelled, they get arrested, they get evicted, they get stomped on in jail, but no matter what, they are still pushing through. They are unstoppable.

There is another funky difference between us, which I heard yesterday from a homegirl from Manila named Roni Villamor: In LFS, pre-marital sex is banned and you have to ask the organization's permission if you want to hit on somebody! I was like, word? I'm fucking terrified. A brother was breaking it down for me. "You see, there are three stages of courting in LFS..." I said, "Well, in YPA there is just one stage."

Norciditha Ganaden, another LFS member, is my guardian angel and political guide through the Philippines. Norchi is not from Manila. She is "from the province." La Union to be exact. We are an unlikely pair walking around: I think she is SO Filipina, she thinks I am SO American. But her laughter went over the average Filipina laughter volume when I downed my first *balut*.

Norchi is also a very good introducer, and that is important if you know how long a Filipino introduction can be, especially for an English-speaking Flip like myself. Endless questions. Yes, a Filipino. From America. No, no Tagalog. No, he doesn't speak Visayan. Yes, both parents from the Philippines. His father is from Mindanao. His mother is from Cebu. No, he's not married. I wish I knew the Tagalog for "None of your damn business!" Luckily, Norchi fields the interrogations. Sometimes it looks like she is arguing on my behalf. "But he is Filipino!" It's a real trip to hear this coming from her. Sitting in the Philippines, I've never felt more American in my life. Whatever that means.

But when my LFS friends and I hang out together and drink Red Horse and tell bad jokes, we feel very much at home with each other. Last night Paul and Amante pulled out the guitar and started singing Joey Ayala songs. Most of the time these activists aren't into talking about moral principles; they mainly talk about strategy stuff. But when they sing, their voices reveal their commitment and their hope in the future. I'm glad that those older Flips had me come out here and see things for myself. Because now I have seen the incredible poverty imperialism has caused, and I have also seen the courage it takes to believe that things can change. Back in the United States, young Filipino Americans must also show that courage, just as Carlos Bulosan did when he left his *carabao* in Pangasinan and organized strikes among the fruit pickers of California. Just as Philip Vera Cruz did when he devoted his entire life to building the United Farmworkers Union in the American Southwest.

My father has walked these streets. Travelling through Manila I wonder, has my father seen this building? Has my mother ever been in this park? One of the colleges I am giving a lecture in is the place my Aunt Sony went to school. I met the woman who took care of my mother when mom gave birth, and she said she held my brother when he was newborn. This unfamiliar country is a part of me, a part of all of us. The search for identity for every Filipino American leads one back to the Philippines. But I don't mean returning on a plane. I mean returning with your heart. Returning to our tradition of struggle, which for almost a hundred years has been the struggle against the imperialistic rule of the United States. Returning to our historical mission as a generation, which is to resist imperialism and the values of white male supremacy and greed that are its superstructure. And working with other Filipinos to help build a future in which all Filipinos are finally free.

Our collective story is one continuous thread, extending from the Philippine past and branching out to all parts of the world, from the nurses in Saudi Arabia, to the busboy on the Carribean cruise liner, to the sex worker in the Japan brothel, to the migrant swinging the bolo in the cane field in Hawaii, to the maid in Toronto, Canada, to the soldier in Luzon, to the business executive in Makati, to you, to me. This thread is not a conceptual thing; it is made of blood. And when we learn to travel that thread of continuity we become grounded in time and space, we can be fully human. bell hooks always quotes the African National Congress Freedom Charter which reads: "Our struggle is the struggle of memory against forgetting." The colonizer is constantly trying to dislocate us from who we are, to dislocate Filipinos from their past. But we shall return. This is our duty.

When we realize our duty, our lives get very complicated. But also, our lives gain meaning, way beyond the meaning we could hope to find in that bullshit American mass culture. Our minds become sharp. That's when we realize that life is not about dying with the most toys. It's about connection, discovery, and hope in the future. It is about justice: Even if we strive and fall and disappoint ourselves and each other, the goals are not the only important thing. We should be militant, but in our militance we should never forget to treat people justly. Liddy Nacpil once told me a long time ago, "It is the process of liberation that is most important. We are not fighting for some utopia out there somewhere. The process of liberation is happening every day." That is what our identity movement is all about.

But still, I knew that my home was the United States. There are enough Filipinos here, they don't need one more. They need us over in America, so that we can raise hell in the belly of the beast. I guess I call my return to the United States "going home." That's kind of funny; coming to the Philippines was also a "going home" of sorts. That reminds me of something Liddy once wrote: "I guess our home is in the struggle."

Why Did YPA Destroy Itself?

This chapter reflects (but does not represent) a lot of the principles of Youth for Philippine Action. YPA believed in taking Asian American identity out of the classroom and turning it into meaningful action against racism, sexism, and imperialism. We thought that nobody in the Filipino American community was saying the things we were saying, and that our organization would become an example for Fil-Ams across the country to start a new activist-oriented identity movement, linking our need for a voice in this country with the need for the Philippines to be liberated from foreign control. On all these things, we were wrong.

In late 1992, YPA wasn't doing much political stuff, mostly just setting up our new office and working for some grant money. During this base-building phase, a lot of that militant energy that we used against enemies got misdirected. First, a couple of members seemed to be caught up in being the victims, sort of like a "more oppressed than thou" thing. They wanted to be versatile in retaining their victim status like it was some heavyweight title. For instance, some members would list in their head all the oppressed nationalities that they bore any relation to, so you would have a person claiming to be Korean, Filipino, Irish, Jewish, Native American, etc., all in the same year. Some folks seemed to have a nationality for every occasion.

Eventually the victim politics went way out of control. Folks were now targeting members of the organization as their main oppressors.

In the space of a few months, members of YPA were accused of serious crimes, from phone harassment to sexual harassment to sexual assault. The membership would either react with disbelief, or would think: It is so outrageous, it has to be true. Accusations of offenses against women were the most effective in halting the progress of YPA: Before the wave of accusations, we discussed sexism pretty regularly, and at some point we had weekly meetings just on curbing sexist conduct in the organization. Whether or not we were going fast enough, all real discussion about sexism stopped when we dealt with the who-did-what-when-and-where of these accusations of sexual harassment and assault.

Most of us did our best to set aside our personal feelings and personal friendships in order to hear the complaints without prejudice. It was damn hard for people to consider their best friends to be suspects accused of violent crime, but we did, which is at once heroic and tragic, because it tested friendships in ways that I wish they never were.

People met for hours and hours to create a grievance procedure, one that protects the rights of the accuser and the accused. In a sense, the members really pulled together in this crisis and poured huge amounts of energy into resolving these accusations as quickly and fairly as possible, even if it meant throwing members out of the organization who were found to have committed any of the offenses those folks were talking about.

Ultimately, no evidence was ever presented to back up any of the accusations. But before YPA could clear an innocent member, a new accusation would come up, and that was the horror of it: YPA's purge would never end. Lost in all of this was our political vision. We were supposed to be a fucking movement, what the fuck happened?

I don't know. I hope you can figure it out. In nationalist youth movements it's probably happened before, and it may happen again. Most of us who tried to save the organization and get to the truth will someday learn from the destruction of YPA.

Some folks saw YPA as a powerful forum for venting anger and dislike at certain members by publicly embarrassing them with accusations. The accusers basically got what they wanted, but the price was that YPA did nothing for six months but investigate, discuss, and attempt to resolve the problems of these few people. But no organization could be disrupted by that kind of bullshit unless the members are willing to get pushed around, are reluctant to make tough decisions. Without clear direction, the organization got more and more off track.

Members wrote and faxed nasty letters to each other. Secret meetings were held. Lawyers got involved. People were sued. One person wrote a letter condemning the U.S. justice system and, in the same letter, threatened to sue the organization. Trusted people in the organization were portrayed as demons, members were actively targeted for smear campaigns.

People in the group who were looked up to would put their credibility on the line to make an accusation and when that accusation proved false, their credibility died. Men who questioned the cultural revolution tactics were called misogynists, and a woman who worked hard for an impartial procedure was called by another woman a "dumb blond." Often we men were silent in order to allow women a voice, but also our silence was an excuse for not taking a stand and our occasional refusal to engage the issues was patronizing to women members.

Instead of understanding our commitment to Filipino people we became completely occupied with ourselves.

Eventually I resigned because we failed to resolve these problems. Many others resigned after I did, and the group eventually died. I was half hoping that the accusers would take up the mantle and continue the goals of the organization, but that didn't happen; they, too, resigned, their work was done. But ours is not.

We still have a duty to carry on the collective story of the Filipino American, to understand ourselves and our place in the world. We must learn to tap the energy of knowing ourselves without destroying ourselves in victim-posing. And we have to be savvy enough in our organizing to protect our organizations from that purge mentality. Most folks in YPA have realized that there's more to activism than just bullshitting and making militant speeches: It's about building organizations that last, with members who are dedicated to the goals, not just themselves. I hope that the great things that YPA has done will become an inspiration to other Filipino Americans. And I hope that our dreadful failures can give you some ideas about how to do things differently.

Notes

1. *Ilustrados* refers to members of the Philippine elite.
2. *Burgis* means bourgeois; Flips is a derogatory slang term for Filipinos.
3. A *barkada* is a club or gang.

16

HOLDING UP MORE THAN HALF THE HEAVENS

Domestic Violence in Our Communities, A Call for Justice

MARGARETTA WAN LING LIN and CHENG IMM TAN

Domestic violence is a disease that knows no boundaries, it cuts across the barriers of culture, race, and political and socio-economic divides. It has claimed countless lives, both literally and figuratively. The precise number of casualties is unknown because most victims do not report domestic violence. They excuse, deny, or bury the violence away, never to be discussed but always remembered in the truth of midnight nightmares.

Few Asian Pacific Americans (APA) would fail to recognize the killings of Vincent Chin and Jim Ming Hai Loo and the massacre of the Stockton schoolchildren: Raphanar Or, 9; Ram Chun, 8; Thuy Tran, 6; Sokhim An, 6; and Ocun Lim, 8, as racially motivated crimes of hate. Anyone who has been called "Chink" or "Gook" or "Dirty Jap" knows that the violence underlying the "harmless" name-calling can, given the wrong circumstances, easily lead to more brutal manifestations of hate. We readily see the tenure denials of Don Nakanishi, Jean Lew, and Rosalie Tung as cases of employment discrimination and civil rights violations. After many decades of struggle by Nisei activists, we now understand that the internment of 120,000 Japanese during World War II was an unlawful deprivation of civil liberties.

What about domestic violence? Few people would consider spouse abuse a crime, much less a hate crime violating victims' civil rights. The American Medical Association's official count is that one in four U.S. women are victimized by domestic violence in their lifetime. This rate translates into two to four million women attacked by current or former partners every year. The surgeon general, Dr. Antonia Novello, has described domestic violence as "more common than automobile accidents, muggings, and rapes combined."[1]

To what extent the cases of APA women contribute to the national statistics is unknown. The marginalized history of Asian Pacific women in the United States—where our lives do not merit inclusion into official data—holds true with domestic violence figures. Activists working to provide support for battered APA women and their children and to eradicate the circle of violence know that domestic violence is pervasive in APA communities. They see the fatalities and the casualties in the women they work with and in their own families.

Battered women are everywhere. They are in ESL classes and community health centers, in multiservice agencies and job training programs, in your office and working side-by-side with you. Because of the stigma, the shame, and the blame we still attach to victims of domestic violence, most simply suffer in silence. No one is immune from the disease, yet there exists a conspiracy of silence whose source lies deeply embedded in the roots of patriarchal perversities. It is a web that holds all of us who hold our tongues out of shame or guilt or need to protect the family's name, the family's honor. It holds all of us who hold our tongues in complicity.

This chapter is a wake-up call to APA activists fighting on the frontlines for the civil rights of Asian Pacific Americans, as well as all peoples. We as a community can never hold our heads high and claim a righteous struggle for civil rights unless we fight hand-in-hand for the rights of our sisters to be free from violence of the body, the mind, the spirit. This is a wake-up call to all Asian Pacific Americans. There will never be a strong and healthy community unless violence in the home—the number one health hazard to women—is eradicated. We can never reach the potential that is our birthright unless we stop denying the impact of domestic violence on our own lives and start dealing with its effects. It is futile to hope and work for a better society when we pass on a legacy of violence and dysfunction. The violence tolerated against our mothers, our sisters, our daughters, our lovers, our wives has shaken, wounded, or devastated every single life in this country.

Defining Domestic Violence

Domestic violence encompasses the whole range of violence in the home among family members and between intimate partners, married or unmarried. Strictly speaking, it includes elderly abuse, child abuse, incest, and partner abuse. In this chapter, we examine domestic violence from the perspective of a woman involved in a heterosexual relationship because our work has focused on that and it is from this perspective we feel best able to discuss the issue.

Most people if asked would say that we should not tolerate domestic violence. Yet, many community leaders still say that a little discipline, an occasional beating now and then to teach the woman a lesson, is not domestic violence. This reveals that a lot of confusion exists about what domestic violence is, or is not. First, let us tell you what domestic violence is not. Domestic violence is not the occasional fight, or conflict, or disagreement between two individuals. Domestic violence is not an interaction between two equal individuals.

Domestic violence is the imposition of total control over a family member, usually an intimate female partner or child (although more and more elderly are also being victimized), by systematic intimidation, isolation, and manipulation through emotional, psychological, physical, and/or sexual abuse or with the threat of physical and/or sexual abuse. Domestic violence usually (though not always) begins mildly with psychological and emotional abuse. It can start subtly with a few criticisms here and there. The criticisms become "put downs and accusations" and develop into a systematic stripping of the victim's confidence and self-esteem. The abuser can also extort control by isolating the victim from friends and family, withholding affection, or destroying her possessions and pets. The message sent is "Submit to my control or I will visit similar violence." Once the violence starts, it always escalates. A push turns into a slap turns into a punch turns into kicks, stabs, burns, and sexual abuse.

Domestic violence is the willful control, use, and abuse of a female partner with impunity. When someone is being stabbed, punched, kicked, burned, or beaten by a stranger, chances are that someone will intervene. At the very least, someone will call the police. But when violence happens behind locked doors—in the privacy and "sanctity" of the home—even when a neighbor can clearly hear screaming, intervention is improbable because no one wants to interfere in a "family" affair. Preserving the family and male control has more value than the life and safety of women and children. This is especially true in APA communities where the family serves as the locus of identity. In addition, APA women who are isolated from mainstream society because of linguistic and cultural barriers rely more heavily on the family structure than they would in their home countries. And to refugee women who have suffered the ravages of war and dislocation, having often lost both family members and worldly possessions, the batterer may be the only family they have left.

Because emotional and psychological abuse usually precede physical abuse, the victim often blames herself for the violence perpetuated against her. It is not only the victim but other people who wrongly believe it is the woman's fault. More often than not, when the woman seeks help, others tell her to be patient, tolerant, or forgiving because he—the abuser—does not mean it. People will ask, "What could she have done to aggravate him so badly? If only she would not nag him so much or be so demanding. If only she would get his dinner on time, argue less, be more understanding of his stress and tensions." She is then sent back with admonish-ments to be a more compliant wife.

This attitude is prevalent among the friends and family members of battered women as well as among many of the profes-sionals who "service" battered women—ministers, doctors, social workers, counselors, police, and court officials. It does not take much to realize that this widespread feeling is based on the irrational but tacit acceptance of male control and superiority that we, living under patriarchy, are conditioned to accept.

To complicate this violence, there is usually a time of repen-tance and remorse right after an outbreak of violence when the batterer promises not to do it again. For a while he is attentive and loving, the man she fell in love with and married. So, she begins to hope that this time he will really change, but then slowly but surely the criticism and emotional abuse begins the whole cycle of violence again.

These difficulties are further exacerbated for refugee women, who are the most isolated members of our society. Refugee men who experience post-traumatic stress tend to express symptoms of uncontrollable rage and angry outbursts, which they often target at the most vulnerable people around them—their partners. The refugee woman who takes courageous steps to learn English, get a job, and become more independent, threatens the traditional balance of power between the husband and wife. This threat will often trigger the male need for greater assertion of his control.

Institutional Barriers from the Outside

In the 15 years since the beginning of the battered women's movement, many activists have galvanized public attention and funneled resources into addressing domestic violence. The marginalization of the Asian Pacific American community, outside of those that serve as tokenized examples of the "model minority" myth, has meant that our problems have also been marginalized. To the extent that the battered women's movement has raised mainstream society's consciousness, it has cut APA women out of the loop.

The rising statistics of domestic violence have reached alarming proportions. Domestic violence is the number one cause of injury and death to women in this country. In 1991, one million women were reported attacked by their husbands or lovers. An estimated three million violent domestic crimes—murders, rapes, and assaults—went unreported.[2] In San Francisco and Boston, as well as in other large cities, domestic violence is spiraling. In San Francisco, domestic violence has increased by 64 percent in the past eight years. In Massachusetts, in 1990, a woman was killed every 22 days as a result of domestic violence; as of April 1992, the rate rose to a woman killed every nine days. These are just the fatality statistics that make the headlines. For those of us who represent the unreported casualties, we know the extent of under-reporting. In Massachusetts, in 1991, over 13 percent of the women and children killed were Asian, even though Asians constitute only 2.4 percent of the state's population.

APA communities are not immune from domestic violence. Yet, no data exists for the number of battered APA women in any given city, much less nationally. While numbers barely begin to tell the whole story, the lack of numerical accounting is a political statement of our exclusion from the fruits of "full-blooded" U.S. citizenship where numbers determine the recognition of a problem and the allocation of limited resources. A coalition effort is in the making uniting the East/West Coast efforts of collecting data on APA victims of domestic violence.

Because of the barriers of language, culture, and economic disparities and the vagaries of racism and sexism, APA victims of domestic violence suffer revictimization at the hands of institutions designed to serve battered women. According to the 1990 U.S. Census, Asians and Pacific Islanders are the fastest growing minority group, totalling nearly seven million. And yet, in the entire United States only two shelters exist for APA women, one safe-home network and one advocacy group that provides culturally sensitive programs and counseling.[3] Of the domestic violence resources available—police, shelters, hotlines, human services programs—few have staff who speak Asian Pacific languages. Given the highly sensitive nature of addressing domestic violence, it is unacceptable not to have linguistically accessible resources. The language barrier, in effect, shuts out most refugee and immigrant women. In addition, many battered women's shelters turn away APA women because of language and cultural difficulties or out of sheer racism. Economic concerns present yet another obstacle. Most women who are victims of domestic violence do not have control of the family's money. Many leave their homes with little besides the clothes on their backs. This means that many battered APA women who have gathered up the strength and courage to flee the violence in their homes must then return there because they have no other viable options. Legal protection is also often both inaccessible because of cultural and linguistic barriers and unavailable because of institutionalized racism and sexism. There are too many examples of the revictimization of battered APA women by institutionalized forces; it would require another whole book just to document the abuses we have seen. We will simply give you a few here. Consider the story of Ling.

One evening, as Ling was cleaning some fish for dinner, her husband who had beaten her repeatedly for the past eight years, who had given her concussions, a broken hip, and a broken jaw, began to pick a fight. Ling did not answer any of his accusations and her enduring silence made him even angrier. He picked up a chair to strike her. She sidestepped the appending blow and screamed at him to stop. The chair broke against the door and he lunged at her, more enraged than before. Ling tried to ward him off by waving the knife that she had been using to clean the fish for dinner that evening. He continued to lunge at her and in attempting to get the knife, fell upon the knife and cut himself open. He continued to strike out at Ling.

Terrified, Ling ran to a nearby store to call the police. When the police came, her husband who spoke good English, accused Ling of attacking him. Ling's English was not enough to defend herself. The police who she called arrested Ling and put her in jail. They set her bond at $2,500. The case against Ling is still pending. This is how our justice system works to protect battered women.

Then there is the case of Thuy, who in desperation to get away from her abusive husband sought the safety of a battered women's shelter with her three children. One day as she was in the bathroom, one of her children fell down and cut himself on the forehead. The shelter staff admonished Thuy for leaving her kids on their own. A few days later, while Thuy was cooking supper, her kids got into a fight with other shelter children. Again, the staff reprimanded Thuy for neglecting her children. Not knowing enough English, Thuy could not counter the staff's judgement of her. A 51A child abuse/neglect form was filed against her. Now, Thuy faces the possibility of losing her children to a system that she does not comprehend and that not only does not understand her but fails to protect her.

The Primacy of Fear of Racist Attacks, The Sacrifice of Our Sisters

Within each ethnic group, male control and domestic violence take on culturally specific expressions. APA communities have tolerated and overlooked domestic violence for some of the same reasons that mainstream society has tolerated and overlooked it for so long—the unquestioning acceptance of patriarchy, of male control and privilege. Some APA activists worry that bringing domestic violence into the open will confirm negative stereotypes about the community, and further fuel the fires of anti-Asian sentiment. To expose the problem within APA communities is not a statement about the greater violence or misogyny in Asian Pacific culture. Instead, the sad reality is that Asian men, like all other men, live in a male-dominated culture that views women as property, objects they must control and possess. Compounding this reality, or underlying it, are cultures that view violence as an acceptable solution to problems.

As a reaction to the pervasive racism and cultural imperialism that threaten to undermine our cultural integrity, APA activists and community leaders have been reluctant to look self-critically at traditional misogynistic attitudes and practices for fear that it would reinforce racist stereotypes about Asian Pacific Americans. This attitude of denial, however, does not keep racism at bay. Instead, it is at odds with cherished notions of our rights as humans and citizens.

The same reasons that inspire the unequivocal and emphatic support of APA activists to have crimes motivated by race, color, and/or national origin identified as hate crimes hold for crimes motivated by gender. As with crimes of racist hate, statistics on domestic violence are inadequate; elected officials will not fund programs until we fully document the violence; keeping such statistics would encourage more public awareness and debate on the crimes.

While there is an emerging effort on the part of APA women activists to include domestic violence as a hate crime, APA civil rights and advocacy groups have not supported their work. We believe that along with sexist motivations, fear of betraying our brothers, of adding to their oppression, plays a role in the glaring absence of their support. Such fear causes APA activists to overlook and ignore domestic violence. It has meant sacrificing the lives of our sisters.

A heinous example of this is Dong Lu Chen's murder of his wife, Jian Wan Chen, and his successful use of the cultural defense. On September 7, 1987, Jian Wan Chen's husband smashed her skull in with a claw hammer after she allegedly admitted to having an affair. Chen's teenage son discovered her body in the family's Brooklyn apartment. The trial judge sentenced Dong to five years probation on a reduced manslaughter charge after concluding, based on the testimony of an anthropologist, that Dong was driven to violence by traditional Chinese values about adultery and loss of manhood. APA activists came out in support of the cultural defense as a necessary tool to protect immigrants in U.S. courtrooms.

Does this mean that Jian Wan Chen's immigrant status is negligible, or that such activists believe that Asian men are traditionally more violent and misogynistic than their white counterparts, or that the status of Jian Wan Chen as an Asian sister, as a human being, is negligible when weighed against the crime of her husband? And what are the repercussions of such outrage? Domestic violence counselors have reported that the case has convinced

329

many battered APA women that they have no protection, period. As for the lawyers, they feel "empowered" to use the cultural defense at any opportunity.[4] What does this say about our society, about our value of human life, about our perception of justice?

The fear of racist attacks on our cultures and communities is so pervasive and deep that it has frustrated our attempts at addressing domestic violence in APA communities. When we first started addressing such issues in the Boston area, we received harassing calls, our tires were slashed, threats and accusations were made that we were family-wreckers. This fear and anger from the APA community has also compromised our strategies in responding to domestic violence. Activists and community leaders have advocated for treatments that do not threaten traditional beliefs and practices, such as mediation, family counseling, and elder intervention. Such measures, however, do not address the underlying attitudes and institutions that uphold violence against APA women and children.

We recognize that APA refugee and immigrant men experience the weight of oppression and stresses from dislocation. Adjusting to a new environment, especially one with racist underpinnings, is stressful, and while many women have found jobs, many men have not.[5] The role reversals and other relocation stresses caused by these factors have often aggravated drinking problems and violence in the home. Adequate multilingual, multicultural programs would have helped many APA refugee and immigrant men manage these stresses. But already inadequate resources provided to refugee populations recently have been cut even more in the Reagan/Bush years.

While APA refugee and immigrant men do have struggles and challenges to cope with, as do the women, this is never an excuse for violence in the home. Violence against another person, for whatever reason beyond self-defense, is unacceptable and illegal.

We are not women who hate our yellow brothers, we do not glorify the white man nor will we allow him to use us as tools of his racist stereotyping. Asian men are not more sexist, more misogynistic, more capable of binding the bonds of patriarchy on women than their white, black, or brown counterparts. What is true and real and must be dealt with, however, is the sickness that pervades our communities, as it does mainstream society. It is not acceptable for us to struggle alongside our brothers to get out the vote, to bring justice to Vincent Chin's murderers, to fight for equal treatment in the work place, schools, courts, and legislatures, and then have our brothers betray us on issues that violate our sacred spaces. We do not shed blood struggling for our equal rights and human dignities on the streets to then turn around and accept subjection to violence in our homes and complicit silence from our communities about our abuse.

Our Struggle Together

Domestic violence demeans and destroys our communities more than any other violence perpetuated on us. It is not an isolated issue. It is not a private family affair protected by the rights of privacy. It is a violent crime of hate that attacks the very fiber of our collective health and we should treat it as such. Symptoms of the sickness spill beyond the confines of the home and taint our participation in the community, our performances in jobs and schools, our personal relationships. It harms every aspect of our lives and the lives that we touch. Because it is premised on unequal relationships and because of its destructive and often fatal impact, domestic violence is not suitable for internal solutions nor should the rights of privacy protect it.

The power to define domestic violence, to give credence to its reality, means much more than validating the experiences of battered women and children. Recognizing the critical dimensions of domestic violence in APA communities translates into accessing resources for dealing with the symptoms, such as making local community health clinics and doctors aware of and able to treat the problems, providing multilingual and multicultural services, and making outside funding sources available to shelters and programs. It means community pressure—saying that domestic violence is unacceptable, that we can no longer sweep it under the proverbial rug or sanction it with patriarchal/misogynist sayings. It means, most of all, empowering victims: stopping the internalization of blame, recognizing their agency to leave, and reaching the empowerment to heal and realize their potentials as humans.

We Asian Pacific Americans in control of our destinies, who are concerned about the well-being of our families and our communities, we must be the ones to break the silence.

Our challenge as leaders and activists in our communities is to strategize ways we can work together to address domestic violence in our own communities. We need to examine and change the underlying attitudes and structures within our communities that maintain violence against women and children. We need to focus on both intervention and prevention. We need to work together on outreach and education to make our communities aware of domestic violence issues and to create intolerance to violence against women and children.

Those of us who work in community health and social services agencies must make information on domestic violence available. We need to have in-house training sessions for our staff so they will understand the seriousness of the problem and know, at the very least, how to approach suspected victims of domestic violence to offer information and resources. We need to take on the responsibility and be the vehicle for change. We need to begin to collect data on domestic violence. As long as no data exist, government agencies at all levels can deny the problem and we will continue to lack the political leverage to advocate for appropriate services.

We need to advocate for multilingual and multicultural services in the human service, legal, and law enforcement systems so that they do not overlook or underserve the needs of Asian Pacific Americans. We need ethnically specific services like Asian women's shelters and resources that are culturally sensitive and appropriate but also connected to the larger resources. Lack of access to services places the lives of Asian Pacific American women and children at unnecessary risk.

We need to support the proposed federal Violence Against Women Act which would allow battered women more opportunities to seek redress for crimes committed against them. The Act would allow women to bring civil cases for attacks committed against them because of their gender, provide educational programs against domestic violence, and mandate stiffer laws against spouse abuse. For example, the bill may make rape a federal offense.

Most of all, we need to go inward, deep within, to examine the effects of domestic violence on our persons, to get rid of the shame and blame we feel as victims, to recognize our responsibility and agency for change if we are perpetrators of the violence, to heal the wounds that keep us silent and complicit.

Conclusion

Our communities face many challenges from the outside. To survive amidst racist hate and violence, we have to put our own house in order first. If our own families are not strong, if our own relationships with one another are not characterized by mutual respect and non-violence, how true is our vision for a world filled with respect, dignity, peace, and justice?

As poet Audre Lorde said regarding Paulo Freire's work in *The Pedagogy of the Oppressed,* "The true focus of revolutionary change is never merely the oppressive situations which we seek to escape, but that piece of the oppressor which is planted deep within each of us, and which knows only the oppressors' tactics, the oppressors' relationships."[6]

The Year of the Rooster, 1993, portends a time when many possibilities come home to roost. Let us, in these times of great hope, learn to dream. Let us choose to love. Let us go hand-in-hand to reach empowerment like bamboo shooting after the rain.

Notes

1. Judy Foreman, "Doctors Urged to Check Women for Abuse Signs," *Boston Globe,* June 17, 1992.
2. "Panel Cites Attacks on Women to Back Domestic Violence Bill," *Washington Post,* October 3, 1992.
3. Centers in San Francisco, Los Angeles, and New York City provide programs for Chinese, Korean, Philippine, Japanese, Indonesian, Laotian, Vietnamese, and Cambodian women, and are staffed with multilingual abuse-hotlines. A program in Boston provides counseling and advocacy services for Vietnamese, Cambodian, and Chinese women.

Bilingual hotlines are available for Koreans in Honolulu and Chicago and for Indians in New Brunswick, New Jersey.

4. Alexis Jetter, "Fear is Legacy of Wife Killing in Chinatown," *Newsday,* November 26, 1989.

5. The ability of refugee women to find work as low paid, unskilled laborers in often unregulated and dangerous conditions, such as sweatshops, is a statement about the capitalist oppression of women's labor rather than any evidence of their advantage over men.

6. Audre Lorde, *Sister Outsider,* New York: The Crossing Press, 1984.

17

BUILDING AN ASIAN PACIFIC LABOR ALLIANCE

A New Chapter in Our History

KENT WONG

On May 1, 1992, the Asian Pacific American Labor Alliance held its founding convention in Washington, D.C. This historic gathering drew 500 Asian Pacific unionists from around the country, including garment workers from New York, hotel and restaurant workers from Honolulu, longshore workers from Seattle, nurses from San Francisco, and supermarket workers from Los Angeles.

Although Asian Americans have been part of the U.S. work force for nearly 150 years, this was the first time a national Asian Pacific American labor organization was established within the ranks of the AFL-CIO. The establishment of the Asian Pacific American Labor Alliance signals a new era in the movement to organize Asian Pacific workers, promote their participation within the ranks of the labor movement, and forge a new path in the larger fight for equality and justice.

A Brief Overview of Asian American Labor History

Asian Pacific American history is inseparably woven with U.S. labor history. Asian Americans have contributed an important, though largely ignored, chapter of U.S. labor history. Asian workers built the transcontinental railroad, worked in mines, planted some of the first crops in California's central valley, developed fishing industries and canneries along the West Coast, and labored in sewing factories, laundries, and restaurants in the emerging cities.

Although Asian Pacific workers have toiled for many generations building this country, the U.S. labor movement historically opposed including Asian American workers in unions. Union leaders feared that owners would use Asian labor to lower wages and break strikes. Union leaders also believed that Asian workers could neither be assimilated nor organized. During the late 1800s and early 1900s, labor unions helped lead racist anti-Asian movements.

The 1882 Chinese Exclusion Act, supported by labor unions, was the first immigration law in the history of the United States that explicitly forbade entry of an entire group of people based on their nationality. Samuel Gompers, founder of the American Federation of Labor, was a lifelong opponent of Chinese immigrant labor and upheld absolute union exclusion of Chinese American workers.

Yet, in spite of the hostility from labor leaders, Asian Pacific workers have consistently organized themselves. As early as 1867, thousands of Chinese American railroad workers organized a strike to demand higher wages. In the 1890s, groups of Japanese American immigrants in California formed labor organizations and attempted to strengthen relations between the labor movements in Japan and America.

In 1903, Japanese American farm workers in Oxnard, California, participated in one of the first farmworkers' strikes in the country. A group of Japanese and Mexican workers joined to launch a strike and form a multiracial union of farm workers. Yet when they applied for a charter with the American Federation of

Labor, they were denied admission because their membership included Japanese Americans.

In the 1930s, Chinese and Japanese Americans helped establish councils of the unemployed, and actively participated in the 1934 general strike on the West Coast. During the same period, Filipino farmworkers established the Filipino Labor Union, and played a key role in organizing agricultural workers throughout California's central valley. Some of these veteran organizers went on to lead the historic Delano grape strike in the 1960s. The formation of the United Farm Workers Union in 1965 was the result of a merger between a Filipino American farmworker organization and a Mexican American farmworker organization.

The strong tradition of Asian Pacific labor activism stands in sharp contrast to the widespread myths that Asians are docile, individualistic, and incapable of being organized, or organizing themselves. These myths led to the U.S. labor movement's failure to embrace immigrant workers and other workers of color.

There are notable exceptions to the labor movement's hostile stance toward Asians. The Industrial Workers of the World, also known as the "Wobblies," was committed to organizing workers of all colors, and recruited Japanese American miners in the early part of the century. The Congress of Industrial Organizations (CIO) also allocated extensive resources to organizing Asian and other workers of color in the 1930s.

The Emerging Asian Pacific American Work Force Since the 1960s

The 1960s and 1970s witnessed a significant rise in Asian American activism, encouraged by the Civil Rights, anti-war, and black and Chicano liberation movements. The majority of activists were college students who organized opposition to the Vietnam War from their campuses. They also took up the struggle for ethnic studies, affirmative action, and others changes within universities.

Asian American student activists later began to develop "serve the people" programs to organize within Asian American communities. They developed numerous youth services, tutorial programs, English as a second language classes, tenant support work, drug programs, health care projects, legal services, and senior services. Greater involvement in the community also led to more interest and support for the struggles of workers and unions.

When the U.S. government lifted racially restrictive immigration quotas with the passage of the Immigration Act of 1966, Asian immigration exploded. The Asian Pacific American population has doubled every ten years since 1960, making Asian Americans currently the fastest growing ethnic group in the country. Asian Pacific Americans will number 10 million by the end of this decade, with over two-thirds immigrants.

The first waves of immigrants from Asia came from China, Japan and the Philippines. Since the 1960s, large numbers of Korean, Southeast Asians, Indians, and Pacific Islanders have come to the United States. Like their counterparts over the years, Asian immigrants are mainly working people, highly urbanized, and generally live in ethnic enclaves. Asian immigrant workers are also frequently clustered in racially segregated occupations, and concentrated in garment, electronic and other light manufacturing, supermarkets and food production, and in service industries such as restaurants, hotels, health care, and maintenance.

Though the Asian Pacific work force has risen dramatically, comprehensive data on it is limited. Even the recently released 1990 census data lacks specific demographic data on employment trends or occupations of Asian Pacific Americans.

Although the level of unionization among Asian Pacific workers is still low, a few unions have a positive track record of organizing Asian Pacific workers. The International Ladies Garment Workers Union, Local 23-25, has over 20,000 Asian members in New York City, most of whom are Chinese immigrant women. The American Federation of State, County, and Municipal Employees (AFSCME) and the Service Employees International Union (SEIU) each have significant numbers of Asian Pacific workers in government and health care, especially in California, Hawaii, and New York. Filipinos in particular comprise a large and growing percentage of the workers in the health care industry.

338

In the area of retail food and food processing, the United Food and Commercial Workers (UFCW) represents large numbers of Asian Pacific workers, especially in California. The International Longshoremen and Warehousemen's Union (ILWU) has a long tradition of organizing Asian workers in Hawaii, beginning with plantation and dock workers, as well as in the Northwest among Asian cannery workers. The hotel and restaurant industry also employs large numbers of Asian Pacific workers, and although the vast majority are still unorganized, a growing number of Asian members have joined the union of Hotel Employees and Restaurant Employees (HERE). There is also a sizable Asian membership within the American Federation of Teachers (AFT) and other unions representing school employees.

Unfortunately, however, the labor movement as a whole has failed to allocate sufficient resources to organize Asian Pacific workers. To ensure the survival of the labor movement, unions must organize the new emerging work force, the majority of whom are people of color, immigrants, and women. At the same time, the best hope for Asian Pacific workers to fight exploitation and discrimination in the work place rests in their active participation in unions.

Why Unions?

Asian Pacific workers need unions, and unions need Asian Pacific workers. Ultimately, Asian Pacific Americans cannot attain full equality until workers of all colors have equality. The conditions faced by many Asian Pacific immigrant workers are similar to those that confronted earlier waves of Asian immigrants. Many work in unskilled or semi-skilled occupations where exploitation and abuse are common, including minimum wage, overtime, child labor, and health and safety violations. Many Asian immigrant workers lack health insurance, vacation or sick pay, or retirement plans.

To ensure their empowerment, workers must organize. The only way to prevent the historic abuse and exploitation at the hands of employers, who are frequently of the same ethnic group, is through banding together and demanding change. Unions offer an opportunity to bargain collectively for improved wages, benefits, and working conditions. Unions also provide an opportunity for greater participation, decision-making, and leadership development. But, when Asian American organizing efforts have remained outside of the national union structure, they have often led to frustration and defeat. Without access to the resources of the labor movement, without a broader knowledge of effective organizing strategies and bargaining campaigns, most independent union efforts are short-lived.

The legacy of racism within the U.S. labor movement is still felt strongly by people of color today. Most labor unions have few people of color in positions of leadership. Change within the labor movement has involved a long, difficult process encouraged by both direct pressure within the unions as well as criticism from outside the labor movement. The future of the labor movement depends on its ability to overcome these past legacies of racism and exclusion and to forge multiracial unity.

And yet, in the broader fight against racism, labor unions are a critical arena of struggle. In some respects, they have a unique advantage. The United States is a highly segregated society. Most churches, social clubs, and community-based groups are segregated organizations. Unions are among the few multiracial institutions. African Americans, Latinos, Native Americans, Asian Pacific Americans, and European Americans work side-by-side within unions. Union members must work together for a common agenda, and fight together for common demands.

Although racism is still pervasive within the labor movement, and within our society as a whole, this potential for advancing genuine multiracial unity exists in few other institutions. With our rapidly changing, multicultural society, the labor movement must aggressively challenge racism and be at the forefront of building multiracial unity to grow. This includes recruiting and hiring union staff that reflect the diversity of the membership, promoting Asians and other people of color to positions of leadership, and opposing all racial barriers and discrimination in the work place.

Changes in the Labor Movement

Significant changes within the labor movement allow greater opportunities for Asian Pacific workers. The U.S. labor movement has been in decline for decades. In the 1960s, unions represented about 35 percent of the United States work force. By 1992, that percentage had dropped to about 17 percent. The changing nature of work, the globalization of capital and labor, the shift from an industrial economy to a service economy, and hostile government policies and labor laws all contributed to this substantial decline. The labor movement has also been unwilling and unable to allocate resources necessary to organize the unorganized.

The changing demographics of the U.S. work force and the rapid rise in immigration, especially from Latin America and Asia, raise new challenges and new opportunities for labor. Although European immigrant workers were instrumental in establishing many U.S. labor unions, unions have paid little attention to organizing Asian or Latino immigrants until recently. But the emergence of new progressive labor activists and their reversal of prior exclusionary policies are transforming the movement.

In 1985, the AFL-CIO published a paper entitled, "The Changing Situation of Workers and Their Unions," which analyzed current developments in the work force. The report advocated a series of changes in unions including addressing new work place issues, experimenting with different types of union membership to allow for a more diverse membership and promoting innovative organizing methods.

In 1986, Congress passed the Immigration Reform and Control Act. This handed unions a unique opportunity as hundreds of thousands of undocumented workers could apply for amnesty, creating a new pool of potential union recruits. Employers have frequently used the undocumented status of workers and the threat of deportation to deter employee organizing.

In Los Angeles, the AFL-CIO established the California Immigrant Workers Association (CIWA) to assist Latino immigrant workers in obtaining legalization, English instruction, and other benefits. CIWA was also an "associate membership" organization

341

allowing immigrant workers to affiliate with the AFL-CIO. Associate members are not part of a bargaining unit nor does a union contract cover them. The organization's goal is to promote good will between the labor movement and Latino community, and to build a foundation for future organizing.

In 1989, the AFL-CIO established the AFL-CIO Organizing Institute to recruit a new generation of union organizers. Designed as a center for strategy, recruitment, and training, the Organizing Institute is committed to advancing the cause of organizing. It assimilates rich lessons within the labor movement, and provides a systematic program to train new organizers through direct internships and placements. It pays special attention to reaching out to women and people of color, and has successfully attracted not only rank-and-file union members, but also community and student activists committed to social change who possess a passion to organize.

New, aggressive leadership within the labor movement has also emerging that is committed to organizing the unorganized and making inroads among more workers of color, immigrants, and women. In 1991, the Teamsters elected insurgent candidate Ron Carey president. This election victory sent shock waves throughout the labor movement, and encouraged other insurgent movements within unions. Carey has assembled a new leadership team committed to improving the image of the Teamsters and to organizing. One of Carey's first steps was to allocate $35 million to organizing.

Community-Based Organizing

These changes within the labor movement have encouraged Asian Pacific labor activists to strengthen unionization efforts within their communities. But they will need new strategies. Traditional union practices, such as shop-by-shop organizing and individual union elections, have proven insufficient to organizing Asian immigrant workers. What is needed is a new community-based model to create labor-community alliances and build on the strength of existing organizations within the Asian American community.

Because many Asian immigrants live and work in ethnic enclaves that have never been unionized, some union activists falsely assume that these communities do not have structure and organization. Important organizations do exist, however, including churches, family associations, social service programs, and mutual aid organizations. The Asian community has its own media, including TV, radio, and newspapers. Any labor organizing strategy should include analyzing and using these existing community structures.

Another false assumption inhibiting organizing efforts is the myth of the "model minority." For many years, certain political leaders and media reports have projected an image of Asians as a model of educational and economic success. This stereotype is a dangerous fallacy that pits Asians against other communities of color and obscures the reality of Asian life.

In truth, a bi-polar situation exists within our community. A number of Asian Americans have attained educational and economic success. Some Asian Americans have family roots in this country dating many generations and have succeeded over the years in spite of discrimination. Others are more recent immigrants who are merchants or educated professionals, who arrived in this country with economic resources. But, at the other end of the economic spectrum, our community has large numbers of Asian Pacific immigrant workers whose lifestyle is far from glamorous. Long hours, low wages, and no benefits are standard. Language and cultural barriers keep them trapped in ghettoes.

These sharp class divisions within Asian Pacific communities also reflect cultural particularities. Paternalistic attitudes by Asian bosses are often an extension of previous class relationships that existed in the native countries. Asian immigrant workers may feel in debt to their boss for the opportunity to work. Bonuses for hard work, or special gifts during holidays, are methods Asian bosses use to foster company loyalty and undermine collective action. In addition, the Asian American merchant class has historically dominated other community and social functions, establishing extensive control over many aspects of workers' lives.

Contract labor is also pervasive in Asian Pacific communities. The garment industry, janitorial services and building maintenance, and construction have used contract labor extensively. Through such labor, employers pay by piece work or on a project-by-project basis. This exacerbates the problems of a transitory work force and limits the bosses' accountability.

Community-based organizing requires thoroughly analyzing the class divisions of the Asian Pacific communities, identifying natural allies, and working with existing leaders who support the goals and ideals of unions. These include progressive religious leaders, elected officials, and social service providers. It also requires genuine reciprocity between labor unions and the Asian Pacific community: forging a common agenda, supporting each other's causes and issues, and building genuine solidarity. Unions must support issues of concern within the community, from redress and reparations for Japanese Americans interned during World War II to voting rights and affirmative action.

The Rise in Asian Pacific Labor Activism

For the past 15 years, Asian American labor activists have been working through meetings and new organizations to strengthen unionization efforts. In San Francisco, the Asian American Federation of Union Members (AAFUM) emerged from this work. AAFUM members helped successfully unionize the Chinese *Times* newspaper workers in the late 1970s. In the mid-1980s, the successful organizing drive of janitors at the San Francisco International Airport resulted in the first group of Korean Americans to be unionized.

In New York, the Asian American Labor Committee organizes annual labor festivals in the Asian community, strengthening the presence of unions in the community and building greater labor-community alliances.

In Los Angeles, the Alliance of Asian Pacific Labor (AAPL), established in 1987, successfully brings together virtually all of the key Asian union staff and rank-and-file leaders throughout Los

Angeles and Orange Counties. Since I have personally been involved in its development, I will describe its work in greater detail.

Although many of the active members had worked for years in the labor movement, few had met to address the specific concerns they shared as Asian Pacific labor activists. Now Japanese, Chinese, Filipinos, Koreans, Vietnamese, and Indians from dozens of unions work to unite immigrant and American-born, women and men. They have sought to ensure diversity within the organization, partly by conducting broad outreach to various Asian Pacific communities. Through its efforts, AAPL has become as an important support network for Asian American unionists, including actively encouraging unions to recruit and promote new Asian American unionists. For example, AAPL has recruited student interns for numerous unions throughout Southern California. With limited numbers of Asians on union staffs, especially with bilingual abilities, internships have provided an opportunity to tap the skills and enthusiasm of these students as well as to encourage them to consider future career options in labor.

Since its inception, AAPL has held monthly membership meetings to promote on-going education for labor activists, build labor solidarity between unions, and encourage labor/community alliances. AAPL has succeeded in establishing a labor movement presence within the Los Angeles Asian American community by sending representatives to conferences, events and meetings, distributing literature, publicizing labor activities through the Asian American media, and promoting union consciousness. AAPL has involved itself in community issues involving language rights, redistricting, voter registration, and political empowerment.

Within the labor movement, AAPL has also worked to oppose "Japan-bashing" and misdirected anti-Asian sentiment. The heated trade wars between the United States and Japan have resulted in many workers blaming Japanese corporations for the demise of U.S. industry. Not only does this let U.S. corporate and governmental policy off the hook, it results in increased anti-Asian violence at home. AAPL believes Asians in the labor movement need to promote fair trade proposals that promote job creation and economic growth, while countering the ugly consequences of racist rhetoric. Toward this goal, AAPL has also sponsored events with labor representatives from Korea, Japan, the Philippines, Taiwan, and China to foster international labor solidarity.

Recent Experiences in Organizing

During one hotly contested campaign in 1989, the United Auto Workers (UAW) contacted AAPL for assistance in preventing a union decertification drive. The union feared a group of Vietnamese workers would vote against them. With help of a Vietnamese speaking student intern, AAPL contacted the Vietnamese workers. The workers raised valid criticisms that the union was completely inaccessible. To remedy the situation, the union began translating its meetings and union fliers and reaching out to Vietnamese workers. It won over the Vietnamese workers who played a crucial role in the UAW victory. Since that time, some of the Vietnamese workers have continued to play a leading role in the union and have also taken on an active role within AAPL.

Another significant victory occurred within the Aluminum, Brick and Glass Workers Union. This union was also facing a decertification vote, and also feared a group of Vietnamese workers would vote against them. The union contacted AAPL member Ho Lai, a Vietnamese American organizer for the United Food and Commercial Workers Union (UFCW), for assistance. He developed a mobilization plan, and set up house meetings with the workers, many of whom the union had never approached. His work was critical in defeating the decertification drive, for which Ho Lai received special thanks and acknowledgment from the vice-president of the union. Since the election, union members have elected a Vietnamese shop steward and developed an active Vietnamese participant on the negotiating committee.

During the height of a contract campaign by the Hotel Employees and Restaurant Employees against the Hyatt Hotels in Los Angeles, AAPL again played an important role in reaching to Asian Pacific Hyatt workers and the larger Asian Pacific community. The Hyatt workers include a large number of Filipino and Chinese immigrants. AAPL mobilized support within the Asian Pacific community by encouraging organizations to honor the boycott and held a special press conference for the Asian press. The campaign ultimately ended in victory, the workers won a favorable contract, and the campaign successfully cultivated an expanding group of union allies within the Asian community.

AAPL was also involved in another, less successful, campaign with workers at Radio Korea, the largest Korean radio station in the country. The radio station required its employees to work seven days a week and holidays for intolerably low wages and no overtime pay. The workers chose to go on strike and demanded union recognition. The strike lasted over four weeks, and was well publicized throughout the Korean community. The strike also attracted considerable support among forces with no prior union experience. Workers from Korean communities across the country learned of the strike and sent letters of solidarity.

The Legal Aid Foundation filed a wage and hour claim on behalf of the workers, one of the first legal actions of this kind within the Korean American community. The station's management refused to negotiate or recognize the union. Instead, it retained a union-busting law firm, cut side deals with some of the workers, and encouraged enough workers to cross the line to break the strike. The failure of the strike reflected the need to have bilingual organizers who could gauge the pulse of the workers and management every step of the way.

Although the strike ultimately failed to unionize Radio Korea this round, the campaign publicized the tremendous exploitation and abuse Asian immigrant workers face, and led to the longest strike in Koreatown history. Already, other promising developments have occurred within the Korean community. In 1992, a new organization, the Korean Immigrant Workers Advocates (KIWA), was established in Los Angeles to set the foundation for future labor organizing among Korean American workers.

Building APALA

Perhaps one of the most important contributions AAPL has made to the national labor movement has been in helping to establish the national Asian Pacific American Labor Alliance. Through AAPL's work in Los Angeles, we realized that in spite of many local accomplishments, we still had to influence the national AFL-CIO in order to organize a significant number of Asian American workers.

Upon the invitation of AFL-CIO Regional Director David Sickler, I attended the 1989 national AFL-CIO Convention to lobby for establishing of a nationwide Asian American labor organization. In March 1990, I met with AFL-CIO President Lane Kirkland to discuss the idea, especially in view of the growing Asian work force and organizing potential. At the following meeting of the AFL-CIO Executive Council, Kirkland appointed a committee of seven International presidents, chaired by ILGWU President Jay Mazur, to establish a national Asian Pacific American labor committee. The first national steering committee, comprised of 37 Asian Pacific labor activists, convened in June 1991. It met for over a year to plan the Asian Pacific American Labor Alliance. The response from Asian Pacific union leaders and rank and file members exceeded all expectations. Five hundred delegates participated in the founding convention in May 1992. At the convention, we honored seven Asian Pacific labor pioneers: 87-year-old Filipino farmworker and former vice-president of the United Farm Workers Union, Philip Vera Cruz, AAFUM founder George Wong of the Graphic Communications Union, AAPL founder Art Takei of the United Food and Commercial Workers, Morgan Gin of the Newspaper Guild, Sue Embrey of the American Federation of Teachers, and Ah Quan McElrath and Karl Yoneda of the Longshoremen and Warehousemen's Union.

During APALA's first year, it has launched two national campaigns. With the first campaign, APALA is working with the AFL-CIO Organizing Institute to recruit a new generation of Asian Pacific labor organizers. At a local level, chapters are actively involved in working with the labor movement to forge labor-community alliances.

The second national campaign involves building a civil rights agenda for Asian Pacific workers. APALA is one of the few national Asian Pacific organizations based in Washington, D.C. It will play an important role in advancing a national agenda to support civil rights legislation, oppose anti-Asian violence, ensure fair representation for Asian Pacific Americans at all levels of politics and promote Asian Pacific political power. While APALA will pay particular attention to the concerns of Asian Pacific workers, it hopes to build multiracial unity.

In spite of APALA's accomplishments to date, the task of organizing Asian Pacific workers is still just beginning. Exploitation of Asian Pacific workers continues on a daily basis, and unions are needed now more than ever. The challenge that lies ahead is to promote multiracial unity within the ranks of the labor movement and to build on the successes of a community-based organizing model for unions. The goals of the labor movement and the Asian American community are one and the same—justice, equality, and empowering workers. The Asian Pacific American Labor Alliance, the AFL-CIO, and other Asian American labor organizations will continue to play an important role in shaping the future for Asian Pacific American workers throughout the country.

18

ASIAN AMERICAN STUDIES

Reevaluating for the 1990s

LANE RYO HIRABAYASHI
and MARILYN C. ALQUIZOLA

Paradigm Lost?

As individuals, we have been engaged in Asian American Studies for a combined quarter-of-a-century, and we are concerned by recent developments threatening our ability to carry out our work in ways faithful to the field's original critical, counterhegemonic stance.

We are grateful to John Hayakawa-Torok, Evelyn Hu-Dehart, Maivân Clech Lâm, and Mary Romero for their comments on this chapter. Also, Ling-Chi Wang organized a discussion at the national meeting of the Association of Asian American Studies, Cornell University, June 4, 1993, that focused in part on an earlier draft of this paper. Our AAAS colleagues offered useful insights that we have drawn from here, especially Greg Mark, Gary Okihiro, and Linda Revilla. Finally, we thank Karin Aguilar-San Juan and Cynthia Peters for their careful editorial inquiries. We alone are responsible for the views expressed herein.

Many of these negative developments can be tied to two salient trends of the 1980s. First, universities have systematically eroded the autonomy of Asian American and Ethnic Studies programs, especially in terms of self-governance and self-determination. Second, the "multiculturalization" and "internationalization" of university curriculum has created opportunities for those who were never, or only peripherally, involved in either Asian American or Ethnic Studies to define these fields and impose criteria that govern them within the academy.

These two trends have a number of very visible manifestations on campuses across the country. In some settings, multiculturalism provides a vehicle to water down and subvert the critical thrust of Asian American and Ethnic Studies curriculum. Concomitantly, a faculty candidate's acceptance by mainstream academic departments has often become a necessary qualification for hire above and beyond the individual's merits as an Asian Americanist. All in all, an Asian Americanist must pursue legitimacy within the university in terms of traditional scholarly criteria, the most important of which involve publication in refereed, disciplinary journals, as well as publishing books through university presses—precisely those vehicles of "intellectual production" that traditionally excluded Asian American issues and perspectives, not to mention scholars.[1]

We can measure the success of this imposed system by the growing hierarchy emerging within Asian American Studies. We, ourselves, can be heard distinguishing among students, graduate students, and those with a "fid" (or, Ph.D.); or among professors who are "lecturers" (basically, grossly underpaid temporary faculty), "tenure-track" (with somewhat better pay, more perks, but still under review), or "tenured" (senior professors with job security). Or, we distinguish based on a given individual's disciplinary, departmental, and institutional status. We have been academically colonized. Asian Americanists have even begun to identify, and even sometimes complain about, colleagues we must tiptoe around because they have become "gatekeepers": senior faculty no one dares offend because their favorable evaluations can literally ensure access to a badly needed job or publication opportunities.

One might well ask if Asian American Studies has lost its critical "counterhegemonic" edge in the 1990s. A brief review of some of the founding principles of Asian American Studies provides one vantage point on where things have gone astray, as well as possible prospects for the future.

Prospectus

We argue below that the first Asian American Studies programs *did* have a cogent vision of, and even a methodology for advancing, the field. We suggest that the implicit theoretical basis of many programs, however, was an Asian American version of *cultural nationalism* that carried within it a set of profound, if not fatal, contradictions. These contradictions became increasingly visible through the 1980s. We argue, then, that lack of critical and reflexive assessment of cultural nationalism has contributed to the present state of the field. In addition, although Asian American scholars have taken steps to organize the students, faculty and staff at a national level, we have only pursued, at best, ad hoc theoretical reformulations of Asian American Studies and have yet to develop effective mechanisms to monitor various practical implementations of the field.

Our approach to evaluating the present state of Asian American Studies within the context of higher education in the United States revolves around analyzing a key case study. The Asian American Studies program at San Francisco State provides a crucial vantage point on the past, as this program had unusually wide powers of self-determination from the very beginning, and was also situated within the only autonomous School of Ethnic Studies in North America.[2] In short, we assess the relative contributions and limitations of Asian American Studies at State as a kind of index to gauge the state of the field as a whole. We conclude by offering a series of suggestions based on our belief that retheorizing is the paramount issue for Asian American Studies at this point in its development. We also argue that, at a national level, practitioners of Asian American Studies should do everything in their power to win autonomy and self-determination as a basis for reconceptualizing the field. We also believe that linking Asian American Studies more tangibly to the larger field of Ethnic Studies is one way to advance and defend this agenda.

Roots and Bases of Asian American Studies

In the university setting, Asian American Studies historically has focused on four substantive topics: history, identity/personality, community and culture, and politics, especially in terms of the politics of empowerment and social change. At first glimpse, what distinguished Asian American Studies perspectives, across the board, was that they attempted to be holistic, and prioritized analyses that integrated insights, concepts, and perspectives that were tied to the actual experiences of the communities. This agenda exploded onto the scene in the late 1960s, largely in response to college and university-level curricula that either ignored Asian Americans or evaluated them in terms of premises and frameworks predicated on assimilation and other misapplied standards.

What some may not know, and many may have forgotten, is that the "administration" of the two earliest Asian American Studies programs was original and radical, if not revolutionary, in intent and practice. In the late 1960s and early 1970s, a coalition of students, lecturers, and community activists organized and ran the Asian American Studies programs at San Francisco State and at the University of California at Berkeley. They collectively controlled all aspects of the Studies, from the courses to the overall curriculum, to the hiring and firing of professors and even administrators. Let us briefly review the genesis of these revolutionary (for the academy, anyway) developments at the San Francisco State campus, noting that the guiding principles for the Berkeley program were quite similar.

From the beginning, the founders of Asian American Studies at San Francisco State University (then a "college") originally conceived and implemented it as an independent, autonomous field of endeavor. The program offered its first set of courses on September 22, 1969, and it was certainly the only program in the United

States to do so within the context of a larger, autonomous Ethnic Studies program (later, "school").

We see the genesis of State's program from the original five demands of the Third World Liberation Front [or TWLF]—the coalition that brought Ethnic Studies at State into being, which itself evolved during a massive and sometimes militant strike. The core of the TWLF's demands, was, first and foremost:

> [T]hat a School of Ethnic Studies for the ethnic groups involved in the Third World strike be set up *with the students in each particular ethnic organization having the authority and control over the hiring and retention of any faculty member, director, administrator, as well as the curriculum in a specific area of study.*[3]

The demands prioritized three immediate goals. The first was "open admissions," which required immediate admission of all "non-white" students, including those that had applied during the fall and for the (then) coming spring semesters of the 1968-1969 academic year. A second goal concerned "community control" of the curriculum content as well as hiring policies. The third goal of self-governance, in fact, became a guiding principle of Ethnic Studies.

It is important to recall here that "autonomy" provided the basis for a specific set of governing and decision-making mechanisms but more fundamentally, autonomy meant freedom from mainstream departments' control of the school (including freedom from their judging it based on traditional academic criteria), as well as freedom from the bureaucratic routine of academic "business as usual." Autonomy enabled Asian American faculty to make links to specific Asian American communities. "Relevance," as defined by curricula that addressed the issues and needs of "the community," was the overriding agenda. Asian American Studies founders envisioned professors and classes facilitating these ends; a collective of students, professors and community-based activists would monitor and evaluate both professors and courses on an on-going basis. Over the longer term, research, analysis, and community organizing would enable political empowerment and social change. This was, in short, a whole new methodology whose code words and phrases were "relevancy," "serve the people," and often "revolutionary change"; this methodology had defined mechanisms within the structure and organization of Asian American and Ethnic Studies to guide it along its intended path.

The earliest available documents regarding the actual organization and operation of Asian American Studies at San Francisco State College are quite revealing in this regard. In contrast to what we might assume, Asian American Studies was far from a unified, egalitarian, pan-Asian collective. More than anything else, the Studies was actually a working coalition of planning committees. Studies intentionally designed these planning committees to be ethnic-specific (that is, Chinese Americans ran Chinese American Studies, Filipino Americans ran the Filipino American Studies component, etc.). The faculty, potential faculty, students, former students, and community-based organizers and community members, who comprised these committees were either directly involved in, or at the very least, supportive of, the Third World Strike and its principles, and/or active in community-based social services. The ethnic-specific planning committees met regularly, established agendas, and retained control over hiring, curriculum, and other matters pertaining to their programs [in an ethnic-specific sense] within Asian American Studies. In fact, it was precisely the principle of self-determination and self-governance that allowed Asian American Studies to set up this arrangement, which technically violated the standard hierarchical governing process of university departments, as specified by University faculty manuals. Traditionally, of course, these rules facilitated the creation of departments that were run by and for the convenience of senior professors, and in terms of the "scholarly" criteria the latter prioritized and imposed.

Again, the purpose of Third World solidarity was to strike for and win the right to self-governance and self-determination. Self-governance provided the aperture to set up ethnic-specific planning groups that would best insure that specific courses and the curricula as a whole were organized by, for, and about specific Asian American communities. Ideally, courses were supposed to be historically framed, holistic, relevant, and committed to empowerment. A key point to emphasize about this set-up is that its creators were concerned about *accountability,* and they designed the rhetoric of "community base" and "community control" specifically to provide and insure a kind of accountability that the university had completely neglected insofar as Asian Americans were concerned.

Innovative principles designed to maximize inter- and intra-ethnic solidarity, as well as smooth decision-making processes, were also adapted within Asian American Studies and within each of the planning groups (at least in contrast to the usual operating procedures found in traditional academic departments). These revolved around establishing "principles of unity" so that differences, whether political or personal, were to be downplayed in order to achieve the common goals of the planning group, Asian American Studies, or Ethnic Studies as a whole. In addition, the Studies adopted a technically illegal "consensus model" of decision-making whereby everyone who was actively involved—regardless of technical rank as a student, lecturer, tenure-track, or tenured professor—was allowed to vote. Furthermore, a "dissenting" vote could effectively table or even veto a proposed policy or action. While often time-consuming, in that groups needed extended discussions to reach consensus, this approach to decision-making was desirable. After all, Asian Americans, because of their relatively small numbers, had become tired of seeing their concerns and priorities subsumed every time an organization took a vote based on "majority rule."

Questioning Cultural Nationalism: The Theoretical Foundation of Asian American Studies

We propose that the political autonomy that the TWLF demanded was in fact an expression of a theoretical position known as "cultural nationalism." Cultural nationalism entails an "ethnic nationalist ideology," as one colleague puts it, which highlights "unique" cultural traits based on language, history, and values.

Ethnic-specificity is thus the hallmark of cultural nationalism, requiring the militant promotion of a unique ethnic identity (note the singular form here), as well as the prioritization of cultural preservation and "community control"—especially economic and political control over neighborhoods or communities which were, ideally, territorially based.[4]

We submit that because the members of Asian American Studies undertheorized their cultural nationalist underpinnings, or in any case never subjected them to sustained, critical evaluation, political contradictions generated a continual, negative undercurrent, which consequently undermined the program.

Problems with the Nationalist Paradigm

During the 1970s, major political battles developed within Asian American Studies. The faculty broke into political factions around issues of sexism (curriculum as well as personnel issues, such as who would obtain access to tenure-track positions or who would become department chair), and the need to incorporate explicit theories of class analysis and struggle. The faculty was also split over whether Asian American Studies should develop a major directed at a select group of committed students, or become a "service-oriented" program. A service-oriented program would be dedicated to fulfilling "general education" requirements, while at the same time providing a comprehensive overview of the Asian American experience, tacitly driven by the premises of cultural nationalism. While serious analysis of these battles entails more space than we have here, suffice it to say that the service-oriented project prevailed; while this meant booming enrollments throughout the 1980s, there was a trade off—tensions arose among faculty over how to staff multiple sections of large, lower-division survey courses, (the content of which was all too often routinized), which cut into ethnic-specific curriculum and research. What is more, Asian American Studies marginalized feminist discourses and courses, as well as "class" as an analytic tool or a method for community organizing. Interestingly enough, these turn out to be precisely the kinds of weaknesses that were often replicated wherever cultural nationalist agendas drove Ethnic Studies programs.

By the 1980s, the strike had become a legend—even, quite frankly, mythologized. This occurred, ironically enough, during the very period that the University began to challenge seriously the School's and its constituent programs' right to autonomy and self-determination. The University staged various attacks including "reconfiguring" general education requirements (usually to the disadvantage of Ethnic and Asian American Studies curriculum), mounting courses in mainstream departments that basically duplicated those offered in the School, and imposing "Ph.D. only" stipulations on any job searches for new hires.[5]

At the same time, the key mechanisms for relevance and accountability—community-base and community-control—began to dissolve. Activists, for one, began to control increasingly large and sophisticated social-service bureaucracies that had little need for the contributions of either full-time faculty or student neophytes. Activists also needed to attend to the many demands of city-, state-, and federal-level politics if they wanted to keep open their lines to the major sources of external funding. As a result, key community-based players had less and less time to be directly involved in monitoring university programs. At the same time, administrators within the School of Ethnic Studies evolved into a full-time bureaucrats, increasingly intent on protecting their "turf." Second, as the bureaucratic politics of survival on campus became increasingly specialized and tactical, faculty at the Studies assumed the entire burden of managing the day-to-day struggles on campus. This institutionalization, in turn, produced a faculty that became like other university faculties who believe that the contributions of community-based and student critics were usually well-intentioned but fundamentally unpragmatic or misinformed.

Moreover, the composition and the nature of Asian American communities changed in the 1980s. For example, it is disheartening but nonetheless true that in the last presidential election the vast majority (almost 70 percent) of the Asian American electorate supported either Bush or Perot.[6] This fact alone muddies romantic characterizations of Asian American communities as unified entities, committed to addressing inequities of class, gender, and race relations, let alone more radical social change agendas.

In response to these changing conditions, Asian American Studies at State became increasingly centralized and self-absorbed. During the 1980s, a "pan-Asian" Asian American Studies agenda emerged, diminishing the importance and role of the ethnic-specific planning groups and courses. Unfortunately, this shift also diminished the original mechanisms designed to insure relevance and accountability. Insofar as there is no specific ethnic community entailed in the concept "Asian American," Asian American faculty at State became both the source that develops and the "community" that evaluates Asian American Studies. By the mid-1980s, the stance of Asian American Studies at State resulted in a situation where *ad hoc* practices and the institutionalization of "old boy" community ties were all that was left as the old ideologies began to crumble.

Toward a Revitalized Asian American Studies

Despite our critical assessment of the field as a whole, and of the program at San Francisco State in particular, we are committed to a struggle to revitalize Asian American Studies nationwide.

Whatever the problems of the past, we believe that the original vision, curricular focus, and radical organization of Asian American Studies are well worth reconsidering today. The question remains, however, how do we reinterpret these to meet our needs both inside the universities and among Asian/Pacific Americans today?

One possibility that could frame this task seems especially promising. The premises, goals, and practices of Asian American Studies can and should be rethought and reconfigured, self-consciously and systematically, within the broader framework of a *theorized* Ethnic Studies. Increasingly, sophisticated histories of the component fields of Ethnic Studies have been published, and it seems imperative that we draw from these explicitly in reformulating Asian American Studies.[7] Advances made in recent research and political struggles framed in terms of transnational and global contexts and perspectives also seem especially promising.

Here we would add that, although the study and inclusion of theory is an activity that certain members of the established power structure in Asian American Studies sometimes regard with suspicion, others have found theory crucial in pointing the way to rupturing hegemony.[8] We feel theory has been useful, as well, in compensating for the limitations of over-historicized and over-empirical approaches to the study of Asian American arts and literatures. Properly deployed, theory has helped us to negotiate the inclusion of minority voices within minority discourses, and can help to insure that we do not replicate the mistakes of the past such as excluding and neglecting our own internal diversity. What we remain sorely in need of, however, is a retheorization of a more diverse and inclusive field that also entails newly framed visions of relevance and accountability.

In terms of the various issues and debates we have discussed above, the bottom line is simple. We can no longer rely upon the exhausted tropes of cultural nationalism, whether these be "ethnic specificity," the essentialized unity of ethnic-specific experience, ethnic solidarity, or even "the community." If we do not take the initiative to redefine what Asian American Studies, as an integral part of Ethnic Studies, is and what it involves—if even on a working and provisional basis—universities and their schools, departments, and faculties will define these for us.[9] The pursuit and evaluation of what constitutes Asian American Studies should be self-determined by a collective body of Asian American scholars, committed to a range of theoretically informed practices, rather than by distanced practitioners of traditional disciplines.[10] Only then can the critical, integrative field of Asian American Studies continue to grow and evolve in its own right, as a component of Ethnic Studies, which was the very point of its creation in the first place.

Notes

1. Lest it be assumed otherwise, some scholars of Asian American descent, including some who ostensibly practice Asian American Studies, are very much in support of such criteria. In our eyes, these Asian Americans tangibly empower that part of the academy that seeks to depoliticize us. For an interesting illustration of this tendency, albeit in a slightly different vein, see Maivân Clech Lâm, "Resisting Inside/Outside Classism," *Forward Motion,* 11 (1992): 59-63.
2. This overview is based on our (combined) experience of 20 years with this program. In addition, we have drawn from a range of sources including formal and informal interviews with the original founders of Asian American Studies at State and its present faculty (many of whom were leaders in the Third World Liberation Front), presentations made at a conference held in honor of the 20th year commemoration of the San Francisco State Strike, and the archives of the School of Ethnic Studies, San Francisco State—especially the folders pertaining to "Asian American Studies" and the "Japanese American Planning Group." Two articles that were also helpful in formulating our view of developments at State were James Hirabayashi, "Ethnic Education: Its Purposes and Prospects," *On Common Ground: A Journal of Ethnic Thought,* 1 (1979), and Karen Umemoto, "On Strike! San Francisco State College Strike, 1968-69: The Role of Asian American Students," *Amerasia Journal,* 15 (1989), 3-41.
3. This quote is from an undated flyer articulating the demands of the Third World Liberation Front. The emphasis in the quote is our own. For the record, we note that the TWLF was a coalition of six student groups, three of which represented Asian Americans: the Asian American Political Alliance, the Philippine-American Collegiate Endeavor, and the Intercollegiate Chinese for Social Action.
4. Our sketch of cultural nationalism is informed by four key sources. These are Robert Blauner, *Racial Oppression in America* (New York, Harper and Row, 1972); Carlos Muñoz, Jr., *Youth, Identity, Power: The Chicano Movement* (New York, Verso, 1989); Michael Omi and Howard Winant, *Racial Formation in the United States: From the 1960s to the 1980s* (New York, Routledge, 1986); and Louis L. Snyder, "Cultural Nationalism," *Encyclopedia of Nationalism* (New York, Paragon House, 1990), 64-66. We note for the record that we could not agree as to the degree to which cultural nationalism was an *explicit* theoretical guide to the majority of individuals who formulated and ran Asian American Studies, or the extent to which the version of cultural nationalism that we describe may have been impacted by the Marxist, Leninist, or Maoist doctrines that were so prevalent in the initial stages of Ethnic and Asian American Studies. These are issues, however, that deserve the extended research that would be necessary to resolve them.

5. During the 1970s, due in no small part to a lack of faculty sensitive to and aware of the conditions provoking strikes for Ethnic Studies, as well as to the complex range of different Asian American experiences, there was a greater degree of flexibility on the part of many universities in regard to the kinds of staff that could be assembled to lecture and teach in Asian American Studies, if only on a part-time or temporary basis.

During the 1980s, this flexibility began to vanish. Increasingly, even at the state college level, let alone the public and private research universities, "Ph.D. required" clauses characterized the hiring requirements for tenure-track and tenured positions. University administrators pressed this requirement, arguing that there was indeed a plentiful pool of such candidates available by the mid-1980s. Since the Ph.D. program in Ethnic Studies at the University of California, Berkeley, established in the mid-1980s, is the only doctoral program in the United States with this explicit emphasis, what in fact ensued was that a growing number of Ph.D. candidates from traditional doctoral programs were either directly studying, or had otherwise gained enough experience with, racial/ethnic minorities in order to qualify as Asian American "experts" within traditional academic fields such as history, psychology, political science, sociology, and so forth.

6. These data appear in a table, "Distribution of Vote for Presidential Candidates" in Milton D. Morris, "Clinton's Vital Minority," *The World and I,* February (1993), 74.

7. A few of the most important examples include Russell L. Adams, "African-American Studies and the State of the Art," in *Africana Studies: A Survey of Africa and the African Diaspora,* Mario Azevedo, ed. (Durham, North Carolina, Carolina Academic Press, 1993), 25-45; Sucheng Chan and Ling-Chi Wang, "Racism and the Model Minority: Asian-Americans in Higher Education," in *The Racial Crisis in American Higher Education,* Philip G. Altbach and Kofi Lomotey, eds. (New York, State University of New York Press, 1991), 43-67; M. Annette Jaimes, "American Indian Studies: Toward an Indigenous Model," *American Indian Culture and Research Journal,11* (1987), 1-16; and Carlos Muñoz, Jr., *Youth, Identity, Power: The Chicano Movement* (New York, Verso, 1989).

8. For examples of such ruptures, see: E. San Juan, Jr., *Racial Formations/Critical Transformations: Articulations of Power in Ethnic and Racial Studies in the United States* (New Jersey, Humanities Press, 1992), and Chela Sandoval, "U.S. Third World Feminism: The Theory and Method of Oppositional Consciousness in the Postmodern World," *Genders,10* (1991): pp. 1-24; Lisa Lowe, "Heterogeneity, Hybridity, Multiplicity: Marking Asian American Differences," *Diaspora* 1 (1991):24-44; and Norma Alarcón, "Traddutora, Traditora: A Paradigmatic Figure of Chicana Feminism," *Cultural Critique* (1989-1990)13:57-87.

9. Our colleague Ray Lou made this very point to the membership of the Association for Asian American Studies almost a decade ago; see

Raymond Lou, "Commentary," *Association for Asian American Studies Newsletter,* Vol. 1 (1984), 1-2. He reportedly received no response. It might be noted that although it has logged a series of important achievements, none of the official documents of the Association, including its constitution and by-laws, specifically defines what Asian American Studies is or what it involves. This, we would argue, has contributed to the current co-optation of the field.

10. We want to emphasize here that the implications of inaction in this regard fall differentially on the shoulders of individual practitioners of Asian American Studies: students, community activists and members, and, of course, junior-level (especially, untenured) faculty members, are the most likely to suffer when the field is left undefined and its constituent activities unspecified.

LIBERATING RACE

M. ANNETTE JAIMES

In passing the editorial baton to Karin Aguilar-San Juan—I edited *The State of Native America* for South End Press—I am fortunate to offer these thoughts, connections, and juxtapositions toward comprehending and combating the insidious, systemic forms that racism has taken in U.S. institutions and society as a whole. As I view it, a major intent of the "Race and Resistance Series" is to liberate all of us by critiquing "white" America and its die-hard assertions of white supremacy and the superiority of "Western civilization" associated with Euroamerican-derived racism. An important base of struggle for oppressed "ethnic minorities" in the United States is to assert our internal sovereignty in maintaining our "ethnic" identities and sustaining our "ethnic" cultures within the U.S. milieu, one that denigrates its own ideals of democracy for cultural diversity and pluralism. The writers and activists brought together in this anthology challenge U.S. race constructs while they work toward a higher vision of humanity.*

---

* In this chapter, "Indian" refers to Native North Americans.

Creating a Notion of Race

What do we mean by the terms "racism" and "race relations"? In my own work, I use the terms in an international context, as illustrated in the global colonization and genocide of indigenous peoples, who are targeted as "a single race" and differentiated from other "races."[1] Robert Miles states in his treatise *Racism*:

> Although the word 'racism' is now widely used in common-sense, political, and academic discourse, it is of very recent origin ... There is no reference to the word in the *Oxford English Dictionary (OED)* of 1910 (although there are entries for 'race' and 'racial'). The *OED Supplement of 1982* defined racism as 'the theory that distinctive human characteristics and abilities are determined by race, and records its first appearance in the English language in the 1930s. [Hence] critics of scientific theories of 'race' prior to this decade did not use a concept of racism to identify their ideological object.[2]

Just as we should challenge the notion that there is such a thing as a pure race, we should be wary of the taboos placed on populations of mixed blood. Among my own people in the Southwest and northern Mexico, biological intermixing between Native peoples and explorers from other continents during pre-Columbian times are well-known facts.[3] Only with the advent of the Europeans to this continent did the indigenous peoples learn that mixing the "races" was abominable.[4] Indeed, racist nationalism in the United States, as in Adolf Hitler's Germany, is predicated on presumptions of Anglo-Saxon superiority and white Protestant supremacy.[5] Hitler clearly saw the expediency of the construction of "race" in rationalizing the Third Reich. In his private conversations with Hermann Raushning,[6] he claimed that even though race cannot be "scientifically" defined, it is an expedient socio-political tool for empire-building, and helps fuel nationalism induced by the State. In the case of the U.S. empire, Indian-hating was a necessary ideological foundation for European conquest.[7]

Miles adds in his assessment that there should be distinctions between the conceptual definition of racism and, say, xenophobia. Yet, in the U.S. treatment of its peoples of color, the two go hand-in-hand, and it doesn't matter which came first, the chicken or the egg, race hatred or fear of foreigners. For example, the English Only movement, which would deny social services and cultural recognition to people who speak other languages, is a pernicious form of racism and xenophobia. The effect is the same, and the need for an anti-racist agenda is urgent in any event.

We—Indian, Asian, African, and Latino—are called peoples of color and are given an "ethnic/minority" substatus, although the demographic reality is that the four "basic" ethnic groups are actually growing in numbers. I prefer to call us *peoples of culture*: We are American Indians or Native Americans, Asian Americans, African Americans, Chicanos/as, Puerto Ricans, and other Latinos/as who are fighting for our communal lifeways at the same time we resist our oppression as substandard peoples in subcultural "ethnicities." We are the bitter legacies of the containment and genocide of Native peoples to Indian reservations allowing European settlement, and of slavery that brought so many black Africans to toil, and suffer, in this hemisphere. We are mostly "lower-class" citizens living in Third World conditions—ghettos, Chinatowns, barrios, and reservations—throughout this nation-state. We have all become part of a diaspora, one that expands as the United States continues its warmongering, intervention, and aggression in Asia and Latin America, the Middle East and Africa, uprooting and decimating local populations.

In the broader scheme of things, we must recognize that racism also has environmental implications; ecological racism treats people of culture as expendable. Native peoples on "national sacrifice lands" are subject to "radioactive colonization" in the Four Corners area and Arizona's Black Mesa, where the Navajo (Diné) and Hopi live, and in New Mexico's Acoma Sky City, home of the Laguna Pueblo.[8] Today, environmental crisis and ecological blight is spreading around the globe, in the forms of toxic waste dumping, chemical contamination, radioactive spheres and pollution, and AIDS and other epidemics. Native people and people of color and their cultures as well as a growing number of non-human life forms are becoming "endangered species" on this planet.

Racism is an Old World Order

In this construction of world affairs into dominant and subordinant actors, there are heavy portents on the horizon that fascism is on the rise. I recently returned from Germany, where I was a Native member of an international human rights delegation invited by German anti-racist and anti-fascist organizations. I was appalled to see that the German state is eradicating any hint of its Nazi history, building over concentration camps that now stand as evidence of Nazi atrocities. In their white-washing efforts, Germany has ignored the plight of the Roma and Sinti peoples, among the approximately 50,000 Gypsies. As maligned descendants of the holocaust victims in that country, their situation has worsened with the repeal of Article 16, a law that is being reversed to close Germany's borders to all refugees. The German authorities have also denied the basic human rights of its Turkish population, many of whom are "guest workers," another group of economically exploited and displaced peoples.

Racism has been institutionalized in many ways during the course of U.S. history. Notorious "Jim Crow" laws forbade black men to look at white women—but legalized the rape of black women and other women of color by white males—and banned miscegenation among whites and people of color, calling such interactions a social disease and a religious sin. Immigrant quotas put caps on primarily Asian populations during the world wars, but only after employers had fully exploited their labor, for example, in building the railroads that opened up the Western frontier, and harvesting valuable crops. In the late nineteenth and early twentieth century, for example, Chinese, Filipino, and Mexican immigrants braved discrimination, racial violence, paramilitary border patrols, and murderous coyotes to seek slave-wage employment here, filling the U.S. economy's need for labor in both agriculture and industry. To this day, the American Dream still drives many people to tolerate economic misery in this country, whether they are running from political and/or economic oppression in their homelands. Foreign exploitation and oppression by U.S.-controlled oligarchies in the "third" world exacerbate racist scenarios, where indigenous peoples have the most to lose, including their lives.

Racism even affects modern-day scientific research, specifically genetic engineering and DNA tinkering, that supports eugenics, the idea that science can improve the human race by controlling hereditary factors. Typically, eugenicists consider such features as maleness, blond hair, and blue eyes to be desirable improvements, as well as a stoic and aggressive character and predatory nature. Concurrently, sexism, homophobia, militarism, and other oppressive "isms" are also important to the foundation of bigotry and racist nationalism.

Challenging Supremacy, Learning from History

Contrary to the history of European and Euroamerican racism, the indigenous peoples of this hemisphere are not known ever to have adhered to a notion of "race" that would differentiate people within the human species. Rather, we have observed and appreciated cultural diversity as variations on cosmological themes. The indigenous worldview encompasses all humanity as well as our relationship with non-human species. Hence, in the traditional Indian Native we can recognize as our brothers and sisters "Red-Black" Indians, and Asian Mexicans, mestizos, métis, mulattos, and other people of "mixed" blood.

Indigenous history includes building alliances across race. Richard Drinnon's *Keeper of the Concentration Camps: Dillon S. Myer and American Racism,*[9] portrays Myer's racist accomplishments while employed by the federal government. In a case exemplifying "the banality of evil," American style,[10] Myers played a key role in establishing and implementing the war relocation camps throughout the country that "contained" Japanese Americans during the 1940s. Myers followed this act with his callous termination, via federal Indian policy, of several American Indian tribes in the 1950s. The missing link between these seemingly unconnected examples of U.S. racism carried out against its "hyphenated

Americans" is that the concentration camps were deliberately located in arid areas with sparse populations, and several were marginal to Indian reservations, such as Leupp in Arizona. The tribal Indians empathized with the plight of Japanese Americans who the federal government forced into the nearby camps. Since the Japanese American situation was much like their own forced removal by the U.S. military to reservations, these Indian neighbors assisted the camp inmates by teaching them farming methods and other survival techniques the duration of their incarceration.

This example of interracial solidarity is crucial for at least two reasons. First, this example challenges the impression that Asian Americans lack common ground with other people of color. Second, it opens up a whole new and important arena for scholars in ethnic studies or other interdisciplinary discourse to transcend Eurocentric parameters in order to obtain a broader analysis of U.S. racism. As Aguilar-San Juan observes in the introduction to this book, radical (ethnic) scholars, and activists such as Yuri and Bill Kochiyama, are driven to take up the causes that cross racial, cultural, and even national (as well as international) boundaries by their analysis of the roots of social and economic injustice. Their work helps "to widen the parameters of a discussion that is often cast solely in black and white terms."

Decolonization demands a "revolutionary politics" that combats the realities of racism, fascism, and imperialism imposed upon us. Radicals among Natives, people of color, and our white allies need to understand how racism works, and also need to build alliances across race. To do otherwise is to let our communities be divided by such ploys as the "model minority myth" by which Asian Americans are touted as having surmounted racism. The myth about Indian "pure bloods" serves a similar divisive function among Native Americans, causing conflict and dissension in the Indian world, "full bloods" vying against "mixed bloods" for a piece of the shrinking pie. We must deconstruct these myths, even negate them, in order to destroy racism as an organizing principle of U.S. society, with its all-pervasive levels of domination and hegemony, culminating in Yankee imperialism and Eurocentric jingoism.[11] For all of us, *The State of Asian America* is one significant step toward our liberation and our search for a universal love of life.

Notes

1. Montague, Ashley, ed. *Statement on Race: An Extended Discussion in Plain Language of the UNESCO Statement by Experts on Race Problems,* Henry Schman, New York, UNESCO stands for United Nations Educational, Scientific, and Cultural Organization. See also Montague, ed., *The Concept of Race* (London: Collier-Macmillan Ltd., 1964) and Montague, *Man's Most Dangerous Myth: The Fallacy of Race,* Fourth Edition (New York: The World Publishing Co., 1964).
2. Miles, Robert. *Racism*, Key Ideas Series (New Jersey: Routledge, 1989), 42-66.
3. Interestingly enough, Canada accepts its métis populations, the product of white (mostly French) and Indian intermixing. On the other hand, the United States does not, and the Spanish category of *mestizo*, representing people of mixed white (mostly Spanish) and Indian blood, is not represented in the official census. I am among those who do not consider the eurocentric term "Hispanic" as an appropriate one for this category.
4. See Gould, Stephen J., The Mismeasure of Man (New York: Norton, 1981): 44-49 on "miscegenation." The author expands on the pseudoscientific case known as *Crania Americana*, made by racist Eurocentrics for "Native inferiority" in the "New World". Gould compares other rationales for theories on race and color, inferior attempts to substantiate "white" race supremacy. See also Stanton, William, *The Leopard's Spots: Scientific Studies Toward Race in America, 1815-59* (Chicago: University of Chicago Press, 1960).
5. Childe, V.G., *The Aryans: The History of Civilization,* (New York: Dorset Press, 1987). Note its arrogant and presumptuous title. Also Horsman, Reginald, *Race and Manifest Destiny: The Origins of American Racial Anglo-Saxonism* (Cambridge, MA: Harvard University Press, 1981).
6. Raushning, Hermann, *The Voice of Destruction,* Chapter XVI, "Magic, Black and White," (New York: Putnam's and Sons, 1940): 230-42.
7. Drinnon Richard, *Facing West: The Metaphysics of Indian-Hating and Empire-Building* (New York: Schocken Books, 1990) and Harvey Pearce, *Savagism and Civilization* (Baltimore: 1965), 244. Both are seminal books on "the metaphysics of Indian-hating for empire-building," and both are predicated on Herman Melville's unpopular novel *The Confidence Man: His Masquerade. See also* Harmon, Alexandra, "When An Indian Is Not An Indian?" "Friends of the Indian" and the problem of Indian Identity, Journal of Ethnic Studies (Seattle, WA: University of Washington) Vol. 18, 2, Summer 1991: 95-123.

8. Churchill, Ward and Winona LaDuke, "Native America: The Political Ecnomy of Radioactive Colonization," *Critical Issues in Native North America,* Vol II., Doc. 68 (Copenhagen, Denmark: International Work Group for Indigenous Affairs, 1991) pp. 25-67. Also see Ward Churchill, *Struggle for the Land* (Monroe, Maine: Common Courage Press, 1992), pp. 261-328.
9. Drinnon, Richard, *Keeper of the Concentration Camps: Dillon S. Myer and American Racism,* University of California Press, 1987. Dillon was ironically called "the Great White Father" by his bureaucratic contemporaries.
10. Arendt, Hannah, *Eichmann in Jerusalem: A Report on the Banality of Evil* (New York: Viking Press, 1963).
11. Haynal, A., et al., *Fanaticism: A Historical and Psychological Study* (New York: Schocken Books, 1983).

INDEX

A

AAFE. *See* Asian Americans for Equality

AAFUM. *See* Asian American Federation of Union Members

AAPL. *See* Alliance of Asian Pacific Labor

AARW. *See* Asian American Resource Workshop

AAUPA. *See* Asian American Union for Political Action

Academic work. *See* Asian American Studies programs

Achebe, Chinua, 190

ACT UP, 12, 282, 285

Activism. *See* Asian American activism

Actor's Equity, 278

Affirmative action, 3, 43, 44, 47

AFL-CIO, 335, 341-42, 348

AFL-CIO Organizing Institute, 342, 348

African American-Korean American relations, 79-80, 109; Black-Korean Alliance, 80-86, 102; and class, 86-87, 111-12; coalition building, 88-89, 93-94; Harlins killing, 79, 80-85, 86, 88, 92, 271, 309; in independent media, 167; and Los Angeles riots/uprisings, 96, 97; and mainstream media, 268-71; and neo-conservatism, 49; Park Tae Sam killing, 84-85; Red Apple boycott, 110, 267, 268; "rudeness" issue, 110-11. *See also* Los Angeles riots/uprisings

African Americans: anti-Asian racism, 247-48n5; and deindustrialization, 107-8; feminism, 147-48, 153; hate crimes against, 247, 249n29, 250n35; in independent media, 166; as inspiration for Asian American activism, 5-6, 91; interracial relationships with, 166-67, 168-69; Latino relations with, 109, 248n7; Los Angeles population, 103-4, 117n6; and model minority stereotype, 63; neo-conservatism, 44, 45, 46-47; and 1970s corporate offensive, 33, 35, 36-37; political power of, 87, 90; and Thomas nomination, 257-58. *See also* African American-Korean American relations; Black/white paradigm; Civil rights movement; Coalitions among people of color; Conflicts among people of color;

K

About the Contributors

Karin Aguilar-San Juan is a writer, activist, and martial artist. Born in Boston and raised in New England, she is a former editor at South End Press and is now a graduate student in sociology at Brown University. Her articles have appeared in *Piece of My Heart: A Lesbian of Color Anthology, Signs: A Journal of Women and Culture,* and *The Women's Review of Books.*

Marilyn Alquizola is currently a Ph.D. candidate in Ethnic Studies at UC Berkeley. With an emphasis in Asian American literature, she has published articles on subversive reading strategies for Carlos Bulosan's *America is in the Heart.* Alquizola has taught Asian American Studies for twelve years. Born and raised in San Francisco, she is a second-generation Filipino American.

Edward Chang is Assistant Professor of Ethnic Studies at UC Riverside. He received his Ph.D. in Ethnic Studies at UC Berkeley where he specialized in the areas of Korean American-African American relations, immigration, and race relations theories. He has recently served as a field reporter and consultant for *LA is Burning: Five Reports from a Divided City,* a PBS special program on the Los Angeles Uprising. He is an author of the Korean-language book, *Who African Americans Are.*

Milyoung Cho is a second-generation Korean American lesbian born in Massachusetts. She was a co-founder of Action for Community Empowerment in New York City, where she organized tenants of welfare hotels and city housing in Central Harlem. Recently, she worked on staff of the Committee Against Anti-Asian Violence, advocating for victims of racist and police violence and organizing communities around related issues. Now in San Francisco, she is free-lancing for *Asian Week* and is a staff member of the Gay Asian Pacific Alliance Community HIV Project.

Steven De Castro is a second-generation Filipino American who grew up in Staten Island, New York. After spending three years as a community organizer and a construction worker, he finished school at Oberlin College and returned to New York, where he was a member of Youth for Philippine Action for two years. He now lives in Jersey City.

Richard Fung is an independent video producer, writer, and community activist. Born and raised in Trinidad, where his family goes back four generations, he has lived in Toronto since 1973.

Born and raised in the Philippines, **Jessica Hagedorn** is well-known as a performance artist, poet, and playwright. Her novel, *Dogeaters,* was nominated for the National Book Award. Her latest book is *Danger and Beauty: Dangerous Music, Pet Food and Tropical Apparitions.*

Lane Ryo Hirabayashi has worked with the Center for Japanese American Studies, the Asian American Theater Company, the Gardena Pioneer Project, and the Japanese Community Youth Council. Currently, he is Associate Professor at the University of Colorado, Boulder and Asian American Studies coordinator at the Center for Studies of Ethnicity and Race in America. He recently published *Cultural Capital: Mountain Zapotec Regional Associations in Mexico City.* Lane is of Japanese American (his father's side) and Norwegian American (his mother's side) descent.

David Henry Hwang is an American of Chinese ancestry and the author of a dozen produced plays, including *M. Butterfly, The Dance and the Railroad, Bondage, 1000 Airplanes on the Roof,* and *FOB.* He wrote the screenplays for the movies *M. Butterfly* and *Golden Gate,* and was librettist for Philip Glass' opera *The Voyage.* Hwang's plays are published by Plume/New American Library.

M. Annette Jaimes is the editor of *The State of Native America: Genocide, Colonialism, and Resistance* and a Lecturer in American Indian Studies at the Center for Studies of Ethnicity and Race in America at the University of Colorado, Boulder. She served as a delegate of the International Indian Treaty Council to the United Nations Working Group on Indigenous Human Rights in 1985 and 1986. An Associate Editor of the journal *New Studies on the Left,* Jaimes was also co-editor of *Hispanic Access to Higher Education* (1984). Her essays have appeared frequently in journals such as *Akwesasne Notes, Wicazo Sa Review, American Indian Culture and Research Journal, Policy Review,* and *Journal of Ethnic Studies.*

Peter N. Kiang is Assistant Professor in the Graduate College of Education and American Studies Program at the University of Massachusetts, Boston. His work in community development and multicultural education has been recognized by the Anti-Defamation League, the Massachusetts Teachers Association, the Massachusetts Association for Bilingual Education, the NAACP, and the Rainbow Coalition.

Bong Hwan Kim is the Executive Director of the Korean Youth and Community Center in Los Angeles. He has also served as co-chair of the Black-Korean Alliance and was a recent recipient of the NAACP Western Region Equality Award in recognition of his efforts to fight for the civil rights of all people.

Elaine H. Kim is Professor of Asian American Studies and Faculty Assistant for the Status of Women at UC Berkeley. She is the author of *Asian American Literature: An Introduction to the Writings and Their Social Context* and co-editor of *Making Waves: Writings By and About Asian American Women* and *Writing Self, Writing Nation: A Collection of Essays on DICTEE by Theresa Hak Kyung Cha.* She is President of the Association for Asian American Studies, on the board of directors of the Korean Community Center of the East Bay, Oakland, and founder of the Asian Immigrant Women Advocates and Asian Women United of California.

Margaretta Wan Ling Lin writes, "I was born in the year of the dragon by the ocean's edge in Taiwan. Immigrating to the U.S. at an early age, I came to experience first-hand the injustices that immigrants of color, particularly women, confront in a society that denies them their dignity and strips away the souls of their men. I have experienced first-hand the cycle of violence, its sources rooted in the perverisities of racist patriarchy, and its impact on the spirit of a community, family, and individual. My life now as a civil-rights lawyer is dedicated to fighting aginst the roots of oppression."

Sophea Mouth is a Cambodian activist and student living in Madison, Wisconsin. He is President of United Refugee Services and a member of the County Office of Commissioners. He also founded the United Refugees Party, which organizes for local Cambodian, Hmong, and Laotian communities.

David Mura is a poet, creative nonfiction writer, critic, playwright, and performance artist. A *sansei* (third-generation Japanese American), Mura is the author of *Turning Japanese: Memoirs of a Sansei,* which won a 1991 Josephine Miles Book Award from the Oakland PEN. His book of poetry, *After We Lost Our Way,* won the 1989 National Poetry Series Contest. He has also written *A Male Grief: Notes on Pornography & Addiction.*

Glenn Omatsu is a staff member of the UCLA Asian American Studies Center and works with community, labor, and solidarity groups. He is associate editor of *Amerasia Journal,* a research publication in Asian American Studies. His writings have appeared in Asian American ethnic publications as well as *Labor Notes* and *Forward Motion.* He is a third-generation Japanese American living in Los Angeles.

E. San Juan, Jr. was born in the Philippines and came to the United States in 1960. After graduating from Harvard University, he taught at UC Davis and Brooklyn College, City University of New York. He currently teaches English and multicultural studies at the University of Connecticut, Storrs. His recent book *Racial Formations / Critical Transformations* received the 1993 National Book Award from the Association for Asian American Studies.

Sonia Shah is an editor at South End Press and the daughter of immigrants from India. She has co-founded a South Asian women's group in Boston, and her writings have appeared in *Sojourner, In These Times, Gay Community News,* and other anthologies. She was formerly managing editor of *Nuclear Times* magazine.

R. Radhakrishnan teaches theory and postcoloniality in the English Department at the University of Massachusetts, Amherst. He has published extensively in collections of essays and in journals such as *Transition, MELUS, differences,* and *Rethinking Marxism.* He is the author of the forthcoming book *Theory in an Uneven World* and is currently working on a book on transnationalism, gender, and the diaspora.

Reverend Cheng Imm Tan is a Unitarian Universalist minister. She is a founding member of the Asian Task Force Against Domestic Violence based in Boston and currently serves as the chairperson. She is also the director of the Asian Women's Project and co-chair of the International Refugee Women's Coalition. She co-led a workshop for Third World Women at the 1985 International Women's Conference in Nairobi, Kenya.

Wen-ti Tsen designed the cover of this book. In the studio, he makes art exploring archetypal and ritualistic images. In the community, he works with others to make murals and graphics and to communicate ideas as a form of "power shield" to ward off the dominant culture and to help make change. He was born in China, educated in Europe and the United States, and now lives in New England.

Kent Wong is Director of the UCLA Center for Labor Research and Education, Institute of Industrial Relations. He teaches Labor Studies and Asian American Studies at UCLA, California State University, Northridge, and California State University, Dominguez Hills and is a member of the American Federation of Teachers. Wong also serves as national President of the Asian Pacific American Labor Alliance.

Yoko Yoshikawa is a 31-year old *nisei* (second-generation Japanese American) who grew up on the East Coast. She moved to Berkeley, California in 1992 and is currently pursuing her interest in the visual arts and writing.

About South End Press

South End Press is a nonprofit, collectively run book publisher with over 175 titles in print. Since our founding in 1977, we have tried to meet the needs of readers who are exploring, or are already committed to, the politics of radical social change.

Our goal is to publish books that encourage critical thinking and constructive action on the key political, cultural, social, economic, and ecological issues shaping life in the United States and in the world. In this way, we hope to give expression to a wide diversity of democratic social movements and to provide an alternative to the products of corporate publishing.

If you would like a free catalog of South End Press books or information about our membership program—which offers two free books and a 40% discount on all titles—please write us at South End Press, 116 Saint Botolph Street, Boston, MA 02115.

Other titles of interest from South End Press:

The State of Native America
Genocide, Colonization and Resistance
edited by M. Annette Jaimes

Breaking Bread: Insurgent Black Intellectual Life
bell hooks and Cornel West

Collateral Damage
The New World Order at Home and Abroad
edited by Cynthia Peters

Year 501
The Conquest Continues
Noam Chomsky